current AW
· Asian studies

Karel Van. Wolferen

Also by Alex Kerr

Lost Japan

Dogs
and
Demons

Dogs
and
Demons

*T*ales *from the Dark Side of Japan*

ALEX KERR

HILL AND WANG
A division of Farrar, Straus and Giroux
New York

Hill and Wang
A division of Farrar, Straus and Giroux
19 Union Square West, New York 10003

Printed in the United States of America
First edition, 2001

Library of Congress Cataloging-in-Publication Data
Kerr, Alex, 1952–
    Dogs and demons : tales from the dark side of Japan / Alex Kerr.
    p. cm.
    Includes index.
    ISBN 0-8090-9521-1
    1. Japan—History—1989– 2. Japan—History—1945– 3. Japan—
Economic conditions—1945– 4. Japan—Industries—1945– I. Title.

DS891 .K47 2001
952.04—dc21

00-061389

The author gratefully acknowledges the invaluable assistance of Bodhi Fishman, who was both chief researcher for and ongoing editor of *Dogs and Demons'* many drafts over the years. Without his collaboration the work could not have been completed.

Designed by Jessica Shatan

To my father, Andy Kerr,
who taught me to observe

Contents

Acknowledgments

When I began work on this book in 1995, I expected to complete it in about a year. I had no idea that it would turn into one of the biggest challenges of my life and, in the end, take over five years to complete, with constant rethinking and revisions. The issues examined in the book are among the most knotty and perplexing in modern Japanese history—and many of them had never been covered systematically. It took an enormous amount of research and conceptualization to bring the story into focus, and I could never have done it without the help of my friends and colleagues.

It began with Merit Janow, with whom I first had the idea for the book, and who gave me constant support and advice.

My greatest thanks are reserved for Bodhi Fishman, whom I have credited chiefly with having researched the book but whose contribution was far greater than that. For five years, Bodhi hunted down thousands of clippings, books, interviews, and articles, reflecting the ever-shifting focus of my writing. In addition, he went over the manuscript countless times and sat with me over the years as we talked over and rethought difficult issues. Bodhi was my true collaborator, and I could not have written the book without him.

In addition, I would like to thank my friends and colleagues in Japan, with whom I have spent many hours discussing these subjects and who urged me to keep writing despite the difficulty of the work. The flower master Kawase Toshiro's and the Kabuki actor Bando Tamasaburo's views on traditional culture were guiding lights to me. Architects Shakuta Yoshiki and Kathryn Findlay filled in my knowledge of architecture, zoning, and city planning. The banker Matsuda Masashi gave me information about the banking crisis.

Karel van Wolferen was a fountain of ideas and advice about Japan's economy and its political dimension; R. Taggart Murphy offered me insights into the financial system; Gavan McCormack was a mother lode of information on the "construction state." Donald Richie heard my analyses of Japan's cultural trauma and offered pithy comments concerning cinema. Mason Florence, guidebook author and my partner in a project to revitalize the remote Iya Valley in Shikoku, was a sounding board for issues about rural life and tourism. Gary DeCoker provided academic resources concerning the Japanese educational system. The painter Allan West shared his experiences as an artist and a cultural adviser. The garden designer Marc Keane counseled me on the ups and downs of Kyoto's preservation movement. David Boggett read the manuscript and made suggestions concerning education. Chris Shannon taught me about the Internet in Japan. The writer Brian Mertens brought a journalist's eye to the process, and was one of my most loyal listeners as well as a source of information on many subjects. The Malaysian artist and cultural manager Zulkifli Mohamad helped me to think about Japan's issues from a wider, Asian point of view.

Some of my advisers did not live to see the completion of the book: the essayist and art critic Shirasu Masako told me the story of "Dogs and Demons" from which the book takes its title; the writer and philosopher Shiba Ryotaro showed me how far modern Japan had wandered from its own ideals; William Gilkey, a longtime resident of Japan and China, was the source of many anecdotes of old times; the psychiatrist Miyamoto Masao brought conceptual power and humor to the subject of the Japanese bureaucracy; and Andy Kerr, my father, advised me concerning the book's overall tone.

With respect to the Japanese translation of the book, Kazue Chida, friend and former secretary, did the early work; Kihara Etsuko later translated the manuscript in its entirety. I used Kihara Etsuko's work as the basis for writing my own version in Japanese, which was corrected by Nishino Yoshitaka. Throughout this process—resulting in years of delay—my publishers at Kodansha showed unending patience and support.

Julian Bach, my agent in New York, guided the book from its inception; Alice Quinn at *The New Yorker* introduced me to Elisabeth Sifton at Hill and Wang, who became my stern but brilliant editor. The book benefited tremendously from her wisdom and professional rigor.

Many others offered advice and help while I was at work on this project: Dui Seid in New York, at whose apartment great stretches of the book were written; my secretary, Tanachanan "Saa" Petchsombat; and my partner Khajorn Khamkong.

As for typing the manuscript, I did that myself. The rest I owe to Bodhi, to my friends and advisers—and to the hundreds of Japanese whom I have never met but who have written or spoken publicly about these issues during the past few years and whose work I consulted. This book belongs to them.

Author's Note

All Japanese names are shown Japanese style: last name first.

The yen/dollar rate has fluctuated widely over the past decade, but for purposes of rough estimation, the rate is about ¥105 to $1 at the time of writing.

As of January 8, 2001, many ministries and agencies of the Japanese government are being merged and retitled. The names I give are those in use at the time of writing.

Dogs
and
Demons

Prologue

What I am about to communicate to you is the most
astonishing thing, the most surprising, the most marvellous,
the most miraculous, most triumphant, most baffling, most
unheard of, most singular, most extraordinary, most
unbelievable, most unforeseen, biggest, tiniest, rarest,
commonest, the most talked about, and the most secret up to
this day.
—MME DE SÉVIGNÉ (1670)

The idea for this book came one day in Bangkok in 1996, as I
sat on the terrace of the Oriental Hotel having coffee with my
old friend Merit Janow. It was a colorful scene: teak rice boats
plied the great river, along with every other type of craft from
pleasure yachts to coal barges. At the next table, a group of
German businessmen were discussing a new satellite system for
Asia, next to them was a man reading an Italian paper, and
across the way a group of young Thais and Americans were
planning a trip to Vietnam. Merit and I had grown up together
in Tokyo and Yokohama, and it struck us that the scene we were
witnessing had no counterpart in the Japan we know today:

very few foreigners visit, and even fewer live there; of those, only a handful are planning new businesses—their effect on Japan is close to zero. It is hard to find a newspaper in English in many hotels, much less one in Italian.

The river, too, presented a sharp contrast to the drab sameness of Japanese cities, where we could think of no waterways with such vibrant life along their shores, but instead only visions of endless concrete embankments. Japan suddenly seemed very far away from the modern world—and the title for a book came to me: *Irrelevant Japan*. Japan kept the world out for so long, and so successfully, that in the end the world passed her by.

However, as I researched this book, it became clear that Japan's problems are much more severe than even I had guessed. Far from being irrelevant, Japan's troubles have serious relevance for both developing countries and advanced economies, for the simple reason that Japan fell into the pitfalls of both. So the title changed.

The key question is: Why should Japan have fallen into any pitfall, when the nation had everything? It reveled in one of the world's most beautiful natural environments, with lush mountains and clear-running streams pouring over emerald rocks; it preserved one of the richest cultural heritages on earth, receiving artistic treasure from all across East Asia, which the Japanese have refined over the centuries; it boasted one of the world's best educational systems and was famed for its high technology; its industrial expansion after World War II drew admiration everywhere, and the profits accumulated in the process made it perhaps the wealthiest nation in the world.

And yet, instead of building the glorious new civilization that was its birthright, Japan went into an inexplicable tailspin in the 1990s. At the start of the decade the stock market collapsed, and by the end of it the Tokyo exchange, the largest in the world in 1989, was capitalized at little more than a fourth of New York's; meanwhile, GNP growth in Japan fell to a minus, while the United States, Europe, and China boomed.

That Japan's economy stumbled is old news. But the media have reported very little about the distress that afflicts other aspects of the nation's life. Few have questioned why Japan's supposed "cities of the future" are unable to do something as basic as burying telephone wires; why gigantic construction boondoggles scar the countryside (roads leading nowhere in the mountains, rivers encased in U-shaped chutes); why wetlands are cemented over for no reason; why the movie industry has collapsed; or why Kyoto and Nara were turned into concrete jungles. These things point to something much deeper than a mere period of economic downturn; they represent a profound cultural crisis, trouble eating away at the nation's very soul.

In the process of researching this book, it became clear to me that Japan's problems have their roots in the 1860s, when the country first opened to the world. At that time, the nation set out to resist the Western colonial powers, and later to vie with them for dominance—and even though Japan succeeded in becoming one of the world's most powerful nations, the basic policy of sacrificing everything for industrial growth never changed. Over time, a wide gap opened up between the goals of this policy, instituted over a century ago, and the real needs of Japan's modern society. Distortions and hidden debts have accumulated, like water dripping into the bamboo poles that can often be seen in Japanese gardens, until finally one last droplet causes the bamboo to tip over, the water spills out, and the other end of the bamboo drops onto a stone with a loud bonk. How Japan went bonk—falling so quickly from being the economic and cultural darling of the 1980s into a profoundly troubled state in the 1990s—is one of the strange and terrible tales of the late twentieth century.

The external view of Japan differs vividly from its internal reality. "A man seeing an X-ray photograph of his own skeleton," wrote Marcel Proust, "would have the same suspicion of error at the sight of this rosary of bones labeled as being a picture of himself as the visitor to an art gallery who, on coming to the portrait of a girl, reads in his catalogue: 'Dromedary resting.' " The Japan that I have described in this book will be equally unfamiliar to many readers. The "land of high technology," lacking the know-how to test for or clean up toxic wastes. The society that "loves nature" concreting over its rivers and seashores to feed a voracious construction industry. An "elite bureaucracy" that has so mismanaged the public wealth that the health system and pension funds are failing, while the national debt has soared to become the highest in the world.

It is an incongruous picture, shockingly alien if one is familiar only with the seductive outer skin of Japan's manufacturing success. How could the winsome *Portrait of a Girl*, presented to the world for forty years by Japan experts, have turned out to be *Dromedary Resting*—ravaged mountains and rivers, endemic pollution, tenement cities, and skyrocketing debt? Why have writers and academics never told us about this?

Since the 1950s, Western observers have come to Japan as worshippers to a shrine. When I majored in Japanese Studies in college in the 1960s and early 1970s, I learned, as did most of my colleagues, that it was our mission to explain Japan to an uncomprehending and unsympathetic world. Japan did everything differently from the West, and this was terribly exciting— for many Japanologists, it seemed to be an ideal society, a utopia. Even the revisionist writers of the 1980s, who warned of a Japanese economic juggernaut, spoke largely in terms of awe.

Many of my colleagues remain convinced that their job is to

present Japan attractively to others, and a high proportion of them depend, in one way or another, on Japan for their livelihood. Let the Japanophile say the wrong thing, however, and he may not be invited back to address a prestigious council; his friends in industry or government back in Tokyo will cease to funnel information to him. So self-censorship rules.

Even stronger than censorship is the power of nostalgia. Japan experts long for the beautiful, artistic, efficient Japan that they continue to believe in, and the unhappy reality makes them cling even more to a vision of utopia. Incurable nostalgia rules this field, and this is why Zen and tea ceremony experts recite to us many an exquisite haiku demonstrating Japan's love of nature but do not speak of the concreting of rivers and seashore. Similarly, economics professors lavish praise on Japan's industrial efficiency without mentioning that factories are free to dump carcinogenic chemicals into neighboring rice paddies. A few writers have raised these issues in recent years, but they were mainly journalists. American academics and cultural experts have uttered not a peep.

This brings me to a personal confession. This is a passionate book, and the reason is that I find what is taking place in Japan nothing less than tragic. Of course, there is much that is wonderful in Japan—I would never say that foreigners conversant with Japan must attack and criticize it. Nevertheless, we must certainly take off the emerald glasses and see modern Japan for what it is. To do otherwise is to condone and even become complicit in the disaster.

People writing about Japan make a big mistake if they believe that to gloss over its troubles is to "support Japan" and to point out difficulties is to "attack" or "bash" Japan. Japan is not a monolithic entity. Tens of millions of Japanese are as disturbed and frightened by what they see as I am. American friends have asked me, "What drove you to write a book that portrays Japan in such a disturbing light?" The answer is an almost embarrassingly old-fashioned Japanese answer: duty.

I came to Japan as a young boy, and spent most of the next thirty-five years in Tokyo, Shikoku, and Kyoto. As someone who loves this country, it is impossible for me to remain unmoved by Japan's modern troubles, especially the doom that has befallen the natural environment. During the past decade, I have spent untold hours with unhappy Japanese colleagues, who deeply deplore what they see happening to their nation's culture and environment but feel powerless to stop it. Halfway through the writing of this book, I took a trip to Ise Shrine, Japan's most sacred site, with two old friends, both of whom are prominent cultural figures. As we walked through Ise's primeval groves, I asked them, "Please tell me honestly whether I should press forward with this book. It's hard work. I could easily let this subject go." They answered, "No, you have to write it. In our position, with our every move scrutinized by the media, we aren't free to speak out publicly. Please write it, for us."

So this book is for my two friends, and millions of others like them. There is a great irony here, for while many foreign experts remain emotionally attached to present-day Japan's way of doing things, a growing and increasingly vocal number of Japanese emphatically are not. They, too, feel nostalgia, but it's for an older, nobler Japan, one that today's Japan denies at every step. As we shall see, much that parades as hallowed tradition is actually new contrivances that would be completely unrecognizable in Edo days or even as recently as the 1960s. People in Japan grieve because they know in their hearts, even if they cannot always express it in words, that their country is no longer true to its own ideals.

A strong streak of dissatisfaction runs through every part of Japanese society, with even a few highly placed bureaucrats questioning the status quo. Commentators in daily newspapers, magazines, and television talk shows here are obsessed with the idea that something is wrong. The title of an article in the influential opinion journal *Shincho 45* sums up the mood: "In the 1990s, Japan Has Lost the War Again!" Another opinion journal, *Gendai*, devoted an entire issue to a series of essays by prominent economists and journalists headlined "As Japan Sinks—How to Protect Your Life and Possessions." The subtitle was "This Country Is Rotting on Its Feet." Unhappy and distressed people number in the millions—and they are Japan's hope for change.

For fifty years after World War II, a favorite theme of writing on Japan was "modernization"—how quickly Japan was changing, catching up with, or even advancing beyond other nations. Over time, Japan became Exhibit A in various theories of modernization, with writers fascinated by how traditional education and culture had contributed to making Japan a successful—some thought the world's most successful—modern state. However, it is a central thesis of this book that Japan's crisis of the 1990s springs from exactly the opposite problem: a failure to modernize.

Japan's ways of doing things—running a stock market, designing highways, making movies—essentially froze in about 1965. For thirty years, these systems worked very smoothly, at least on the surface. Throughout that time Japanese officialdom slept like Brünnhilde on a rock, protected by a magic ring of fire that excluded foreign influence and denied citizens a voice in government. But after decades of the long sleep, the advent of new communications and the Internet in the 1990s were a rude awakening. Reality came riding on his horse through the ring of fire, and he was not a welcome suitor. In the world of business, the stock market and banks crumbled; on the cultural front, citizens began to travel abroad by the tens of millions to escape drab cities and ravaged countryside.

The response by the bureaucrats who run Japan was to build monuments, and this they are doing on a scale that is bankrupting the nation. It was the only thing they knew to do. Hence the new title of this book: *Dogs and Demons*. The emperor of China asked his court painter, "What's easy to paint and what's hard to paint?" and the answer was "Dogs are difficult, demons are easy." Quiet, low-key things like dogs in our immediate surroundings are hard to get right, but anybody can draw a demon. Basic solutions to modern problems are difficult, but pouring money into expensive showpieces is easy. Rather than bury electric wires, officials pay to have telephone poles clad in bronze; the city of Kyoto spent millions on building a Cultural Zone in its new railway station, the design of which denies Kyoto's culture in every way; rather than lower Internet connection fees, the government subsidizes "experimental Internet cities," and so forth.

One of the recurring ideas in this book is the concept of "Japan at the extremes." As Karel van Wolferen documented in *The Enigma of Japanese Power*, in Japan's political system the actual exercise of power is mostly hidden and widely denied, people dare not speak out, and the buck is passed indefinitely. The "Enigma" lies in how smoothly Japan Inc. seems to work despite a lack of strong leaders at the helm, and many an admiring book tells of how subtle bureaucrats gently guide the nation, magically avoiding all the discord and market chaos that afflict the West. But while the experts marveled at how efficiently the well-oiled engines were turning, the ship was headed toward the rocks. Japan's cleverly crafted machine of governance lacks one critically important part: brakes. Once it has been set on a particular path, Japan tends to continue on that path until it reaches excesses that would be unthinkable in most other nations.

Led by bureaucracies on automatic pilot, the nation has carried certain policies—notably construction—to extremes that would be comical were they not also at times terrifying. In recent years, *manga* (comics) and *anime* (animated films) have come to dominate major portions of Japan's publishing and cinematic industries. The popularity of *manga* and *anime* derive from their wildly imaginative drawings, depicting topsy-turvy visions of the future, with cities and countryside transformed into apocalyptic fantasies. One might say that the weight of *manga* and *anime* in modern Japanese culture—far out of proportion to comics or animation in any other nation—rests on the fact that they reflect reality: only *manga* could do justice to the more bizarre extremes of modern Japan. When every river and stream has been re-formed into a concrete chute, you are indeed entering the realm of sci-fi fable.

Extreme situations are interesting. Physicists learn the most from accelerated particles colliding at high energy levels not usually found in nature. What happens when bureaucrats control financial markets? One could do no better than study Japan, where one may view firsthand the crash at the end of the road for the most elaborate vehicle of financial control ever devised. What happens to cultural heritage when citizens have been taught in school not to take responsibility for their surroundings? Although temples and historical sites have been preserved, the destruction of traditional neighborhoods in all of Japan's old cities makes a good test case.

Destruction of *all* old cities? The words come easily, but the fact that such a thing is occurring strikes at the very heart of everything Japan once stood for. "Cultural crisis" is not, in fact, the best description of Japan's problems, for "crisis" implies a moment of truth, when issues come to a head and are resolved, whereas what is taking place in Japan is far more chronic and long-term. "Cultural malaise" is closer to the truth, a malaise that came about because of a severe mismatch between Japan's bureaucratic systems and the realities of modern life. This book is the story of that mismatch, and of how Japan wandered so far off on a lonely side road, removed not only from the world at large but from her own true self.

I The Land

The Construction State

Our country, as a special mark of favor from the heavenly gods, was begotten by them, and there is thus so immense a difference between Japan and all the other countries of the world as to defy comparison. Ours is a splendid and blessed country, the Land of the Gods beyond any doubt.
—HIRATA ATSUTANE (1776–1843)

Writers on Japan today mostly concern themselves with its banks and export manufacturing. But in the greater scheme of things, for a wealthy nation does it really matter so much if its GNP drops a few percentage points or the banks falter for a few years? The Tang dynasty poet Du Fu wrote, "Though the nation perishes, the mountains and rivers remain." Long before Japan had banks, there existed a green archipelago of a thousand islands, where clear mountain springs tumbled over mossy stones and waves crashed along coves and peninsulas lined with fantastic rocks. Such were the themes treasured in haiku, bonsai and flower arrangements, screen paintings, tea ceremony, and Zen—that is, everything that defined Japan's traditional culture. Reverence for the land lies at the very core of Shintoism, the native religion, which holds that Japan's mountains, rivers, and trees are sacred, the dwelling place of gods. So in taking stock of where Japan is today, it is good to set economics aside for a moment and take a look at the land itself.

When we do, we see this: Japan has become arguably the world's ugliest country. To readers who know Japan from tourist brochures that feature Kyoto's temples and Mount Fuji, that may seem a surprising, even preposterous assertion. But those who live or travel here see the reality: the native forest cover has been clear-cut and replaced by industrial cedar, rivers are dammed and the seashore lined with cement, hills have been leveled to provide gravel fill for bays and harbors, mountains are honeycombed with destructive and useless roads, and rural villages have been submerged in a sea of industrial waste.

Similar observations can be made about many other modern nations, of course. But what is happening in Japan far surpasses anything attempted in the rest of the world. We are seeing something genuinely different here. The nation prospers, but the mountains and rivers are in mortal danger, and in their fate lies a story—one that heretofore has been almost entirely passed over by the foreign media.

H. P. Lovecraft, describing a creepy New England hamlet doomed to be the setting for one of his horror stories, would say, "On viewing such a scene, who can resist an unutterable thrill of ghastliness?" For a modern traveler seeking something of that Lovecraftian thrill, nothing would do better than a trip to Japan's countryside.

During the past fifty-five years of its great economic growth, Japan has drastically altered its natural environment in ways that are almost unimaginable to someone who has not traveled here. In the spring of 1996, the Japan Society invited Robert MacNeil, the retired co-anchor of *The MacNeil/Lehrer News-*

Hour, for a month's stay in Japan. Later, in a speech presented at the Japan Society in New York, MacNeil said that he was "confused" about what he saw, "dismayed by the <u>unrelieved banality</u> of the [800-kilometer] stretch from Hiroshima to Tokyo . . . the formless, brutal, utilitarian jumble, unplanned, with tunnels easier on the eyes."

Across the nation, men and women are at work reshaping the landscape. Work crews transform tiny streams just a meter across into deep chutes slicing through slabs of concrete ten meters wide and more. Builders of small mountain roads dynamite entire hillsides. Civil engineers channel rivers into U-shaped concrete casings that do away not only with the rivers' banks but with their beds. The River Bureau has dammed or diverted all but three of Japan's 113 major rivers. The contrast with other advanced industrial nations is stark. Aware of the high environmental cost, the United States has decided in principle not to build any more dams, and has even started removing many that the Army Corps of Engineers constructed years ago. Since 1990 more than 70 major dams have fallen across America, and dozens more are scheduled to be dismantled. Meanwhile, Japan's Construction Ministry plans to add 500 new dams to the more than 2,800 that have already been built.

To see at close hand how the construction frenzy affects one small mountain village, let us take a short journey to Iya Valley, a picturesque fastness of canyons and peaks in the center of the southern island of Shikoku. When I bought an old thatch-roofed farmhouse in Iya in 1971, people considered this region so remote that they called it the Tibet of Japan. Villagers subsisted on crops such as buckwheat and tobacco, as well as forestry.

Over the next twenty-five years, young people fled Iya for the prosperous cities, and local agriculture collapsed. With its dramatic landscape and a romantic history going back to the civil wars of the twelfth century, Iya had a golden opportunity to revive its local economy with tourism and resorts in the 1980s. Yet in a pattern that repeats itself in countless regions across Japan, Iya failed to develop this potential. The reason was that the village suddenly found itself awash with cash: money that flowed from building dams and roads, paid for by a national policy to prop up rural economies by subsidizing civil-engineering works. Beginning in the 1960s, a tidal wave of construction money crashed over Iya, sweeping away every other industry. By 1997, my neighbors had all become construction workers.

Most foreigners and even many Japanese harbor a pleasing fantasy of life in the Japanese village. While driving past quaint farmhouses or perusing lovely photographs of rice paddies, it's tempting to imagine what bucolic country life must be: oneness with the seasons, the yearly round of planting and harvesting, and so forth. However, when you actually live in the countryside you soon learn that the uniform of the Japanese farmer is no longer a straw raincoat and a hoe but a hard hat and a cement shovel. In 1972, for example, my neighbor Mrs. Omo farmed tea, potatoes, corn, cucumbers, and mulberry for silkworms. In 2000, her fields lie fallow as she dons her hard hat every day to commute by van to construction sites, where her job is to scrape aluminum molds for concrete used to build retaining walls. In Iya Valley, it makes no sense to ask someone, "What line of work are you in?" Everyone lives off *doboku*, "construction."

More than 90 percent of all the money flowing into Iya now comes from road- and dam-building projects funded by the Construction, Transport, and Agriculture ministries. This means that no environmental initiative can possibly make headway, for

Iya has become addicted to dams and roads. Stop building them, and Mrs. Omo and most of the other villagers are out of work. Without the daily pouring of concrete, the village dies.

The most remarkable paradox is that Iya doesn't need these roads and dams; it builds them only because it must spend the construction subsidies or lose the money. After decades of building to no particular purpose, the legacy is visible everywhere, with hardly a single hillside standing free of giant slabs of cement built to prevent "landslide damage," even though many of these are located miles from any human habitation. Forestry roads honeycomb the mountains, though the forestry industry collapsed thirty years ago. Concrete embankments line Iya River and most of its tributaries, whose beds run dry a large part of the year because of the numerous dams siphoning water to electric power plants. The future? Although traffic is so sparse in Iya that in some places spiderwebs grow across the roads, the prefectural government devoted the 1990s to blasting a highway right through the cliffs lining the upper half of the valley, concreting over the few scenic corners that are left.

If this is what happened to the "Tibet of Japan," one can well imagine the fate that has befallen more accessible rural areas. To support the construction industry, the government annually pours hundreds of billions of dollars into civil-engineering projects—dams, seashore- and river-erosion control, flood control, road building, and the like. Dozens of government agencies owe their existence solely to thinking up new ways of sculpting the earth. Planned spending on public works for the decade 1995–2005 will come to an astronomical ¥630 trillion (about $6.2 trillion), *three to four times* more than what the United States, with twenty times the land area and more than double the population, will spend on public construction in the same period. In this respect, Japan has become a huge social-welfare state, channeling hundreds of billions of dollars through public works to low-skilled workers every year.

It is not only the rivers and valleys that have suffered. The seaside reveals the greatest tragedy: by 1993, 55 percent of the entire coast of Japan had been lined with cement slabs and giant concrete tetrapods. An article in a December 1994 issue of the popular weekly *Shukan Post* illustrated a ravaged coastline in Okinawa, commenting, "The seashore has hardened into concrete, and the scenery of unending gray tetrapods piled on top of one another is what you can see everywhere in Japan. It has changed into something irritating and ordinary. When you look at this seashore, you can't tell whether it is the coast of Shonan, the coast of Chiba, or the coast of Okinawa."

Tetrapods may be an unfamiliar word to readers who have not visited Japan and seen them lined up by the hundreds along bays and beaches. They look like oversize jacks with four concrete legs, some weighing as much as fifty tons. Tetrapods, which are supposed to retard beach erosion, are big business. So profitable are they to bureaucrats that three different ministries—of Transport, of Agriculture, Forestry, and Fisheries, and of Construction—annually spend ¥500 billion each, sprinkling tetrapods along the coast, like three giants throwing jacks, with the shore as their playing board. These projects are mostly unnecessary or worse than unnecessary. It turns out that wave action on tetrapods wears the sand away faster and causes greater erosion than would be the case if the beaches had been left alone.

It took some decades for this lesson to sink in, but in the 1980s American states, beginning with Maine, began one by one to prohibit the hard stabilization of the shoreline; in 1988, South Carolina mandated not only a halt to new construction but removal of all existing armoring within forty years. In

Japan, however, armoring of the seacoasts is increasing. It's a dynamic we shall observe in many different fields: destructive policies put in motion in the 1950s and 1960s are like unstoppable tanks, moving forward regardless of expense, damage, or need. By the end of the century, the 55 percent of shoreline that had been encased in concrete had risen to 60 percent or more. That means hundreds of miles more of shoreline destroyed. Nobody in their right mind can honestly believe that Japan's seacoasts began eroding so fast and so suddenly that the government *needed* to cement over 60 percent of them. Obviously, something has gone wrong.

The ravaging of the Japanese countryside—what the writer Alan Booth has called "state-sponsored vandalism"—is not taking place because of mere neglect. "State-sponsored vandalism" is the inexorable result of a systemic addiction to construction. This dependence is one of Japan's separate realities, setting it apart from every other country on earth.

At ¥80 trillion, the construction market in Japan is the largest in the world. Strange that in the dozens of books written about the Japanese economy in the past decades, it is hard to find even a paragraph pointing out the extent to which it depends on construction. And even fewer observers seem to have noticed the most interesting twist: that from an economic point of view the majority of the civil-engineering works do not address real needs. All those dams and bridges are built by the bureaucracy, for the bureaucracy, at public expense. Foreign experts may be fascinated by Sony and Mitsubishi, but construction is not a sexy topic for them, and they have largely ignored it. Here are the statistics: In the early 1990s, construction investment overall in Japan consumed 18.2 percent of the gross national product, versus 12.4 percent in the United Kingdom and only 8.5 percent in the United States. Japan spent about 8 percent of its GDP on public works (versus 2 percent in the

United States—proportionally four times more). By 2000 it was estimated that Japan was spending about 9 percent of its GDP on public works (versus only 1 percent in the United States): in a decade, the share of GDP devoted to public works had risen to nearly ten times that of the United States. What these numbers tell us is that the construction market is drastically out of line with that of other developed countries. The situation is completely artificial, for government subsidy, not real infrastructure needs, has bloated the industry to its present size.

The construction industry here is so powerful that Japanese commentators often describe their country as *doken kokka*, a "construction state." The colossal subsidies flowing to construction mean that the combined national budget devotes an astounding 40 percent of expenditures to public works (versus 8 to 10 percent in the United States and 4 to 6 percent in Britain and France).

Public works have mushroomed in Japan because they are so profitable to the people in charge. Bid-rigging and handouts are standard practices that feed hundreds of millions of dollars to the major political parties. A good percentage (traditionally about 1 to 3 percent of the budget of each public project) goes to the politicians who arrange it. In 1993, when Kanemaru Shin, a leader of the Construction Ministry supporters in the National Diet, was arrested during a series of bribery scandals, investigators found that he had garnered nearly $50 million in contributions from construction firms.

Construction Ministry bureaucrats share in the takings at various levels: in office, they skim profits through agencies they own, and to which they award lucrative contracts with no bidding; after retirement, they take up sinecures in private firms whose pay packages to ex-bureaucrats can amount to millions of dollars. The system works like this: the River Bureau of the Construction Ministry builds a dam, then hands its operation over to an agency called the Water Resources Public Corporation (WRPC), many of whose directors are retired officials of the River Bureau. The WRPC, in turn, with no open bidding, subcontracts the work to a company called Friends of the Rivers, a very profitable arrangement for the WRPC's directors, since they own 90 percent of the company's stock. Hence the ever-growing appetite at the River Bureau for more dam contracts. When it comes to road building, the four public corporations concerned with highways annually award 80 percent of all contracts to a small group of companies managed by bureaucrats who once worked in these corporations. Similar cozy arrangements exist in every other ministry.

Thus, with the full force of politicians and bureaucracy behind it, the construction industry has grown and grown: by 1998 it employed 6.9 million people, more than 10 percent of Japan's workforce—and more than double the relative numbers in the United States and Europe. Experts estimate that as many as one in five jobs in Japan depends on construction, if one includes work that derives indirectly from public-works contracts.

The secret behind the malaise of the Japanese economy in the 1990s is hidden in these numbers, for the millions of jobs supported by construction are not jobs created by real growth but "make work," paid for by government handouts. These are filled by people who could have been employed in services, software, and other advanced industries. Not only do my neighbors in Iya valley depend on continued construction but the entire Japanese economy does.

The initial craving for the drug of construction money came from the profits made by politicians and civil servants. But for a craving to develop into a full addiction, there needs to be a reason why the addict cannot stop himself at an early stage—in other words, some weakness that prevents him from exercising self-control. In Japan's case, addiction came about through the existence of a bureaucracy that was on automatic pilot.

Bureaucracy by nature tends toward inertia, for left to themselves bureaucrats will continue to do next year what they did this year. In Japan, where ministries rule with almost no supervision or control by the public, bureaucratic inertia is an irresistible force. The world of official policy functions like a machine that nobody knows how to stop, as if it had only an "On" button, no "Off."

With essentially no accountability to the public, Japanese ministries know only one higher power: the Ministry of Finance, which determines the national budget. Whatever original purpose each government department may have had, over time its aim has devolved to the very simple goal of preserving its budget. Dr. Miyamoto Masao, a former official in the Ministry of Health and Welfare (MHW), relates the following exchange with a superior in his book *Straitjacket Society*:

Miyamoto: "You mean that once something is provided for in the budget you can't stop doing it? Why not?"

MHW official: "In the government offices, as long as a certain amount of money has been budgeted for a certain purpose, it has to be used up."

"Surely it wouldn't matter if there was a little left over."

"It's not that easy. Returning unused money is taboo."

"Why is that?"

"Leftover money gives the Finance Ministry the impression that the project in question is not very important, which makes it a target of budget cuts the following year. The loss of even a single project means a smaller budget for the whole department. The director is going to take a dim view of that, since it affects his career prospects."

True to their reputation for efficiency, Japanese ministries have done an extremely good job of enlarging their budgets by meticulously observing the principle that each ministry should get the same relative share this year that it received last year. The allowance for construction in the general budget for 1999 was thirteen times larger than it was in 1965, around the time of the Tokyo Olympics. Although more than thirty years have passed since that time, when small black-and-white television sets were common and most country roads were still unpaved—years during which Japan's infrastructure and lifestyles have changed radically—each ministry continued to receive almost exactly the same share of construction money it has always had, down to a fraction of a percentage point. "Bureaucrats are very skilled at spending it all. It is a fantastic waste, done in a very systematic way that will never stop," says Diet member Sato Kenichiro.

Budgets that must be spent and programs that must expand in order to maintain the delicate balance among ministries—such is the background for the haunting, even weird aspect of Japan's continued blanketing of its landscape with concrete. The situation in Japan enters the realm of *manga*, of comic-strip fantasy, with bizarre otherworldly landscapes and apocalyptic visions of a topsy-turvy future. This is what the Construction Ministry is busy building in real life: bridges to uninhabited islands, roads to nowhere honeycombing the mountains, and gigantic overpasses to facilitate access to minute country lanes.

The story of Isahaya Bay is a good example of the "unstoppable" force of bureaucratic inertia. In the mid-1960s the Min-

istry of Agriculture, Forestry, and Fisheries (MAFF) drew up a
plan to reclaim this bay near Nagasaki, Japan's last major tidal
wetland. The tides in Isahaya can rise to five meters, among the
highest in Japan, and they nurtured a rich sea life in the bay's
wetlands, where about three hundred species lived, including
rare mudskippers and a number of endangered crabs and clams.
On April 14, 1997, everything began to die when officials
closed off the waters behind the first part of a seven-kilometer
embankment.

The original idea was to provide new fields for farmers in
the area. But the number of farmers, which had begun to drop
in the 1960s, fell rapidly thereafter, and was reduced to almost
half between 1985 and 1995. That nobody would farm these
new fields posed a serious problem for MAFF, because the Isahaya drainage project, at ¥237 billion, was a very large civil-
engineering program, a keystone of the ministry's construction
budget. So it relabeled the plans a "flood-control project," even
though experts believed that the last flood, in 1957, had been of
the sort that comes only once every hundred years.

Major projects involve decades of bargaining with vested interests as to the amount of their payoffs, or "compensation," and
at Isahaya this long preparatory period ended in the early
1990s. The fishing and farming groups in Isahaya could not
refuse a largesse that amounted to hundreds of millions of yen.
But this compensation was the gold for which such local
groups sold their souls to the devil, for once they received the
payoff they could never refund it. Many towns in Japan, having
decided to reconsider a dam, nuclear plant, or landfill they have
agreed to, learn to their sorrow that the citizens have received
more money than they can possibly repay. In the late 1980s, a
group of environmentalists began to object to the Isahaya
drainage project. Opposition grew, but MAFF went on steadily
building the seven-kilometer dike that shut the wetlands off

from the sea. By the time the villagers began to question the project, it was too late.

Enter the Environment Agency, whose role shows how the Construction State has led to strange mutations in the shape of the Japanese government, rather like those crabs that grow an enormous claw on one side while the other side atrophies. While the River Bureau of the Construction Ministry, originally a minor office, has burgeoned into a great empire with a budget surpassing those of many sovereign states and with almost unlimited power to build dams and concrete over rivers, the Environment Agency has shriveled. Starved of a budget and without legal resources, it has ended up a sleepy back office with a dusty sign on the door and very little to do, having been reduced to rubber-stamping the projects of its bigger and stronger brother agencies.

In 1988, only a year before construction of the Isahaya dikes was to begin (but decades after MAFF began planning and negotiating the payoffs), the Environment Agency made a "study" of it all, followed almost immediately by approval with a few minor restrictions. When MAFF closed the dikes in April 1997, it was clear that the Environment Agency's study had been a cursory travesty. Assailed by the media, the only comment of agency chief Ishii Michiko was this: "The result might have been different if the assessment had followed today's environmental standards. . . . But it is unlikely that we will ask the Agriculture Ministry to re-examine the project."

In other words, although the Environment Agency was aware that the drainage of the Isahaya wetlands was a disaster, it did not move to stop the project. And why should it? Allowing Japan's last major wetland to die shouldn't concern anyone. MAFF chief Fujinami Takao commented, "The current ecosystem may disappear, but nature will create a new one."

And so it stands. The tideland is dead now, and for no better reason than the necessity for MAFF to use up its construction budget. When asked what Isahaya would do with the drained land, the town's mayor, its most strenuous supporter, had no clear idea. "We are considering using the reclaimed land for growing crops, raising dairy cows, or breeding livestock," he replied. But apparently there are even better uses for land that no one knows what to do with. He added, "We have also studied setting up a training center for farmers from Southeast Asia or conducting biotechnology research."

Having seen how Japan killed its largest wetland, let's take a look at the mechanisms behind the attack on its rivers. One of the biggest businesses spawned by the Construction State is the building of dams and river-erosion levees. Under the name of flood control, Japan has embarked on what the British expert Frederick Pearce calls a "dam-building frenzy." This frenzy costs ¥200 billion per year, and by 1997, 97 percent of Japan's major rivers were blocked by large dams. This figure is deceptive, however, because concrete walls now line the banks of *all* Japan's rivers and streams; in addition, countless diversion canals have brought the total of river works to the tens of thousands. The Construction Ministry justifies the dams and canals on the pretext that Japan faces a water shortage. Yet it is a well-known fact that this is not true. The River Bureau uses projections for population and industrial growth that were calculated in the 1950s and never revised, despite drastic changes in the structure of water use since then. The estimates are so far out of line that, according to *Sankei Shimbun* newspaper, the additional demand projected by the River Bureau is 80 percent above and beyond all the water used in Japan in 1995.

An example of the construction bureaucracy's modus operandi is the Nagara Dam, an enormous facility spanning the Nagara River, where three river systems meet in Mie, Gifu, and

Aichi prefectures. The cost of this facility (¥1.5 trillion, roughly $12 billion) makes it one of the world's most expensive civil-engineering projects. The *Kozo*, or "concept," of the dam took shape in 1960, but while water needs changed completely in the ensuing decades, the plan did not, for too many bureaucrats and politicians stood to gain from the construction money. By 1979, new water-use projections showed that the three prefectures would have more water than they needed for at least thirteen to twenty years—possibly forever.

The governor of Mie, well aware of the water surplus, was concerned about the tremendous expense that his prefecture would have to shoulder. At the same time, he was afraid to cancel the project because the Ministry of International Trade and Industry (MITI) was subsidizing its construction, and if the prefecture turned down the dam MITI would deny it money in the future. In 1979, Mie dispatched Takeuchi Gen'ichi, the director of its Office of Planning, to present the new figures to MITI and to beg for a delay in construction. But MITI's manager of the Office of Industrial Water Use dismissed Takeuchi, saying, "You can't just tell us now that there will be too much water!" MITI couldn't allow the fact of water surplus in 1979 to interfere with the inexorable concept adopted in 1960. Environmental groups loudly protested the damming of Japan's last major river in its natural state, but their voices went unheard. Construction began in the 1980s, and today the central dam stands complete while work goes forward on a vast web of canals and subsidiary flood works spanning the three rivers.

Once a concept, always a concept. As in the case of the Isahaya wetlands, no opposition and no change in outward realities would affect the concept. Students of Japan's bureaucracy must understand this simple truth: A bureaucratic concept is like a Terminator robot programmed with commands that no one can override; the Terminator may stumble and lose a leg or an arm, but it will pick itself up and go forward relentlessly until it has fulfilled its mission. It is beyond the power of any man to stop it.

An old poem reads: "Though the mills of God grind slowly, yet they grind exceeding small; / Though with patience He stands waiting, with exactness grinds He all." So grind the mills of Japan's government agencies. In August 1998, public opposition forced Kyoto's city office to cancel plans to build a bridge that would have altered the ambience of the old street of Pontocho, but when the dust settled it became clear that the city had canceled only the present *design* of the bridge, while reserving the right to build another bridge with a different design at the same location later. No matter how misguided or unpopular—give it five, ten, or twenty years—the bridge at Pontocho will be built.

Across Japan, gigantic earthmoving projects—among the largest and most costly in the world—continue to advance, many long after their original purposes have disappeared. There is hope, however, in new citizens' opposition movements that are beginning to stir, such as the one that stopped the Pontocho bridge. Other projects are being canceled or "extended indefinitely" because their costs have run too high even for Japan's profligate ministries. One such example is Shimane Prefecture's plan (dating back to 1963) to create new agricultural land by filling in part of Lake Nakaumi at a cost of $770 million, even though the number of farmers in the area, the people for whom the plan was intended, has dropped. The few farmers who remain vigorously oppose the landfill because of the damage it will do to the water quality of the lake, but the project continued on course—until recently. In August 2000, the government, as part of a review of the most notoriously wasteful public-works projects, decided to halt the landfill. While this is progress, it does not mean that Lake Nakaumi or the area around it will remain in pristine condition. For one thing, 40 percent of the reclamation has already been completed; meanwhile, on learning of the news of cancellation, local governments scrambled to present new proposals for roads, and even for reclamation of other parts of the lake to "revitalize the local economy." Shimane governor Sumita Nobuyoshi told reporters that he would do everything in his power to make sure the replacement proposals get funded. The Concept at Lake Nakaumi will live on, although under different names.

The roots of Japan's environmental troubles go much deeper than the mere greed of bureaucrats and politicians. Japan is a sobering case study, for it calls into question what may befall the landscape of other countries in East Asia or across the world. What happens if "developing countries" never become "developed countries"? The great modern paradox of Japan is the mismatch between its present-day economic success and its governing mentality, which is that of a still-undeveloped country.

Japan suffers from a severe case of "pave and build" mentality. "Pave and build" is the idea that huge, expensive, man-made monuments are a priori wonderful, that natural surfaces smoothed over and covered with concrete mean wealth, progress, and modernism. Nakaoki Yutaka, the governor of Toyama Prefecture, summarized this attitude when he argued, in September 1996, for the construction of a new railroad line to rural areas, although there was no apparent need for it. Building the new line, he said, "is needed to develop the social infrastructure so that people *can feel they have become rich.*"

Before World War II, Japan was a poor nation, with industrialization limited to its cities. The war devastated the cities, and afterward the pave-and-build mentality took root. Although today Japan is wealthy—by some measures, the wealthiest nation in the world—and every tiny hamlet has "developed," the postwar view that progress means building something new and shiny remains unchanged.

President Dwight Eisenhower once remarked that when he was growing up his family was very poor. "But the wonder of America," he said, "is that we never felt poor." The wonder of Japan lies in precisely the opposite feeling: though rich, people do not feel rich, and hence need a constant supply of new train lines and freshly cemented riverbanks to reassure them.

Kata is an important Japanese word that means "forms," a term that derives from traditional arts and refers to fixed movements in dance, the tea ceremony, and martial arts. Once the *kata* of an art take shape, it is nearly impossible to change them fundamentally, although practitioners may make slight adjustments and embellishments. In the tea ceremony, *kata* require that the tea master first fold a small silk cloth and wipe the tea container with it. Followers of the Urasenke school fold the cloth in thirds, while those of the Mushanokoji school fold it in half, but the essential *kata* is the same for both schools.

Kata apply to modern life in Japan as well. Japan's school system, established in the 1880s, took as its model the Prussian system, complete (for the boys) with black military uniforms with high collars and brass buttons. Today, even though the boys have dyed hair and wear earrings, they must continue to wear these uniforms—a *kata* that never changed. In general, most of Japan's modern *kata* do not go back as far as the Prussian uniforms; they can be traced to the early postwar years, roughly 1945–1965, the period during which Japan experienced its highest growth rate and its modern industry, banking, and bureaucracy took shape. The mismatch between the realities of the 1990s and ways of thinking established in the decades before 1965 is the keynote of Japan's modern troubles—and it is visible in every art and industry. The *kata* were set in their present shape almost forty years ago and are now out of step with the modern world.

Pave-and-build involves another mismatch—with Japan's own tradition. In their historical culture, the Japanese have all the ingredients necessary to counter or, at least, to temper this mentality. "Love of nature" is a cliché in the standard literature about Japan, and there was much truth in it, as can be seen in the haiku poems of Basho or the intensively cared for gardens of Kyoto. Japan was once the land of love of autumn grasses and mossy hillsides covered with the falling leaves of gingko trees and maples; Japanese art is almost synonymous with the words *restraint* and *miniature*, with the use of unpolished wood and rough clay. Yet modern Japan pursues a path that is completely at variance with its own tradition.

Shigematsu Shinji, a professor at the Graduate School of International Development at Nagoya, discovered this to his surprise when he did a survey of the sacred groves of Japan's local shrines, stands of trees preserved even in the middle of large cities, which Shintoists hold up as the very essence of Japan's love of nature. People complained, he learned, that "the forests are a nuisance because the trees block the sunlight and fallen leaves from extended branches heap up on the street and in front of their houses." That fallen leaves have become a "nuisance" goes straight to the heart of Japan's present-day cultural crisis, and it raises sobering questions about what the future may bring to other developing nations in East Asia.

If we were to divide modern cultural history into the three basic phases—pre-industrial, industrial, and postindustrial life—we might say that in the first phase, which ended about two hundred years ago in the West and as recently as twenty years ago in many countries of East Asia, people lived in harmony with nature. For Japan, the primal image is that of a peasant family living in a thatched house nestled in the foothills at the edge of the rice paddies.

The second industrial phase is marked by a rude awakening. Because the contrast between unheated, dark old houses and sparkling new cities is too great, a rush to modernism takes place in which people reject everything old and natural as dirty and backward in favor of shiny, processed materials as symbols of wealth and sophistication. The world over, the paradigm is well-dressed salaried workers commuting from their concrete apartment blocks to new factories and offices.

In the third, postindustrial state, most people have reached a certain level of comfort—everyone has a toaster, a car, a refrigerator, and air-conditioning—and societies move on to a new view of modernism, in which technology recombines with cultural heritage and natural materials. In the United States, the image is that of young people gentrifying nineteenth-century brick town houses in Brooklyn, or of Microsoft computer nerds dwelling in solar-heated houses in the mountains of Washington State. In the first phase, man and nature live happily as one family; in the second, they divorce; and in the third, they are reunited.

What about this third phase in East Asia? In the case of Japan, although all the elements that can propel the nation into a postindustrial culture are present, the process seems blocked. Instead, Japan is speeding forward into a culture where the divorce is final and irreparable, in which everything old and natural is "dirty" and even dangerous.

Someone once asked Motoori Norinaga, the great eighteenth-century Shinto thinker, to define the word *kami*, a Shinto god. True to Shinto's ancient animist tradition, he answered, "*Kami* can be the Sun Goddess, the spirit of a great man, a tree, a cat, a fallen leaf." Yet in modern Japan, fallen leaves are anything but divine; it would be hard to exaggerate the extent to which the public now dislikes them. Most cities, including my own town of Kameoka, near Kyoto, lop off the branches of roadside trees at the end of summer, before the leaves begin to change color and fall onto the streets. This accounts for the shadeless rows of stunted trunks lining the streets in most places. I once asked an official in Kameoka why the city continued this practice, and he replied, "We have sister-city relationships with towns in Austria and China, and when we saw the beautiful shady trees on their streets, we considered stopping. But the shopkeepers and homeowners in Kameoka objected. For them, fallen leaves are dirty and messy. After receiving a number of angry telephone calls, we had no choice but to continue."

In 1996, NHK television produced a documentary reporting on the difficulties of growing trees in residential neighborhoods in Tokyo. One neighborhood had a stand of *keaki* (zelkova), which grow tall, with graceful soaring branches resembling the stately elm trees that once marked the towns of New England. Residents complained that the trees blocked the sunlight, shed too many leaves in autumn, and obscured road signs. Many wanted the trees chopped down altogether, but after discussion the city of Tokyo reached a compromise in which it cut down some of them and pruned the tall, arching branches off the rest, reducing them to the usual pollarded stumps found along streets in other parts of the city.

Nor is it only fallen leaves that earn angry calls to city offices. In May 1996, the *Yomiuri Daily News* reported that the city of Kyoto received only four calls during the previous year objecting to the noise from sound trucks chartered by rightist fringe groups, which circulate through the city year-round, blaring nationalist diatribes and martial anthems so loudly that the noise echoes on hillsides miles outside town. On the other hand, there were a number of complaints about frogs croaking in the rice paddies in the suburbs. Itakura Yutaka, the chief of Kyoto's Pollution Control Office, reported, "They say, 'Please kill all the frogs.' "

The stigma of being "messy" extends beyond trees and animals to natural materials in general. The writer and photographer Fujiwara Shinya witnessed once, in the 1980s, a mother in Tokyo guiding her son away from handmade crafts in a shop because they were "dirty." This was an example of "how Japanese women had come to prefer shiny, impeccable plastic with no trace of human labor to products made by hand from natural materials," he wrote. The idea that nature is dirty, that shiny smooth surfaces and straight lines are preferable to the messy contours of mountains and rivers, is one of the strangest attitudes to have taken root in modern Japan, given the country's traditions.

But take root it has. The Japanese often use the word *kirei*, which can mean both "lovely" and "neat and clean," to describe a newly bulldozed mountainside or a riverbank redone with concrete terraces. The idea that smoothed-over surfaces are *kirei* is a holdover from the "developing country" era of the 1950s and 1960s, when most rural roads were still unpaved—one can imagine people's joy at having rutted dirt lanes overlaid with smooth asphalt, and rotting wooden bridges replaced by reinforced steel. That feeling of joy has never faded; the nation never stopped to catch its breath and look back, and the result is that Japan has become a postindustrial country with preindustrial goals.

It's a dangerous combination, and the effect is sterility. Drive through the countryside and you can see the sterilization process everywhere, for the damage lies not only in large-scale projects that flatten the curves of beaches and peninsulas but in many an aluminum or asphalt detail: be it a trail in a national park or a humble path through the rice paddies, every track must be paved, lined with concrete borders, and fenced with high chrome railings. To give some sense of the sterility of the new Japanese landscape, here is an image from close to my home: in Kameoka, a walkway goes alongside a pond that used to be the moat of the local castle, and on the other side is a small park that until a few years ago was a shady, grassy hideaway, where people sat on the lawn and boys played soccer. The grass and the shade were hopelessly "messy," though, so the city recently redid the park, paving over the grass and cutting down the trees. Now few people linger in the park's empty expanse of masonry edged with neat borders of brick and stone. In the middle stands one official cherry tree, with a granite monument in front engraved with calligraphy that reads "Flowers and Greenery."

Japan's traditional culture sprang from a oneness with nature, but it is sterile industrial surfaces that define modern Japanese life. It's a stark contrast, but a real one. The gap between Japan's traditional image of itself and the modern reality has riven the nation's present-day culture. Artists must make a hard choice: try to re-create a vanished world of bamboo, thatched houses, and temples (but in a cultural context in which sterility rules and all these things have become irrelevant) or go with the times, giving in to dead, flat industrial surfaces. Cut off from the latest trends in Asia or the West, designers find it hard to conceive of natural materials used successfully in a modern way, or of modern designs that blend happily into a natural context. This unresolved cultural conflict is a secret subtext to art and architecture in Japan today.

It is not, of course, only the Japanese who find flat sterile surfaces attractive and *kirei*. Foreign observers, too, are seduced by the crisp borders, sharp corners, neat railings, and machine-polished textures that define the new Japanese landscape, because, consciously or unconsciously, most of us see such things as embodying the very essence of modernism. In short, foreigners very often fall in love with *kirei* even more than the Japanese do; for one thing, they can have no idea of the mysterious beauty of the old jungle, rice paddies, wood, and stone that was paved over. Smooth industrial finish everywhere, with detailed attention to each cement block and metal joint: it looks "modern"; ergo, Japan is supremely modern.

In this respect, as in many others, Japan challenges our idea of what modernism consists of. *Kirei*, in Japan, is a case of industrial modes carried to an extreme, an extreme so destructive to nature and cities as to turn the very concept of modernism on its head. An inability to let anything natural stand, a need to sterilize and flatten every surface—far from being comfortable with advanced technology, as Japan is so often portrayed, this is a society experiencing profound difficulties with it.

The cultural crisis might be easier to resolve if it were simply a matter of Japanese tradition versus Western technology. But the situation is made more complex—and also chronic and severe—by the fact that the roots of the problem lie in tradition itself. People who admire the Japanese traditional arts make much of the "love of nature" that inspired sand gardens, bonsai, ikebana flower arranging, and so forth, but they often fail to realize that the traditional Japanese approach is the opposite of a laissez-faire attitude toward nature. These arts were strongly influenced by the military caste that ruled Japan for many centuries, and they demand total control over every branch and twig.

Indeed, total control is one of Japan's exemplary traits, father of some of its greatest cultural marvels and of its high quality on the assembly line. The kind of sloppiness that is taken for granted in the West has no place in Japan. But a trait like total control is a double-edged sword, for it has cruel and deadly results when married to the powers of modern technology and then applied to the natural environment.

Writers on Japan commonly lament the contrast between the nation's contemporary ugliness and its traditional beauty. Discussion focuses on the conflict between modernity and traditional values, but this is to neglect one of the most thought-provoking elements of Japan's twentieth-century disasters: the problem is not that traditional values have died but that they have mutated. Maladapted to modernity, traditional values become Frankenstein's monsters, taking on terrifying new lives. As Donald Richie, the dean of Japanologists in Tokyo, points out, "What's the difference between torturing a bonsai and torturing the landscape?"

In 1995, the citizens of Kamakura woke one day to find that the municipality was felling more than a hundred of the city's famed cherry trees—Kamakura's official symbol—in order to build a concrete support barrier on a hillside. The reason? Some residents had complained of rocks rolling down the slopes, and officials had condemned the hill, which was within temple grounds, as an "earthquake hazard." In modern Japan, it requires a surprisingly small threat from nature to elicit this "sledgehammer to a mosquito" reaction. Every bucket of sand that might wash away in a typhoon, every rock that might fall from a hilltop is a threat the government must deal with—using lots of concrete.

Quietly, almost invisibly, a strong ideology grew up during the past fifty years to support the idea that total control over every inch of hillside and seashore is necessary. This ideology holds that nature is Japan's special enemy, that nature is exceptionally harsh here, and that the Japanese suffer more from natural calamities than do other people. One can taste the flavor of this attitude in the following excerpt from a publication of the Construction Ministry's River Bureau:

Earthquakes, volcanoes, floods, and droughts have periodically wreaked havoc on Japan. For as long as Japanese history has been recorded, it has been a history of the fight against natural factors. . . . Although Japan is famous for its earthquakes, it is perhaps water-related problems which have been the true bane of Japanese life. In the Japanese islands, where the seasons are punctuated by extremes, extremes which have required people to take vigilant precautions in order to assure survival, water is a constant issue.

The idea that the nation's history is one of a "fight against natural factors" goes back a thousand years, and the tradition is that the main work of government was *Chisan Chisui*, "control of rivers and mountains." An extensive literature bemoans the damage done by natural and man-made disasters, typified by the *Record of the Ten-Foot-Square Hut* by Kamo no Chomei (1153–1216), a classic of Japanese philosophical literature. In his *Record*, Kamo no Chomei dolefully relates a series of disasters ranging from fires, wars, and whirlwinds to famines and earthquakes. His point is that life is impermanent, that "the world as a whole is a hard place to live in, and both we and our dwellings are precarious and uncertain things."

As a matter of historical fact, Japan has suffered far less from wars, famines, and floods than China, for example, where these disasters have resulted in the loss of millions of lives and the destruction of much of China's perishable physical heritage. Many more ancient wooden buildings and artworks on paper and silk remain in Japan than in China, despite China's far greater size. Italy, likewise, has endured volcanoes and earthquakes far more severe than Japan has ever experienced, yet "impermanence" is not the abiding theme of Italian or Chinese literature. That it so dominates Japanese thought may have something to do with the ancient desire for *Wa*, "peace" or "stasis." Any sudden change, whether in politics or the weather, is an insult to *Wa*. Hence the fear of and fascination with "impermanence."

One of the persistent myths about Japan held by many Japanese and accepted unthinkingly by Western observers is that in the golden age before Commodore Perry arrived, the Japanese dwelled innocently in harmony with nature and that only with the arrival of Westerners did they learn to attack and subdue the environment. The romantic in all of us would like to believe this. "It was only when Japan modernized (and therefore Westernized) that it learned the ambition of conquering nature," writes Patrick Smith in *Japan: A Reinterpretation*. According to Smith, Japan regrets what it "has taken from the West: its excessive corporatism and materialism, the animosity toward nature that displaced the ancient intimacy."

That is the myth. Now the reality. Where is the "animosity to nature" that is supposedly such an inbred feature of the West? Obviously, modern technology has led to environmental destruction all over the earth. Yet in the West this destruction has been tempered in local communities, where people have fought to preserve their villages, houses, and fields. Nothing remotely like what is happening in Japan has occurred in Europe or the United States. In England, France, Italy, and even industrial Germany, thousands of square miles of lovingly tended fields, picturesque thatched villages, un-dammed rivers and un-concreted seashore are preserved. Europe and the United States, not Japan, are in the forefront of environmental movements; in case after case—from the logging of rain forest in Malaysia and Indonesia to drift-net fishing—Japan fights these movements with every political and economic tool at its disposal. Where are the Westerners who are teaching Japan to destroy its landscape? From Lafcadio Hearn in the early 1900s to

Donald Richie's *The Inland Sea* in the 1970s and Alan Booth's *Looking for the Lost* in the 1980s, Western observers have been lamenting what they saw as Japan's destruction of its natural heritage. They have certainly not been urging Japan toward further destruction.

The key to the misunderstanding lies in the telltale words "modernized (and therefore Westernized)." If there is one important contribution that the so-called revisionist writers on Japan of the past fifteen years have made, it is in their recognition that Japan is modern but definitely not Western. Its financial world, its society, and its industry function on surprisingly resilient principles, with roots set deep in Japanese history.

When Japan opened up to the world in 1868, the slogan of Meiji-period modernizers was *Wakon Yosai*, "Japanese spirit, Western technology," and Japan has never diverged from this basic approach. That it managed to become modern without losing its cultural identity is an achievement of which it can be very proud, and writers on Japan have universally seen this as a great success. On the other hand, *Wakon* (Japanese spirit) did not always adapt well to *Yosai* (Western technology), and sometimes the mix has been extremely destructive. The *Wakon* of militarism led to the disaster of World War II, and the *Wakon* of total control is leading Japan to ravage its environment today. *Yosai* was only the means; *Wakon* was the motive.

The impulse to subdue natural forces arises in every traditional society, from the Egyptians and the building of the Pyramids to the Chinese and the construction of the Grand Canal. In China, legends teach that Yu, one of the mythical first emperors in 3000 B.C., gained the right to rule because he tamed the Great Flood. Japan, too, has a long history of restructuring the landscape. It began in the eighth century, when the capitals of Nara and Kyoto were laid down according to vast street grids, tens of square kilometers across, on what had been semi-wild plains. Another spate of civil engineering took place at the end of the Muromachi period, in the late sixteenth century, when warlords mobilized hundreds of thousands of workers through the corvée to dig moats and build gigantic castles, the walls of which can still be seen today. Hideyoshi, one of the generals who unified Japan at this time, changed the course of the Kamo River in Kyoto, moving it somewhat to the east of its former channel. During the Edo period (1600–1868), cities poured so much landfill into their harbors that the livable area of ports like Hiroshima, Osaka, and Tokyo nearly tripled. Historians cite landfill as an example of a technology in which Japan had long experience before Perry arrived.

With the advent of modern technology, every society made mistakes. The United States, for example, embarked on enormous civil-engineering programs, such as the Hoover Dam and the Tennessee Valley Authority. Intended to address urgent needs for water and electric power, some of these programs were not wholly beneficial, although it had been claimed that they would be. After a certain point, however, Americans reconsidered these projects. In other East Asian nations, environmental destruction, serious as it is, slows down when it ceases to be profitable. Not so in Japan. It is tempting to blame this on an evil Western influence, but that does not explain Japan's rampant and escalating assault on its rivers, mountains, and coasts, which is so at variance with anything to be found in the West.

In this, Japan teaches us a lesson about a cultural problem that every modern state faces: how to rise above antiquated cultural attitudes that have dangerous consequences for modern life. Another case in point is the "frontier mentality" that still makes so many Americans cherish the right to possess firearms. The right to bear arms enshrined in the Second Amendment made sense for poorly protected frontier communities, but in modern America it leads to the slaughter of thousands of people every year. No other advanced nation would tolerate this. Yet Americans still find it impossible to legislate gun control. From this we may see that Japan is very unlikely to rethink its environmental policies, for the very reason that channeling small streams into concrete chutes is something learned *not* from the West but from Japan's own tradition. As with other stubborn cultural problems, change will come when enough people become aware of them and demand solutions. Unfortunately, as we will see throughout this book, change is the very process that Japan's complex systems work to prevent at all costs.

In Kamo no Chomei's time, changes caused by nature seemed to be irrevocable acts of karma. There was simply no alternative but to submit to impermanence. With the help of modern technology, however, it seems possible to banish impermanence once and for all, and thus the concept of impermanence has mutated into a relentless war on nature. The self-pitying perception that Japan, punished viciously by the elements, is "a hard place to live in" features in the media and in school curricula, and serves as the official reason that Japan cannot afford the luxury of leaving nature alone.

A 1996 editorial in the major daily newspaper *Mainichi Shimbun* says it well: "This country is an archipelago of disasters, prone to earthquakes, typhoons, torrential rains, floods, mudslides, landslides, and, at times, to volcanic eruptions. There are 70,000 zones prone to mudslides, 10,000 to landslides and 80,000 dangerous slopes, according to data compiled by the Construction Ministry." In the numbers quoted at the end of the editorial, the reader may experience a true Lovecraftian "thrill of ghastliness": these official figures tell us that the Construction Ministry has already earmarked tens of thousands of additional sites to be covered in concrete in the near future.

Everywhere in Japan, one encounters propaganda about the rivers being the enemy. Typical of the genre is a series of advertisements written in the guise of articles called "The Men Who Battled the Rivers," which ran every month from 1998 to 1999 in the influential opinion journal *Shincho 45*. Each article features antique maps and paintings or photographs of the tombstones of romantic personalities in history, such as the sixteenth-century warrior Takeda Shingen, who subdued dangerous rivers. The message was that fighting against rivers is traditional and noble.

Agencies with names like the River Environmental Management Foundation, whose money comes from the construction industry and whose staff have descended from the River Bureau, pay for "nature as the enemy" ads, and cultural figures happily lend their names to these ads. In the West, we are so accustomed to seeing and hearing "save the earth" preachments in magazines and on television that it may be hard to believe that the media in Japan are following a different tack, but it is indeed different. Here is an example of what the Japanese public reads every day in popular magazines and newspapers: a long-running river-works series printed in *Shukan Shincho* magazine was called "Speaking of Japan's Rivers." The September 9, 1999, issue features a color spread of the award-winning writer Mitsuoka Akashi standing proudly on a stone embankment along the Shirakawa River in Kyushu. In the first few paragraphs, Mitsuoka reminisces about his childhood memories of swimming in the river; then the article gets to the point:

It was in 1953 that this Shirakawa River showed nature's awesome power and unsheathed its sword. It was on June 26,

1953. That natural disaster is known as the June 26 River Disaster. At the time, our house was near Tatsutaguchi Station near the riverbank. At about eight o'clock at night there was a loud rumble. The steel bridge had been washed away. We rushed to the station platforms but the water level kept rising, so we took refuge at Tatsuyama hill just behind. I could hear people in the houses along the riverbank screaming "Help!" and before my eyes I saw one house and then another washed away. But there was nothing we could do.

Mitsuoka concludes: "For me, Shirakawa River has much nostalgia, for [I remember] the surface of the water sparkling when I was a little boy. At the same time, it was a terrifying existence that could wipe out our peaceful lives in the space of one night. With regard to Shirakawa, I have very complicated emotions in which both love and hate are mixed." It's a sophisticated message reminding the public that Japan has no choice but to hate its rivers, that they are dangerous and need to be walled in or they will unsheathe their fearful swords. Similar warnings of nature's destructive power, issued by respected intellectuals, flood the media.

The media campaign is related to Japan's special Law of Inertia as it applies to bureaucratic policy. Newton's law is that an object will continue to move in the same direction at a constant speed unless it is acted on by an outside force. In Japan, the rule has a special and dangerous twist, for it states that if there is no interference the object (or policy) will speed up. Former prime minister Lee Kwan Yew of Singapore once commented:

One particularly outspoken chap told me, "I don't trust us, the Japanese people. We get carried away to the extreme. It starts off small. It ends up by going the whole hog." I think it's in their culture. Whatever they do, they carry it out to the apex, whether it's making samurai swords or computer chips. They keep at it, improving, improving, improving. In any endeavor, they set out to be No. 1. If they go back to the military, they will set out to be No. 1 in quality, in fighting spirit. Whatever their reasons, they have built total dedication into the system, into the mind.

Total dedication drives Japan's self-sacrificing workers, and underlies the quality control that is the hallmark of Japanese production. But the tendency to take things to extremes means that people and organizations can easily get carried away and set out to "improve" things that don't need improving. Recently, driving home from Iya Valley, I passed a small mountain stream, no more than a meter wide, which the authorities had funneled into a concrete chute, flattening the mountain slopes down which it flowed and paving them for fifty meters on each side. One could see the "fail-safe" mentality of the Construction Ministry's River Bureau at work: if ten meters of protection will prevent a landslide for a hundred years, why not fifty meters, to make sure there will be no landslide for a thousand years?

Take the ideology of "An Archipelago of Disasters" and marry it to "Total Dedication." Sweeten the match with a dowry in the form of rich proceeds to politicians and bureaucrats. Glorify it with government-paid propaganda singing the praises of dam and road builders. The result is an assault on the landscape that verges on mania; there is an unstoppable extremism at work that is reminiscent of Japan's military buildup before World War II. Nature, which "wreaks havoc" on Japan, is the enemy, with rivers in particular seen as "the true bane of Japanese life," and all the forces of the modern state are made to focus on eradicating nature's threats.

———————

In the coming century, under pressure of population, erosion, and climatic changes, nations will be making crucial decisions about the proper way for people to live in their environment. Two opposing schools of opinion and technology will influence these decisions: the natural-preservation group (which at its extreme includes the "tree huggers," who fight to preserve the environment at all costs); and the pave-and-build group, represented at its most far-reaching by the planners of massive dam systems on the Yangtze or the Mekong River, who seek to dominate nature with big man-made structures.

In the West, most governments are trying to chart a middle course, with environmental protection given high priority. They are decreeing the removal of shoreline buttresses and funding vast projects to undo mistakes already made. In Florida, for example, there is now a multibillion-dollar program to remove some of the drainage canals in the Everglades and restore them to their natural condition. "If someone's got a dam that's going down," U.S. Secretary of the Interior Bruce Babbitt told his friends, "I'll be there." But Japan's Minister of Construction will very definitely not be there. He's busy planning Japan's next monster dam system, similar to the one at Nagara, this time on Shikoku's Yoshino River, another mega-project designed to protect against a flood that comes only once every few centuries. The majority of registered voters in the area signed a petition requesting that the project be put to a referendum, but it moves forward regardless. So weak is Japan's democracy in the face of officialdom that in twenty-five out of thirty-three such cases, between 1995 and 1998, legislatures have refused to conduct referendums.

So Japan has staked its position at the far end of the pave-and-build spectrum. Redressing old mistakes is not on the agenda; the momentum within Japan is for increasing, rather than decreasing, humanity's impact on its mountains and seas. Even as Japan fell deeper and deeper into recession during the 1990s, it continued to provide more funding for civil-engineering works than ever before. In 1994, concrete production in Japan totaled 91.6 million tons, compared with 77.9 million tons in the United States. This means that Japan lays about *thirty* times as much per square foot as the United States.

In fiscal 1998, spending on public works came to ¥16.6 trillion (about $136 billion at 1999 exchange rates), the kind of money that dwarfs the cost of building the Panama Canal and far surpasses the budget of the U.S. space program. It meant an almost incalculable quantity of concrete and metal structures overlaying rivers, mountains, wetlands, and shoreline, in just one year—and a "poor" year at that, since Japan was mired in a recession. One can only imagine what heights the expenditures may rise to when the economy begins to grow again.

Meanwhile, through its Overseas Development Assistance (ODA), Japan is exporting the building of dams and river works to Asian countries such as Indonesia and Laos, where cash-starved governments welcome ODA largesse regardless of need. Through ODA-funded projects, Japanese construction firms profit during a time of economic downturn at home while establishing themselves abroad at ODA expense. Igarashi Takayoshi, a professor of politics at Hosei University and the author of a book on Japan's construction policies, commented, "They are exporting the exact same problems Japan has at home to the rest of the world."

At international forums, Japanese participants are usually to be found speaking warmly in favor of environmental protection. And while these individuals are often sincere—even tragically sincere—their speeches and papers should not blind us to the path that Japan as a nation is following. Projects such as the destruction of wetlands at Isahaya, the damming of river systems at Nagara, the blasting of forest roads, and the armoring of the seashore are not marginal ones. They lie at the core of modern Japanese culture. Bureaucrats educated in the best universities plan them, consulting with the most respected professors; the finest engineers and landscape artists design them; top architects draft far-reaching civil-engineering schemes for the future; companies in the forefront of industry build them; leading politicians profit from them; opinion journals run ads in their pages in support of them; and civic leaders across the nation beg for more. Building these works and monuments consumes the mental energies of Japan's elite.

This means that Japan's money, technology, political clout, as well as the creative powers of its designers, academics, and civic planners, will be exerted in favor of pave-and-build—on a massive scale—during the next few decades. Scholars and institutions seeking to predict the way the world is going have overlooked one simple truth: the world's second-largest economy—Asia's most advanced state—is set firmly on this path.

One can already see the effect on Japan's intellectual life. While expertise in the technologies of protection of wetlands, forests, and seacoasts languishes at a primitive level, land sculpting heavily influences the direction of study both in the humanities and in engineering. The design of land-stabilizing material has become a specialty of its own. Gone are the days when the Construction Ministry simply poured wet concrete over hillsides. Today's earthworks use concrete in myriad inventive forms: slabs, steps, bars, bricks, tubes, spikes, blocks, square and cross-shaped buttresses, protruding nipples, lattices, hexagons, serpentine walls topped with iron fences, and wire nets. Projects with especially luxurious budgets call for concrete modeled in the shape of natural boulders.

Land sculpting has also become a hot topic in contemporary art. The photographer Shibata Toshio has built an international reputation with his images that capture in black and white the interplay of cement textures laid down over Japan's newly molded mountains and seasides. Shibata is documenting the haunting visual results of this disaster, and his work is very ironic. Yet foreign critics, faithful converts to what they believe is "Japanese aesthetics," and ignorant of the ongoing calamity on the ground, fail to get the point. Art critic Margaret Loke enthused, "For the Japanese—who seem to bring a graphic designer's approach to everything they touch, from kitchen utensils to food packing to gardens—public works are just another chance to impose their exquisite sense of visual order on nature." Japan is indeed imposing its exquisite sense of visual order on nature, on a scale almost beyond imagining.

At the far reaches of the Construction State the situation reaches Kafkaesque extremes, for after generations of laying concrete to no purpose, concrete is becoming a purpose in its own right. The River Bureau prides itself on its concrete technology, the amount of concrete it lays down, and the speed at which it does so. "In the case of Miyagase Dam," one of its publications brags, "100,000 m^3 of concreting was possible in one month. While this record numbers third in the history of dam construction, the other records were set through seven-day workweeks. So this is the best record for a five-day workweek." At times, the fascination with concrete reaches surreal heights. In June 1996, the Shimizu Corporation, one of Japan's five largest construction companies, revealed plans for a lunar hotel—with emphasis on new techniques it has developed for making cement on the moon. "It won't be easy, but it is possible," said the general manager of the company's Space Systems Division. "It won't be cheap to produce small amounts of concrete on the moon, but if we make large amounts of concrete, it will be very cheap."

The Ministry of Construction, like many businesses and

public institutions in Japan, has its own anthem. The lyrics of this Utopia Song, unchanged since 1948, include "Asphalt blanketing the mountains and valleys . . . a splendid Utopia."

Japan will not have long to wait for Utopia. At home, the Construction Ministry is well on its way to blanketing all of the country's mountains and valleys with asphalt and concrete. The next challenge will be the natural landscapes of Southeast Asia and China, which are already destined for numerous dams and roads paid for by ODA money.

And then—it shouldn't take many more five-day work-weeks—the moon!

2 Environment

Cedar Plantations and Orange Ooze

The Moving Finger writes; and, having writ,
Moves on: nor all thy Piety nor Wit
Shall lure it back to cancel half a Line,
Nor all thy Tears wash out a Word of it.
—OMAR KHAYYÁM, *The Rubáiyát*

In the construction frenzy described in the previous chapter, we can see that Japan's economic woes are linked with deep cultural trouble. The sterility of Japan's new landscape, so far from everything the nation once stood for, denotes a true crisis of the spirit. Something has driven this nation to turn on its own land with tooth and claw, and simplistic reasons like "modernization" do not explain it.

In seeking the roots of today's crisis, we need to take another look at what happened in the nineteenth century, when Japan first encountered the West. Japan woke from centuries of isolation to find itself a poor and weak nation in a world many ancient kingdoms were rapidly being swallowed up by European colonial powers. Shocked at the nation's precarious position, Japan's new rulers set out on a crash program to build up the economy and the army, first to resist the Western powers and later to challenge them for dominance. From the beginning, this meant making industrial output a top priority to which almost everything else had to be sacrificed.

Japan's defeat in World War II had the effect of intensifying the emphasis on manufacturing, for it burned into the national memory the desire to build power so that Japan could never be defeated again. In the process, the environment, quality of life, legal system, financial system, traditional culture—everything— suffered. It was all part of a "poor people, strong state" policy, which gave Japan's economy tremendous competitive strength. However, the sacrifice of all to achieve an ever-expanding GNP spawned policies that in many ways harmed the country's mountains, rivers, and seas. One such policy is the state-sponsored stripping of native forest cover and the planting of commercial cedar; another, which has had even more serious effects, is the deliberate turning of a blind eye to industrial pollution.

Foreign analysts have admired a population trained to obey bureaucracies and large corporations as the source of Japan's industrial might. But it also means that the country has no brakes. Once the engine of policy begins to turn, it moves forward like an unstoppable tank. One might say this inability to stop lies at the root of the disaster of World War II, and it is also behind the environmental destruction of postwar Japan.

Soon after the end of the war, Japan's Forestry Agency embarked on a program to clear-cut the mountainsides and plant them with commercial timber. The aim was to replace the native broadleaf forest with something more profitable that would serve Japan's industrial growth. Tens of billions of dollars flowed to this ongoing project, with the result that by 1997 Japan had replanted 43 percent of all its woodland with a monoculture of coniferous trees, mostly *sugi*, or Japanese cedar.

In the process, Japan's rural landscape has been completely transformed. Today, across the country, tall stands of cedar planted in regimental rows encroach upon what remains of the bright feathery greens of the native forest cover. It is nearly impossible to find an undamaged view of the scenery that for millennia was the essence of traditional Japanese art and literature: a mix of maple, cherry trees, autumn grasses, bamboo, and pines.

Apart from the aesthetic and cultural damage, the cedar monoculture has decimated wildlife, since the cedars' dense shade crowds out undergrowth and destroys the habitat for birds, deer, rabbits, badgers, and other animals. Anyone who has hiked these cedar plantations will know how deathly silent they are, empty of the grasses, bushes, and jungly foliage that characterize Japan's native forest. Stripped of ground cover, the hillsides no longer hold rainwater, and mountain streams dry up. In Iya Valley, droughts have affected streams in my village so severely that many of them are dry for months at a time. The villagers call this "*sugi* drought." Erosion from the cedar plantations also leads to landslides and to the silting up of rivers, bringing these slopes and streams into the fatal purview of the Construction Ministry.

That is not all. Allergy to *sugi* pollen, an ailment almost unknown a few decades ago, now affects 10 percent of all Japanese. Dr. Saito Yozo, an allergy specialist at Tokyo Medical and Dental University, observes that there is no medical treatment to eliminate pollen allergy, though he recommends wearing protective gear such as masks and goggles. And, indeed, masks and goggles are what you see on streets in the springtime in Tokyo. Some of the mask-wearers are trying to avoid contracting or spreading the common cold, but hundreds of thousands of others are trying to protect themselves against the man-made plague of *sugi* pollen.

The final touches in this picture are the roads that the Forestry Agency builds to bring the cedar plantations within easy reach of vehicles for harvesting. The agency has spent billions of dollars on forestry roads in every remote wilderness, including national parks—and they have involved a degree of damage to steep hillsides that one must see to believe. In Yamagata Prefecture, the government-backed Forestry Development Corporation put forward a plan in 1969 to build 2,100 kilometers of roads in the mountains, costing ¥90 billion. Residents and environmental groups opposed the project, and engineering problems plagued it for decades. "If we had this kind of money at our disposal," says the mayor of Nagai, a town in Yamagata, "we'd do something else with it—but if the national government insists [on building forestry roads], we're happy to cooperate." Fat government subsides drive the program on.

All this for an industry that contributes less than a fraction of 1 percent to the GNP! For economically, reforestation has been a total washout. The Forestry Agency is about ¥3.5 trillion in debt as the result of decades of its subsidies to support reforestation and to build roads. Lumber prices have been declining for years, and Japan's dependence on foreign wood is now 80 percent (up from 26 percent three decades ago). Back in the 1940s, when the reforestation policy was set in motion, planners expected mountain dwellers to prune and log the *sugi* trees, but today nobody wants to do the backbreaking labor required to harvest timber on Japan's hillsides. Villages are depopulated, and the Forestry Agency has reduced its workforce from a peak of 89,000 in 1964 to only 7,000 by March 2001. A recent survey found that the few Japanese mountain villages that have not suffered severe depopulation are those with a low percentage of cedar plantations, where villagers can make a living from harvesting shiitake mushrooms, collecting wild herbs, firing charcoal, and hunting the wildlife of the native broadleaf forest.

One might expect the Forestry Agency to have second thoughts. This is what happened in China after a similar reforestation program: in 1996, its Forestry Ministry made a dramatic U-turn, requesting that the State Council lay out new logging and timber regulations to make conservation "more important than production." But in Japan the program goes on. Today, logging of virgin forest and replanting with cedar continue at a heightened pace. The Forestry Agency has promised to develop a new "low pollen" cedar, although even with such an innovation it will be decades, perhaps centuries, before pollen levels begin to drop. And in place of human labor, the government is introducing mammoth "all-in-one deforestation machines" that fell, log, and haul out lumber. Eight hundred of these are already at work.

What is in store for the future is mechanized mountains— with giant machines marching across the land via concrete strips of forest roads that have been gouged through the hillsides. It is a scene from the movie *The War of the Worlds*. The social critic Inose Naoki comments, "We've passed into another dimension altogether. It hardly matters what people say: so long as the present system remains unchanged, the forests will disappear, like rows of corn mowed down by bulldozers." Shitei Tsunahide, a forestry expert and the former president of Kyoto Prefectural University, adds, "The reforestation policy was a failure. During the high-growth years of the economy, the Forestry Agency was dragged into this fast-growth atmosphere and focused only on commercial concerns. . . . They completely ignored the fact that a forest involves considerations other than business. A tree does not exist just for economic gain." Alas, Professor Shitei has put his finger on the very crux of Japan's modern cultural malaise: not only forests but *every-thing* was sacrificed for economic gain.

The story of Japan's poisoning of its environment is not a new one. It dates to the two famous cases of Minamata and *Itai-itai* disease in the 1950s and 1960s. Minamata disease takes its name from a bay near Kumamoto, Kyushu, where more than a thousand people died from eating fish that were contaminated with mercury discharged into the bay by the Chisso Corporation. *Itai-itai*, which means "it hurts, it hurts," was a bone disease contracted by farmers who ate rice from cadmium-tainted paddies in Toyama Prefecture. The buildup of cadmium made the bones so brittle that they disintegrated inside the body, causing excruciating pain.

Industry and government collaborated for forty years to hide the damage and prevent compensation from being paid to the victims of these disasters. At the outset of the Minamata scandal, Chisso hired gangsters to threaten petitioning victims; goons blinded Eugene Smith, the pioneering photographer who documented the agony and twisted limbs of the Minamata sufferers. Doctors investigating at Kumamoto University had their research money cut off. As recently as 1993, the Ministry of Education told a textbook publisher to delete the names of the companies responsible for Minamata, *Itai-itai*, and other industrial poisonings, even though they are a part of the public record.

Despite harassment, groups of victims managed to file their first suit for compensation in 1967, yet it was in the courts that the government had its ultimate victory. As has been eloquently described by Karel van Wolferen, Japan does not have an independent judiciary. The secretariat of the supreme court keeps judges strictly in line, and they dare not rule against the government; the police have broad powers to imprison without trial and to elicit confessions with methods verging on torture. An incredible 95 percent of lawsuits against the state end in rulings against the plaintiffs.

The primary tool of the government is delay. Legal cases in Japan, especially those filed against the government, take decades to resolve. A citizen suing the government or big industry stands an excellent chance of dying before his case comes to a verdict. This is precisely what happened at Minamata. In July 1994, the Osaka District Court finally passed judgment on a later suit filed in 1982 by fifty-nine plaintiffs. In the meantime, sixteen of them had died. The verdict: the court found no negligence on the part of either the national government or Kumamoto Prefecture for failing to stop Chisso from discharging mercury into the bay. The court turned down twelve of the surviving plaintiffs because the statute of limitations had, due to the long court case, run out. The judge ordered Chisso to pay surprisingly small damages of ¥3–8 million to each of the remaining plaintiffs. Only in 1995 did the main group of Minamata sufferers, representing two thousand plaintiffs, accept a mediated settlement with the government—almost forty years after doctors detected the first poisonings.

In two separate cases, in October 1994 and December 1996, courts resolved air-pollution suits that were more than ten years old by stipulating that damages should be paid to nearby residents, while rejecting demands that the responsible companies be required to halt toxic discharges. In other words, according to Japanese law, you may—after a lapse of decades—have to pay for the pollution you are causing, but the courts rarely require you to stop.

One might be tempted to put down what happened in the 1950s or the 1960s to haste and ignorance on the part of a newly developing country. But Japan enters the new millennium with only the most primitive regulation of toxic waste.

There are more than a thousand controlled hazardous substances in the United States, the manufacturing and handling of
which fall under stringent rules that require computer monitoring and free public access to all records concerning storage
and use. In Japan, as of 1994, only a few dozen substances were
subject to government controls—a list that has changed only
slightly since it was established in 1968—and there is no com-
puterized system in place to manage even these. In July of that
year, the Environment Agency announced that it was considering creating a registration system like the American one—but
computer monitoring and public access to records were not on
the agenda. And it would be too much to ask companies to
stop dumping these materials. They would merely be required
to report to the agency the amount of these chemicals they are
disposing of.

Japanese laws do not call for environmental-impact studies
before towns or prefectures approve industrial projects. In having no environmental-impact assessment law, Japan is alone
among the twenty-eight members of the Organization for
Economic Cooperation and Development (OECD), though
such assessments have been proposed eight times during
the past quarter century. In October 1995, the U.S. air base at
Atsugi complained to Tokyo about cancer-causing emissions
from nearby factory incinerators, only to find that there are no
cancer-risk regulations in Japan. "It's difficult to deal with the
case if there is no violation of Japanese legislation," an Environment Agency official said.

Despite serious incidents such as the arsenic poisoning of
hundreds of farmers in the 1970s in Miyazaki Prefecture, the
government has no controls for arsenic, either. The few toxic-
waste regulations that do exist have hardly been revised since
1977, and the new regulations have no teeth. Only in 1990 did

Japan begin to draw up standards concerning dioxins, which are among the most lethal poisons on earth. In August 1997, driven by a popular outcry after the discovery of shockingly high concentrations of dioxin around incinerators, the government finally approved new regulations to monitor dioxin, adding it to the list of controlled substances. However, so unprepared were officials that the first study, made in 1996, had to rely on foreign data to judge toxicity, and the new regulations affected only steel mills and large-scale incinerators. Operators of small incinerators (the vast majority) would need to control dioxin only "if necessary," according to the Environment Agency. The situation in Japan is especially urgent because, unlike other developed countries, Japan burns most of its waste rather than burying it. In April 1998, researchers found that the ground near an incinerator in Nosecho, near Osaka, contained 8,500 picograms of dioxin per gram, the highest recorded concentration in the world. It was only in November 1999 that Japan brought its dioxin soil-contaminant regulations in line with those of the rest of the developed world—and the nation is still years away from putting them into practice.

Why the long delay on dioxins? "To single out dioxin as a toxic substance, we needed more data," a manager of air-pollution control at the Environment Agency claims. Yet it's hard to see why the agency needed more data when research worldwide has so clearly established dioxin toxicity that in 1986 the state of California ruled that there is *no* safe threshold for dioxin emissions, and state law there requires incinerator operators to reduce emissions to the absolute lowest level possible, using the best technology available. The real reason for the delay in Japan was simple: the dioxin problem was a *new* one, and Japan's bureaucrats, as we shall see, are woefully ill equipped to deal with new problems. Dioxin disposal had not been budgeted within the Ministry of Health and Welfare, and there were no officials profiting from it or business cartels pushing for it, so the ministry felt no urgency to pursue the matter.

The Japanese tradition of hiding disadvantageous facts means that it is impossible to discover the true extent of toxic waste in Japan. On March 29, 1997, Asahi Television did a special report on dioxin contamination in the city of Tokorozawa, outside Tokyo. Studies had shown that dioxin levels in the milk of mothers there were twelve to twenty times the level that even Japan considers safe for infants. The news team showed a videotape of waste-disposal techniques there to experts in Germany, who were aghast. One commented that the techniques were "pre-modern," and the program made it clear that these were standard across Japan. A study in Fukuoka revealed similar levels of dioxin, and there is every reason to believe that the situation is the same throughout the country.

The pièce de résistance was the following interview with a section chief at the Ministry of Health and Welfare (MHW):

Interviewer: Does the Ministry of Health and Welfare have any policy for dealing with dioxin?

Section chief: There is no policy whatsoever.

Interviewer: Has the MHW conducted any investigation concerning dioxin?

Section chief: No idea.

Interviewer: Do you have any idea how much dioxin is out there?

Section chief: No, we have not.

Interviewer: Have you set any guidelines for dioxin?

Section chief: No, we have not.

Interviewer: Do you plan to?

Section chief: No.

Interviewer: Do you have controls on dioxin emissions?

Section chief: No.

It is remarkable that the section chief gave this interview at all. The interview was granted before public concern over the dioxin situation became so strong that the Ministry of Health and Welfare was forced to listen to it. If the section chief had had any inkling that the dioxin situation was embarrassing or scandalous, the television crew would never have gotten in the front door. The MHW was so unconcerned about dioxin that the section chief exuded an air throughout of "Why are you asking me this stuff—how should I know?"

Only scattered accounts give a shadowy sense of the scale of the vast, unstudied problem of toxic dumping in Japan. In September 1997, the media revealed that the city of Tokorozawa and its prefecture had colluded in concealing data on dioxin discharges from local incinerators and that the levels for 1992–1994 were more than 150 times the legal limit. In one notorious case, the Yatozawa Waste Water Cooperative, a public agency representing twenty-seven municipalities in the Tama area outside Tokyo, continues to withhold data on water conductivity, a measure of contamination, despite being ordered by a court to release the data. In December 1995, the Environment Agency announced that spot surveys had found carcinogenic substances exceeding allowable levels in well water in forty-one of Japan's forty-seven prefectures. Among the serious cases was a well in Tsubame, Niigata Prefecture, that contained trichloroethylene (a metal solvent) at 1,600 times the safe level. Although trichloroethylene is a known carcinogen and has turned up in 293 sites across the nation, no regulations to control its use or disposal existed at the national level.

The issue of toxic waste brings up the larger issue of "modern technology," in which Japan is reputed to be a world leader. Unfortunately, the cutting-edge techniques studied by the experts have almost exclusively to do with manufactured goods. In the meantime, Japan has missed out on a whole world of modern technology that has been quietly developing in the West since the 1960s. This world includes the science of ecological protection. Although it flies in the face of the established image of an "advanced Japan," the nation limps along at a primitive level in this science, decades behind the West.

From 1987 to 1989, I was involved in a joint development between Trammell Crow, a real-estate company based in Dallas, Texas, and Sumitomo Trust Bank in building a fashion mart in Kobe. The designers from the United States were astounded to find that the local contractor's plans called for asbestos-containing plastic tiles for the hallways. "There is no law against asbestos flooring," the architect said. "In fact, these tiles are standard. Most buildings in Japan use them."

The results of continued use of asbestos materials became evident after the 1995 Kobe earthquake, when the collapse of tens of thousands of buildings released asbestos and other carcinogens into the environment. Waste-removal operators rushed to Kobe to sign lucrative contracts, which encouraged them to dispose of the rubble quickly—without shields or other health safeguards. Although the national and Kobe governments provided much of the money for cleanup, they offered almost no guidance. A Kobe city official recalls that he approved a thousand disposal contracts in a single day. "We were in a great hurry, because we thought that removal of the rubble would lead to reconstruction," he said.

While the cleanup continued during the next two years, the amount of asbestos in the air rose to fifty times the normal level, and more than two hundred grams of cancer-causing dioxin (enough to kill millions of people in concentrated form) entered the soil and atmosphere in quake-hit areas. The Geological Survey of Japan set up a task force that found carcinogenic chemicals in 55 of the 195 Kobe sites studied. "We are astonished at the results. The situation is very bad," said Suzuki Yoshikazu, the chief of the task force. Yet the official survey of the quake-hit area, made by the Hyogo prefectural government, found carcinogens in only six sites; Kawamura Kazuhiko, in charge of soil protection at the Environment Agency, dismissed Suzuki's concerns about chemical seepage into the soil with the comment, "Even if underground water in Kobe is contaminated by chemicals, few people drink the water."

It's time to take a little tour of the countryside, as reported by the weekly journal *Friday* in May 1995. We begin at the small town of Iwaki, in Fukushima Prefecture, with a pile of 30,000 oil drums rusting and leaking behind a sign that says *Anzen Daiichi*, "Safety First." In 1989, this cheap disposal facility had reached the point where it had a seven-year backlog, after which the operators began dumping excess sludge into an abandoned mine south of town in the dead of night. By 1992, when the illegal dumping ended, the waste pile came to more than 48,000 drums. The owner could not pay the $6 million bill for the cleanup, and the prefecture, unwilling to set a precedent, has cleared away only 17 percent of the mess. Near the mine, only a few yards from the closest house, a landfill contains radioactive thorium. In response to residents' complaints, the company responsible spread a thin layer of dirt over the landfill;

after this there were no government studies or legal follow-up.

From Iwaki, we travel to the mountains of Nara, where we can see *Showa Shinzan*, "The New Mountain of Showa." This fifty-meter hill takes its name from its origin in the late Showa period (1983–1989), when an Osaka construction company illegally dumped refuse there. The president of the company later sold the land and disappeared, and since then neither Nara Prefecture nor the national government has dealt with it. Recently, farmers have noticed a strange orange ooze on their rice paddies. *Friday* reported that in 1992 the police uncovered 1,788 cases of illegal dumping amounting to 2.1 million tons of waste in Japan. Even so, the arrest rate for illegal dumping is no better than 1 percent, with as much as 200 million tons going undetected each year. Fines are ludicrously small, as in the case of Yoshizawa Tamotsu, who was found guilty of cutting down 3,000 cypress trees and then dumping 340,000 cubic meters of construction-site wastes in a state-owned forest. Although Yoshizawa made about $6 million from the business, he paid a fine of only $5,000.

Scenes like these are repeated by the thousands across the length and breadth of Japan. Ohashi Mitsuo, the executive director of the Japan Network on Waste Landfills in Tokyo, notes that cities have been dumping industrial wastes in rural areas for decades. "If this continues, local areas will be turned into garbage dumps for big cities," he cautions.

In one celebrated case, the Teshima Sogo Kanko Kaihatsu company dumped half a million metric tons of toxic waste on the island of Teshima, in the Inland Sea. For this the company paid a fine of only $5,000, and the island's inhabitants were left to deal with fifteen-meter-high piles of debris filled with dioxin, lead, and other toxins. As is the common refrain in such cases, for a decade Kagawa Prefecture refused to take responsibility for or dispose of the waste. Suzuki Yukichi, the managing director of the National Waste Association, said, "Almost all waste disposal facilities are very small-scale operations. Enterprises are not prepared to foot the bill for proper waste treatment. If consumers are not prepared to pay for waste disposal, then the job won't get done."

It is not consumers who are to blame, of course, for in Japan they have little say in national industrial policy. The problem lies with government policy that favors industry at all costs. "Why do we have to shoulder the cost of removing illegally dumped waste while the government seems to go easy on licensed agents who dump illegally?" asks Ohta Hajime, the director of the industrial affairs bureau of Keidanren, the Japanese Federation of Economic Organizations. "Japan's economy is supported by illegal dumping," the operator of one disposal facility concludes. And it is true that central and local governments consistently support industrial polluters by means of cover-ups and lies. A typical example is the town of Nasu, near Utsunomiya (the site of ninety-four landfills for supposedly nontoxic waste). When animals started dying in Nasu, the villagers requested a survey, and the government insisted there was no problem with the water. A private research firm then found high levels of mercury, cadmium, and lead in the water supply.

This accumulated mess—and the lack of expertise to deal with it—arose because those in charge of framing national industrial policy factored waste treatment out of the equation. There are few legal or monetary costs for poisoning the environment, and Japanese companies have consequently felt no need to develop techniques for handling wastes. And they weren't the only ones who overlooked this problem. Foreign commentators, as they lauded Japan's "efficient economy," never stopped to ask where the factories were burying sludge or why the government couldn't—indeed wouldn't—keep track of toxic chemicals. One would think that waste disposal and management of industrial poisons have an intimate bearing on the true efficiency of a modern economy; and the evidence of run-away pollution was there to see. It's a case of what some economists call "development on steroids," for a high GNP achieved without strict controls on toxic waste is fundamentally different from one that has such controls.

Unquestioned at home, and basking in the praise lavished on them abroad, the bureaucrats in Japan's Ministry of International Trade and Industry (MITI) and the Environment Agency have sat back and taken it easy. They have only the haziest idea of the many techniques for testing and controlling hazardous waste that have become the norm in many advanced countries. The central and local governments simply have no idea how to test for or dispose of toxic chemicals. The reason that waste disposal after the Kobe earthquake took place in such confusion was that the agencies in charge didn't know anything about waste incineration; they didn't know about shields; they didn't know how to monitor toxic discharges.

In September 1994, the Environment Agency announced tightened regulations on industrial-waste-disposal sites. Current rules, unchanged since 1977, did not cover chemicals produced in the 1990s, and disposal sites were still mostly unprotected holes in the ground, without waterproofing, and with no devices to process leachate. There are 1,400 such unprotected disposal pits, representing more than half of all reported industrial-waste sites in Japan. (There are tens of thousands of unreported sites.) What were the Environment Agency's "tightened regulations"? A study of twenty sites over several years.

This lack of environmental technology became vividly clear on January 2, 1997, when the Russian tanker *Nakhodka*, carrying 133,000 barrels of oil, ran aground and split in half off the coast of Ishikawa Prefecture, west of Tokyo. Although bioremediation (using microbes to break oil down into water and

CO_2) has been in standard use as a means of cleaning up oil spills in other parts of the world since the 1980s, the Japanese government had not yet approved its use. The Environment Agency therefore did not apply microbes to the 300-meter oil slick, and untold damage to marine life in the region resulted. Finally, a group of fishermen took matters into their own hands and used a small supply of American-manufactured microbes on what they said was "an experimental basis."

Besides bioremediation, another common technique to contain oil spills is to have surfactant sprayed by airplanes and vessels or to have the oil that reaches the surface burned. Neither of these technologies was available in Japan. Although the tanker ran aground in an established tanker lane, there were no disaster plans in place and no large oil-recovery vessels stationed in the Sea of Japan. One had to sail all the way from Japan's Pacific coast, which took days. The actor Kevin Costner was moved to donate $700,000 of high-tech cleanup devices to the affected areas. And in the end farm women scooped oil off the beaches with *hishaku*, old-style wooden ladles. As Yamada Tatsuya reported in the *Asahi Evening News*, "This time the old-fashioned *hishaku* ladies—something of a museum piece in our modern society—suddenly became a symbol of the cleanup effort."

In April 1997, the Maritime Self-Defense Force discovered a giant oil slick forty kilometers long and ten kilometers wide that threatened to reach the west coast of Tsushima Island within two days. Two destroyers rushed to the scene—carrying, according to the newspapers, "a large number of blankets used to soak up oil, as well as plastic buckets and drums." In technologically advanced modern Japan, this is how you clean up an oil spill: with old ladies using wooden ladles, blankets, and plastic buckets. This raises a fundamental question of what we should include in our definitions of modern technology. In

general, economists have used a very limited definition, judging
a nation's technological level by its ability to manufacture cars
or memory chips, or by its academic resources in advanced science. But many more fields of human endeavor with high degrees of sophistication are qualified to be called technologies.
What types of skills and knowledge are really essential for a
modern state, and how high is the price for ignoring them?

Consider the simple example of forest management. In the
United States, thousands of people study its fine points, and
tens of millions of dollars are poured annually into numerous
disciplines of forest science. In Japan, all the effort—billions
of yen every year—goes into supporting the tired old scheme
of cedar monoculture. While Canada supports 4,000 forest
rangers, Japan has only 150, with no professional training; while
the United States spends the equivalent of ¥190 billion on
public-park management and Canada ¥50 billion, Japan devotes
only ¥3.6 billion. Forestry management is only one technology
that Japan has failed to master; there are hundreds more.

From a strictly economic point of view, Japan has not calculated the cost of environmental cleanup. For an environmental
mess that may be close to impossible to remedy, the next generation of Japanese will face an unpaid bill of trillions of yen.
Or maybe not. Solving such problems is very low on Japan's list
of priorities, which is now a century and a half old and is set as
hard as concrete. When we find the Environment Agency itself
taking the attitude that it doesn't matter that ground water is
contaminated because, after all, "few people drink the water,"
we can predict that environmental cleanup is one unpaid bill
Japanese industry may never have to settle.

Yet recently there has been talk of strengthening controls
over waste disposal, because the government is beginning to realize that this is an industry with growth potential. In 2000, the
government began to institute a new law requiring that house-

hold electric goods such as television sets and refrigerators be recycled when discarded; the recycling will be paid for by consumers, who will buy recycling coupons at the post office. It's a great step forward, but it leaves open the question of who will pay for cleaning up the sort of pollution that doesn't involve consumers directly. Japanese business built its global competitiveness partly thanks to the free ride it got on issues of environmental destruction. Now that the Japanese economy has slowed to a crawl and exports face threats from newly industrialized Asian countries, it will be very difficult suddenly to force industry to pay the costs.

The best the Environment Agency has done for soil pollution is to set up a secret panel in 1992 to study the merits of establishing something similar to the United States' Super Fund Act, whereby industry would foot the bill for cleaning up toxic-waste sites. But powerful business leaders and bureaucrats opposed the scheme as being too expensive, so the agency quietly put the idea to sleep. The panel still meets, but its discussions go nowhere. One panelist has said, "If we dig up landfills, it's clear that they're contaminated. But if safety measures were to be applied to all such landfills, an enormous amount of money would be needed. It just wasn't realistic."

The Japanese public exerts very little political pressure on the government to address issues of industrial pollution, and the few lawsuits are mostly ineffectual, mired in decades of delay. The central and local governments, deeply in debt after decades of funding massive construction boondoggles, cannot afford the responsibility for monitoring or disposing of toxic wastes. The Environment Agency gave up before it even started. There will be no cleanup.

One could view this runaway waste problem itself as a toxic by-product of Japan's vaunted schoolrooms. Students in Japa-

nese schools are made to memorize huge numbers of facts, far
more than is required of students in other countries, and they
also learn to be docile and diligent workers. The system that
teaches students so many facts and such unquestioning obedience has been the wonder and envy of many writers on Japan.
But there are huge liabilities. Items of low priority on the national list for manufacturing success, such as environmental
consciousness, do not appear in the Japanese curriculum. And
what is the result? Mason Florence, an American resident of
Kyoto and the author of *Kyoto City Guide*, says, "In the States
there is a negative buzz to litter. If you drop a cigarette pack or
a can out the window, there is a good chance of having a guy
or girl next to you saying 'Hey, man!' " Not so in Japan. Discarded bottles and old refrigerators, air conditioners, cars, and
plastic bags filled with junk line country roads. Plastic bottles
clutter the beaches. As Mason says, "Drive through the hills of
Kitayama [north of Kyoto], and you see garbage everywhere. It
would be unthinkable, for example, in Colorado." Or in the
countryside of most nations of Europe. Or in Singapore or
Malaysia.

Another subject that Japanese schools very definitely do not
teach is social activism. Citizens' groups in Japan have patheti-
cally low memberships and budgets. For example, Greenpeace
has 400,000 members in the United States, 500,000 in Germany, and only 5,400 in Japan. The World Wildlife Fund has
fewer than 20,000 members in Japan, versus millions in the
United States and Europe. This adds up to powerlessness. As
Professor Hasegawa Koichi of Tohoku University stresses,
"Japan's nature conservation groups are not powerful enough to
influence the policy-making process, unlike their Western
counterparts."

On the other side, government agencies keep up a barrage of

propaganda, at public expense, to support their programs, as we have seen in the case of construction. In October 1996, newspapers revealed that the River Bureau of the Construction Ministry collected ¥47 million from ten nationally funded foundations under its own jurisdiction to pay for public relations that included magazine advertisements warning of the risk of massive rains and floods, a series of events commemorating the centennial of modern river-control methods in Japan, and two international symposiums on water resources and flood control. Needless to say, it was not revealed that retired River Bureau bureaucrats served on the boards of those foundations. Nor was it mentioned that the same officials hold stock in the companies that have the contracts to manage dams, channeling billions of yen directly into their own pockets.

A full-color advertisement sponsored by the Electrical Resource Development Company, in the popular weekly *Shukan Shincho* in December 1995, was typical of the propaganda effort. In front of a photograph of a large hydroelectric dam stands the attractive Ms. Aoyama Yoshiyo, who is traveling in the mountains of scenic Wakayama. "Ah," says Ms. Aoyama in the text. "What lovely cedar trees. They're so nicely tended, and their trunks, shorn of branches, grow up tall and straight to the sky. And there is such abundant water here, of course, the result of this being a region of high rainfall. Why, it's just perfect for an electrical generating station!" When she reaches her destination, Ikehara Dam, she exclaims, "My, there's no water in the river on the other side of the dam. When I asked where the water went to, I found that it now takes a shortcut via a winding river on the other side of the dam. Where the old river was," she cries with delight, "is now the area below the dam where there is a sports garden and places for relaxation." One of these places for relaxation is a golf course, which the electric company kindly contributed to the village when it built the dam. "If I'd known about the golf course, I would have come a day earlier," Ms. Aoyama concludes.

You can hardly pick up a major magazine without coming across this sort of thing—the public-relations barrage is nearly overwhelming. In contrast, scattered citizens' groups bravely take on the government or companies in certain isolated cases, but there is no strong movement on a national scale.

Japan's schools are instilling a mind-set in children that accepts every dam as glorious, every new road as a path to a happy future. This locks Japan permanently into its "developing country" mode. When the U.S. Department of the Interior ordered the dismantling of Maine's Edwards Dam (which was more than a century old), church bells chimed and thousands cheered at the sight of their river regaining its freedom. In Japan, where civic organizations continue to raise flags and beat drums to announce the latest civil-engineering monuments, such a reaction would be unthinkable. "Welcome to Hiyoshi Dam!" proclaims *Ninomachi*, the local citizens' magazine of my town of Kameoka. We see glossy photos of concrete-flattened mountainsides, and learn that Hiyoshi is a "multipurpose" dam providing not only flood control but a visitors' center that allows the public to learn and to play:"We expect that it will play a large role in improving local culture and activity not only in the hometown of Hiyoshi but also in the surrounding regions."

Dams like Hiyoshi are precisely where Japanese children go to learn and play, and they certainly contribute to culture—indeed, they are rapidly *becoming* the culture, with schools, courts, and industry all functioning as one closely knit whole. Allan Stoopes, who teaches environmental studies at Doshisha University in Kyoto, told me that his students want to subscribe to journals published by "green" groups like Friends of the Earth and Greenpeace, but they dare not, for fear universities and companies will learn of it and turn them down when they apply for jobs. Citizens' groups such as those that fought the *Minamata* and *Itai-itai* cases for four decades truly deserve to be called heroic.

Millions of Japanese who do not have a clear sense of the mechanisms involved nonetheless grieve at the steady disappearance of all that was once so beautiful in their environment. Since I began writing in Japanese ten years ago, my mailbox has been full of letters from people who share my concern: One tells me how his hometown has become ugly, another describes how she came home to find her favorite waterfall buried in a concrete coffin. The letters frequently say, "I feel as you do, but I never dared to voice it before." In a typical letter to me, Ms. Kimoto Yoko writes: "I have come to realize that Japanese themselves do not realize how ugly their surroundings have become. I was of course one of these people that didn't realize it. When I talked to people around me about the sorts of things discussed in your book, I found I was speaking to people who had no idea of these things. While the place I live in is not Iya Valley, it is still a rural village. And yet here too, I've seen that what was ugly already is becoming increasingly ugly."

People feel that beauty in their surroundings is doomed and that they are powerless to stop it. The landscape artist Harada Taiji, interviewed in the *Nihon Keizai Shimbun* newspaper, said, "Whenever I find a small village I rush to it on my bad legs. It's not quite that the scenery is running away from me, but I feel, 'I've got to capture this quickly or it will disappear. When I find a wonderful place, I worry that someone will come and take it away from me.'"

The decline of domestic travel in Japan and an explosive growth of foreign travel in recent years indicate a large measure of national malaise. I believe it is possible that most Japanese know, somewhere deep in their hearts, that they are despoiling their own country, but what they know in their hearts they find difficult to think about consciously, given the array of government ideology and misinformation pitted against them. Other factors, too, make it unlikely that environmental destruction will become a mainstream political issue. One is the deep-rooted Japanese concentration on the instant or small detail, as in a haiku poem. This is beautifully expressed in the paintings on the sliding doors at Ryoanji Temple in Kyoto: a few parrots, their feathers brightly painted in red and green, sit on gray branches in a landscape drawn in stark shades of black ink on white paper. The Zen message of the painting is that the parrots are the focus of our attention—hence we see them in color, while the background black-and-white trees are nearly invisible to the mind's eye. The architect Takeyama Sei says that it is this ability to "narrow their focus" that leads the Japanese people to ignore the ugliness in their environment. You can admire a mountainside and not see the gigantic power lines marching over it, or take pleasure in a rice paddy without being disturbed by the aluminum-clad factory looming over it.

While human beings may color in what we want to see and leave the rest in black and white, this is not an easy task for a camera. Photographers and moviemakers in Japan must carefully calculate how to frame each shot to preserve the illusion of natural beauty. The Japanese are surrounded by books and posters that feature precisely trimmed shots of nature—mostly close-ups of such details as the walkway into an old temple grounds or a leaf swirling in a mountain pool—with accompanying slogans praising the Japanese love of nature, the seasons, and so forth. Often the very agencies whose work is to resculpt the landscape have produced and paid for such advertisements.

Well-selected words and photos remind the Japanese daily that they live in a beautiful country. They also impress upon foreigners who buy books on gardens, flowers, architecture, and Kyoto that Japan is blessed above all nations in the world with its exquisite "love of the four seasons." No country in the world has so rich a heritage of symbols and literature extolling nature. Signs for restaurants and bars read "Maple Leaf," "Firefly," "Autumn Grasses"; a major bank, formerly Kobe Taiyo Mitsui Ginko (Kobe Sun Mitsui Bank), even changed its name to Sakura Ginko (Cherry Blossom Bank). Myriad ceremonies such as *Mizutori*, the Bringing of Spring Water, at the Nigatsudo Temple in Nara, survive from traditional culture, and people perform such rituals in private homes and at temples or watch them broadcast in some form or another almost daily on television. From the emperor's ceremonial planting of spring rice on the palace grounds in Tokyo to moon-viewing parties in autumn, millions of people celebrate the passing of the seasons. Shopping arcades hang branches of plastic cherry blossoms in the spring and plastic maple leaves in the fall. But this wealth of seasonal reminders obscures the devastation taking place throughout Japan. It is easy to forget, or never even to notice, that the Forestry Agency is replacing Japan's maples and cherries with *sugi* cedar, that fireflies no longer rise from concrete-encased riverbanks.

It is impossible to get through a single day in Japan without seeing some reference—in paper, plastic, chrome, celluloid, or neon—to autumn foliage, spring blossoms, flowing rivers, and seaside pines. Yet it is very possible to go for months or even years without seeing the real thing in its unspoiled form. Camouflaged by propaganda and symbols, supported by a complacent public, and directed by a bureaucracy on autopilot, the line of tanks moves on: laying concrete over rivers and seashores, reforesting the hills, and dumping industrial waste. Advancing as inexorably as the "Moving Finger" of Omar Khayyám, the bureaucracy carves its "concepts" upon the land, and neither our Piety nor our Wit shall lure it back to cancel half a Line, nor all our Tears wash out a Word of it.

3 The Bubble

Looking Back

Naturam expelles furca, tamen usque recurret.

If you drive nature out with a pitchfork, she will soon find a way back.

—HORACE

We are ready to take a look at the long financial travail Japan has been experiencing since 1990, the aftermath of wild speculation known as the Bubble. The meltdown of the stock market and property prices has wiped away assets worth $10 trillion, with another $3 trillion likely yet to go. These vanished assets are not trivial, for they make up one of the most grievous declines of wealth experienced in human history, the sort of loss that usually happens in war or at the fall of an empire. To see how Japan could have got itself into this incredible situation, we must go back to the heyday of Japanese financial power more than a decade ago.

When, toward the end of 1987, black limousines began lining up each afternoon in front of Madame Onoe Nui's house in

Osaka, the neighbors thought little of it. The cars disgorged blue-suited men carrying briefcases who disappeared inside, sometimes not to emerge until two or three the next morning. Nui operated a successful restaurant, and it appeared that she had expanded her dinner business into earlier daylight hours. Only later did the neighbors learn that Madame Nui's visitors were not coming for the good food. The men in blue suits were coming to pay homage to a shadowy resident of Nui's house, a figure later revealed to be the single most important player in the Japanese stock market at the time. He was Nui's pet ceramic toad.

Toads, as is well known, are magic beings that like badgers and foxes are adept at weaving spells, especially those involving money. People like to have as charms in their gardens ceramic statues of badgers with a jug of wine in one paw and ledgers of receipts in the other. Toads, though less popular, are more mysterious, as they can transform themselves into demon princesses, and they know ancient sorcery from China and India.

The blue-chip Industrial Bank of Japan (IBJ), Japan's J. P. Morgan, especially favored Madame Nui's toad. Department chiefs from IBJ's Tokyo headquarters would take the bullet train down from Tokyo to Osaka in order to attend a weekly cere-mony presided over by the toad. On arriving at Nui's house, the IBJ bankers would join elite stockbrokers from Yamaichi Securities and other trading houses in a midnight vigil. First they would pat the head of the toad. Then they would recite prayers in front of a set of Buddhist statues in Nui's garden. Fi-nally Madame Nui would seat herself in front of the toad, go into a trance, and deliver the oracle—which stocks to buy and which to sell. The financial markets in Tokyo trembled at the verdict. At his peak in 1990, the toad controlled more than $10 billion in financial instruments, making its owner the world's largest individual stock investor.

Madame Nui was also the world's largest individual bank borrower. "From the mouth of the toad," she proclaimed, "comes money," and she seems to have called considerable Chinese and Indian sorcery into play, for she parlayed a small initial set of loans made in 1986 into a vast financial empire. By 1991, in addition to IBJ, which lent Nui ¥240 billion to buy IBJ bonds, twenty-nine other banks and financial institutions had extended her loans totaling more than ¥2.8 trillion, equal to about $22 billion at the time.

Onoe Nui was riding the success of the so-called Bubble, when Japanese investors drove stocks and real estate to incredible heights in the late 1980s. In 1989, the capitalization of the Tokyo Stock Exchange (TSE) stood slightly higher than that of the New York Stock Exchange; real-estate assessors reckoned that the grounds of the Imperial Palace in Tokyo were worth more than all of California; the Nikkei index of the TSE rose to 39,000 points in the winter of 1989, after almost a decade of continuous climb. At that level, the average price-to-earnings ratios for stock (about 20 to 30 in the United States, the United Kingdom, and Hong Kong) reached 80 in Japan. Yet brokers were predicting that the stock market would soon rise to 60,000 or even 80,000. Euphoria was in the air. Japan's unique financial system—which is based on asset valuation, rather than on cash flow, as is the norm in the rest of the world—had triumphed.

When the crash came, it hit hard. In the first days of January 1990, the stock market began falling, and it lost 60 percent of its value over the next two years. Ten years later, the Nikkei has still not recovered, meandering in a range between 14,000 and 24,000. When the stock market collapsed, so did real-estate prices, which fell every year after 1991 and are now about one-fifth of Bubble-era values or lower. Many other types of speculative assets also evaporated. Golf-club memberships, which during their heyday could cost $1 million or more, today sell for 10 percent or less of their Bubble price, and bankruptcy looms over many golf-club developers, who must return tens of billions of dollars taken in as refundable deposits from members.

Despite the best efforts of Madame Nui's bankers and the toad, her empire crumbled. In August 1991 the police arrested her, and investigators found that she had based her first borrowings on fraudulent deposit vouchers forged by friendly bank managers. Nui's bankruptcy resulted in losses to lenders of almost ¥270 billion, the resignation of the chairman of the Industrial Bank of Japan, and the collapse of two banks. The "Bubble Lady," as the press called her, spent years in jail, along with her bank-manager patrons.

Banks, which lent heavily to speculators like Madame Nui to buy stock and land, found themselves saddled with an enormous weight of nonperforming loans. For years the Ministry of Finance claimed that bad loans amounted to ¥35 trillion, only grudgingly admitting, in 1999, that they surpass ¥77 trillion. Even so, most analysts believe the figure is much higher—perhaps twice that. Taking the more conservative figure favored by many analysts, ¥120 trillion, Japan's bank fiasco dwarfs the savings-and-loan crisis of the 1980s in the United States. The S&L bailout, at $160 billion, came to about 2.7 percent of GNP at the time, but the cost of rescuing Japan's banks could reach as much as 23 percent of GNP, a crushing burden. By the end of the century, despite a decade of rock-bottom interest rates maintained by the government to support banks, and despite a massive ¥7.45 trillion bailout in 1999, Japan's financial institutions had written off only a fraction—perhaps 20 percent—of the loan overhang.

What were the policies that caused a supposedly mature financial market to fall prey to a mania completely askew with economic realities? The answer is simple. It applies not only to this question of finance but to questions in almost every area in which Japan is presently suffering: Japan's financial system rests on bureaucratic fiat, not on something that has intrinsic value. What occurred in Japan is an elegant test case, better even than that of the U.S.S.R., of what happens when controlled markets defy reality. For fifty years, the Ministry of Finance (MOF), the most powerful of Japan's government agencies, has set levels for stocks, bonds, and interest rates that nobody has dared to disobey. The financial system was designed to enrich Japan's manufacturing companies by providing cheap capital, and in this it succeeded spectacularly well for thirty years. Money from savings flowed to the big manufacturers at very low rates—in the late 1980s, the cost of capital in Japan was about 0.5 percent. (In contrast, American and European companies paid rates ranging from 5 percent at the lowest to more than 20 percent.) And while in other countries investors and savers expected returns and dividends, in Japan they did not.

In the West, financial gurus sometimes lament that Wall Street holds corporate earnings captive to shortsighted demands for profit, whereas in Japan, rather than paying dividends to greedy stockholders, companies retain most of their earnings and pour them back into capital investment. Even though they didn't pay dividends, stocks kept climbing throughout the 1970s and 1980s. Thus arose the myth that stocks in Japan were different from those in other countries: they would *always* rise. When in 1990 Morgan Stanley began issuing an advisory that included warnings of which stocks to sell, MOF viewed this as an ethical lapse out of tune with the moral tradition of the Japanese stock market.

Concentrating only on the benefits to companies that need not pay dividends leaves out several important factors. We all know there are various standard ways to value stock. Most important of these is the price-to-earnings ratio (P/E ratio), which tells you what percent of your investment you can expect a company to make as earnings. A P/E ratio of 20 means that in one year the company will earn one-twentieth, or 5 percent, of the price of the stock, some or all of which it will pay out to you, the shareholder, in the form of dividends. These dividends will be your basic return on investment.

Calculating the true value of a stock gets complicated if you expect the company's earnings to grow dramatically in the future—which is why investors have snapped up Internet stocks in America even though many dot-coms have never made profits and have even suffered losses. But the general principle still applies; that is, the investor expects to be paid dividends, now or in the future, on earnings.

This has not been true in Japan, where the accepted wisdom held that stocks needn't pay out earnings; before the Bubble burst, P/E ratios reached levels undreamed of elsewhere in the world. The Dow Jones average, at its most inflated in early 2000, averaged P/E ratios of about 30, at which point analysts screamed that it was overheated. In contrast, average P/E ratios in *depressed* Japan reached 106.5 in 1999, more than three times the American level. A P/E ratio of 106.5 means that the average earnings per share of companies listed in the Japanese market is essentially zero.

A situation like this is paradise for industry, because it means that companies can raise money from the public for practically nothing. It works for investors, however, only if stocks always magically rise somehow, despite producing no earnings. That is to say, it works only as long as the stocks continue to find eager buyers. As part of the recovery after World War II, Japan's Ministry of Finance engineered just such a system, and it was a modern miracle. It worked partly because there was then relatively little stock available to the public, given a policy called "stable stockholding," by which companies bought and held each other's stock, which they never sold. The purpose, as with many of MOF's stratagems, was not economic (which is why Japan's system baffles classical Western theorists) but political, in the sense that it was a means of control. It prevented mergers and acquisitions, which MOF could not allow: the threat of a takeover forces a company's management to manage assets to produce high returns, and this would go against the government policy of building up industrial capacity at any cost.

In order to restrict the stock available to the public, MOF raised high barriers for new companies coming to market. Only long-established firms could ever consider a new listing on the Tokyo Stock Exchange. Even Japan's over-the-counter market (OTC), equivalent to the NASDAQ exchange in the United States, followed this "bigger and older is better" approach. The average *review period* for a company to list on the OTC was 5.7 years, and typically companies listing on the OTC have been around for decades, not a few years or months, as is the case with NASDAQ. "It's a cold, hard fact that in Japan newly launched companies have had no way of raising direct capital. In America they can; in Japan they can't," says Denawa Yoshito, the founder of an over-the-counter Internet stock market for unlisted venture companies.

Matters began to change only in 1999, when, borne on the crest of a new wave of Internet euphoria, the OTC spurted upward, its index quadrupling in just one year. Even so, the OTC remains so dysfunctional, so far from the Internet-friendly marketplace that Japan's new entrepreneurs will need, that in the summer of 2000 Son Masayoshi, Japan's Internet wizard, set up a Japanese version of NASDAQ ("Jasdaq"). In addition to easing the way for Japanese investors to buy American NASDAQ stocks, Jasdaq envisions listing promising Japanese ventures in New York, where they can source funds denied to them in

Japan. The Tokyo Stock Exchange meanwhile set up its own emerging stock market, named Mothers. The pieces would seem to be in place for a brand-new form of stock investing. At the same time, all the old rules still apply over at the Tokyo Stock Exchange, where P/E ratios are still astronomical. It remains to be seen whether Mothers, the OTC, and Jasdaq can nurture stock that pays dividends and rewards investors—or whether they will follow the pattern of the Tokyo Stock Exchange in the 1980s and merely engineer another big Bubble.

During much of the past half century, money poured into the Tokyo Stock Exchange, driving stocks relentlessly upward. After decades in this hothouse atmosphere, Japan's financial community came to believe in the "magic of assets": assets would always rise in value, especially when calculated by a technique, dear to MOF's heart, known as "book value accounting." According to this system, owners of stocks, bonds, and property do not need to assess their holdings at market value. Instead, balance sheets show stock at the price purchased—the stock you bought at 100 seven years ago, though now worth 200, still appears on the books at 100.

This is a complete fiction, and it spawned a concept known as "latent profits," which is the difference between purchase value and current value. The concept of "latent losses" did not exist. Investors have ignored dividends and looked exclusively at "asset value" and "latent profits."

The same principles have ruled in real estate, where returns have averaged 2 percent or lower; even minus returns were common. The crash came even harder for real estate than it did for stocks, and by 1996 official land prices for Japan as a whole had dropped to half their 1991 peak (real prices were 88 percent off or lower at auction) and stayed low for the rest of the decade. Vacancy rates in Tokyo's commercial sector grew as high as 15 to 25 percent, and rents were half or a third of what they had been in 1988.

The "magic of assets" leads to a distorted view of Japan's strengths, since so much energy has gone into making banks and securities houses bigger but not necessarily better. In 1995, when ranked by assets, the top-ten banks in the world were all Japanese, with twenty-nine banks in the top one hundred (versus only nine U.S. banks). However, when Moody's Investors Service quantified liabilities, it found that only five of Japan's eleven city banks had assets in excess of bad loans; no banks rated A, only one rated B, three C, and twenty-six banks D. By early 1999, the average rating of major banks had slid to E+, meaning that they were essentially bankrupt. Obviously, size alone is not a good measure of financial health, since liabilities may equal or even exceed assets, and the truest measure of health is profitability, in which case not a single Japanese bank got into the top one hundred.

Lack of profits sapped the energy of Japanese banks, so that in time foreign banks outstripped them through profitable growth and mega-mergers. By July 1999, only two Japanese banks had made it into the world's top ten. One had a negative return on assets, the other nearly zero—at a time when Citigroup and BankAmerica, the top two on the list, were making more than 1.3 percent returns on much larger asset bases.

In Japan's asset-based system, size meant everything; in time, therefore, MOF mandated a wave of mergers so that Japan's banks could reclaim their position as the world's largest. Moriaki Osamu, the director of the Restructuring Agency, is reported to have said, "In order to preserve the financial system we have to shut our eyes [to unprofitable banks]. But, since they can't survive on their own, we've ordered them to merge." In other words, Japan's bank mergers simply combined small hills of losses into larger mountains of losses. In August 1999, three banks—DKB, IBJ, and Fuji Bank—merged to create the world's largest bank by assets, yet the merger did nothing to make the resulting behemoth profitable. The well-known consultant Ohmae Ken'ichi compares the bank to the *Yamato*, Japan's giant warship in World War II that sank before it had a chance to fire its guns. By mid-2000, Japan once again had four of the five largest world banks—all of them huge money-losers.

This did not disturb MOF, however, because in Japan's credit system losses and debt have no consequences. Banks rarely make unfriendly recalls of debt within their *keiretsu* (industrial groupings), allowing companies within their grouping to borrow safely far more than their counterparts in the rest of the world. It has been in a company's best interest to borrow as much as it can so as to acquire more and more capital assets and never to sell them. A company would borrow against assets such as land, and then reinvest that money in the stock market. The market would rise, and the company would then have "latent profits" against which to borrow more money, with which to buy land. And on to the next round.

This cycle of assets–debt–assets is the background for the madness that seized Japan during the Bubble. It explains why IBJ lent Madame Nui money to buy IBJ's own bonds in a deal that cost her $30 million the moment she signed the contract. IBJ knew well why she wanted those bonds. She took her bondholdings to other banks, which were glad to lend her more billions because she had such blue-chip collateral.

This system flies in the face of Western economic theory, but it worked brilliantly in Japan for the first years after World War II, allowing Japan to pull itself up by its own bootstraps. Karel van Wolferen calls the system "credit ordering," and it is important to remember that it really did achieve great success, turning Japan in a few decades into the world's second-largest industrial power. Since then the South Koreans have Japan's credit ordering and so to a greater or lesser extent have most of the so-called Asian Tigers.

This new paradigm of capitalism once appeared to have triumphed over old-fashioned Western values such as the law of supply and demand. There was just one little flaw. As Nigel Holloway and Robert Zielinski wrote back in 1991, "The competitive advantages that Japanese companies gain from their stock market depend on a single factor: share prices must go up." The Ministry of Finance patched together an intricate machine to support this market: stocks that yielded no dividends, real estate that produced no cash flow, debts that companies never needed to repay, and balance sheets that legally hid losses and liabilities. In this market, no Japanese company could ever go wrong. It was the envy of the developed world.

It was a powerhouse, but it also was a Ponzi scheme. Ponzi schemes work well as long as money keeps flowing in; when the flow stops or slows down, trouble ensues. During the period of high growth that lasted until the late 1980s, Japan's financial system seemed invincible. The economy grew at an annual rate of 4 to 6 percent for so long that everyone took it for granted that this would continue indefinitely. When, in the early 1990s, it slowed to 1 percent or less, the system began to fall apart.

The aim of the contraption the Ministry of Finance had rigged up for Japan's financial world was peace or, rather, stasis. No bank could ever fail; no investor could ever lose by playing the stock market. Everywhere, cartels and monopolies ruled, guided by the firm hand of bureaucrats. This desire for peace, for no surprises, is such a strong factor in traditional Japanese culture that the Law of No Surprises comes first in my personal Ten Laws of Japanese Life. There is no better paradigm for this than the tea ceremony, where detailed rules determine in ad-

vance every slight turn of the wrist, the placement of every object, and virtually every spoken word. No society has ever gone
to such extreme lengths to rein in spontaneity. In the industrial
arena, employees rarely change companies; small start-ups do
not challenge established large firms. Concrete slabs armor riverbanks and seacoasts to guard against any unwelcome surprises
from nature.

The Law of No Surprises means that people find it difficult
to let go of failed policies and cut their losses—a process that
we will see at work in many fields in Japan. The inability to cut
losses is what underlay the Daiwa Bank scandal of July 1995,
when the U.S. Federal Reserve discovered that Daiwa had hidden $1.1 billion of trading losses from federal authorities, and
also the Sumitomo Trading scandal of October 1996, in which
a copper trader for Sumitomo Trading in Great Britain ran up
$2.6 billion in secret losses. Both cases involved a spiraling se-
ries of bad trades that lasted years—in the case of Daiwa, for
more than a decade. Neither the traders nor their parent companies were able to call a halt at an early stage.

Traditionalists hold the hallowed word *Wa* (peace, or harmony) as Japan's ultimate ideal, even going so far as to use *Wa*
as an alternate name for Japan itself. The nation's first constitution, promulgated by Prince Shotoku in 604, began with the
words "Harmony [*Wa*] is to be valued, and an avoidance of
wanton opposition to be honored." To update this to the twentieth century, read "market forces" for "wanton opposition."
There is a hankering after a peaceful golden age, when everyone knew his place and all human relations worked like clock-
work—the quiet harmony of the feudal era. In the words of
the seventeenth-century novelist Ihara Saikaku, Japan is the
land of peace, with "the spring breezes stilled and not a ripple
upon the four seas."

The trouble is that the world does in fact change, and as it does, inflexible systems grow increasingly removed from reality. Small losses accumulate into torrents of red ink, as Daiwa Bank and Sumitomo Trading discovered. A beautiful stock exchange, lovingly engineered with a thousand clever devices so that prices will always rise, results in the biggest banking fiasco the world has ever seen. With a twist: in banking fiascos elsewhere, banks typically go under; in Japan, with a few exceptions, the government cannot allow that—so the nation has paid the price in other ways.

There is a moral to the story, and it strikes at the root of authoritarian societies everywhere. The Soviet Union under Brezhnev, Japan under its bureaucracy—each is an example of a society that believed it had achieved eternal balance: central planners had everything under their control. Change, and all the social chaos to which it gives rise, had been banished. But alas, we can never banish change. Machiavelli writes: "If a man behaves with patience and circumspection and the time and circumstances are such that this method is called for, he will prosper; but if time and circumstances change he will be ruined because he does not change his policy. . . . Thus a man who is circumspect, when circumstances demand impetuous behavior, is unequal to the task, and so he comes to grief."

One aspect of Japan's failure to keep in touch with reality was that the Ministry of Finance and Japan's banks and brokerage firms failed to acquire the technology used in financial markets elsewhere. This may be one of the most surprising aspects of the Bubble, for it runs against the common wisdom about Japan's alleged gift for high technology.

If debts need never be repaid and stocks produce no yields, what is the measuring rod of value? There was none, aside from Madame Nui's toad. In the 1980s Japan's securities houses, dominated by Nomura, towered over all competitors and many

believed them to be practically invincible. But traders at Nomura and other brokerage houses did not learn the mathemati-
cal tools that Wall Street brokers developed in the 1980s, and
that led to the complex computer trading and new financial in-
struments that dominate the market today. Since 1991, they
have seen one long series of retrenchments, with Nomura consistently losing money, or barely scraping by in the United
States and Great Britain. Daiwa cut its foreign branches from
thirty to eighteen in 1999; Nikko reduced its overseas operations; and Nomura is closing foreign desks. By January 1998,
Japanese securities firms had fallen completely out of the ranking for the world's top-ten bond dealers. Nomura made it only
to No. 13; the other firms did not get into even the top
twenty. And by then foreign brokerage houses were handling
almost 40 percent of all trades on the TSE. In the fall of 1997,
Yamaichi Securities, one of the Big Four brokerages, declared
bankruptcy when more than $2 billion in losses surfaced in
hidden offshore accounts. And then there were three. "Just as
the U.S. brokers toppled England's largest securities firms, the
same thing is happening here in Japan," said Saito Atsushi, Nomura's executive managing director.

However, there was to be one last mission for MOF's financial machine to accomplish, albeit a suicide mission. MOF decided that it should expand into Asia, which it considered
Japan's natural sphere of influence. Land prices had been rising
in Thailand, Malaysia, and Indonesia for decades—all the old
Bubble rules still seemed to apply there. So Japan in effect ex-
ported its Bubble to Asia, lending heedlessly to build office
towers, shopping centers, and hotels, as was done in Tokyo and
Osaka years ago. "We are just asset eaters," says Sanada Yukimitsu, an associate director at Tokyo Mitsubishi International in
Hong Kong. "The Europeans and Americans consider profitability, they manage their assets. If there is no profit, those

banks just withdraw. But Japanese banks lend even when the price isn't so good."

And lend they did. Asian countries modeled their markets on Japan: under the leadership of strongmen such as Indonesia's Suharto and Malaysia's Mahathir, governments set values, and told large investors what to buy, and they obeyed. From MOF's point of view, Southeast Asia was one last blessed corner of Eden that was still free of dangerous wild animals like P/E ratios and cash-flow analysis. From the mid-1990s on, Japanese banks doubled and tripled their loans to Southeast Asia, providing the lion's share of loans to Korea, Malaysia, and Indonesia, and more than half of all foreign money lent to Thailand.

There is an old Yiddish joke that asks: Question: What does the saying mean, Though he slips and falls on the ice, the Avenging Angel will still catch up with you? Answer: He's not called the Avenging Angel for nothing! Alas for MOF. In the fall of 1997, the Avenging Angel arrived in Southeast Asia waving the flaming sword of "real value." The Korean, Thai, Malaysian, and Indonesian currencies collapsed overnight. Suharto and Mahathir watched in helpless rage as the markets, long used to obedience, went their own way: down. The mistake of the Asian nations was to lower the walls around their credit systems, something Japan would never do—hence when the crash came they could not control it as MOF did in Japan.

A massive financial meltdown of the sort that had been taking place slowly in Japan over seven years happened within a few months. Japan's banks, whose loans to the region were four times those of U.S. banks, are writing off tens of billions of dollars of bad debt. The results for Japan, however, are not entirely negative, for while the banks lost heavily, Japan's manufacturers benefited from the Asian crisis to snap up businesses and properties at bargain prices. Much is at stake in MOF's new offensive in Asia. Japanese banks and stockbrokers are in such trouble at home, and have lost so much business in the United States and Europe, that if their Asian policy does not succeed they may languish permanently as second-class citizens in world finance. "What's left if this fails?" asks Alicia Ogawa, the head of research for Nikko Salomon Smith Barney. "That's a good question."

Meanwhile, what about the *size* of the stock exchange? In 1989, the New York and Tokyo stock markets stood very nearly equal in market value (Tokyo's was slightly larger). Eleven years later, in August 2000, the New York exchange had reached a total capitalization of about $16.4 trillion; Tokyo's had $3.6 trillion, making it less than *one-fourth* the size of New York's. Even more sobering, while Japan's OTC market for emerging stocks fizzled, NASDAQ grew to be a giant in its own right. Indeed, NASDAQ, with a market cap of $2.9 trillion, came within striking reach of the Tokyo Stock Exchange; when the TSE dipped in June 1999, NASDAQ even surpassed it! Together, monthly turnover at NASDAQ and New York exceeded Tokyo by eleven times.

One of the more puzzling aspects of post-Bubble Japan has been the unwillingness to reform a market that has obviously failed. By 1996 it was clear that drastic changes would be necessary, and MOF came up with the idea of a Big Bang, a deregulation modeled on the market-opening of the 1980s in London, when the "Big Bang" sparked dramatic growth in the London financial world.

The problem is that Japan's banks and securities firms rely for their very life on unreal values. Like Japan's rural villages and their dependence on dam building, the banks are hooked on the narcotics of these unreal values, and kicking the habit will bring about severe withdrawal symptoms. Deregulation in Japan, scheduled to take place over several years starting in

1999, has turned out to be anything but a Big Bang. Speaking on the subject of Japan's reforms in 1996, Sakakibara Eisuke, the director of MOF's International Finance Bureau, announced, "We bureaucrats are giving up all of our power." This was followed, according to *The Wall Street Journal*, by "a quick outline of how Mr. Hashimoto's Big Bang program would unleash market forces. But then Mr. Sakakibara made an important qualification. 'Of course,' he said, giggling, 'we can't allow any confusion in the markets'—a phrase bureaucrats often invoke to justify a go-slow approach to reform."

The go-slow process began immediately. The insurance industry, due to open to newcomers in 1998, won a reprieve until 2001—or later. The Ministry of Finance announced that banks must set aside capital against bad loans under a system known as "prompt and corrective action" but quickly began to water down the standards, phasing in the rule piecemeal, applying it first to large banks and only later—if ever—to small banks, where most of the trouble lies. As Japan entered the twenty-first century, the hype about the Big Bang had died out, and it was consigned to dusty shelves as just another government report. It was business as usual in Tokyo.

This brings us to a striking feature of Japan's post-Bubble trauma: paralysis. Instituting a real Big Bang is simply out of the question, for the whole edifice of Japanese finance might crumble if MOF allowed economic rationalism to infiltrate. It has been said that the Bubble losses were not as severe as they seem because they were merely "paper losses"—but for Japan, paper losses are a serious issue because the very genius of MOF's system was its ability to inflate assets on paper: Japan's rapid postwar development depended on it. So when troubles began to appear, MOF trod very gently, afraid to make any sudden moves.

The concept of "latent profits" has come home to roost in

the form of "latent losses." Banks lent heavily to real-estate companies that own land now valued at a fifth or a tenth of the price they paid for it a decade or two ago. As the real-estate companies go under, these properties become the problem of their lenders, but rather than write down the losses year by year on a present-value basis, the banks have kept these properties on their books at purchase value; the moment they sell, they must suddenly report huge losses. So the market came to a near-complete stop in the 1990s: banks didn't sell because of "latent losses," and few bought because not enough transactions occurred to lower the prices to profitable levels.

Paralysis also rules in the stock market. The amount of money raised by new stock offerings in 1989 was ¥5.8 trillion; by 1992, it had fallen to ¥4 billion, a shocking 0.07 percent of what it had been three years earlier. By 1998 this figure had crawled back up to ¥284 billion, still a tiny fraction of its earlier height. Another telling statistic is the number of companies listed on the exchange. In Tokyo, that number remained almost flat during the 1990s, while that of the New York Stock Exchange rose by 45 percent.

Overall, the Tokyo and Osaka stock exchanges raised about ¥1.5 trillion (about $13 billion) in initial and secondary public offerings in 1995–1999; the equivalent for the same period on the combined New York and NASDAQ exchanges was considerably more than $600 billion, a truly staggering difference. To get a sense of the scales of magnitude involved, consider that in the first three months of 2000 alone the NYSE and NASDAQ raised $92 billion through public offerings, far more than the total raised in Tokyo and Osaka over the entire past *decade*. The original purpose of a stock market is to provide a forum for companies to sell equity to the public, but the TSE abandoned this role for ten years; for most intents and purposes, it was shut down.

Remarkably, in spite of all this, very little has changed in Tokyo. It is important to realize that as Japan enters the new millennium its financial system remains essentially intact, with only a nod to what Americans and Britons would consider universal reality. Banks and real-estate companies continue to keep properties on their books at exorbitant values; the stock market remains high when measured by P/E ratios, and the big players stay obedient to the system and never blow the whistle. It might seem that Japan has gotten away with it. Western theorists, convinced of certain invariant laws of money—like the laws of physics—find themselves baffled.

The paradox lies in the fact that money is to a great degree determined by society and its belief systems. If everyone agrees that Japan's failed banks are still functioning, then they function. If everyone agrees that unrealistic land and stock values are acceptable, then this is indeed so. And this explains the paralysis, because all these artificial values are linked, each propping up the other.

One must also remember that the collapse of the Bubble was slow, not fast. When it began to deflate, MOF officials took the situation in hand and did their best to manage events, and so controlled was the deflation that some have even speculated that MOF itself initiated and directed the entire crisis. While the theory of MOF invincibility is unrealistic—during most of the 1990s the ministry was fighting one long rearguard action—the fact remains that Japan escaped with remarkably little apparent pain.

Or did it? Japan's success over several decades shows that the laws of money are not immutable; they can be altered to a great degree by such systems as Japanese-style credit ordering. However, post-Bubble paralysis shows that the laws will reassert themselves if such systems are carried to an extreme. Most interestingly, the pain may come in unexpected places. Japan protected its system on the surface: bankrupt banks kept their doors open for business, and the stock market appeared to have stabilized—but the trouble, driven underground, surfaced elsewhere.

The authorities are in a position similar to a player of the Whack-a-Mole game in arcades a few years ago. In front of you is a big box punctured with little portholes out of which a mole pops up now and then. You grab a rubber hammer, and your job is to hammer the mole. As the game goes on, the mole moves faster and faster—when you hammer the mole over here, it pops up over there. One of the busiest mole games played by MOF goes by the name of the Bank of International Settlements. BIS, the world's central banks' central bank, prescribes that banks must maintain a minimum "capital adequacy ratio" of 8 percent of capital to outstanding loans. This means that in order to lend $100, I need to have at least $8 of my own money as supporting capital. If a bank's capital falls too low, it will face restrictions on its international lending ability.

The Japanese mole game began in the early 1990s, when stocks began to fall. Banks, which own large stock portfolios, found their BIS ratios sinking below the 8 percent cutoff point, so MOF ordered insurance companies and pension funds to buy stock to support the market, pounding the BIS mole back into its hole. But soon other moles were popping up in unexpected places: insurance companies and pension funds, after years of investing in low-yield stock, are receiving near-zero, or even negative, returns on their assets. Save the stock market, and you bankrupt the pension funds and insurance companies. Relieve them, and the banks have to curtail international lending. Allow the Nikkei to fall below 10,000, and P/E ratios would return to health, attracting domestic and foreign investors, but at that level it would no longer be possible to pretend that the banks are solvent—and belief in the system is the keystone that props it all up. So, on goes the mole game, fast and furious.

One unexpected consequence of the Bubble was the discovery that Japan's financial community was becoming irrelevant to the developed world. The barriers raised by MOF were so high that when the crash came, others could hear the sound of crumbling columns and smashing glass, but it had very little impact on local economies elsewhere. Japan lost more money than any nation had ever lost in all of human history, from the Sack of Rome to the Great Depression of 1929, but it affected the United States and Europe not a jot, and the bourses in London and New York went on to flourish as never before.

The Ministry of Finance assumed that Japan's national borders are absolute barriers, and within them it did indeed command absolute obedience for decades. But with money now flowing in an instant from one country to another at the news that interest rates have shifted one-tenth of a percentile, old ways of controlling the market no longer work. MOF discovered this when it tried to restrict the futures market in Osaka, only to find that Singapore and Chicago had grabbed the lead in Osaka's absence.

There is one important area in which Japan's financial system may not be globally irrelevant, and this is the nation's enormous dollar holdings. This brings us to another artificial financial system, one that has perhaps the most far-reaching repercussions of all: Japan never took the dollars earned over decades of trade surpluses and exchanged them back into yen.

The economist R. Taggart Murphy and Mikuni Akio, a pioneer of independent rating agencies in Japan, have examined this issue in some detail, and the gist of their analysis is as follows: For Japan to repatriate all the dollars earned abroad (net holdings came to a colossal $1.3 trillion by the end of 1998) would put pressure on the yen and drive it upward, increasing imports and weakening Japan's ability to export, and the point of MOF's financial system was to repress imports and allow Japan to keep exporting at all costs; so manufacturing firms and the government left these dollars abroad, while funding their external balance with "virtual yen"—that is, yen borrowed at almost no interest from domestic lenders. This system worked well for decades, but by the 1990s it had come under huge strain. It is now more difficult than ever for Japan to repatriate its foreign reserves, since if it did, the dollar would drop like a stone, which would drive up inflation in the United States, raise interest rates, and put an end to America's long economic expansion; at the same time, it would result in a shockingly high yen, bringing Japan's exports to a crawl. So it is not only Japan that wields power over the United States; it goes both ways. Murphy says, "Japan and the United States have realized the financial equivalent of the nuclear balance of terror—mutually assured destruction."

It's sobering to realize that the supposedly "rational" United States, too, relies on an artificial system to support its economy, persistently ignoring the mountain of dollars piling up in foreign ownership—it has been called America's "deficit without tears." For the time being, foreigners continue to finance the U.S. economy with money earned from America's huge trade deficits, but sooner or later they will cash in those dollars and the American economy will suffer severe pain.

Or maybe not. If Japan suddenly sold off its dollars, it would hurt the U.S. economy but damage Japan's far more. Furthermore, Japan is not the only country to hold dollars; all of America's trading partners do, and China, running the largest trading surplus with the United States, is building up the biggest reserves of all. In coming years, Japan may not necessarily exert the determining influence on what happens to the dollar. The very existence of so many dollars abroad is also a plus for the United States, because it makes the dollar the de facto world currency—so there is less need for foreign nations to trade their dollars in for local money. Perhaps the United States will turn out to have practiced a bit of financial magic of its own, holding those dollars hostage indefinitely—or, at least, until a time beyond the horizon when economists can make predictions.

Meanwhile, Japan continues to keep most of its dollars abroad, diverting ever more "virtual yen" at home to fund its huge external surpluses, and this is getting harder and harder to do. Uncontrolled bank lending in the 1980s (the Bubble) could be seen as an early attempt to inflate the domestic money supply without bringing the dollars home. We have seen what the effects of the Bubble were. In the 1990s, the government tried another approach: pumping money into the economy through public works, paid for with a burgeoning national debt. This, too, cannot go on forever. Another crash may be coming, and this one could drag Japan down—and with it the entire world economy.

It might seem incongruous that while a great sword hangs over the world's head in the form of Japan's external dollars, its domestic markets are becoming irrelevant. The paradox, however, lies in the fact that each is the complement of the other: Japan's external reserves exist only because domestic markets, in order to preserve MOF's system, are cut off from the world.

The most vivid demonstration of the irrelevance of domestic markets to world finance is the collapse of the Tokyo Stock Exchange's foreign section, launched in the late 1970s in a bid to make Tokyo an international capital market. At its height in 1990, the TSE's foreign section boasted 125 companies. However, the rules hedging in foreign firms were so restrictive that fees far outweighed the anemic trading in foreign stocks. By the spring of 2000, the number of companies had dropped to 43. Average trading volume shrank nearly to the vanishing point: during the week of June 1–5, 1999, only 19 of the remaining companies traded at all on an average day. In an era of international finance, such a foreign section goes beyond failure to farce.

In the meantime, foreign listings on other stock markets skyrocketed. By April 2000, London listed 522 foreign firms, the three American stock exchanges featured 895 foreign firms, and even Australia (60 foreign listings) and Singapore (68) had surpassed Tokyo. Foreign stocks in New York accounted for just under 10 percent of all trading, while trading volume on the TSE's foreign section came to a fraction of 1 percent of the trading on NASDAQ's foreign section alone.

Embarrassed by the TSE's poor showing, MOF relaxed some of the restrictions and lowered costs in 1995, but this failed to stem the withdrawals. Starting in 1994, the listing department began sending delegations to Asian capitals beating the drum, and after almost two years of soliciting, it managed to persuade Malaysia's YTL Corporation to debut on the TSE's foreign section, which it did with great fanfare in February 1996. YTL's offering raised $44 million (versus the $700 million raised by Korean Mobile Telecom and more than $1 billion raised by Telkom Indonesia in New York around the same time). A year later, only one more Asian firm joined the Tokyo exchange, and in 1999 none did.

Once known as the "land of technology," Japan is now out of touch with the times. While Merrill Lynch and Goldman Sachs were developing elaborate computer algorithms to predict the future of the market, brokers at Nomura were still using aba-cuses, on which they knew how to do only one operation: add. That is why Madame Nui's toad held such sway over the In-dustrial Bank of Japan. The toad's utterances were as good a predictor as any of which direction the market would go.

The lesson of the Bubble is not that Japan should be casti-gated for departing from Western norms. Credit ordering, Japanese style, was a huge success, and it has helped other Asian nations to expand their industrial bases with great speed. To some degree, the Japanese system is still providing benefits to the nation, just as America's "deficit without tears" aids its economy. Both these systems, however, stretch underlying laws of money and have the potential to become dangerous when carried to extremes. For the United States, the danger of sur-plus dollars abroad is a real one, but the threat is not total: mar-ket forces do rule large segments of the U.S. economy, thus lending stability to the structure. In Japan, on the other hand, inflated assets, "virtual yen," and imaginary balance sheets rule all, making the structure much more fragile. The issue is one of balance. As in the case of the construction industry, Japan's fi-nancial world carried things to extremes, pushing credit order-ing beyond reasonable limits. In the process, the Ministry of Finance, Nomura, bank executives, and pension-fund managers lost all idea of what a healthy financial position really consists.

Indeed, in following Madame Nui's toad, the IBJ deserves credit, for in the never-never land of late-twentieth-century Japanese finance, toad magic and spells from ancient China were the best available predictors of the market. The toad told Madame Nui sometimes to buy and sometimes to sell, and as a result she lost only $2.1 billion out of combined loans of $22 billion, fairly respectable damages of about 10 percent; MOF and Nomura, on the other hand, advised investors only to buy—and never, ever, to sell—and as a result those who stayed in the market squandered 50 to 60 percent of their investments between 1989 and 1999. The Ministry of Finance is still ordering pension funds and insurance companies to buy. Japan might be in better shape today if the banks had gone on listening to Madame Nui's toad.

4 Information

A Different View of Reality

Men take their misfortunes to heart, and keep them there. A gambler does not talk about his losses; the frequenter of brothels, who finds his favorite engaged by another, pretends to be just as well off without her; the professional street-brawler is quiet about the fights he has lost; and a merchant who speculates on goods will conceal the losses he may suffer. All act as one who steps on dog dung in the dark.

—IHARA SAIKAKU, "What the Seasons Brought to the Almanac-Maker" (1686)

A countryside of legendary beauty is ravaged, and what was once reputed to be the richest nation in the world runs out of money. To understand how such things can happen, we must come to grips with an issue that disconcerts writers on Japan so badly that when faced with it they ordinarily set down their pens and look away. It is the quality of sheer fantasy.

We have entered a twilight zone where dams and roads carve their way through the landscape without reason and money comes from nowhere and goes nowhere. We cannot dismiss the air of unreality in Japan's public life lightly, as it is the very air that its officials breathe. The facts about much of Japan's social, political, and financial life are hidden so well that the truth is nearly impossible to know. This is not just a matter of regret for academic researchers, for a lack of reliable data is the single most significant difference between Japan's democracy and the democracies of the West. Why have so many students of Japan and commentators by and large ignored the issue of how the nation handles information? I believe it is because our cultural biases run much more deeply than we think. While experts on Japan know all about the commonly encountered difference between *tatemae* (an official stated position) and *honne* (real intent), they tend to view the discrepancy as a negotiating ploy. It hasn't occurred to them that the fundamental Japanese attitude toward information might differ from what they take for granted in the West. But it does differ, and radically so.

Traditionally, in Japan "truth" has never been sacrosanct, nor do "facts" need to be real, and here we run up against one of the great cultural divides between East and West. We can see the two approaches clashing in the Daiwa Bank scandal of 1995, when the Federal Reserve ordered Daiwa's American branches closed after finding that Daiwa, in collaboration with the Ministry of Finance, had hidden more than a billion dollars of losses from U.S. investigators. MOF reacted angrily with the comment that the Fed had failed to appreciate "cultural differences" between American and Japanese banking. The cultural difference goes back a long way, to a belief that ideal forms are more "true" than actual objects or events that don't fit the ideal. When an Edo-period artist entitled his screen painting *A True View of Mount Fuji*, he did not mean that his painting closely resembled the real Mount Fuji. Rather, it was a "true view" because it captured the perfect shape that people thought Mount Fuji ought to have. This principle of valuing the ideal above the real is far-reaching, and one may see it at work in the play between *tatemae* and *honne* that dominates daily life in Japan. People will strive to uphold the *tatemae* in the face of blatant facts to the contrary, believing it is important to keep the *honne* hidden in order to maintain public harmony.

Tatemae requires an element of reserve, for it presumes that not everything need be spelled out. It relies on communication through nonverbal means, and in interpersonal relations there is much to be said for *tatemae*, for from it springs the flower of harmony. *Tatemae* helps to make Japanese society peaceful and cohesive, with a relative lack of the aggressive violence, family breakups, and lawsuits that plague the West. The statistics professor Hayashi Chimio puts the case for *tatemae* very elegantly:

> When people say "There's no communication between parents and children," this is an American way of thinking. In Japan we didn't need spoken communication between parents and children. A glance at the face, a glance at the back, and we understood enough. That was our way of thinking, and it was because we had true communication of the heart. It's when we took as our model a culture relying on words that things went wrong. Although we live in a society replete with problems that words cannot ever solve, we think we can solve them with words, and this is where things go wrong.

Discreet reliance on *tatemae* is one of Japan's truly excellent features, infusing daily life with a grace and a calm that are rare in the fractious West. The problem arises when *tatemae* goes beyond its natural limits. As we saw earlier, when Japan began to modernize after 1868, the rallying cry was *Wakon Yosai* (Japanese spirit, Western technology). *Tatemae*, the idea that an unruffled surface takes precedence over stating the facts, is an old bit of *Wakon*, of Japanese spirit, and, like the *Wakon* of "total control," it runs into trouble when it does not adapt to modern systems. *Tatemae* is a charming attitude when it means that everyone should look the other way at a guest's faux pas in the tearoom; it has dangerous and unpredictable results when applied to corporate balance sheets, drug testing, and nuclear-power safety reports.

As we saw earlier, Japanese finance companies lend money to bankrupt borrowers or subsidiaries so that they can continue to pay interest and make bad loans fly off the books. This is *tobashi*, "flying"—one popular technique for which is to have a bank sell a troubled property to a subsidiary, to which it then loans the money to pay for the property: real-estate problem solved! The docile Japanese press meekly reports *tobashi* transactions as if they were real ones; one must learn this in order to understand how to read a Japanese newspaper. A headline announces "Nippon Trust sells choice Kyoto site" or "Hokkaido Bank sells assets to write off loans," and one might imagine that the banks were disposing of assets. However, in both cases the banks were selling to their own subsidiaries in *tobashi* transactions. The headlines should have read "Nippon Trust fails to sell choice Kyoto site" and "Hokkaido Bank finds no bona fide buyer to help it write off loans."

The National Land Agency accepts *tobashi* sales as real ones, which further distorts land-value statistics. Hence while the agency estimates that land prices have dropped in half from their peak, the results at actual auctions show that the fall is more than 80 percent. This is a classic example of an official statistic based on skewed data, but, unfortunately, we have even less to go by in estimating the true situation in most cases.

Tobashi is only one of several techniques of *funshoku kessan*, "cosmetic accounting." Another technique is, as we have seen, "book accounting," whereby banks value their holdings at purchase value, although they may be worth much less today than what was paid for them. Or unsightly liabilities are simply brushed away, such as pension-fund deficits, which Japanese companies have not had to report, even though they face huge exposure to their underfunded pensions. When all else fails, outright falsification comes into play—with encouragement from the ministries of Finance and of International Trade and Industry. In the Jusen scandal of 1996, when Japan's seven housing-loan corporations (known as Jusen) went bankrupt, leaving bad debts of ¥8 trillion, former MOF men (*amakudari*, or "descended from heaven," because after retirement they descend to the management of companies under MOF's control) ran six of the seven Jusen, which together had extended loans of which an astonishing 90 to 98.5 percent were nonperforming. In the years before the final collapse and exposure, the *amakudari* executives guided the Jusen banks in a game of elaborate trickery. At Juso, for example, the bank showed investigators and lenders three different sets of figures for the total of bad loans: ¥1,254 billion, ¥1,004 billion, or ¥649 billion. MOF was aware of the scale of the Jusen disaster as early as 1992, but it must have chosen to work only with the C List, because a report at that time concluded that the Jusen were "not approaching a state of danger." This decision to put off the reckoning led to the public's having to pay hundreds of billions of yen more in 1996 to clean up the mess.

Tobashi and "cosmetic accounting" are endemic; one could say they are defining features of Japanese industry. As embarrassing as revelations of serious abuses are when they come, MOF cannot do without either, because Japanese banks are addicted to them. Only with such techniques can the banks maintain the capital-to-assets adequacy ratio of 8 percent mandated by the Bank of International Settlements (BIS), failing which they cannot lend abroad. Nakamori Takakazu of Teikoku Databank estimates that if Japanese banks were to disclose the true state of their finances, their BIS ratios would fall to 2 to 3 percent at best.

As the Japanese economy sank lower and lower during the 1990s, each year the government announced rosy predictions for growth. Likewise, MOF has consistently downplayed the financial crisis, with Vice Minister Sakakibara Eisuke announcing in February 1999 that the crisis would be over "in a week or two." The wolf is at the door, yet the government keeps crying "Sheep!" It is indeed precisely because MOF has been the Little Boy Who Cried Sheep that experts estimate bad loans to be two or three times higher than the government admits, and the true national debt to be as much as triple the official numbers. Ishizawa Takashi, the chief researcher at Long Term Credit Bank's research institute, says, "Even if we told the truth people would think there is more being hidden. So we put out lower numbers on the assumption people believe the true figure is higher."

Nevertheless, there is much to be said for *tobashi*. *Tobashi* is a form of make-believe in which Japan's banks pretend to have hundreds of billions of dollars that they don't have. But, after all, money is a sort of fiction. If the world banking community agrees to believe that Japan has these billions, then it essentially does.

For the time being, *tobashi* seems to be working just fine. In any case, Japan's ministries have at their disposal a further "management of information" technique, perhaps the strongest: denial. *Shiranu, zonsenu*, means "I don't know, I have no knowledge," and it is the standard response to most inquiries. We saw an example of this when Asahi TV questioned a section chief at the Ministry of Health and Welfare about dioxin pollution, and he responded, "I don't know, I have no idea." A similar process was at work in the same ministry when for seven years its officials denied that they had any records of AIDS-contaminated blood products which had infected more than 1,400 people with HIV in the 1980s. In March 1996, however, when Health Minister Kan Naoto demanded that the "lost" records be found, they turned up within three days.

The writer Inose Naoki describes an encounter he had with officials of the Water Resources Public Corporation (WRPC), the special government corporation that builds and maintains dams. Inose inquired about a company called Friends of the Rivers, to which the WRPC had been awarding 90 percent of its contracts and most of whose stock was owned by WRPC ex-directors, and this is what the WRPC official told him: "Contracts are assigned by local units across the nation, so we have no way of knowing how many go to Friends of the Rivers. Therefore I cannot answer you." "But isn't it true that many of your employees have transferred to Friends of the Rivers?" Inose asked. "Job transfers are a matter for each individual employee" was the reply. "If someone transfers in order to make use of his superb ability and expertise acquired while at the Corporation, it is his individual decision. The Corporation can say nothing about these individuals' choices."

The Corporation "cannot answer you," "can say nothing." There is no recourse against this. In 1996, newspapers reported that auditors at government agencies turned down 90 percent of the public requests for audits during the decade from 1985 to 1994. And if a citizens' group presses too hard, documents simply vanish: this is what happened when citizens of Nagano demanded to see the records of the money (between $18 and $60 million) the city spent courting the International Olympic Committee in 1992. City officials put ninety volumes of records in ten big boxes, carried them outside town, and torched them. Yamaguchi Sumikazu, a senior official with the bidding committee, said the books had taken up too much space and contained information "not for the public," such as "who had wined and dined with IOC officials and where." Neither the tax office nor the city administration asked any questions. Case closed.

One reason for the vast waste and hidden debts in the "special government corporations," *tokushu hojin*, is precisely that they don't need to open their books to the public. The WRPC does not publish its balance sheets; neither does the New Tokyo International Airport, nor dozens of other huge special corporations, all of which function in near-total secrecy. For those who believe that reform is on its way to Japan, it was sobering to learn of a law proposed by the Ministry of Justice in 1996 that would tighten, not loosen, the bureaucrats' hold on information. According to the new law, agencies need not divulge information about committee meetings and may even refuse to disclose whether requested information exists.

This brings us to the critical factor in MOF's delay in closing down the Jusen: the Jusen hid their debts so well that they fooled *everybody*. A high-ranking MOF official admits "it was impossible at the time to get a handle on the scale of the situation." This was true not only of the Jusen companies but of other banks that went belly-up in the mid-1990s, such as Hyogo Bank and Hanwa Bank, which turned out to have debts ten or twenty times larger than their stated liabilities. Today, the Ministry of Finance cannot find its way out of the labyrinth it created when it encouraged banks and securities firms to cook their books, bribe regulators, and consort with gangsters. It is lost in its own shell game.

Kawai Hayao, a leading academic and government adviser, says, "In Japan, as long as you are convinced you are lying for the good of the group, it's not a lie." It's all part of what Frank Gibney, Jr., a former Japan bureau chief at *Time*, calls "the culture of deceit." A few examples will show how deeply rooted this culture is, and how the policy of hiding unattractive facts prevents citizens from learning the true depth of their nation's problems or doing much about them.

Ladies and gentlemen, step right this way to a junior high school in the town of Machida, outside Tokyo. In 1995, the school board commissioned a study of a large crack that had opened up on the school grounds, since local residents were concerned that the landfill on which the school was built might be sinking. It was, but no need to panic: the board instructed the consulting firm to alter its report. Where the original had read, "It is undeniable that subsidence could re-occur," the revised version stated, "The filled-in areas can be thought to have stabilized." To prove this was so, the consultant set up meters at a school far away, in Yamanashi Prefecture, calibrated them to show no tilt, and attached photos of those meters to the report. So, although the Machida crack was 120 meters long, 10 to 20 centimeters wide, and up to 3 meters deep—and growing—the land was, according to the report, magically ceasing to sink. This fiction troubled very few people, for the school board granted another large contract to the same consultant immediately after it was revealed that the report had been doctored. A company representative commented, "We just want to avoid misunderstandings and make the phrasing of the text easy to understand."

Government officials work hard to make sure that reports are easy to understand and eyesores pleasant to look at. Here is another example. At Suishohama Beach in Fukui, on the Sea of Japan, a large nuclear power plant regrettably detracts somewhat from the beach's picturesque charm. So while preparing its tourist poster, officials simply air-brushed the plant out of the picture. "[We did it] believing the beauty of the natural sea can be stressed when artificial things are removed," they said.

Police departments provide special training materials to educate officers in how to shield the public from situations that they would be better off not knowing about. In November 1999, on the heels of a scandal in which Kanagawa police destroyed evidence in order to protect an officer who was taking drugs, newspapers found that the Kanagawa Police Department had an official thirteen-page manual expressly for covering up scandals, entitled "Guidelines for Measures to Cope with Disgraceful and Other Events."

All this should come as no surprise—it's the natural consequence of Japan's political structure, which puts officialdom more or less above the law. What is surprising is that the media, in a democratic country with legally mandated freedom of the press, collude in these deceptions. It comes down to the fact that the press is essentially a cartel. Reporters belong to press clubs that specialize in police or finance or politics, and so forth (which do not admit foreigners), and these clubs dutifully publish handouts from the police or the politicians in exchange for access to precious information. If a reporter shows any true independence, the agency or politician can exclude him from further press conferences.

Shinoda Hiroyuki, the chief editor of *Tsukuru* magazine, says, "Investigative reporting isn't rewarded." In fact, it is often punished. Kawabe Katsurou is the reporter who in 1991 led TBS Television to investigate the trucking company Sagawa Kyubin's connections to gangsters and politicians. By 1993, prosecutors had filed charges against Kanemaru Shin, one of the nation's most powerful politicians, and soon thereafter the government fell. But far from rewarding Kawabe, TBS transferred him to the accounts department in 1996, and eventually he quit. Today, he survives precariously as a freelance journalist. "Many journalists have become like salarymen," Kawabe says. "They want to avoid the difficult cases that will cause trouble."

In the old days, the populace waited for their feudal masters to issue the *O-sumitsuki*, the Honorable Touch of the Brush, a written proclamation against which there was no recourse. The function of the press today is to publicize modern *O-sumitsuki* issued by major companies and bureaucrats. It means that you must read the newspapers with great care, as it's easy to mistake official propaganda for the real thing. Okadome Yasunori, the editor of the controversial but widely read monthly *Uwasa no Shinso* (*Truth of Rumors*), says, "With such a close relationship between the power and the media, journalists can be easily manipulated and controlled. Just study the front-page articles of major Japanese dailies. They are almost identical. Why? Because they just print what they are given."

For example, *Nihon Keizai Shimbun* (*Nikkei*) is Japan's leading economic journal. *Nikkei* gives out technology awards every year, and in 1995 its winners included, along with Windows 95, NTT's PHS handphone and Matsushita's HDTV. Though both were notoriously unsuccessful—PHS is an enormous money-loser, and one could fairly say that HDTV (high-definition television with an analog rather than digital base) ranks as one of the biggest technological flops of the twentieth century—both are favorites of the Ministry of International Trade and Industry, so *Nikkei* dutifully celebrated them.

The most entertaining rooms in the press wing of the Hall of Mirrors are the television studios where producers cook up documentaries. So common is the staging of fake news reports that it has its own name, *yarase*, meaning literally "made to do it." Japanese television is filled with faked events. In a mild version of *yarase*, villagers dress up in clothes they never wear to enact festivals that died out years ago. For truly sensational effect, television producers will go much further, as in reports of young girls tearfully admitting to being prostitutes—in what turn out to be paid acting stints. In November 1999, one of the longest-running and most elaborate *yarase* came to light when it was revealed that Fuji Television, over a period of six months, had paid prostitutes and call girls ¥30,000 per appearance to act as wives on its supposedly true-life series, *Loving Couples, Divorcing Couples*. Nor is *yarase* limited to television. In 1989, the president of *Asahi Shimbun* newspaper resigned after it came to light that a photographer had defaced coral in Okinawa in order to create evidence for a news story on how divers were damaging the reef.

The most elaborate *yarase* often involve foreign reporting. Here's how *Far Eastern Economic Review* describes a report on Tibet by NHK, Japan's national broadcasting company: "[In 1992] an NHK documentary on harsh living conditions in the Tibetan Himalayas featured a sand avalanche, footage of a monk praying for an end to a three-month dry spell, and an explanation that his horse had died of thirst. NHK later admitted that a crew member had deliberately caused the avalanche; it had rained twice during the filming; and the monk, whom it paid, did not own the dead horse."

The common thread in the *yarase* for foreign documentaries is to show how poor, miserable, seedy, or violent life is elsewhere, with the implied message being that life in Japan is really very nice. For reports on the United States, scenes of low life and violence are obligatory, and a practiced producer can manage to set these up almost anywhere. In 1994, NHK did a special on the city of Missoula, Montana, a state famed for its natural beauty and national parks. Most of the program, however, took place in a seedy bar, which offered just the atmosphere NHK felt was right for America. Here's how the program was filmed, according to a Missoula citizen:

> The camera is focused on the door, waiting for a man to come in. He looks nervous and is squeezing out some tears.

The camera follows him as he comes up to the bar, and sits down, then moves in for a close-up on his tears. He looks up and confesses that he has just been mugged. . . . Making it even more suspicious was the man's claim to have been beaten, struck several times in his face, which had not a mark on it. His face was as clean as a baby's behind. Then we learn he had had his money and clothes and Amtrak [train] ticket stolen, even though he is carrying a beautiful new bag that wasn't taken. And Amtrak doesn't come through Missoula. It doesn't come anywhere near Missoula.

Yarase documentaries and government misinformation do succeed to some extent in quelling people's misgivings about their country, but unfortunately some pretty scary skeletons are hidden in Japan's bureaucratic closets. At a sinister agency called Donen, the hiding of information becomes downright terrifying. Donen, a Japanese acronym for the Power Reactor and Nuclear Fuel Development Corporation, manages Japan's nuclear-power program.

At Monju, the fast-breeder nuclear reactor near Tsuruga, which suffered a major leak of liquid sodium from its cooling system in 1995, Donen officials first stated that the leakage was "minimal." It later turned out to be more than three tons, the largest accident of its type in the world. But they could easily remedy the trouble by hiding the evidence: Donen staff edited film taken at the scene, releasing only an innocuous five minutes' worth and cutting out fifteen minutes that showed serious damage, including the thermometer on the leaking pipes and icicle-like extrusions of sodium.

Donen's attitude to the public at the time of the Monju scandal says much about officials who take for granted that they can always hide behind a wall of denial. The day after the accident, the chairman of the Tsuruga city council went to visit the

Monju plant—and Donen officials simply shut the door in his face. Kishimoto Konosuke, the chairman of Tsuruga's Atomic and Thermal Energy Committee, said, "Donen was more concerned with concealing the accident than with explaining to us what was happening. That shows what they think of us."

Still, there was widespread public anger and concern over Monju (which remained shut down for the rest of the decade), yet the same scenario repeated itself in March 1997, this time when drums filled with nuclear waste caught fire and exploded at a plant at Tokai City north of Tokyo, releasing high levels of radioactivity into the environment. In May 1994, newspapers had revealed that seventy kilograms of plutonium dust and waste had gathered in the pipes and conveyors of the Tokai plant; Donen had known of the missing plutonium (enough to build as many as twenty nuclear bombs) but did nothing about it until the International Atomic Energy Agency (IAEA) demanded an accounting. To this day, Donen claims to have no idea where the plutonium is clustered or how to remove it. "We know that the plutonium is there," an official said. "It's just held up in the system."

Given that several nuclear bombs' worth of plutonium dust were lost somewhere inside the Tokai plant, there was great public concern over the Tokai fire. Yet Donen's initial report was a shambles, in some places saying, "Radioactive material was released," and in others, "No radioactive material was released"; claiming that workers had reconfirmed in the morning that the fire was under control, though they had not (managers had pressured the workers to change their stories); misstating the amount of leaked radioactive material, which turned out to be larger than reported by a factor of twenty. Incredibly, on the day of the explosion, sixty-four people, including science and engineering students and foreign trainees, toured the complex, even visiting one building only a hundred meters from the site of the fire—and nobody ever informed them of the accident.

Several weeks later, Donen revealed that it waited thirty hours before reporting a leak of radioactive tritium at an advanced thermal reactor, Fugen. This was an improvement, though, because in eleven cases of tritium leaks during the previous two and a half years, Donen had made no reports at all. Reform, however, was on the way: Donen was "disbanded" and renamed Genden in May 1998, supposedly to appease an angry public. Today, under this new name, the nuclear agency continues to operate with the same staff, offices, and philosophy as before.

Nor is it only government agencies such as Donen-Genden that are falling behind in nuclear safety. The same problems beset private industry. The troubles at the Tokai plant came to a head at 10:35 a.m. on September 30, 1999, when employees at a fuel-processing plant managed by JCO, a private contractor, dumped so much uranium into a settling basin that it reached critical mass and exploded into uncontrolled nuclear fission. It was Japan's worst nuclear accident ever—the world's worst since Chernobyl—resulting in the sequestration of tens of thousands of people living in the area near the plant. The explosion was a tragedy for forty-nine workers who were exposed to radiation (three of them critically) but at the same time a comedy of errors, misinformation, and mistakes. It turned out that Tokai's nuclear plant had not repaired its safety equipment for more than seventeen years. The workers used a secret manual prepared by JCO's managers that bypassed safety regulations in several critical areas: essentially, material that workers should have disposed of via dissolution cylinders and pumps was carried out manually with a bucket.

Measures to deal with the accident could be described by no

other word than primitive. Firefighters rushed to the scene after the explosion was reported, but since they had not been
told that a nuclear accident had occurred they did not bring
along protective suits, although their fire station had them—
and they were all contaminated with radiation. In the early
hours, no local hospital could be found to handle the victims,
even though Tokai has fifteen nuclear facilities. There was no
neutron measurer in the entire city, so prefectural officials had
to call in an outside agency to provide one; measurements were
finally made at 5 p.m., nearly seven hours after the disaster.
Those measurements showed levels of 4.5 millisieverts of neu-
trons per hour, when the limit for safe exposure is 1 millisievert
per year, and from this officials realized for the first time that a
fission reaction was still going on! Many other measurements,
such as for isotope iodine 131, weren't made until as many as
five days later.

The accident at Tokai came as a shock to other nuclear-
energy-producing nations. The director of the China National
Nuclear Corporation commented, "Improving management
techniques is the key lesson China should learn from the Japan
accident, since the leak happened not because of nuclear technology but because of poor management and human error."
And, indeed, poor management, combined with official denial,
was at the root of the disaster. "Oh no, a serious accident can't
happen here," a top Japanese nuclear official declared some
hours after the fission reaction at Tokai had taken place.

The level of sheer fiction in Japan's nuclear industry can be
gauged from the story of how Donen misused most of its
budget for renovation work between 1993 and 1997. The
problem lay in 2,000 drums of low-level radioactive waste
stored at Tokai, which began rusting in pits filled with rainwater. Records show that the problem dated to the 1970s, but
only in 1993 did Donen begin to take action, asking for money

to remove the drums from the pits and to build sheds for temporary storage. So far so good. Four years and ¥1 billion later, Donen still had not taken the drums out of the pits or built the sheds. Nobody knows where the money went—semipublic agencies like Donen are not required to make their budgets public—but the suspicion was that Donen secretly spent it doing patchwork waterproofing in the pits to hide evidence of radioactive leakage. There is no problem, the agency said. One official remarked, "The water level has not dropped, so radioactive material is not leaking outside."

Donen went on to request more money for 1998, stating that renovation was going smoothly, and asking for ¥71 million to remove the sheds it had never built! It even attached drawings to show how it was reinforcing the inner walls of the storage pits. The Donen official in charge of technology to protect the environment from radioactive waste said, "It's true that the storage pits will eventually be reinforced. So I thought it would be all right if details of the project were different from what we had stated in our request for budgetary approval."

When Donen gets money from the government to remove sheds it never built and shore up the walls of pits it never drained, we are definitely moving into the territory of Escher and Kafka. A final surreal touch is provided by an animated video produced by Donen to show children that plutonium isn't as dangerous as activists say. "A small character named Pu (the chemical symbol of plutonium), who looks like an extra from 'The Jetsons,' gives his friend a glass of plutonium water and says it's safe to drink. His friend, duly impressed, drinks no less than six cups of the substance before declaring, 'I feel refreshed!' "

There is a lesson to be learned from Donen's madness, and it is that if you disguise the truth long enough you eventually lose touch with reality yourself. This happened at MOF, which can no longer figure out the true state of bank finances, and it happened to the nuclear industry, which doesn't know the standard techniques of nuclear-plant management common elsewhere in the world. Why invest in technology when with a stroke of the pen an official can bring fires under control and make leaks dry up? At Tokai in 1997, so unconcerned were Donen officials that seven maintenance employees played golf on the day of the fire—and went back to play another round the day after.

Japan is like the spaceship in *2001: A Space Odyssey*. The computer Hal runs all life systems aboard the ship with benevolent wisdom, speaking to the crew through the public-address system in a resolutely calm and cheerful manner. Later, when Hal goes mad and starts murdering people, he continues to placidly assure crew members in an unwaveringly upbeat voice that all is well, wishing them a good day. In Japan, articles in magazines paid for by the bureaucrats who cement over rivers and lakes assure the public that their natural environment is still beautiful. Bureaucrats at Donen instruct children that plutonium is safe to drink. Every day in Japan we hear the soothing voice of Hal telling us not to worry. Since 1993, the government has predicted economic rebound every year, despite an ever-deepening recession. In February 1999, as the nation prepared to inject $65 billion into the banks, with the prospect of even larger bailouts ahead, Yanagisawa Hakuo, the chairman of the Financial Revitalization Committee, announced, "By the end of March, the bad loans will be completely cleared and we will have confidence at home and overseas." Problem over, have a good day.

While it runs against the conventional wisdom that Japan is a technological leader, there is no question that Japan has fallen drastically behind in the technology of nuclear-power management and safety. Let's examine what happened at the Tokai plant in 1997 more closely. Workers checked the state of the blaze by looking in the window—they used no other monitoring devices and did not check again. A team of three people, including an untrained local fireman, entered the building with no protection and proceeded to seal it up—with duct tape! Dozens of other workers were sent into or near the site, unprotected by masks, and inhaled radioactive fumes. In the 1999 fission incident at Tokai, rescue workers were not warned to wear protective suits, neither measuring devices nor hospital care was readily available, and national authorities had no disaster plan to cope with the emergency.

What is in the manual for nuclear facilities in Japan has been duct tape or, in the case of the nuclear plant in Hamaoka, in Shizuoka Prefecture, paper towels, which were used to wipe up a hydrogen peroxide solution that had been spilled during cleaning of radioactively contaminated areas there. So many paper towels accumulated by January 1996 that they spontaneously combusted. This is reminiscent of the situations concerning waste removal after the Kobe earthquake (no shields or other safeguards), dioxin (no data), leachate from chemical waste pools (no waterproofing), and oil spills (cleaned up by women with bamboo ladles and blankets).

Since the 1970s, Japanese quality has become a byword, and many a book and article has been penned on the subject of *Kaizen*, "improvement," a form of corporate culture in which employers encourage their workers to submit ideas that will polish and improve efficiency. The writers on *Kaizen*, however, overlooked one weakness in this approach, which seemed minor at the time but has seriously impacted Japan's technology. *Kaizen*'s emphasis is entirely on positive recommendations; there is no mechanism to deal with negative criticism, no way to disclose faults or mistakes—and this leads to a fundamental problem of information. People keep silent about embarrassing errors, with the result that problems are never solved. Kato

Hisatake, professor of ethics at Kyoto University, argues that the Tokai fission disaster came about because although people knew for years that the wrong procedures were being followed, nobody said a word. In the United States, he said, "in the case of the Three-Mile Island accident, whistle-blowing helped prevent a far worse disaster."

The problem is endemic in Japanese industry, as is evidenced by a survey made by Professor Kato, in which he asked workers in Tokyo if they would disclose wrongdoing in their company; 99 percent said they would not. A major case of such a cover-up surfaced in July 2000, when police found that for twenty-three years Mitsubishi Motors had hidden from investigators most of its documents on customer complaints. At first Mitsubishi kept its records in a company locker room, but after 1992 it created a state-of-the-art computer system for storing dual records: those to be reported to regulators, and those to be kept secret. Only after inspectors discovered the ruse did Mitsubishi begin to deal with suspected problems, recalling over 700,000 cars for defects including bad brakes, fuel leaks, and failing clutches. A similar scandal arose in June 2000 at giant milk producer Snow Brand, whose tainted milk poisoned 14,000 people, as the result of careless sanitation procedures that had gone unchecked for decades.

At Tokai's nuclear plant, Mitsubishi Motors, and Snow Brand, no worker or manager ever drew attention to a situation dozens or even hundreds of people must have been aware of for many years. Meanwhile, complacent officials meekly took the information they were served and never bothered to investigate. Multiply these stories by the tens of thousands and one begins to get a shadowy view of slowly accumulating dysfunction afflicting almost every field in modern Japan. From the outside, the machine of *Kaizen* still looks bright and shiny, but inside, an accretion of bad information is gumming up the works.

On February 17, 1996, the *Mainichi Daily News* ran an article headlined "DA [Defense Agency] chief richest among Cabinet ministers," and then listed his and other ministers' assets. However, they were not valued at actual market prices, ministers are not culpable if they give false reports, and the assets did not include business interests. In other words, the official numbers had near-zero credibility—yet the newspaper diligently computed rankings and averages for the group, and publishes similar rankings every year.

These small bits of misinformation pile up into mountains of misleading statistics, which lead government planners, businessmen, and journalists to very wrong conclusions. Journalists, beware—reporting on Japan is like walking on quicksand. Take an innocent-looking number like the unemployment rate. With unemployment hovering around 3 percent in Japan for most of the 1980s and early 1990s, it would seem that Japan's unemployment has been far below the 5 or 6 percent reported for the United States.

But was it really? Japan uses its own formula to calculate unemployment, with several important differences. For example, in the United States you are unemployed if you were out of work for the previous month; in Japan, it is for the previous week. While economists differ on the exact numbers, everyone agrees that the Japanese rate would rise by 2 to 4 percent if it were calculated in the American way. Japanese officials publicly admit that employment data are as unreliable as corporate balance sheets; in early 1999, Labor Minister Amari Akira, when pressed to provide realistic information, responded, "It's my corporate secret." And yet—and this is the notable part of the story—journalists continue to use the Japanese unemployment figures and to compare them with the American ones without warning their readers that they are comparing apples and oranges. Karel van Wolferen writes: "Systematic misinformation is a policy tool in Japan. Unsuspecting foreign economists, especially those of the neo-classical persuasion who must be reassured that Japan, after all, is not embarrassing evidence contradicting mainstream theory, are easy targets. . . . We simply do not know, even approximately, the level of unemployment, the amount of problem loans, assets and debts in most corporate sectors."

Suppose you were a delegate at the Third UN Convention on Climate Control, which was held in Kyoto in December 1997. You would have been delighted to learn that according to a report issued by its Environment Agency, Japan spent a total of ¥11 trillion for projects aimed at averting global warming. However, if you took a closer look at the agency's report, you would have discovered that of ¥9.3 trillion labeled "finding ways to reduce emissions of carbon dioxide," ¥8.35 trillion went into the construction and maintenance of roads. The Natural Resources and Energy Agency spent an additional ¥400 billion promoting nuclear energy. Of ¥1.2 trillion listed as spent for "preservation and enhancement of forests," about half went into labor expended in stripping the native forest cover and replanting it with *sugi* monoculture and paying the enormous interest on debts piled up by the Forestry Agency in this ill-fated project. Money spent on solar- and wind-power generation came to only ¥90 billion. "The report is not ideal in terms of representing the current state of affairs," an Environment Agency official admitted. Indeed, the agency's report inflated the true numbers by a factor of *120*.

Skewed numbers are endemic in every field, and as we have seen, the discrepancies can be huge. Official estimates of the bad debt crisis went from ¥27 trillion in the early 1990s to ¥35 trillion in 1996, ¥60 trillion in 1997, and ¥77 trillion in 1999—and even then MOF was far from admitting the true figure, which might be double that amount. The national budget, as solemnly announced every spring by the press, is not all that it seems. There is a "second budget," called Zaito (or FILP, Fiscal Investment and Loan Program), out of which MOF distributes funds independently of parliamentary control. Zaito, which is almost never reported in the newspapers—indeed, many people have never even heard of it—amounts to as much as 60 percent of the official budget. We shall have more to say about Zaito in chapter 6.

In the case of medical costs, Japan's expenditures appear to be far below those of the United States—but that's because published costs do not include the payments of ¥100,000–200,000 that patients customarily hand to their doctors in plain white envelopes when they have surgery. There is no way to calculate how much under-the-table money boosts Japan's national medical bill. Indeed, medicine is a statistical *Alice in Wonderland* where the numbers verge on comedy. As for drug testing, the Ministry of Health and Welfare has never enforced scientific protocols, and payoffs from drug companies to doctors are commonplace, with the result that Japanese medical results have become a laughingstock in world medical journals.

It is no exaggeration to say that no technical or academic field in Japan stands on firm factual ground. In November 2000, *Mainichi Shimbun* revealed that Fujimura Shinichi, Japan's leading archaeologist, had been caught red-handed burying prehistoric artifacts at an excavation site. He later "discovered" these artifacts and used them as evidence that human habitation in Japan occurred one hundred thousand years earlier than previously thought. Fujimura had worked on 180 sites; the scandal undoes much of the work of prehistoric archaeology in Japan over the last fifteen years. No one knows how the mess can ever be cleaned up.

In short, everywhere you look you find that information in Japan is not to be trusted. I will admit to a twinge of fear myself, for this book is filled with statistics whose accuracy I cannot gauge.

Sapio magazine calls Japan *Joho Sakoku,* "a closed country for information." This blockage—or screening—of information about the rest of the world happens not just because of overt government controls but because of systemic bottlenecks encountered everywhere. News arrives in Japan, and then, like a shipment of bananas held up at port, it rots on the dock. With the exception of a few industrial areas where it is vitally important for Japan to acquire the latest techniques from the West, information rarely makes it into daily life, beyond the television screen or the newspaper headline. This is because for new concepts from abroad to be put into practice, certain prerequisites must be met.

One is the active involvement of foreigners. When Shogun Hideyoshi imported new ceramics techniques to Japan at the end of the sixteenth century, he shipped entire villages of Koreans to Japan and settled them in Kyushu. In early Meiji (1868–1900), Japan brought over hundreds of *yatoi gaikokujin,* "hired foreigners," who designed railroads, factories, schools, and hospitals, and trained tens of thousands of students. Indeed, the very term used by *Sapio* magazine, *sakoku* ("closed country"), is an old one, dating to the shogunal edict that closed Japan in the early 1600s; despite the opening in the Meiji period, the tradition never died. After the *yatoi gaikokujin* served their purpose, the government sent most of them away, and for a good century foreigners have not been permitted to have influence in Japanese society.

In the 1990s, the Ministry of Education forced national universities to dismiss foreign teachers, including those who had been in Japan a long time, and to hire new teachers from abroad only on short-term contracts. Foreigners who had lived in Japan for a decade or more, who could speak the language, and who were familiar with local issues could presumably teach their students dangerous foreign knowledge. This policy is still in force as Japan enters the twenty-first century. Even so, academia is wide open compared with medicine, law, and other skilled professions. No foreign architect of stature, such as I. M. Pei, resides in Japan. Foreign architects come to Japan on short-term contracts, erect a skyscraper or a museum, and then leave. But subtle and sophisticated approaches to services and design—the core elements of modern building technology—cannot be transmitted in this way. Japan is left with the empty shells of architectural ideas, the hardware without the software.

The second requirement for making use of information is a hungry public. As taught in the ancient Chinese classic *I Ching*, the symbol of education is a claw over an egg: the parent taps on the egg from outside at the same moment that the chick pecks from the inside. In Japan, the chick is not pecking. In order for a business or a government agency to use information, the people in charge must realize they *need* it. But, soothed by the reassuring voice of Hal, surprisingly few executives recognize that their businesses or agencies are in a state of crisis.

The third requirement is a solid statistical base. New data make sense only if they stand upon solid old information. For example, foreign dioxin studies can be useful only if the Environment Agency has done its homework and knows which neighborhoods are contaminated and to what degree. Lacking this information, once you've brought in the foreign studies there is little you can do with them. It made sense for Hideyoshi to bring Korean potters to Japan because there was a demand for Korean pottery. Not so for much of the information Japan receives from abroad today. What use, for example, does Japan have for number-crunching techniques developed by trading houses in New York when the numbers that Japanese companies put in their financial statements are largely fictional?

This attitude toward information has proved to be an obstacle to Japanese use of the Internet. Log on to the Internet home pages of important Japanese entities and you will find a few meager pages, as poor in quality as in quantity, consisting mostly of slogans. From university home pages, for example, you would never get a clue to any serious data, such as Tokyo University's budget, Keio University's assets, the makeup of the faculty, a cross section of the student body, and so forth, only "What Our University Stands For." Most serious information about these schools is secret, not available in any medium, much less on the Internet. In the end, you would find it difficult—perhaps even impossible—to put your hand on any practical information about these universities. In doing research for this book, I have found a striking contrast between the availability of information in Japan and in the United States and Europe. Visit the U.S. Army Corps of Engineers Web site, for example, and you will find yourself deluged with so many pages of data that you can hardly process it. Japan's Construction Ministry and the River Bureau provide a few pages of slogans, and some dead links.

As of summer 2000, both the Tokyo and Osaka stock exchange sites failed to offer *any* information of substance (for example, the value of new or secondary listings) and did not even have something so rudimentary as a ticker with current index levels. By contrast, the Singapore exchange's Web page was light-years ahead. The failure of the Internet to bring openness to Japan bodes ill for the nation's future. Take, for example, the concept of "industrial secrecy." In the old manufacturing economy, it was in every company's interest to patent its techniques or, even better, to lock them up in a vault and keep them absolutely hidden from outsiders. And Japan was very good at that. One journalist, praising the Japanese for their efficiency in keeping secrets, commented, "Patents are only for a time; a secret is forever." But in the new economy people don't have time to wait forever. Time moves too fast; today's secret is tomorrow's failed idea. The explosion of software and new Internet technologies bursting out of Silicon Valley has been a collaborative effort in which a young engineer calls up his friend and says, "I have these parts of the puzzle, but I'm missing other parts. What do you think?" His friend listens, supplies another piece, and everyone benefits. In Japan, such free and easy give-and-take is nearly inconceivable. Hobbled by secrecy, new ideas in Japan will continue to come slowly—and in the new economy there is no greater sin than to be slow.

One could say that Japan poses a fascinating challenge to the very idea of the modern state at the start of the twenty-first century. Information—its processing, analysis, collection, and distribution—stands at the core of postindustrial technology. Or does it? Japan has made a big bet otherwise. Wisdom in the West has it that high quantities of precision data and the ability to analyze them are what make banks and investment houses succeed, nuclear power plants run safely, universities function well, archaeologists build up a credible picture of the past, engineers design efficiently, doctors prescribe drugs properly, factories produce safe cars and hygienic milk, and citizens play a responsible role in politics. From that perspective, one would expect that the lack of such information—a preponderance of fuzzy information—would become an increasing liability.

The value of factual data would seem to be only common sense, and for all that traditional Japan valued the ideal above the real, canny merchants in Edo days well understood the importance of keeping their accounts straight. The seventeenth-century novelist Saikaku comments, "I have yet to see the man who can record entries in his ledger any which way or ignore

details in his calculations and still make a successful living."
One could argue that the modern Japanese bureaucracy's utter
disdain for facts is something new—a tenet from traditional
culture that was carried to extremes. It could result from something as simple as the fact that officials got away with it. In
Saikaku's day, sloppy accounting soon dragged a shopkeeper
into trouble. In present-day Japan, bureaucracies with unlimited
funding and no public accountability can hide their mistakes
for decades.

Nevertheless, authoritarian leaders in East Asia favor the
modern Japanese model of development. They see merit in
having the bureaucracy keep information secret and manipulate
it for the national good, not letting the public get involved in
wasteful disputes over policy. For these leaders, freedom of information is chaotic, controlled information more efficient.
Until now, the dialogue on this issue has been carried on between Asian authoritarians and Western liberals largely in political terms: whether people deserve or have a human right to be
informed. In Japan's case, it might be helpful to disregard these
political aspects for a moment and question whether such control of information really does make government and business
more efficient. Those who favor information managed by the
bureaucracy assume that while the general public stays in the
dark, all-knowing officials will guide the nation with an unerr-
ing hand.

For Japan, the results of such a policy are now coming in,
and they indicate that, far from being all-knowing, Japan's bureaucracy no longer has a clear understanding of the activities
under its control. What we see is officialdom that is confused,
lazy, and behind the times, leading to incredible blunders in the
management of everything from nuclear plants to drug regimens and pension funds. Until a decade ago, very few people
noticed that there was anything going wrong in Japan; rather,

the emphasis was on Japan's "efficiency." It is now becoming possible to see what happens to a nation that develops without the critical ingredient of reliable information.

Much money and millions of words have been spent on the question of whether Japan will catch up with the West in new information industries. But few have even noticed that Japan has a fundamental problem with information itself: it's often lacking and, when it does exist, is fuzzy at its best, bogus at its worst. In this respect, Japan's traditional culture stands squarely at odds with modernity—and the problem will persist. The issue of hidden or falsified information strikes at such deeply rooted social attitudes that the nation may never entirely come to grips with it. Because of this, one may confidently predict that in the coming decades Japan will continue to have trouble digesting new ideas from abroad—and will find it more and more difficult to manage its own increasingly baroque and byzantine internal systems. The nation is in for one long, ongoing stomachache.

For the time being, bureaucrats and foreign academics alike are tiptoeing around embarrassing situations, "as one who steps on dog dung in the dark." This is comfortable for those in charge, since it relieves them of any urgency to solve Japan's pressing problems. Defaulted bank loans, unemployment, rising national debt, lost plutonium, out-of-date analog television, waste dumps in the countryside, tilting schoolyards, ugly beachfronts, global warming, defective cars, poisonous milk—Japan has them firmly under control. There is just one little problem with this approach. Abraham Lincoln pointed it out once to a delegation that came to the White House urging him to do something he felt wasn't feasible. He asked the members of the delegation, "How many legs will a sheep have if you call the tail a leg?" They answered, "Five." "You are mistaken," Lincoln said, "for calling a tail a leg don't make it so."

5 Bureaucracy
Power and Privilege

Therefore a wise prince must devise ways by which his
citizens are always and in all circumstances dependent on
him and on his authority; and then they will always be
faithful to him.
—MACHIAVELLI, *The Prince* (1513)

Japan's bureaucracy has been much studied, mostly with admiration, by Western analysts, who marvel at its extremely subtle means of control, its tentacles reaching downward into industry and upward into politics. And there is no question that Japan's bureaucracy can lay claim to being the world's most sophisticated—several rungs up the evolutionary ladder from the weak, constrained officialdom in most other countries. Bureaucrats in the United States or Europe are hedged in by politics, local activism, and above all by laws that mandate freedom of information as well as punish their receipt of favors from businesses under their control. In Communist countries, such as China, bureaucrats may be corrupt, but in the end the Party rules, and officials can see their most elaborate schemes overturned in a minute by the stroke of a Politburo member's pen.

Not so in Japan. A largely ritualistic form of democracy in force since World War II has given the bureaucracy far-reaching control over society. Ministries not only are shielded from foreign pressures but function outside Japan's own political system. Schools teach children not to speak out; hence activists are rare. The police investigate only the most flagrant cases of corruption and courts rarely punish it; cozy under-the-table give-and-take between officials and industries has become institutionalized. It is no exaggeration to say that government officials control nearly every aspect of life from stock prices to tomatoes in supermarkets and the contents of schoolbooks. From this point of view, too, Japan is a test case: what happens to a country that chooses an extreme form of bureaucratic rule?

The bureaucracy's techniques of control have a strong bearing on what is happening to Japan's rivers, cities, schoolyards, and economy, especially because of the *amakudari*, "descended from heaven," the retired bureaucrats who work in the industries that ministries control. MOF men become bank directors, Construction Ministry men join construction firms, ex-policemen staff the organizations that manage pachinko parlors, and so forth. The pickings are fat: a retiring high-level *amakudari* bureaucrat can earn an annual official salary of ¥20 million plus an unofficial ¥30 million in "office expenses" and, after six years, a retirement of ¥20 million, which adds up to about ¥320 million in six years!

The ministries meet any efforts to restrict *amakudari* with vigorous resistance. "It's because we are assured of a second career that we are willing to work for years at salaries below those in the private sector," says an official at the Ministry of Agriculture, Forestry, and Fisheries. The result is an incestuous system where businesses hire and pay ex-bureaucrats, and in exchange receive favors from government ministries.

While *amakudari* in private industry have garnered most media attention, there is another, even more influential type:
amakudari who run the vast web of semi-government agencies
through which subsidy money trickles downward. The largest
and most powerful of these are the *tokushu hojin*, "special government corporations," almost half of whose directors are
amakudari. After these directors retire from *tokushu hojin*, they
descend another rung, becoming directors of a second group of
agencies, *koeki hojin*, or "public corporations." These agencies
function with hardly any public scrutiny, and they are protected
by ministry colleagues who look forward to enjoying *amakudari*
benefits when their own time comes.

Consider the Japan Automobile Federation (JAF). Theoreti-
cally, JAF exists to provide road service for Japan's drivers.
However, JAF spends only 10 percent of its annual ¥48 billion
budget on road service, paying much of the rest to *amakudari*
officials from the Transport and Police ministries who draw
double incomes from JAF and its shell subsidiaries. Where the
lion's share of JAF's money goes nobody knows for sure, and
this is typical of the secret jugglings and cooked books of the
tokushu hojin.

Tokushu hojin are the very keystone of Japan's bureaucratic
state, and they represent yet another economic addiction. Although there has been much talk of reducing or abolishing
their largely anachronistic activities, they and their subsidiaries
employ 580,000 people; if you count the families and depen-
dents, they support more than 2 million people. The government can no more afford to suddenly cut back on *tokushu hojin*
than it can afford to reduce the construction budget, since such
a large percentage of the workforce depends on income from
these agencies.

Other soft landing sites for *amakudari* bureaucrats with
golden parachutes are government advisory councils and *kyo-*

kai, "industry associations." Groups such as the Electronics Communications Terminal Equipment Testing Association and the Radio Testing Association administer standards and recommend new policies. This helps to explain why Japan's industry is so slow to update technical standards, for as one journalist has observed, "When you seek to abolish certain regulations, a stone wall is immediately erected. Abolishing regulations translates into destroying these cushy post-bureaucratic careers."

Politicians exert influence through their relations with bureaucrats, and the press call the latter *zoku giin*, "tribal Diet members," according to which ministry tribe they belong to. Former prime minister Hashimoto, whose prime area of influence lay in the Ministry of Health and Welfare, derived his power from being a member of that ministry's tribe. Industry pays vast sums to tribal members who can secure contracts for them through their associated ministries. Construction Ministry tribalists sit at the top of the heap, as was illustrated in a major scandal of the 1990s in which it was found that Diet kingmaker Kanemaru Shin had made more than $50 million.

"Power," said Mao Zedong, "springs from the mouth of a gun." In Japan, even greater power springs from the issuing of rules and permits. Rules exist in every area and in a bewildering variety, most of them in the form of unpublished "administrative guidance." How do you know what the rules are? Only by maintaining close ties with government officials through the practice of *settai*, "wining and dining." *Settai* means giving expensive meals, but it extends into a gray area that most other advanced nations would call bribery at high levels: free golf-club memberships, use of corporate cars, and gifts of money.

Departments lower in the food chain need to curry favor with those higher up, which requires that officials practice *settai* with one another as well. Government bureaucrats spend billions of yen every year to wine and dine functionaries from other agencies. In this rich stream of slush funds, they have found ways to pan for gold—overbilling and charging for fictitious trips and nonexistent functions that cost prefectural governments millions of dollars a year.

Bureaucrats alone have the power to issue permits, and permits do not come cheap, as may be seen in the following example from the sports-club business. In the 1980s, although relatively new to Japan, sports clubs attracted the interest of men working in the Ministry of Health and Welfare (MHW) and the Ministry of Education. They saw ways of enriching themselves through the time-honored techniques of giving mandatory lectures and study sessions, issuing facilities permits, and creating credentials and "levels" for sports-club professionals; agencies staffed by *amakudari* would administer the study sessions and permits, as the social critic Inose Naoki has described. Nothing better illustrates the baroque structures of Japan's bureaucracy.

First, the MHW created the Foundation for Activities Promoting Health and Bodily Strength, which licensed two categories of workers: "health exercise guides" and "health exercise practice guides." The MHW and the Ministry of Education then jointly sponsored a Japan Health and Sports Federation, which granted permits to the first category, while the MHW alone founded a Japan Aerobics Fitness Association, which granted permits to the latter category. Not to be outdone, the Ministry of Education set up a Japan Gymnastics Association, which devised two credentials for Sports Programmer at the First Level and Sports Programmer at the Second Level. To gain a First Level certificate, an aerobics instructor has to pay ¥90,000, for the Second Level ¥500,000. In addition, something called the Central Association for Prevention of Labor Disabilities requires the instructor to attend twenty days of study sessions—at a cost of ¥170,000—before obtaining a permit to be either a "health-care trainer" or a "health-care leader." In short, if you want to teach aerobics, you must run the gamut of four agencies and pay for six permits. No laws explicitly require them, but nobody dares do business without at least some of these permits. The fees do not go back to the public purse but straight into the pockets of the *amakudari* who run the permit agencies.

With regulations earning so much money for bureaucrats, it is no wonder Japan has become one of the most heavily regulated nations on earth—former prime minister Hosokawa Morihiro once said that when he was the governor of Kumamoto he couldn't move a telephone pole without calling Tokyo for approval. Yet these regulations have created a strange paradox: they are a priori and exist solely on their own terms— they do not necessarily make business honest and efficient, products reliable, or citizens' lives safe.

The key to the paradox is that the regulations control but do not regulate in the true sense of the word. Industries in Japan are largely *unregulated*. There is nothing to stop you from selling medication that has fatal side effects, dumping toxic waste, building an eyesore in a historic neighborhood, or giving investors fraudulent company statements. But just running a noodle shop requires you to fill out lots of forms in triplicate, with stamps and seals. The point of Japan's red tape is bureaucratic control—the restriction of business to routine paths along which officials may profit.

Just as there is no environmental-assessment regulation, there is no product-liability law, no lender-liability law, very few rules against insider trading or other market manipulations, few testing protocols for new medicines—and no cost-benefit analyses for the gigantic building schemes of government agencies. Banks and securities firms routinely falsify financial information at the direction of the Ministry of Finance. When Ya-maichi Securities went belly-up in late 1997, investigators found that MOF had instructed it to hide more than $2 billion of losses in offshore accounts. Hamanaka Yasuo, the trader who cost Sumitomo Trading $2.6 billion through his dubious commodities dealing, violated no Japanese law. While home builders must contend with a welter of ordinances that happen to keep construction-company profits high, there is no city planning in the true sense of the word.

Because of the paradox of control versus regulation, the world of rules in Japan has a *Through the Looking-Glass* quality. A store must wait three years after getting a liquor license before it can sell domestic beer—but vending machines sell beer freely, even to minors, everywhere. The supermarket chain Daiei had to apply for two separate licenses to sell hamburgers and hot dogs if it displayed these products in different sections of the same store—but meat-processing standards for food manufacturers had not changed since 1904. If a supermarket sells aspirin, a pharmacist must be present and have medical tools on hand—yet nowhere else in the developed world are physicians free to dispense drugs themselves, and as a result the Japanese use far more drugs, of dubious efficacy, than any other people on earth. The *Through the Looking-Glass* nature of Japanese regulations goes a long way toward explaining such preposterous prices as $100 melons and $10 cups of coffee. The aggregate cost to the economy is simply incalculable. These outrageous prices, absurd regulations, weird and inexplicable public works—all the ingredients of a *manga*-like world—exist for the simple reason that bureaucrats profit from them.

Officials have devised many ingenious ways of channeling funds into their own pockets. The River Bureau, as we have seen, has made a particularly lucrative franchise of its work.

While bureaucrats get the lion's share of the profits from construction work, a goodly percentage flows to political parties. The rule of thumb has been that contractors pay 1 to 3 percent of every large public-works project to the politicians who arranged it, in which practice the Tax Office colludes by recognizing "unaccounted-for expenditures" (i.e., bribes to politicians and bureaucrats) as a corporate-expense line item, which in the case of the construction industry amounts to hundreds of millions of dollars annually.

In *Mito Komon*, a long-running Japanese television series set in the Edo period, Lord Mito, the uncle of the Shogun, travels around the country incognito righting wrongs done to innocent people. The scene changes with each episode, but the villain is invariably a corrupt samurai *machi bugyo*, or town administrator, whom we see seated in his spacious mansion before an alcove decorated with rare and expensive art, counting gold from ill-gotten gains. His victims have no recourse against him. Only at the climax of each episode does Lord Mito's attendant raise high his paulownia-flower crest and reveal his true identity, whereupon the administrator falls to the ground in obeisance and is carried off for punishment.

The difference between Edo and modern Japan is that today we have no Lord Mito. The public suffers from chronically expensive goods and services, while bureaucrats and politicians prosper to a degree that verges on the fantastic, nowhere more than in construction, where *amakudari* reap post-retirement fortunes. With more than 500,000 construction firms in Japan, no ex-official will ever find himself out of a job. Their personal future income at stake, Construction Ministry bureaucrats support and encourage bid-rigging, which is endemic in Japan's construction industry, inflating the cost of public construction by 30 to 50 percent. (According to some estimates, inflated bids

provide 16 to 33 percent of the industry's profits, which is between $50 and $100 billion every year.)

Just as leftist writers in the 1930s were so in love with the "dic-
tatorship of the proletariat" that they were unwilling to admit
the brutal reality of Stalinism, so mainstream Western commentators have kept up a long love affair with Japan's bureaucracy.
As recently as 1997, Ezra Vogel of Harvard University, the author of *Japan as Number One*, described Japan's "elite bureaucracy" as one of its distinctive strengths, which "compare very
favorably around the world." "Japanese civil servants enjoy the
priceless advantage of the moral high ground," Eamonn Fingleton wrote in his book *Blindside*, which aimed to show "why
Japan is still on track to overtake the U.S. by the year 2000."
"Their actions," he continued, "will be judged only in terms of
how well they serve the overall national interest. Their objective is to achieve the greatest happiness of the greatest number
of people. Moreover, they take an extremely long-term view in
that they seek to represent the interests not only of today's
Japanese but of future generations."

    In the 1980s, the Ministry of International Trade and Indus-
try (MITI) was the darling of foreign commentators; today, that
honor goes to the Ministry of Finance. "MOF men truly are
Nobel caliber," continued Fingleton adoringly. MOF men are
"brilliant, creative, tenacious, public spirited." They have "not
only grit and technical brilliance but an uncommon sense in
reading people and their needs." Unlike the "greed-is-good"
West, "MOF today is living proof that top officials can be
'rightly oriented in their own minds and hearts.' " This is due
to "pride in a distinctive (and distinctively masculine) way of
life, a concern to earn the good opinion of comrades, satisfac-
tion in the largely symbolic tokens of professional success."

    What could be more attractive, more worth emulating in

other countries? Nevertheless, the greedy *machi bugyo* of the Lord Mito series, sitting in his embroidered kimono eating off fine gold lacquer, represents a cold fact of bureaucratic life: corruption. It's a genteel, smoothly organized, even institutionalized, form of corruption, so endemic as to be called "structural" and thus not usually seen as corruption as we ordinarily understand it.

The sad reality is that the Japanese bureaucracy thrives on shady money: in small ways by cadging extra expenses with falsified travel reports; in larger ways by accepting bribes from businessmen and as favors from organized crime. Shady money is the oil that greases the wheels of Japan's smooth-running relationship between the bureaucracy and business, and that features in the expensive practice of *settai*.

The bureaucratic scandals that periodically rip through the Japanese media are efforts, as van Wolferen points out, to rectify outrageous excess, but they do nothing to address the structural corruption that is the normal state of affairs. In 1996, for example, newspapers revealed that Izui Jun'ichi, the owner of an Osaka oil wholesaler and a "fixer" in the Japanese oil business, had spent more than ¥75 million on wining and dining government officials, including forty-two from MITI and thirty from MOF, reaching all the way up to MITI's vice minister, Makino Tsutomu, and MOF's vice minister, Ogawa Tadashi. MITI, stung by these fierce press reports, investigated 138 employees and reprimanded six top officials. A former vice minister of the Transport Ministry, Hattori Tsuneharu (in the *amakudari* position of president of the Kansai International Airport), had received from Izui ¥4.9 million in cash, gift coupons, a bar of gold, and an expensive painting. (Paintings, easy to hide and difficult to value, are gifts of choice.) Izui was also reported to have given a painting worth several thousand dollars to Wakui Yoji, the chief of the MOF Secretariat—in exchange for which favor newspapers speculated that Wakui may have pressured Tax Bureau officials to relax their investigation of Izui's tax evasion.

Part of MOF's admirably "masculine way of life" involves enjoying the fun at hostess bars and other sleazy venues that are paid for by banks' *settai* budgets. In September 1994, Dai-Ichi Kangyo Bank treated Miyakawa Koichi, the chief of MOF's Inspectors' Office, to an evening at a "no-pants *shabu-shabu*" restaurant, featuring waitresses in the nude from the waist down. Miyakawa was so grateful that he let the bank people know about a surprise inspection due to take place the next day. A cartoon in a weekly magazine showed a devil at the gates of hell consulting his notebook and commenting, "For a bureaucrat from Japan's Ministry of Finance to sell his soul for no-pants *shabu-shabu* and *yakitori*, that's really cheap!"

That these scandals are chronic, not mere flukes in an otherwise honest system, is obvious not only from the sheer number of officials involved but also from their seniority. In the government ministries, a politician takes the largely ritual top position as minister, while true executive power lies with the senior career bureaucrat, the vice minister. Vice ministers from *all* major ministries have been implicated in recent *settai* and bribery scandals, and then the takings extend downward in diminishing amounts. For example, Okamitsu Nobuharu, the vice minister of Health and Welfare, was arrested in December 1996 for receiving more than ¥100 million in gifts and favors from Koyama Hiroshi, a developer of nursing homes subsidized by his ministry. At the same time, Wada Masaru, in a lesser position as the ministry's councilor, received ¥1 million from Koyama, and other officials further down the line benefited in various degrees from *settai*. The MHW, anxious to avoid further public scandal, carried out an in-house investigation and later fined or reprimanded sixteen employees.

Where in the past decade, in Europe, America, Malaysia, or Singapore, could we find a bureaucrat convicted of the ¥100 million garnered by MHW vice minister Okamitsu? Or the $600,000 paid by Takahashi Harunori, the president of real-estate company EIE Corporation, to Nakajima Yoshio, the former vice director of MOF's Budget Bureau in 1991? Such are the takings of those who have the "priceless advantage of the moral high ground" and stand as "living proof that top officials can be 'rightly oriented in their own minds and hearts.' "

One feature of MOF's superior moral quality is its links with organized crime. Under MOF's guidance, gangsters play a large role in Japan's financial system. In 1998, another scandal broke with the news that Dai-Ichi Kangyo Bank, one of Japan's top-ten commercial banks, extended collateral-free loans of ¥30 billion to Koike Ryuichi in 1989 so that he could buy stocks in Nomura Securities and other brokerage firms. Koike was in a business unique to Japan known as *sokaiya*, which is the disturbance of shareholder meetings by asking difficult questions. In other countries, people who ask hard questions at shareholder meetings are simply stockholders, but in Japan they are usually extortionist gangsters. Most large companies try to conclude their annual meetings in less than an hour, so *sokaiya* is a considerable threat. The answer is to pay the gangsters off. Nomura paid Koike as much as ¥70 million to keep quiet, and later it was revealed that all the other top stockholders and major banks had paid Koike as well.

The fact that officials enrich themselves at public expense is not considered to be more than a minor evil in Japan and the rest of East Asia, because people expect these same officials to manage the resources of the state in a wise and efficient manner. There is an ongoing debate in East Asia over the virtues of open, Western-style bureaucracy versus the paternalistic "crony-capitalism" found in Japan. Apologists for "crony-capitalism" admire the way that officials can easily and freely channel funds to pet industries and projects without having to engage in raucous policy debates in public. However, in this very freedom lies the source of danger.

The muckraking journalist Lincoln Steffens, who exposed Tammany Hall–style corruption in American cities a century ago, defined "privilege" as the essential problem of corruption. What Steffens meant by "privilege" was that those with money get access to government resources; those who don't pay up go without. This is why corruption has to be taken seriously: privilege skews the way the state assigns its resources. Herein lies the key to modern Japan's mismanagement. Official support doesn't go to those who need it but to the privileged—those who pay bureaucrats the most. Looking forward to *amakudari* rewards, officials lavish funds on building up massive overproduction in one old-fashioned industry after another, rather than support new business involving services and the Internet. The pachinko industry hires ex-policemen as *amakudari*, and pachinko parlors overrun the country. River Bureau officials profit from dams, so dams go up by the hundreds. Useless monuments sprout and the seashore disappears under cement because of the privileged position of construction companies. The shady money flowing into officials' pockets is molding the very look of the land.

6 Monuments

Airports for Radishes

Aujourd'hui rien.
—LOUIS XVI, writing in his diary on the day the
Bastille fell (1789)

Information is unreliable, knowledge of new techniques used abroad scarce, and public funds distributed not to the sectors that need them but to those who pay bureaucrats the most—in this dim twilight world, Japanese officials are losing touch with reality. Government agencies feel they should be doing something and, unable to see what the basic problems are or how to address them, they turn to building monuments. Monument construction is profitable, too. Anyone who travels in Japan will be familiar with the multipurpose cultural halls, museums, and communications centers that are becoming the predominant features of urban life. Even tiny villages have them. Halls and centers that cost tens or hundreds of millions of dollars each go up across the nation, it is said, at the rate of three a day.

In the ancient Chinese philosophical treatise *Han Feizi*, the emperor asked a painter, "What are the hardest and easiest things to depict?" The artist replied, "Dogs and horses are diffi-

cult, demons and goblins are easy." By that he meant that simple, unobtrusive things in our immediate environment—like
dogs and horses—are hard to get right, while anyone can draw
an eye-catching monster. Japan suffers from a severe case of
"dogs and demons." In field after field, the bureaucracy dreams
up lavish monuments rather than attend to long-term underlying problems. Communications centers sprout antennas from
lofty towers, yet television channels and Internet usage lag.
Lavish crafts halls dot the landscape while Japan's traditional
crafts are in terminal decline. And local history museums stand
proud in every small town and municipal district while a sea of
blighted industrial development has all but eradicated real local
history.

In libraries devoted to Japan, shelves sag under the weight of
hundreds of volumes written about the gardens of Kyoto, Zen,
Japan's youth culture, and so forth. Yet we must concede, after
looking at the Construction State, that these are not the areas
into which the energies of Japanese society are really flowing.
The real Japan, sadly ignored by travel writers so far, lies in its
many modern monuments; visiting a few of them will give us a
taste of the true Japan.

Our first stop is Tokyo's Teleport Town, a waterfront construction project like the ones that almost every Japanese city with
access to the sea now boasts. These utopian visions of high-tech
"cities of the future" are Japan's pride, with their expensive
landfill in harbors, followed by museums, convention halls, and
superexpensive "intelligent buildings." The costs are astronomical, high enough to drag Osaka Prefecture and Tokyo, Japan's
two major metropolitan regions, into bankruptcy. But the local
governments are pressing on regardless.

Teleport Town was built on land reclaimed from Tokyo Bay
by the Tokyo metropolitan government and developed with

state-of-the-art infrastructure. Time 24, one of its "intelligent buildings," boasts fiber-optic wiring and other equipment, and is serviced by a shiny new train system. The trouble is that there was no need for Teleport Town. Time 24 has been almost empty since it opened, and so has the train. So few tenants moved in that in February 1996 Time 24 tried to lease floors to the Fisheries Department, to be filled with fish tanks—unsuccessfully. Projections indicate that Teleport Town will run up a ¥5 trillion shortfall over the next three decades.

From here we move on to Tega Marsh Fountain, built by the Chiba prefectural government, northeast of Tokyo. This fountain, spouting water from the most polluted inland body of water in Japan, was built to "symbolize the community's hopes for the future." So poisonous is the spume that operators halt the fountain when the wind is blowing hard or when there is an outbreak of toxic algae. In a newspaper interview, one man summed up the view of local residents: "I don't have a good feeling when I see the fountain."

While Teleport Town is a monument in progress and Tega Marsh Fountain is in its terminal stages, in Gifu, between Kyoto and Nagoya, we can see a monument at its inception. The town of Gifu is a dreary conglomeration of little shops, home to thousands of low-end manufacturers of T-shirts and cheap clothing. This local industry, at a sharp disadvantage to China and other cheap foreign producers, is mired in chronic depression, hardly an encouraging sight, but in December 1995 Gifu Prefecture announced that it intended to become the "Milan of Japan." At great expense, it redeveloped the wholesale market near the train station, raising a gleaming new complex that Gifu hoped would solve the problem of structural decline in Japan's apparel industry.

Northwest of Gifu, the Hokuriku Express, a spur train line, was built for ¥130 billion during the course of almost thirty years simply to shave fifteen minutes off the rail time between Tokyo and Kanazawa, and it is now to be overshadowed by a newer monument. In addition to the fact that there was no real need for it in the first place, it appears no one will ever use the line because Japan Railways is extending the bullet train to Kanazawa. A Hokuriku Express executive says, "Although no one openly says so, everybody's worried. We hope to attract passengers by developing tourist attractions." In other words, more monuments.

Last, there is the Hakata Bay project, a container port being built on mud flats in the harbor off Fukuoka City. When completed, the 448-hectare island, second in size only to Teleport Town, will destroy bird habitat, the last remaining place in Hakata Bay for migratory birds. There was some opposition to this project in the early 1990s, but Fukuoka Prefecture claimed the port would be needed for new commerce with Southeast Asia, though this is unlikely, given the high yen and increased competition from other ports in Asia and Japan. Kaneko Jun, a manager at Evergreen, a company that handles the largest volume of containers at Fukuoka, said, "As far as our company is concerned, the island is not necessary." Would Fukuoka protect the birds, cancel the plan, and save itself ruinous expense? The answer is predictable. Although the World Wildlife Fund Japan petitioned the national government to review the project, the Environment Agency approved it and construction began in April 1996.

Japan's monument mentality is in evidence everywhere. Not only the Construction and Transport ministries raise monuments—every department does. One of the biggest builders is the Ministry of Agriculture, Forestry, and Fisheries (MAFF), which receives 20 percent of the public-works construction budget, far more than it needs. Nevertheless funds, once budgeted, *must* be spent. MAFF devotes as much money as it can to creating untraveled forestry roads and fishing ports where no boats call, but even this isn't enough to soak up the surplus. To spend it all, MAFF officials have cooked up some truly bizarre schemes, the most fanciful among them being rural airports devoted to airlifting vegetables. The idea was to improve Japan's agricultural productivity by speeding vegetable delivery from rural areas to big cities. The veggie airports are a classic Dogs and Demons project, because the problems in Japanese agriculture have little to do with delivery and everything to do with other factors—such as artificially high prices and a declining workforce—which MAFF would rather not address.

There are four veggie airports already built, and five more under construction. However, as it turns out, flying vegetables costs six to seven times as much as trucking them, and far more labor to load and reload them from trucks to aircraft to larger aircraft and back to trucks. Kasaoka Airfield flies vegetables to Okayama City, only a few dozen kilometers away, even though flying them takes just as long as sending them by road.

Boondoggle fever is infectious. It has expanded beyond government into endowed foundations and cultural groups. Even the Red Cross, it seems, is not immune. In March 1997, newspapers revealed that the Japan Red Cross had secretly diverted much of the $10.3 million in earthquake-relief donations that came from Red Cross organizations in twenty-six countries to build a facility called the Hyogo Prefecture Disaster Treatment Center.

"This money was collected for victims of the Kobe earthquake," said Vedron Drakulic, the public-affairs manager of the Australian Red Cross. "We didn't know about other uses." One could hardly blame the Australians for not understanding the way things work in modern Japan. The socially prominent Japanese who sit on the Japan Red Cross board and the millions of contributors across the nation who support it are sincere in their desire to be philanthropic. They, too, are victims, for they are no match for the bureaucrats who manage the organization like every other, programmed to make construction a priority.

Mitsuie Yasuo, a Construction Ministry official who has argued in support of higher public-works budgets, makes the claim that "Japan is still a developing country compared with Western Europe and the United States." This open admission of the Construction Ministry's ineptitude is, incredibly enough, a truthful one. Perhaps the single exception is Japan's rail network, one of the most extensive and efficient in the world. Railroad building is an example of a policy that grew far beyond its original aims and became one of officialdom's unstoppable tanks. A high priority in the postwar years, railways took on a life of their own as the ultimate pork barrel beloved of politicians, with the result that gigantic new lines continue to expand across the nation regardless of economic need or environmental impact. As Richard Koo, the chief economist for the Nomura Research Institute, puts it, "Good projects are a luxury. Recovery is a necessity. How money is spent is not important. *That* money is spent is important."

That so much money has brought so little real improvement to life is an aspect of Japan's modern development that most defies comprehension. As boondoggles burgeon madly over the landscape, the sorely needed improvements that would really enhance life remain in the future: burial of power and phone lines, construction of sewage lines (still lacking for a third of Japan's homes), provision of good public hospitals and educational institutions, cheap and efficient air travel (Japanese domestic air travel is the most expensive in the world, and Narita Airport in Tokyo features such poor design and management that travelers recently voted it the forty-second worst airport in the world out of forty-three), and waterproof waste-disposal sites. This is not to mention a massive *de-construction* program to remove the Construction Ministry's worst mistakes—such as the asbestos found in almost every large building in the country. Yet money does not flow to such projects. It flows to museums with no artworks, rail lines with no passengers, container ports with no ships, new cities with no tenants, and airports for radishes. The trillions of dollars poured into construction during the past decades have been going, quite simply, to the wrong places.

To understand how the monument frenzy can continue at fever pitch, we need to take another look at how these projects are funded. Where do the bureaucrats get their money? They get it from Zaito, or FILP (Fiscal Investment and Loan Program). Zaito is Japan's second budget, the shadow budget, through which MOF's Trust Fund Bureau draws on a huge pool of deposits in the postal-savings system to fund its agencies and programs—with almost no parliamentary overview. Zaito is the bureaucracy's private piggy bank.

Zaito works like this: The government grants tax exemptions and other preferential treatment to postal-savings accounts managed by local post offices; interest on postal-savings deposits is consistently higher than in the private sector. Lured by these higher interest rates and by the convenience of banking at post offices, the Japanese people have put more and more of their money into postal savings, to the extent that by the end of the twentieth century they accounted for about a third of all bank deposits in Japan.

This enormous pool of capital—trillions of dollars' worth—is handed over to MOF's Trust Fund Bureau to manage. With the funds from postal savings, pension funds, and other special accounts combined, the Trust Fund Bureau has, in effect, become the world's largest government bank. It invests much of the money in Japanese government bonds, which helps to explain why these bonds, which paid interest of only 1 to 2 percent or less for most of the 1990s, still found buyers—or, at least, one large buyer, the government itself, using captive savings deposits managed by the Trust Fund Bureau.

With money like this at its disposal, how could MOF resist the temptation to dip into the honey pot? It didn't take long. In 1955, only three years after the American Occupation ended, MOF borrowed a little money from the Trust Fund Bureau to support certain items for which there was not enough allocation in the general budget; the purpose was obviously to get around the official budget process in the National Diet.

It worked all too well. By 1999, Zaito borrowings had skyrocketed to ¥52.9 trillion annually, including ¥39.4 trillion overseen by the Trust Fund Bureau and another ¥13.5 trillion lent by the Postal Life Insurance system. In 1999, the ¥52.9 trillion Zaito program amounted to two-thirds of the money disbursed in the official "first budget." The beauty of Zaito, from MOF's point of view, is that it flows from an inexhaustible pool of public savings and is largely invisible to politicians and the press. So far so good. The problem is that the people who manage Zaito are the same "brilliant, creative, tenacious, public spirited" MOF men who have run Japanese banks into the ground. With an endless supply of money at their disposal and no public accountability, the fifty-seven *tokushu hojin* and other agencies on Zaito support have racked up debts as they have spent trillions on all these wasteful monuments and shell agencies supporting ex-bureaucrats.

When these corporations and agencies found themselves unable to repay their Zaito borrowings, the *tobashi* started.

Tobashi, or "flying," is a word we have met before as the term used by banks to describe the method whereby they pass bad loans on to subsidiaries, thus causing them to "fly" off the books. In the case of Zaito, MOF lent more money to Zaito borrowers to cover the interest payments. By 1997, troubled Zaito loans were estimated to be as high as ¥62 trillion, although even this is a conservative figure. These Zaito obligations, added to the cumulative deficits of the central and local governments, the "hidden debts" (such as ¥28 trillion for the old Japan National Railroad Resolution Trust), and the juggling of inter-governmental accounts, raise Japan's real national debt to a level higher in absolute value than the U.S. national debt, equal to as much as 150 percent of Japan's GNP.

To see where all the Zaito money went, one must step boldly into the swamp of bureaucratic finance. The breeding habits of *tokushu hojin* are remarkable: ninety-two *tokushu hojin*, grouped under various ministries, have spawned thousands of *koeki hojin*, of which the central government oversees 6,922 and regional governments 19,005. *Amakudari* run most of the *koeki hojin* associated with the government, while ex-officials and employee welfare funds of the various ministries own a major portion of their stock. The *koeki hojin* in turn breed grandchildren, owned by the same people: full-fledged private profit-making enterprises that, without having to make public bids, gain a large share of public-works contracts. The various corporations fall under the jurisdiction of different ministries, which use them like cattle to be milked. MITI sponsors a herd of 901 *hojin*, the Ministry of Education 1,778. All these *hojin* feed on Zaito money. Their breeding ground is the ministries that oversee them. They have no natural predators. Their droppings take the form of huge pellets known as monuments.

At the top of the list is the Highway Public Corporation, *Doro Kodan*, the largest of all the swamp creatures, king of the jungle. To build and manage Japan's highways, it has an operating budget of ¥4.4 trillion, roughly half of which comes from road tolls and other highway receipts; Zaito borrowings supply the rest. (The Highway PC is in fact Zaito's single largest borrower.) Over the years, the Highway PC has sunk into a quagmire of unrepayable debt; its cumulative red ink had come to well over ¥20 trillion by the end of the century. At this level, it rivaled even the notorious Japan National Railroad debt (¥28 trillion) and by 2002 might even surpass it. This desperate financial situation lies behind the high tolls, such as the ¥1,700 charge to drive for three minutes over the bridge to the New Kansai Airport.

The management of highways has its profitable side, however—the operation of service and parking areas along the freeways, with their attendant food and drink concessions, as well as telephone and car-radio monopolies. These monopolies lend themselves to schemes whereby bureaucrats make money for themselves. Here's how it works: The Highway PC creates a *koeki hojin* known as the Highway Facilities Association, which owns and manages the thousands of service and parking areas and has annual revenues of ¥73 billion, making it Japan's seventh-largest real-estate company. For this it pays the Highway PC only ¥7 billion in fees (less than 10 percent of revenues); the rest goes to the *amakudari* who run it. In turn it contracts out the work of operating the service areas and parking areas to agencies whose qualifications are that ex-bureaucrats from the Highway PC and the Construction Ministry employee-welfare funds own most of their stock. These companies have combined sales of ¥545 billion and employ 26,000 people, almost three times more than the number employed by their grandfather, the Highway PC. Add in the sales earned by the Highway Facilities Association, and the earnings of these subsidiaries come to more than ¥600 billion annually, a large part of which is pure profit, since the Highway PC awards cushy bloated contracts with no public bidding.

What all these numbers tell us is that the retired bureaucrats from the Construction and Transport ministries who run the Highway PC have neatly removed the profits in road management from the Highway PC's budget and funneled them into their own pockets. Every time the Highway PC builds a new highway, the public pays high tolls, shouldering the burden of paying off the Zaito debt, while the bureaucrats profit from new service- and parking-area concessions. Therefore it is imperative to build more and more highways.

Everywhere you look, you find parasitic tendrils sucking nourishment from the flow of Zaito money. The favorite technique is *marunage*, "tossing it on," by which an agency midway in the food chain receives a contract from the government and then tosses the project on to a subcontractor. The agency receives hefty fees in spite of not having done any work.

An example of *marunage* is the New Development Materials Company, an enterprise in the purview of the Ministry of Posts and Telecommunications (MPT). Anyone who has been awarded a contract to build a new post office must order materials through this company, although its business is entirely *marunage*—it simply channels orders to the suppliers that the builder would have used anyway. The contractors who design new post offices do not particularly mind, however, as there are only four of them and MPT employee funds own most of their stock. MPT has dozens of other profitable *marunage* subsidiaries, such as Japan Post Transport, which subcontracts the job of collecting letters from mailboxes and delivering them to post offices. This explains why the post office charges some of the world's highest postage rates. In recent years, postage rates have risen so steeply that people send letters to Hong Kong in bulk and have them re-posted to Japan one by one. International airmail from Hong Kong is cheaper than the domestic post.

The shell game goes on. Just as MOF found a way, via Zaito borrowings, to remove much of the budget from the overview of the Diet, individual ministries have found ways to raise money on their own account, thus bypassing MOF. A favorite technique is to establish a gambling venue from which the ministry takes a share of the proceeds via a *koeki hojin*. Thus the Transport Ministry has ¥6.6 billion at its disposal earned from boat racing, while MITI rakes in ¥16 billion from auto and bicycle racing. The police, meanwhile, make sums that dwarf those of all other ministries combined from their involvement with pachinko.

What happens to all this money is a mystery. In the case of MITI, the subsidiaries that handle the gambling earnings do not publish the names of the agencies to which they distribute the money. The official reason is that the United States might sue Japan at the World Trade Organization if it learned that MITI was subsidizing certain industries. The real reason is that most of the money flows to comfortable *amakudari* nests, such as the Industrial Research Center—the recipient of roughly $1 million a year for each of its twenty-three *amakudari* employees—for no work that anyone has been able to discover. A disgruntled MOF official remarked, "[Racing money] is not checked by MOF. It's MITI's pocket money. It's a warm bed of privilege that MITI will guard to the death."

On the day the Bastille fell in 1789, Louis XVI went hunting and had a rather nice day; the news of the fall of the Bastille meant very little to him. In hindsight, we know that it was one of the pivotal events in world history and that it cost the king his head. But on that day hunting took priority, and in the evening the king wrote in his diary: "*Aujourd'hui rien,*" "Today, nothing."

The Japanese bureaucracy does not realize that the Bastille has fallen. When a reporter from the *Nikkei Weekly* pointed out that the value of the collateral on which banks granted their bad loans—mostly land—had dropped to the point that the banks can never recover the principal, a senior official at the Banking Bureau scoffed that it was, after all, "just collateral." He went on to say, "There is enough cash flow for most companies to make payments on these loans, especially with current low interest rates."

As we have seen, corruption in MOF is widespread and well documented. Scandals in 1997 and early 1998 resulted in a public raid of MOF's offices by police investigators, and two suicides, not to mention lots of salacious details about no-pants *shabu-shabu.* Yet, in an interview by the *Mainichi Daily News* in February 1997 concerning the bribery scandal of Nakajima Yoshio, the recipient some years earlier of $600,000 from the EIE Corporation, Sakakibara Eisuke (then vice minister of MOF) responded that this had been "emotionally magnified," "an anomaly." In February 1999, as the government was about to infuse ¥7 trillion into the failing banking system, he claimed that the financial crisis would end "in a week or two." This despite the fact that admitted bad loans (at that time) amounted to ¥49 trillion, seven times the amount of the government bailout.

Alas, the crisis will not end in a week or two, because the world has changed. For MOF, no harkening after the old days of protected local markets will save Japan's depressed stock market, bankrupt pension funds, banks submerged in red ink—and a national debt that is the highest in the world. Fundamental problems beset other ministries as well. And yet the bureaucrats have still not been called to account. When the official at the

Environment Agency remarked, "Even if underground water in Kobe is contaminated by chemicals, few people drink the water," he was essentially responding, "*Rien.*" Dioxin in the water table? Not to worry. As for the destruction of Japan's last great wetlands at Isahaya, well, said the chief of the Ministry of Agriculture, Forestry, and Fisheries, "The current ecosystem may disappear, but nature will create a new one."

For those looking to what the future is likely to bring to Japan during the next few decades, the answer "*Rien*" is an important one to understand. It rules for a simple reason: the Zaito piggy bank is still flush with postal savings. No force on earth can stop the forward march of Japan's bureaucracy for the simple reason that there is ample money to support it.

"*Rien*" does not mean just business as usual. As we have seen earlier from the Law of Bureaucratic Inertia, it means gradual acceleration: more of the same business, and faster. Most readers will be familiar with Dukas's music for *The Sorcerer's Apprentice*, which was featured in a famous animation sequence in Walt Disney's *Fantasia.* The story is that a sorcerer asks his apprentice to fetch water while he is away, but the boy is too lazy to do it himself. He uses a bit of magic stolen from his master by which he empowers a broom to fetch the water for him. For a while, all goes well. But the water keeps accumulating, and the apprentice realizes that he doesn't know the spell that will make the broom stop. The broom multiplies. Soon hundreds of brooms are pouring torrents of water. The music builds to a climax—there is no stemming the flood now—but finally the sorcerer returns, and in an instant the brooms stop and the waters recede.

Japan's bureaucracy is like this. Before World War II, the bureaucrats had already consolidated power but had to share it with the armed forces and the big *zaibatsu* business cartels. After the war, with the army and the *zaibatsu* discredited, politicians, the press, and the public consigned their fate to bureau-crats, allowing them near-dictatorial powers and asking no questions. For a while, the system worked reasonably well. But in the 1970s, things started to get out of hand. Government agencies began to bury cities and countryside under ever more aggressive building schemes, piling dam on top of dam and landfill on top of landfill. The tempo of the music sped up. Agencies started multiplying. First there were *tokushu hojin*, then there were *koeki hojin*, and finally there were companies like Friends of the Waters—all dedicated to building more dams, more roads, more museums, more harbor landfill, more airports for vegetables. By the end of the 1990s, there were thousands of brooms fetching water, most of it the color of red ink.

In Japan's case, unlike that of the sorcerer's apprentice, there is no wizard who knows the charm that will stop the brooms. The scale of public works on the drawing board for the next two or three decades is mind-boggling: 500 dams planned, be-yond the more than 2,800 already built; 6,000 kilometers of expressways beyond the 6,000 already managed by the High-way PC; another 150,000 kilometers of mountain roads on top of the 130,000 kilometers already built by the Forestry Bureau. Nagara Dam, which resulted in three large river systems being concreted, was just for openers. "Why not go and connect those systems to Lake Biwa?" asks Takasue Hidenobu, the chair-man of the Water Resources Public Corporation. For yet an-other Lovecraftian thrill, one need only look at a map of Japan to see what he is suggesting—nothing less than the demolition of a mountain range, as Lake Biwa sits on the far side of one, in a completely different prefecture from that of the Nagara Dam river systems. Meanwhile, Osaka Prefecture has plans to fill in all of Osaka Bay to a depth of fifteen meters. The music is building to a crescendo.

The process has the insistent quality of Japan's march to war in the 1930s. Inose Naoki writes:

> At the moment, our citizens are waiting again for the "End of the War." Before World War II, when Japan advanced deeply into the continent, it was like the expansion of bad debts [today], and unable to deal with the consequences, we plunged into war with the United States. We should have been able to halt at some stage, yet even though we were headed for disaster, nobody could prevent it. At this point, lacking an "Imperial Decree," there is absolutely nothing we can do to stop what is going on.

7 Old Cities

Kyoto and Tourism

To be happy at home is the
ultimate result of all ambition.
—DR. SAMUEL JOHNSON, *The Rambler* (1750)

In the opening scene of the Kabuki play *Akoya*, the courtesan
Akoya walks sadly along the *hanamichi*, the raised walkway that
passes through the audience, to the stage where she faces trial.
The chanters describe her beauty in captivity as "the image of a
wilted peony in a bamboo vase, unable to draw water up her
stem." This verse neatly captures the irony of modern Japan:
the contrast between its depressed internal condition and the
wealth of industrial capital and cultural heritage it has to draw
on. There is water in abundance, but something about the system prevents it from being drawn up the stem.

A friend of mine once remarked, "What is modernism? It's
not the city but how you live in the city. It's not the factory but
how you manage and maintain the factory." Technology involves far more than products running off an assembly line or
computer software. It could be defined as the science of managing things properly. How to design a museum exhibit, how

to manage a zoo, how to renovate an old building, how to build and operate a vacation resort—these all involve very sophisticated techniques and fuel multibillion-dollar industries in Europe and the United States. None of them exist in Japan today except in the most primitive form.

Yet managing things properly is what traditional Japan did in a way that put virtually every other culture of the world to shame. The tea ceremony, for example, is nothing but an intense course in the art of managing things. The way to pick up or put down a tea bowl involves sensitivity to many different factors: the harmonious angle at which the bowl sits on the tatami brings pleasure to the eye; turning the bowl is a symbolic ritual that connects us to deep cultural roots; when the bowl is set down, the movements of the arm, elbow, and hand are utterly, even ruthlessly, efficient. Well into the twentieth century, Japan perfected quality control on the assembly line and built the world's largest and most efficient urban public-transportation systems. The care for detail and the devotion to work are certainly there—Japan has all the ingredients necessary to become the world's supremely modern country. Yet this hasn't happened.

The reason the flower is unable to draw water up its stem is that Japan has resisted change; and modernism, by definition, requires new ideas and new ways of doing things to keep up with a changing world. When the cold gray hand of the bureaucracy settled on the nation in the mid-1960s, Japan's way of doing things froze. Quality control in manufacturing and public transportation continued to develop, but Japan ignored many of the drastic changes that swept the rest of the world in ensuing decades.

Let's look at the technology of renovating old buildings. Recently, I read an article by Philip Langdon in the November

1998 issue of the *Yale Alumni Magazine*, describing the renovation of Linsly-Chittenden Hall, one of Yale's older but more run-down buildings. The $22 million renovation included raising the roof to accommodate new faculty offices; installing high-tech devices in the basement; building a new facade to the main entrance with an attractive handicapped-accessible ramp, a tiered lecture hall with data ports, electrical outlets for every seat, and the latest in sound and lighting systems. At the same time, the university stipulated that the renovation "maintain the traditional architectural character of the undergraduate teaching spaces."

> To that end, most of the technological improvements are tucked out of sight inside floors, walls, and ceilings, while the old chalkboards—which were removed, refurbished, and then reinstalled—provide reassurance that the character of the classrooms remains intact. Where new hallways have been constructed or old corridors have been extended, their new oak-veneer paneling looks practically identical to the solid oak of the original halls. Where windows have been replaced, the new panes recreate the appearance of old.

What Yale is doing to its buildings—at a cost of $1 billion over a twenty-year period—involves some very complex processes. At the Sterling Memorial Library's periodical reading room, University Librarian Scott Bennett points out, "We literally tore the outside skin of the building off." Yale removed the stone surface, installed modern anti-moisture systems, and then reattached the stone.

Here is how renovation is done the Japanese way: Starting around 1990, an heiress named Nakahara Kiiko purchased eight châteaus in France. She and her husband then proceeded to strip them of their interior decorations, after which they carted away statues and marble basins from the gardens and cut down the trees, leaving the properties in ruins. The saddest case was the Château de Louveciennes, in suburban Paris, where Madame du Barry once entertained King Louis XV. *The New York Times* reported:

> Today, the celebrated dining room that the courtesan had lined with finely carved oak wainscoting is just a shell of bricks and plaster, stripped of the paneling. In the salons and bedrooms the marble fireplaces have been ripped out of the walls leaving large black hollows. The three-floor chateau seems a haunted place now, with shutters flapping in the wind and dark puddles on the wooden landing when rain drips through the roof.

In January 1996, French authorities jailed Nakahara on charges of "despoiling national heritage." Concerned about her adverse effect on Japan's image in Europe, the Japanese press pilloried her for her gross insensitivity to history and cultural heritage.

Yet one could argue that Nakahara was treated unfairly. What she did to the châteaus in France is nothing other than standard practice in Japan. It is exactly what businesses, home-owners, and civic officials have done and are still doing in Kyoto, Nara, and every other city, and to tens of thousands of great houses and temples across the country. In uprooting old trees and stripping historical buildings, Nakahara was only following the customs of her native land.

In seeking the roots of Nakahara's actions, the best place to begin is the city of Kyoto. Professor Tayama Reishi of Bukkyo University in Kyoto has written:

> How must Kyoto appear to one who has never visited here? Passersby clad in kimono going to and fro along quiet nar-

row streets between temples, rows of houses with black wooden lattices, glimpsed over tiled roofs the mountains covered with cherry blossoms, streams trickling at one's feet. Well, even if we don't believe such a city really exists, nobody can help imagining such things about a town one is about to visit for the first time. The traveler's expectations must be high—until the moment when he alights from the Bullet Train.

He leaves the station, catches his first sight of Kyoto Tower, and from there on it is all shattered dreams. Kyoto Hotel cuts off the view of the Higashiyama hills, and big signs on cheap clothing stores hide Mount Daimonji. Red vending machines are lined up in front of the temples, Nijo Castle rings with taped announcements, tour buses are parked right in front of the main halls of temples. It's the same miserable scenery you see everywhere in Japan, and the same people oblivious to it all. And so the traveler spends his day in Kyoto surrounded by boredom.

It wasn't always miserable scenery and boredom. In fact, the city that the traveler dreams of was still largely intact as recently as thirty years ago. When I asked the art collector David Kidd why he chose to live in Japan, he told me the story of his arrival in Kyoto in 1952: it was Christmas Eve, and snow was falling on tiled roofs and narrow streets lined with wood-latticed shops and houses. It was a dreamlike evening, quiet, a scene from an ink painting. Kyoto worked its magic. That magic had entranced pilgrims for centuries, and was celebrated in scrolls and screens, prints and pottery, songs and poetry. The haiku poet Basho sighed, "Even when in Kyoto, I long for Kyoto." With its refined architecture shaped by the tea ceremony and the court nobility, and its many crafts of weaving, paper-making, lacquer, and others, Kyoto was regarded by people around the world as a cultural city on a par with Florence or Rome.

In the last months of World War II, the U.S. military command decided to remove Kyoto from the air-raid list. Although Kyoto was a major population center of some strategic importance, the State Department argued that it was more than just a Japanese city—it was a treasure of the world. As a result, old Kyoto survived at the end of the war, a city of wooden houses, its streets lined with bamboo trellises. The first thing an arriving visitor saw as a train pulled in was the sweeping roof of Higashi Honganji Temple, like a great wave rising out of the sea of tiled roofs.

To the eyes of city officials, however, this sea of tiled roofs was an embarrassment, a sign to the world that Kyoto was old and impoverished. They felt the need to prove to the world that the city was "modern," and in order to do this, at the time of the Tokyo Olympics in 1964, the city administration arranged for the construction of Kyoto Tower, a needle-shaped, garish, red-and-white building erected beside the railroad station. Hundreds of thousands of residents petitioned against this building, but the city government pushed the project through. It was a symbolic stake through the heart.

Kyoto's history since then has been one long effort to sweep away its past. Thirty-five years later, most of its old wooden houses have been torn down and replaced with shiny tile and aluminum. I have seen ancient gardens flattened, historic inns bulldozed, and mansions as gorgeous as any French château razed. The city of Kyoto legislates only the most primitive protection of old neighborhoods, and the national tax bureau allows almost no incentives for protecting historic properties. The destruction goes on as these words are being written. The Kyoto art dealer Morimoto Yasuyoshi tells me that when he takes coffee at a shop on the corner of Kita-Oji and Kawaramachi streets, he sees trucks driving by laden with rubble from demolished old houses almost daily.

In June 1997, my friend Mason Florence (the author of *Kyoto City Guide*) and I took a week off to drive one of those trucks ourselves, loaded with timbers from an Edo-period *kura* (storehouse) in the heart of the old city. Its owners were tearing it down to replace it with a new house, and they gave the wooden framework to me and my friends. We took it up to Iya Valley, on the island of Shikoku, where it sits in storage; one day we will rebuild it next to the farmhouse Mason and I own there. In 1998, Mason salvaged another truckload of beautiful old beams and sliding doors from the wreckage of one of Kyoto's largest traditional inns. But Mason's saving material from these old buildings is an exception, for by and large the owners of old structures in Kyoto simply discard the material of these ancient houses and inns as rubbish. At the antiques auctions there, old cabinets and lacquered doors sell so cheaply (or, more often, don't sell at all) that dealers pile them up outside in the rain, hardly bothering to bring them indoors for shelter.

Readers may be pardoned for wondering if the situation could possibly be so bad, since Japan's destruction of its cities and houses has received very little press abroad. One would have thought that a book like Ezra Vogel's *Japan as Number One* would take these issues into account, for surely any measurement of being "number one" would include the quality of the rural and urban environment.

Yet it is one of the mysteries of Western experts writing about modern Japan that they happily forgive circumstances they would never countenance in their own countries. They would hardly see the destruction of Paris or Rome or San Francisco as praiseworthy, or describe the bureaucrats who ordered it as "elite" public servants taking a "long-term view."

Could it be that in their hearts they still see the Japanese as quaint natives struggling out of poverty, not really entitled to the sophisticated quality of life that is taken for granted in the West?

The heart of foreigners' tendency to go soft on Japan is an overlay of two conflicting images: even as they praise the nation for its economic success, they see Japan with pitying eyes, as a struggling, "developing" country. It's a natural mistake, given that Japan is essentially a postindustrial state with pre-industrial goals. Westerners feel some guilt and sympathy for Japan's devastation at the end of the war, and there is also the fact that Japan's economic system is configured to benefit industry and not to improve citizens' lives, with the result that its cities and countryside really do seem backward and shabby by Western standards. But Japan as "number one" and as a poor "developing" country cannot both be true. If Japan is truly an advanced society—even, as some have suggested, the world's most advanced society and a model for us all—then the destruction of heritage and environment that is accepted as a necessity in newly developing countries should not be happening here.

The tearing down of the old city of Kyoto was by no means limited to the 1950s and 1960s, when every city in the world made similar mistakes. The city's destruction really gathered speed in the 1990s, by which time Japan was a mature economy, with a per-capita income exceeding that of the United States. According to the International Society to Save Kyoto, more than forty thousand old wooden homes disappeared from the inner city of Kyoto in that decade alone. What remains is the temples seen on picture postcards, preserved along the outskirts. In the city where people live and work, the bamboo lattices and wood have largely disappeared. With no guidelines to ensure that new construction harmonizes with the old, owners have crudely remodeled wooden houses with tin and plastic, and where people have gone to the trouble of preserving an old house, they find themselves submerged in a morass of electrical wires, flashing signs, and pachinko. Professor Tayama of Bukkyo University in Kyoto describes how to do away with the beauty of an old city:

In its scale, and for its natural beauty, this city [Kyoto] had a close to ideal environment. Now let's see what we can do to destroy this environment: First let's chop up the soft line of the hills with high apartment buildings with laundry hanging from their terraces. As for places where we can't build anything, not to worry, we can darken the sky by stringing a web of telephone wires and electric lines. Let's have cars drive through Daitokuji Temple. Let's take Mount Hiei, the birthplace of Japanese Buddhism, and turn it into a parking lot, and on its peak let's build an entertainment park. . . . Let's have gasoline stations and city buses broadcast electronic noise under the name of "music". . . and let's paint the buses with designs of children's graffiti. If we make sure that all the buildings are mismatched and brightly colored, that will be very effective. . . . And to finish it off, let's fill the town with people who happily put up with unpleasantness. This Kyoto I have described is actually a fairly generous portrait.

In the early 1990s, there was a popular movement against the rebuilding of the Kyoto Hotel. City Hall next door had waived height limitations so that the rebuilt hotel, as with Kyoto Tower twenty-five years earlier, would set a precedent for the construction of more high buildings in the heart of town. Despite vigorous opposition by citizens' groups and temples such as Kiyomizu Temple, the hotel went up—and, to everyone's surprise, this grim granite edifice, wholly at odds with the traditional scale of the city, ended up looking not particularly out of place. For, in the meantime, the city had changed: a grim granite edifice fit right in.

Kyoto Hotel was just light introductory music for the triumphal march that came next in the shape of the New Kyoto Station, completed in 1997. This construction, one of Japan's most grandiose modern monuments, built at the cost of ¥150 billion ($1.3 billion), dwarfs everything that came before. Straddling the railway tracks along almost half a mile, its massive gray bulk towers over the city. True to Kyoto's postwar tradition, it aggressively denies the history of the place, almost shouting this denial to the world. A local architect, Mori Katsutoshi, says sadly, "In a historic city like this, you have to think of the quality of the design. This looks almost like some kind of storehouse, or a prison."

Except, of course, there are Dogs and Demons touches. Tawdry artificial "culture" replaces the real thing. As reported in *Far Eastern Economic Review*, "Visitors can enjoy the classic Kyoto image of cherry-blossom petals falling without ever going outside: A coffee shop features a light show that imitates the effect. The Theatre 1200 turns Kyoto's 1,200 years of history into a musical that promises 'first-class hi-tech entertainment.' Afterwards visitors can dine at an Italian restaurant with frescoes that include a copy of Raphael's 'School of Athens.' "

A woman named Kato Shidzue, writing on her hundredth birthday in *The Japan Times*, lamented: "There must be many foreigners who come to Japan full of dreams about the country's scenery after having read Lafcadio Hearn only to be surprised and upset at the sight of the Japanese so heartlessly destroying their own beautiful and unparalleled cultural legacy." Sadly, Ms. Kato is wrong. One looks in vain in the foreign media for expressions of surprise or concern at what has happened to Kyoto.

It would seem that Western visitors fail to distinguish—perhaps it is part of their condescension toward Asia—between well-preserved tourist sites and a thoroughly unpleasant cityscape. The fact that Kyoto has nice gardens on its periphery is enough to make them overlook the unwelcoming mass of glass and concrete cubes in the rest of the city. Yet though gardens and temples are wonderful things, world-heritage sites do not a city make. Streets and houses make a city, and in Kyoto, with the exception of three or four indifferently cared for historic blocks, the old streets have lost their integrity.

In Paris or Venice, travelers do not overlook the city and focus only on its cultural sites. Who goes to Paris just to see the Louvre, or to Venice only for the Basilica of San Marco? In both these cities, the joy lies in walking the streets, "taking the air," eating at a nondescript hole-in-the-wall somewhere on a picturesque alley where old textures, worn stone, cast-iron street lamps, lapping water, and carved wooden shutters regale the senses with a host of impressions. On the other hand, perhaps visitors to today's Kyoto are to be excused for not expecting much. What they see must seem inevitable. How could they imagine that the destruction was deliberate, that it did not happen because of economic necessity, and that the worst of it took place *after* 1980?

It's part of the phenomenon of foreigners' exotic dreams of Japan. Mason Florence says, "People come to Japan seeking enchantment, and they are bound and determined to be enchanted. If you arrived in Paris or Rome and saw something like the new station you would be utterly revolted, but for most foreigners coming to Kyoto it merely whets their appetite to find the old Japan they know must be there. When they finally get to Honen-In Temple and see a monk raking the gravel under maple trees, they say to themselves, 'Yes, it does exist. I've found it!' And their enthusiasm for Kyoto ever after knows no bounds. The minute they walk out of Honen-In they're back in

the jumbly modern city, but it doesn't impinge on the retina—
they're still looking at the dream."

Even so, it is true that in the end Kato Shidzue is right: however attached they may be to the dream of old Japan, visitors are
in fact largely not happy in Kyoto. There has been a steady decrease in the number of tourists, both domestic and foreign,
during the past ten years, and those who do come visit largely
out of what one might call "cultural duty" to do the round of
famous temples; it's rare for visitors to come to Kyoto to rest
or merely enjoy a vacation. A vacation is by definition a period
of taking life easy, but in Japan beauty no longer comes easily;
you have to work hard to see it. Kyoto, despite its tremendous
cultural riches, has not become an international tourist mecca
like Paris or Venice. There are few visitors from abroad, and
their stays are short. After they've seen the specially preserved
historical sites, what other reason is there to stay on?

For the reader curious to see with his own eyes the reality of
today's Kyoto, I advise taking the elevator to the top of the
Grand Hotel, near the railroad station, which is more or less ge-
ographically at the center of the city. Examine all 360 degrees
of the view: with the exception of Toji Pagoda and a bit of the
Honganji Temple roof, all one sees is a dense jumble of dingy
concrete buildings stretching in every direction, a cityscape that
could fairly be described as one of the drearier sights of the
modern world. It is hard to believe that one is looking at
Kyoto.

Beyond the jumble is a ring of green hills, mercifully spared
development, but the urban blight does not stop there. To the
south, the industrial sprawl stretches, unbroken, to Osaka and
the coast of the Inland Sea. Across the hills and to the east lies
another jumble of concrete boxes called Yamashina, and the
same landscape continues interminably, past Yamashina to the
drab metropolis of Nagoya, home to millions of people, but

very nearly devoid of architectural or cultural interest. And on it goes for hundreds of miles, all the way to Tokyo, which is only mildly more interesting to look at than Nagoya. When Robert MacNeil looked out of the train window during his 1996 tour of Japan and felt dismay at the sight of "the formless, brutal, utilitarian jumble, unplanned, with tunnels easier on the eyes," he was confronting an aspect of Japan that is key to its modern crisis.

If the administrators of Kyoto could so thoroughly efface the beauty of its urban center in forty years, one can well imagine the fate that befell other cities and towns in Japan. Kyoto's eagerness to escape from itself is matched across Japan. It is not only Edo-period wooden buildings that get bulldozed. Tens of thousands of graceful Victorian or Art Deco brick schools, banks, theaters, and hotels survived World War II, but of the 13,000 that the Architectural Institute of Japan listed as historical monuments in 1980, one-third have already disappeared.

In 1968, the management of the Imperial Hotel in Tokyo tore down a world-renowned masterpiece of modern architecture, Frank Lloyd Wright's Old Imperial, one of the few buildings in that district of Tokyo to have survived the Great Earthquake of 1924. Wright's fantastical hotel, built of pitted stone carved with Art Deco and Mayan-style decoration, fell to the wrecker's ball without a peep of protest from Japan's cultural authorities. The hotel management was so desperate to make its point about being ruthlessly indifferent to the past— the same point made by the erection of Kyoto Tower in 1964— that when Wright's widow gave a speech at the hotel in 1967 protesting its destruction, workers were ordered to enter the hall and remove bricks even as she spoke.

Here is another example: Fukagawa, a neighborhood of willow-lined canals that was one of the ten scenic sights of pre-war Tokyo, is today another concrete jumble. As a Japanese journalist reported in *The Japan Times*: "Work has started on the last remaining canals; soon they will be choked, buried and flattened with cement. As appeasement or perhaps a feeble attempt at apology, the Tokyo government turned some of the concrete space into playgrounds, equipped with a couple of swings and what must be the world's tackiest jungle gyms."

The jungle gyms are the obligatory Dogs and Demons touch. So important are such monuments to modern Japanese culture that I have taken them up as a subject in their own right in chapters 9 and 10. One could formulate a rule of thumb to describe the fate of Japan's old places: whenever something essential and beautiful has been destroyed, the bureaucracy will erect a monument to commemorate it. Perhaps the tacky gyms are a form of atonement. It was traditional in old Japan to raise *kuyo* or *tsuka*, "atonement tombstones," for animals and objects that humans had thrown away or used harshly for their own purposes. Thus, by Ueno Pond in Tokyo, one will find a stone monolith, the *tsuka* for needles, donated by seamstresses who had used needles until they were worn out and then discarded them. There are also *kuyo* for fish and turtle bones, sponsored by fishermen and cooks, and so forth. In that sense, Kyoto Tower and the New Kyoto Station are massive *kuyo* raised in honor of a civilization that was thrown away. Japan's towns and villages are littered with *kuyo* monuments donated by an uneasy officialdom, shiny new tombstones for lost beauty.

Decades ago, when the decline of Fukagawa began, the novelist Nagai Kafu wrote: "I look at Fukagawa and I see the sadness of a woman no longer beautiful, whom men had used and abused to suit their needs. She's tired, stripped of her dignity, waiting to die." The same sad words could be written about most of Japan's historical neighborhoods, for the burying of the old Japan under slipshod new buildings is by no means limited to big cities. It is a simple objective truth that, with the exception of a few corners preserved for tourists in showpiece cities such as Kurashiki (and even in Kurashiki, says Mason Florence, "travelers must shut their eyes between the station and the three preserved blocks"), today not a single beautiful town—and only a handful of villages—is left in all Japan. There is the occasional old castle, or a moat with lotuses, but step ten feet away and you are back in the world of aluminum and electric wires.

The phenomenon is not, of course, unique to Japan. China, Korea, Thailand, and other fast-growing economies in Asia are not far behind. Modernity came to East Asia so rapidly that it was as if there simply wasn't enough time to learn how to adapt its old houses and cities to modern comforts. And old meant dirty, dark, poor, and inconvenient.

The lovely traditional houses of Japan, Thailand, and Indonesia may have been reasonably clean and comfortable when they were occupied by people who were close to nature and were temperamentally suited to living in such houses. But for people accustomed to modern lifestyles, one must admit that these houses are often prone to mud and dust, dark, and inconvenient; they need to be restored with amenities to make them clean, airy, and comfortable. Kyoto residents complain, "Why do we have to live in a museum? Do people expect us to go back to the Edo period and also wear *chonmage* [traditional hairdos, such as sumo wrestlers wear]?"

The tragedy is that people in Kyoto have equated preserving the old city with enduring the old lifestyle, when in fact it is eminently possible to restore Asia's old houses in harmony with the needs of a modern society. With the right skills, the work can even be inexpensive, at least compared with the cost of building a new house. You don't need to go back in time, fold yourself into a kimono, and have your hair styled in a *chonmage* in order to live in an old house, yet, lacking the experience (that is, the technology) to combine old and new, people find it difficult to imagine this. This story, which was related to me by Marc Keane, a garden designer living in Kyoto, gives a sense of the prevailing ethos:

I visited an old couple the other day who live in an old house—a magnificent old house with fine wood and work-manship throughout, even a pillar in the *tokonoma* alcove made of rare black sandalwood. We were trying to convince the couple, who plan to tear the house down, sell half the property and live in a pre-fab house on the other half, that their house was very special, an important heritage in fact, and with a little fixing in the kitchen and bath, would be the best for them to live in. The lady of the house said an in-teresting thing—a horrible thing really. She said that her friends, and members of the local community (you know, the local nosy old grandmothers), on seeing the way they live, in an old wooden house with a bath using a wood-stove, and an old earthen-floored kitchen, would say to her, "Mrs. Nishimura, your lifestyle is so un-cultured." Can you get that: "UN-cultured." Everything about their lifestyle, for me, is an embodiment of the best of Japanese culture, and yet many people (in fact the old couple themselves, I guess) see the very same things as "un-cultured."

Keane suggested a little fixing of the kitchen and bath, ad-vising the couple to preserve but modernize the house. Sadly, most Japanese today don't realize that this is possible—at least, not without overwhelming expense and difficulty.

You will hear similar responses from people living in traditional structures almost anywhere in East Asia. Interestingly, in nations that were formerly European colonies, such as Indonesia, Malaysia, Singapore, and Vietnam, the influence of the West somewhat mitigates the situation. Although this influence is a contentious issue, the West has had centuries of experience in coping with modern technology. Ex-colonies of European powers inherited Western-trained civil-service regimes, and it is partly due to this that beautiful modern cities such as Hong Kong, Singapore, and Kuala Lumpur have developed.

Outside Japan, the demands of international tourism have encouraged architects to experiment with designs that successfully combine Asian art with new technologies. It is common to find foreigners like Marc Keane in Kyoto, who appreciate traditional culture with an enthusiasm that local people have forgotten—and who inspire them to rediscover and re-create their own heritage. Thailand, with its remarkable openness to foreigners, has benefited from the efforts of people such as the legendary silk magnate Jim Thompson, whose mansion in Bangkok, built in the traditional Thai style, has exerted an incalculable influence on Thai designers and architects. Bali, a bastion of thriving ancient culture, and with a relatively unspoiled environment, likewise owes its salvation partly to generations of Dutch, German, American, and Australian residents who loved the island and joined the Balinese in preserving it.

Occasionally one sees foreigners having an impact in certain out-of-the-way niches in Japan, such as Iya Valley in Shikoku, where the Chiiori Project, a volunteer movement centered on Mason Florence's and my old farmhouse, is drawing numerous foreign travelers and exchange teachers. The sight of all these foreigners trekking to such a remote place is reawakening local interest in reviving Iya's natural beauty. Another case is that of Sarah Cummings, a native of Pennsylvania, who took on the management of a traditional sake brewery in the town of Obuse in Nagano Prefecture. Although the brewery was housed in a spectacular old building, its sales were declining and the business was on the verge of failure when Cummings joined. To everyone's surprise, she chose tradition as her sales pitch. She refurbished the building and got the company to brew its sake in authentic cedar vats for the first time in fifty years, becoming one of only a few firms in the country to do so. Today the brewery is thriving and its sake has achieved a national reputation. "I was surprised when Sarah chose a traditional ceramic bottle," said the brewery's owner, "but it appeals to young people. Since wine has become so popular, it's really important to attract a new generation to sake."

Unfortunately, Iya Valleys and Sarah Cummingses are all too rare. Japan chose, for better or for worse, to go it alone. Japan generally has not allowed foreigners to play an important role in its society, and, given its neglected tourist industry, it sees few foreign travelers. The idea that "old equals inconvenient" set hard and fast in Japan, along with many other ideas from the 1960s, since the country was all but closed to Western influence in every area except industrial technology. Since then, having failed to train designers and city planners to adapt the old architecture to new lifestyles, the idea has become self-reinforcing. Most old buildings in Japan are unloved and have been repaired cheaply, if at all; they are indeed uncomfortable and inconvenient. Unfortunately, so are the new buildings, which are constructed of cheap materials, cramped, poorly lit, badly heated, and uninsulated. Because of its pervasive fear of discomfort and inconvenience, the Japanese public never quite feels that it has escaped the squalid old lifestyle.

By now, the equation of old and natural with inconvenient is made obsessively. Recently, a village in Gifu built a hamlet in the prehistoric style as a tourist attraction. As part of the ambience, "inconvenience will be deliberately added," said press reports. "There will be no electricity in the hamlet except for probably a naked bulb in the hut," said Okuda Toshio, a local official in charge of tourism. "We'd like visitors to have a rare experience of inconvenience and enjoy rich natural life."

Meanwhile, of course, if you travel around Japan you will see many old temples that the Cultural Ministry has restored to perfection, not to mention flawlessly repaired and polished old houses in "Old House Parks." The work that goes into these buildings is a credit to Japan's famed perfectionism. Yet these restored structures tend to be sterile, uncomfortable spaces; their restoration is predicated on the assumption that the buildings will never be used again. Or, if people continue to live in them, they must abandon most modern conveniences.

On the other hand, the National Museum or the Craft Museum in Tokyo are examples of historical buildings that also function as places to live or work, and both are shabby and poorly maintained. In the Cultural Ministry's main offices in Ueno, paint is peeling off the walls, dim fluorescent lights flicker, electric wires are pinned to the walls, gloomy offices are filled with piles of dusty papers, there is no proper heating or ventilation—all this in a grand historic building just a block from the National Museum.

The technology of restoration, when applied to living cities, involves sophisticated techniques of combining old and new, as was demonstrated by Yale University. Restoration technology in Japan came to a halt in about 1965, and since then officials have concentrated on ways of perfectly preserving the old. When it comes time to make an old building functional, or to build a new building with old touches that have warmth and texture, nobody knows what to do. Because of its frozen technology, Japan is torn between two extremes—old-shabby or

new-sterile—and often a combination of the worst of both de-
fines the look of modern Japan.

The preservation of vibrant old cities, sophisticated resort management, and high-quality residential and furniture design don't
occur in a vacuum. Like all other arts and industries, they
thrive only when watered with liberal amounts of money. The
readiest source of such money would be tourism—an industry
in which Japan has very conspicuously failed. The story of this
failure is one of the most remarkable tales of modern Japan, for
it occurred not through accident but as the result of a deliberate national policy.

During the boom years of postwar manufacturing, Japan's
industrial leaders considered tourism a minor business, a side-
show to the real work of the nation, which was to mass-
produce things. While Europe, the United States, and other
Asian nations were developing sophisticated tourist infrastructures, Japan was trashing Kyoto, concreting Iya Valley, and designing resorts out of chrome and Formica.

Some economic writers have seen the lack of attention paid
to tourism as a great success, for it was part of what has been
called the "war on service-ization." According to such views,
any work except that of producing objects on an assembly line
or building things is a waste of national effort. Tourism, according to this analysis, merely supports menial low-paid jobs, unlike manufacturing, which creates high-tech, high-salaried jobs.
Such an argument presumes that everyone involved in tourism
is a waiter or a maid, and neglects the economic activity gener-
ated by architects, landscape artists, makers of furniture and dining ware, painters and sculptors, electricians, manufacturers of
lighting equipment, tour-company operators, hotel managers,
taxi and charter companies, airline companies, lawyers, accoun-
tants, travel agents, performers and musicians, interior decora-

tors, instructors of swimming, scuba diving, dance, and language, owners of souvenir shops and restaurants, printers, visual artists, PR and advertising firms, and much more. The "anti-services" theorists also forget that in Japan more than 10 percent of the workforce is engaged in low-paying, hard-hat construction work—financed by government subsidy—and there is no alternative industry to sop up the excess labor force.

In any case, it is undoubtedly true that Japan succeeded in repressing service industries. Unfortunately, some of the services, such as software design, communications, and banking, turned out to be enormous moneymakers. Tourism, likewise, surprised everybody by becoming transformed, overnight, from a lackluster wallflower into a glamorous starlet wooed by all.

Elsewhere in the world, an explosive growth of the international tourist industry began in the late 1980s and picked up pace in the 1990s. By the turn of the century, international tourism accounted for about 8 percent of the world's total export earnings, ahead of autos, chemicals, food, computers, electronics, and even oil and gas. The dramatic growth of tourism didn't fit into Japan's strategies, for it is based on mobility, a concept not dear to Japan's bureaucrats, whose complicated operational structures depend on borders being sacrosanct and people, ideas, and money not traveling easily. When newly enriched populations around the world began to travel by the tens of millions, it became clear that tourism would be one of the most important industries of the twenty-first century. Many states and cities in Europe and the United States, not to mention Asian countries such as Singapore, Indonesia, and Thailand, earn a considerable proportion of their income from tourism. The World Tourism Organization (WTO) estimates that 657 million tourists visited a foreign country in 1999, spending $532 billion.

Meanwhile, tourism within Japan has been dwindling across the board. In the years 1992–1996, the number of people traveling in their own country grew by less than 1 percent, and the value of domestic tours dropped 3 percent every year. For many local areas the fall has been severe, as, for example, on the Ise-Shima promontory of Mie Prefecture. Though it is home to Ise Shrine, Japan's holiest religious site, as well as Mikimoto pearl culturing, Ise-Shima's tourist arrivals in 1999 dropped to a twenty-year low, 40 percent below its height decades earlier. As domestic tourism waned, the number of Japanese traveling abroad nearly quadrupled, from 5 million in 1985 to almost 16 million people in 1998, soaring by 25 percent in just two years (1993–1995). By 1999 this had risen to a record 17 million, with no end to the increase in sight; significantly, a high percentage of these travelers were what the Japan Travel Bureau (JTB) calls "repeaters," for whom travel abroad is a "habitual practice." One reason the Japanese are making a habitual practice of travel abroad is that it is cheaper than travel in Japan: it costs roughly the same to fly from Tokyo to Hong Kong as to take the train from Tokyo to Kyoto. It costs me more to travel for a few days to Iya Valley in Shikoku than to spend a week in Honolulu.

Traveling abroad, the Japanese cannot help noticing that they find quality in hotel design and service, in life in general, which they cannot find at home. The contrast is especially strong in Southeast Asia, where resort design and management are highly advanced, and where hotels have been built with natural materials and a sensitive regard for local culture.

Dr. Johnson said, "To be happy at home is the ultimate result of all ambition." In the decline of domestic travel lies the paradox of modern Japan: After decades of economic growth providing a per capita income many times their neighbors', the

Japanese are not able to enjoy their own country. They are not happy at home.

The number of foreign visitors to Japan, never large, has grown only sluggishly, from about 3.5 million in 1990 to 4.5 million in 1999. Japan ranks thirty-second in the world for foreign tourist arrivals, far behind Malaysia, Thailand, and Indonesia—and light-years behind China, Poland, or Mexico, each of which admits tens of millions of tourists every year. For all the literature about Japan's international role, it's sobering to realize that Japan has very nearly fallen off the tourist map. Every year more people visit Tunisia or Croatia than visit Japan. Another way to assess the amount of tourism is the number of foreign visitors against national population. In Japan, the ratio is only 3 percent, ranking eighty-second in the world. (The corresponding number for South Korea is more than double: 8 percent.)

The economic consequences of Japan's failed tourist industry are serious. In 1998, when 4.1 million foreign visitors came to Japan, the United States had 47 million visitors and France had 70 million. The United States earned $74 billion, France raised about $29.7, and Japan had only $4.1 billion. Looking at it from a balance-of-payments point of view, we see that U.S. citizens spent $51.2 billion in tourism abroad but earned $23 billion more than that. Japan, by contrast, spent $33 billion overseas but had a $29 billion tourism deficit.

It is commonly believed that among the many reasons tourism in Japan has lost its appeal to both foreigners and the Japanese people, the most important are the high yen and the cost of travel within Japan. But these arguments are not entirely persuasive. Well-heeled foreign travelers think nothing of spending thousands of dollars to stay in posh resorts in Phuket or Bali, but give Japan a wide berth. The real reason is that the rewards in scenic beauty and travel amenities are very slim. However much tourists enjoy a quiet Zen rock garden in Kyoto, they confront a chaotic and trashy modern cityscape the minute they walk out of the garden. At the hotel, they will seek in vain for anything to remind them that they are in Kyoto, and instead be oppressed by an environment of shiny polyester wallpaper and garish chandeliers. The visitor to a famous waterfall or stand of pine trees on a beach has to frame the view very closely to shut out the concrete embankments that are the universal mark of the modern Japanese landscape. No one will write an idyllic book about Japan like *Summer in Provence* or *Under the Tuscan Sun.*

With Japan's old-fashioned manufacturing and construction economy beginning to stagnate in the 1990s, it came as a jolt to the government to realize that perhaps services do matter to a modern economy, and a few officials began looking at the long-ignored issue of tourism. It quickly became clear that Kyoto, Nara, and Japan's once lovely rural villages were nearly beyond help, but there was hope: theme parks. Today, the Japanese flock to theme parks featuring reconstructed European cities, such as Huis Ten Bosch (Dutch) in Kyushu and Shima Spain in Mie, or a replica of Mount Rushmore (at one-third the scale) under construction in Tochigi Prefecture. These are spotless and completely artificial, like the enormous Seagaia complex in Miyazaki, which, though located on the coast, boasts a fully enclosed artificial beach. The number of adult tourists visiting these theme parks (close to 8 million touring Huis Ten Bosch and Shima Spain as early as 1994) will soon surpass the number visiting Kyoto. The designers of Huis Ten Bosch used natural materials such as rough bricks, incorporated sign control, buried power lines, and established design guidelines; with its lovingly tended lawns, it is much more appealing than a cluttered and unloved Kyoto. It would seem that Japan's premier tourist destinations will end up having nothing to do with its own culture, becoming watered-down copies of Western originals.

Obviously, these cannot have much appeal to Westerners, but the hope is that they will draw Asian tourists. "For Hong Kong's Wong Chun Chuen, [neither Mount Fuji nor Kyoto] compares with that hallowed sanctum of the Japanese soul, Sanrio Puroland," writes Tanikawa Miki. Sanrio Puroland is a mini–medieval Europe on the outskirts of Tokyo, built indoors with a nymphs' forest, floating riverboats, and cartoon characters such as Hello Kitty. Sanrio's 150,000 Asian visitors represented 10 percent of the total number of visitors in 1996, while at Huis Ten Bosch, Asian visitors numbered 330,000, about 8 percent of the total.

In January 1999, China ended its ban on visiting Japan, and many in the tourism industry see it as Japan's last great hope. "China has the potential to become our largest foreign market," says Shimane Keiichi, the president of Japan Travel Bureau's subsidiary Asia Tourist Center. "China has a population of over 1.2 billion. If about 1 percent of Chinese a year come to Japan, we will get about 12 million visitors." The long-term problem is that if tourism will depend on gimmicky theme parks, there is competition ahead when Hong Kong, Thailand, Korea, and Taiwan jump on that bandwagon. It bodes ill that the Japanese site that most travelers from mainland China want to see is Tokyo Disneyland, for at the beginning of 1999 Disney announced that it was negotiating to build a new Disneyland in or near Hong Kong.

Since badly conceived development is defacing beyond recognition the attractions that were unique to Japan, it is time to build new attractions, and this suits the Construction State. The government has announced its plans for another wave of halls and monuments. The Japan National Tourist Organization (a wing of the Transport Ministry) says that its Welcome Plan 21 involves "*building a broad range of tourist attractions* [italics mine]. For example, Japan could create *rekishi kaido,* or 'Japanese historic highways,' as well as theme districts around the country, complete with roads and international exchange facilities." An example is the Ise Civil War Era Village, near the Grand Shrine of Ise, a wholly artificial medieval town that is meant to evoke Japan during the civil wars of the sixteenth century.

In the coming decades, we can look forward to the raising of hundreds of facilities designed specially for travelers under the banner of "international tourism." Japan must build these monuments—that is a certainty, for the construction industry requires it. Typical of what the next wave will probably be is ASTY Tokushima, a monument that sits at the confluence of two rivers in the town of Tokushima, on the island of Shikoku. ASTY Tokushima features a multipurpose hall and the Tokushima Experience Hall, where, as the prefectural tourism bureau puts it, travelers can discover "passionate romantic Tokushima." The passionate romantic experience includes the Yu-ing Theatre, where two robots perform traditional puppet-ballad drama, and a corner where visitors can gaze at photographs of Tokushima's scenery as it changes from season to season.

The end of the road for the domestic tourism industry is when it gives up on natural or historical attractions altogether and makes concrete itself an attraction. This is beginning to happen, for Japan Railways and local towns are sponsoring package tours of their dams and cement fortifications. Flyers advertising dam tours are often seen in subways and buses. "At

Atsui Dam, everywhere you look, it's huge!" trumpets a publicity pamphlet from the Construction Ministry, urging travelers to join a bus tour and come and see cement being poured. "It's almost the last chance to see Atsui Dam while under construction," the pamphlet says invitingly.

There is hardly the need to create fake tourist facilities or to rely on cement-pouring at dams for excitement when Japan has plenty of the real thing. Still, the modern malaise seems to have created an inability to distinguish between what is fake and what is real. Kyoto prides itself on being Japan's "cultural capital," yet for the past fifty years it has put all its energies into destroying its old streets and houses. The Cultural Zone in the New Kyoto Station typifies the confusion; there a tearoom provides a light show of cherry blossoms instead of the real thing, and the restaurant features a copy of a Raphael fresco—"culture" with no particular connection to Kyoto at all.

Recent events in Kyoto show that a sizable minority of its citizens are angry about all this. In November 1998, one group miraculously succeeded in halting a very destructive project. The story began more than a year earlier, when the city office announced plans for its newest monument—right in the middle of Pontocho, one of the few historic city blocks left, a narrow street of bars and geisha houses running alongside the Kamo River, with the Sanjo Bridge to the north and Shijo Bridge to the south. The city proposed to demolish a segment in the middle of Pontocho and build a new bridge modeled on one that spans the Seine—not even one of the famous old bridges, with picturesque stone arches, but a modern structure of steel girders and tubular concrete pilings of no distinction. To add insult to injury, the city fathers actually proposed to call this copy the Pont des Arts, and enlisted the support of France's President Chirac, who in a classic case of foreign misunderstanding of Japan endorsed the project because it was French-inspired. For many, this was the last straw. Professor Saino Hiroshi wrote:

> Pontocho is part of our cultural heritage, representing Kyoto's cityscape based on a wood-based culture. It was built as an integral piece of the space along the river. [The new bridge] will conflict with traditional architecture such as Shimbashi [an old neighborhood on the other side of the river], and furthermore [Pontocho] has something rarely seen in other cities—traditional architecture extending continuously 600 meters down it—and one feels a sense of historical atmosphere. This will be split in two by a modern European-style bridge right in the middle of it, which will greatly decrease its cultural value.

This time the protests of Saino and others did not go unheard, as they had in 1964 with Kyoto Tower, in 1990 with Kyoto Hotel, and in 1994 with the design competition for the New Kyoto Station. The concerned citizens of Kyoto amazed everyone by gathering such overwhelming support for their anti-bridge petition that the project was discontinued.

For now. One must keep in mind that the Law of Concepts still applies: once a concept, always a concept. After all, the city has been planning this bridge for a long time, perhaps decades, so it canceled only the French *design*, reserving the option to build another bridge at Pontocho later, with a different design. Sooner or later, the old street of Pontocho is probably doomed.

Yet some parts of Kyoto could in fact be saved. Hundreds of temples and shrines and thousands of wooden homes still stand. The bones of the old city are still there. With well-planned zoning and design guidelines, some parts of it could be revived. And this is also true of other cities and towns in Japan, which still boast numerous wooden houses in the traditional style. For the most part, these houses are in a shambles, their roofs leaking and their pillars leaning, or fixed up with slapdash improvements featuring tin and vinyl. A house or a neighborhood that is in reasonably good repair can be picked out from its unsightly surroundings only with difficulty, but it is still there. It is another case of "a wilted peony in a bamboo vase, unable to draw water up her stem." The water—a proud and ancient culture—exists in abundance.

Or does it? The supply of beautiful old places is not inexhaustible, and the time may come in the not very distant future when Japan will have damaged its old cities beyond hope. Some fear this time is already here. The Japanese realize that something is amiss. Recently, a television drama featured the following wry segment:

A hotel manager is entertaining a foreign guest, taking him to the finest restaurants and hotels. Finally, the foreigner says, "Fine meals, fine hotels, entertainment parks. I can get that anywhere in the world. But where can I see the Thirty-six Views of Mount Fuji portrayed by the print artist Hokusai? What about the Fifty-three Stations of the Tokaido, where the feudal lords used to stay on their trips to Tokyo, and which featured in so many prints and paintings?" Of course, the Thirty-six Views and the Fifty-three Stations have completely disappeared. The hotel manager thinks he must have misunderstood. What could the foreigner be talking about? So at the end of the segment he decides to take English lessons!

8 New Cities

Electric Wires and Roof Boxes

Stricken on a journey
My dreams go wandering round
Withered fields.
—MATSUO BASHO (1694)

Since the entire thrust of development in Kyoto since its Tower
was built has been to escape from the old and build a modern
city, it seems only fair to measure the place by its own standards. What if Kyoto were to wipe away its ancient heritage entirely? A dedicated modernist might feel this was justified if it
meant creating a city of leading-edge contemporary culture.

This is what has happened in Hong Kong, where a tree-
lined harbor filled with quaint junks gave way to a cityscape
of dazzling office towers, one of the wonders of the modern
world. The same may well happen in Shanghai and Bangkok,
where developers have treated the charming old city centers
brutally, but where dramatic new buildings are rising from the
dust—hotels, restaurants, office towers, and apartments that vie
with the best in Hong Kong or New York.

This did not happen—and is not happening—in Japan. The

ugly view from the top of the Grand Hotel in Kyoto is less a consequence of the loss of the old than a result of the low quality of the new.

Nothing could run more contrary to the trend of Western commentary on Japan for the past fifty years than the argument that Japan has failed in its pursuit of modernity. However, that is the truth. Instead of an advanced new civilization, Japan has tenement cities and a culture of cheap industrial junk. Homes are cramped and poorly built; public environments, whether in hotels, zoos, parks, apartment buildings, hospitals, or libraries, are sadly lacking in visual pleasure and basic comforts, at least compared with those available in other advanced nations. This failure to achieve quality in the new is perhaps Japan's greatest tragedy—and it lies at the very core of its cultural meltdown today.

It's the unexpected result, a devastating boomerang, of the policy that economists and social scientists once believed was Japan's greatest strength: the policy of "poor people, strong state"; the policy of having its citizens accept a low level of consumption and limited outlets for pleasure and relaxation in their personal lives so that the nation's resources could be invested in unlimited industrial expansion. That happened, and in the process Japan nurtured a bureaucracy uneducated in modern technologies and several generations of Japanese who are ignorant of what true modernity might offer—ignorant, one might say, of the finer things of modern life. And this has had not only cultural but economic consequences.

To get some sense of contrast with other nations, consider Malaysia. As you drive between Port Klang on the Strait of Malacca and the capital, Kuala Lumpur, the highway passes through spectacular valleys of rocky cliffs. While building this road, Malaysia called in a French landscaping firm to advise on how to make it beautiful, including how to sculpt the cliffs through which the highway passes. The result of their efforts is that there was no unnecessary destruction, no concrete in sight, and the cliffs appear to be natural. It's a classic example of modern technology, in the true sense of the word, in road building. Such a highway does not exist the length or breadth of Japan, for calling in foreign consultants would have been unthinkable, and road-building techniques froze in about 1970.

In downtown Kuala Lumpur itself, high-rises are springing up everywhere, and the city is beginning to take on the sleek, elegant look one also sees in Hong Kong, Singapore, Jakarta, and parts of Bangkok but rarely in cluttered Tokyo. By looking closely, one can discern the details that make the difference.

One is the lack of junk on rooftops. In Japan, electrical machinery and air-conditioning units appear to have been tacked onto rooftops as afterthoughts. It is possible to put unsightly mechanical components inside a building's internal structure and to integrate them architecturally, but in Japan a regulation dating from the 1950s and never altered punishes a builder for using internal space for such machinery by subtracting that space from his allowable floor-area ratio (FAR).

Japan has no regulations limiting billboards; in fact, its construction laws actively encourage billboards on top of buildings because of another regulation concerning height limits. Builders may increase the height of their structures by a story or two if the added height is merely empty boxes on the roofs. Naturally, the next step is to mount enormous logos and advertisements on these boxes. Back in Kuala Lumpur, you will not see many such signs, and most of the ones you do observe belong to Japanese-owned businesses and were designed by Japanese architectural firms that know no other way. Looking out of my apartment window in Bangkok, I can see dozens of skyscrapers, only one of which sports a large rooftop billboard—Hitachi. In Japan, there is so little understanding of sign control that Hitachi has even made a deal with the Cultural Agency to place advertisements beside all buildings designated as National Treasures or Important Cultural Properties. In Kyoto, you will see scores of metal Hitachi signs placed prominently in Zen gardens and before the gate of every historical temple and pavilion. A short walk through the grounds of Daitokuji, the fountainhead of Zen arts, yields a count of no fewer than twenty-five Hitachi signs, with four in one sub-temple, Daisen-In, alone.

Other East Asian cities—Singapore, Kuala Lumpur, and Hong Kong—go far beyond Bangkok in regulating advertisements; Jakarta boasts some of East Asia's best sign control through a taxation policy that makes the raising and maintenance of large ads expensive. In Japan, in contrast, architects learn nothing about signage in their university courses. During the 1980s, the concept of "visual pollution" spread through the international design community, and attention began to be paid to observations that bright, flashing lights disturb the peace of residential neighborhoods, garish signs lower the tone of five-star hotels, fluorescent lights destroy the romance of parks at nighttime, and towering billboards detract from the beauty of scenic countryside. The science of avoiding and ameliorating this sort of visual pollution is a modern technology.

Visual pollution in Japan has resulted from the same vicious cycle we have seen in other aspects of its life: in the case of the environment, construction breeds dependence on more construction; in banking, deception leads to greater deception; in urban design, ugliness gradually comes to be taken for granted, which leads to ignorance and thus to more ugliness. An architect friend of mine, Lucilo Pena, helped to design the Four Seasons Hotel in Barcelona, in which the Japanese department store Sogo was one of the investors. Lucilo tells of acrimonious discussions between the hotel operators and the Japanese owners concerning signs, for Sogo wanted a huge flashing sign on the outside of the hotel, and it seemed impossible to convince Sogo's management that in Barcelona this was considered a plan that would damage the ambience of the city and lower the prestige of both the department-store owners and the hotel. Sogo gave in when its representatives realized that in the West citizens might resort to boycotts of a company that flouts local concerns, but it came as a shock.

In Japan, there are almost no zoning laws, no taxation policy, and no sign control to regulate urban or rural development—so giant billboards tower over rice paddies, vending machines stand in the lobbies of ritzy hotels and Kabuki theaters, and bright plastic signs hang in even the most stylish restaurants. People who are born, grow up, live, and work in such an environment know of no alternative; and the result is that the general public, as well as planners and architects, think this kind of look is an inherent part of modernization. It is thus not surprising that Hitachi would blazon its name across the Bangkok skyline when few American, European, Thai, or Chinese corporations feel the need to do so.

Zoning—the political and social science of making the most efficient use of different types of land—is a crucial skill that Japan's bureaucrats have failed to master. The distinction between industrial, commercial, residential, and agricultural neighborhoods hardly exists. In the residential neighborhood of Kameoka, near Kyoto, where I live, I need walk only about five minutes to find—right next door to suburban homes and rice paddies—a used-car lot, a gigantic rusting fuel tank filled with nobody knows what, a plot surrounded by a prefabricated steel wall twenty feet high in which construction waste is dumped, rows of vending machines with blinking lights, a golf driving range half the size of a football field surrounded by wire mesh hung from giant pylons and illuminated at night, a vast number of signs of every type (pinned onto trees, propped up by the roadside), and, of course, a pachinko parlor, with towers of spiraling neon and flashing strobe lights. This is the typical level of visual pollution in the suburban neighborhood of a Japanese city, and nobody considers it odd, because every structure scrupulously obeys the rules: FAR ratios, footprint quotas, allowable building materials, location of telephone poles, and so forth. It is the *Through the Looking-Glass* world of bureaucratic management: there is no lack of regulation, yet chaos reigns.

Many of the regulations exist to protect cartels of architectural firms and construction companies. Others, such as those that effectively prohibit residential homes from having basements, are cobweb-covered relics. Their original purpose is lost in time, yet no one considers changing them. Indeed, the complete inflexibility of these rules and regulations creates more of the clutter and crowding that characterize Japanese cities.

Kyoto, for example, had a golden opportunity in the 1960s, when it was working on renovations for the Olympic Games. Had it zoned the city differently north and south at the train station (most of the historic center lies north of the station), the old center could easily have been protected and saved. To the south, where most of the buildings except a few large temples were poor, shoddily built, and ripe for redevelopment, Kyoto could have created a new satellite city—like La Défense, the supermodern suburb of Paris. But of course this did not happen. Instead, bureaucrats applied rigid FAR and height limitations everywhere, which led to a cycle of rising land prices, high inheritance taxes, and destruction in the city center, and at the same time prevented the development of good new architecture. Rather than having a truly new city in the south and a beautiful old city in the north, Kyoto today has neither new nor old but a conglomeration where everything looks equally shabby.

The two regulations that have had the most devastating effect on Japan's cities are those concerning the inheritance tax and the so-called Sunlight Law. Japan's inheritance tax is one of the highest in the world; as land prices have risen continually for a half century, inheritors of old houses almost invariably have to sell them in order to pay the tax. For the purchasers, these prices are so high that it is uneconomical to leave single-story old wooden buildings standing, so they tear them down and build apartment blocks. The Tax Office grants very few exemptions for buildings in historic neighborhoods, and the tax guidelines, determined by the central government, are inflexible, so that local administrations cannot easily structure their own neighborhood systems. Faced with laws like this, Kyoto didn't stand a chance.

The Sunlight Law was passed in the 1960s as a well-meaning effort to restrict high buildings that would shroud their neighbors in shade. It created a formula whereby buildings must fit within a diagonal "shadow line," which means that the higher they rise the narrower they must be. This accounts for the stepped, pyramidal look of most Japanese buildings. Americans made a similar mistake in the 1960s and 1970s, when "street setback" was a magic phrase. This had disastrous effects on thousands of American cities, for it turns out that buildings that come right up to the sidewalk create an intimacy that setback structures lack. New York City learned this to its cost when zoning laws encouraged the sterile office towers on the Avenue of the Americas, which are set back from the street and fronted by wide vacant plazas.

Japan's Sunlight Law also restricts building because on a given plot of land a higher structure often cannot use to the full whatever is allowed by local FAR regulations. As a result, Tokyo has an average FAR of less than 2 to 1, the lowest of any world capital, including Paris and Rome. "Low density" sounds attractive—until one realizes what this means for the inhabitants of a metropolis with 30 million people: the highest land prices in the world, cramped apartments and homes (millions of Tokyo residents dwell in spaces even smaller than the official minimum of fifty square meters), exorbitant commercial rents, and crowded commuter trains that must transport people several hours from their homes to work. With buildable land in Tokyo expensive and scarce, the Construction Ministry favors plans by big construction companies to build giant cities underground. From their underground apartments, it imagines, residents will speed on subways to subterranean office buildings. So effective is the Sunlight Law that future homeowners in Tokyo need never see the light of day.

Japan is the world's only advanced country that does not bury telephone cables and electric lines. While a handful of neighborhoods, such as the central Marunouchi business district of Tokyo, have succeeded in laying cables underground, these are mostly expensive showpieces. Even the most advanced new residential districts customarily do not bury cables, as I discovered when I was working on the Sumitomo Trust Bank/Trammell Crow project on Kobe's Rokko Island in 1987. Kobe City touted the island—brand-new landfill in the harbor—as a supermodern, futuristic neighborhood. With telephone poles. In the countryside, a "priority policy" dictates that until every large city has buried every one of its power lines, which the Construction Ministry is encouraging them not to do, no rural area can do the same with support from the central government.

Here, in a nutshell, is Japan's bureaucratic dynamic at work. The first stage, the starting point after Japan's defeat in World War II, is the poor people, strong state principle. Central planners considered the extra effort and expense required to do such things as burying cables luxurious and wasteful, drawing needed resources away from industry.

The second stage, policy freeze, came in the early 1970s. Unaccustomed to burying cables, Japan's bureaucrats came to believe that the nation shouldn't, indeed couldn't, bury them. They cooked up justifications for the policy, such as the added dangers in the event of earthquakes. (In fact, a nation that is likely to have frequent earthquakes *should* bury lines, as became clear in the Kobe quake of 1995. Toppled poles carrying live wires were one of the biggest dangers, blocking traffic and wreaking havoc with rescue efforts.) Another argument was that Japan had uniquely damp soil, which made it harder to bury lines there than in other countries. (This belongs to the "Special Snow" school of thought, made famous when trade negotiators in the 1980s asserted that "Japanese snow is unsuitable to foreign skis.") The inner logic is that Japan's uniqueness forbids it to bury cables. Since burying cables is not what Japan has done, it is un-Japanese to do so.

The third stage is addiction. Making concrete and steel pylons has become a profitable cartelized business; meanwhile, utilities have a free hand to plan power grids without regard for the look of urban or rural neighborhoods, for the inconvenience posed by poles jutting into narrow roads, or for anything else. And since the power companies have not learned the skill of efficient, safe, and well-designed cable laying and have never had to factor in the costs, today they simply cannot afford them. Meanwhile, the Construction Ministry, driven by the "uniquely damp soil" ideology, has mandated protective cover-

ings for underground cable strong enough to survive the apoc-
alypse, making it the most expensive in the world.

My friend Morimoto Yasuyoshi recently moved to Sanjo
Street, in the heart of historic Kyoto. When people in the
neighborhood got together to discuss revitalizing this famous
but now shabby street, he suggested that the city remove the
clutter of aboveground wires and lines and bury them. He
learned that this would be close to impossible, because of a rule
that says when a street decides to bury its lines, property owners must forfeit their right to a few square feet of space on the
pavement to allow for electrical boxes every fifty meters or so.
(Why there must be boxes so close together, and above ground,
is not clear. After all, the basic idea is to put all the apparatus
underground. It would seem to spring from bureaucratic resistance to the very idea of burying wires. *Something* should be
above ground!) Japan's land values being what they are, no one
can afford to give up those precious square feet.

Mild addiction results in total addiction when Japan ends up
relying on technologies that actually require the existence of
poles. In the 1990s, Japan began pushing the PHS cellular
phone as its big contender in the mobile-phone business. Unlike other new systems, which are truly wireless and satellite-
linked, PHS sends signals to small relay boxes that must be set
up every few dozen meters on traffic-light or telephone poles.
With the full weight of officialdom thrown behind PHS, Japan
will never bury its power lines and phone wires.

We have reached the final stage: decoration. Since about
1995, the trend has been to replace the old concrete poles in
certain city blocks with fancy ones clad in polished bronze.
Rather like the "designer concrete" (shaped like hexagons or
molded to look like rocks) that Japan is developing for its rivers
and mountains, designer telephone poles are now in evidence.

It's a classic Dogs and Demons approach to city planning: The city feels it has done something. Each pole, up close, looks prettier. However, the street, festooned with wires, looks as cluttered as before.

Combine the Sunlight Law with regulations that encourage machinery boxes and billboards on rooftops, and you get the chaotic look of the typical Japanese cityscape. Add to this the absence of zoning and sign control, and factor in vending machines and electric and phone wires—and you get the visual clutter that is a defining feature of daily life in Japan. Japanese architects have become so accustomed to it that they can imagine no alternative. Despite manifold evidence to the contrary in garden-filled, neatly organized old Kyoto and Beijing—not to mention Penang, Kuala Lumpur, Hong Kong, and Jakarta—Japanese architects justify shadeless trashy cities as somehow uniquely "Asian." When Baba Shozo, a former editor of *Japan Architect* magazine, was asked whether there might be some improvement in city planning, such as more parks (the average is 14 percent open space for cities in Japan, versus 35 percent in Europe and 40 percent in the United States), he is reported to have responded, "It's absolutely not necessary. Tokyo's population is totally satisfied with the way things are. . . . After all, we are living in an Asian city. It's natural the way it is. Parks and open spaces are not required. Who needs green space?"

Foreign writers on Japanese architecture condescendingly accept this line of reasoning. Christine Hawley writes of a Tokyo neighborhood: "The scale was distinctly 'sub' urban, and architectural grain identifiably oriental. There was of course the visual compression of space, the use of low, horizontally defined buildings covered in banners, signs, and the ubiquitous web of service lines as they run in and around the buildings." City planners in Singapore and Malaysia, the most vociferous champions of "Asian values," would be surprised to learn that poorly regulated advertisements and unburied service lines are "identifiably oriental."

Clutter is not the whole story. People crave open views and clean city lines, so planners respond with monumental "new cities," boasting wide avenues and enormous office towers surrounded by pavemented parks and windswept plazas. The pendulum swings in the direction of total sterility. One cannot fail to be struck by the complete inhumanity of the new urban landscape at Kobe's Port Island or Tokyo's Makuhari and Odaiba. Gigantic office towers are surrounded by empty access roads, vacant squares, and shadeless rows of pollarded trees. There is no middle ground in Japan's cities—only the two extremes of shabby or sterile.

"New Japan does not like trees," Donald Richie wrote in *The Inland Sea* back in 1971. In Richie's day, this truth was expressed in the tendency to bulldoze parks and plazas; in the 1980s it developed into an aversion to falling leaves, which was discussed in an earlier chapter; in the 1990s, it became an attack on branches. Until very recently, in Tokyo, shady tree-lined avenues surrounded the zoo side of Ueno Park and Tokyo University, but not anymore. A desire on the part of civic administrators to widen the streets and do away with shade has led to new rules that require the pruning of all branches that extend over a roadway; this policy has been carried out all over the country.

Keats wrote, "the trees / That whisper round a temple become soon / Dear as the temple's self"—a sentiment clearly not in the mind of the Cultural Ministry when it restored Zuiryuji Temple in the town of Takaoka in 1996. In the true spirit of Nakahara Kiiko, it cut down and uprooted a grove of ancient *keaki* and pine trees that had stood for hundreds of years in the temple courtyard and replaced them with a wide expanse of raked gravel. Although the temple's founder had expressly designed the courtyard to conjure up the cypress groves of Zen temples in China, the ministry decided that flat gravel was more Zen to their liking—and certainly more beautiful than those messy old trees that interfered with the view.

The new war on urban trees is baffling. I cannot fathom its causes, but I can proffer a guess. The inconvenience posed by trees hardly compares with the telephone poles that take up space on both sides of narrow roads, but perhaps the trees, with their unruly branches going this way and that, offend the authorities' spirit of order. Perhaps the long decades of sacrificing everything to industrial growth have had their effect: sterility has become a part of modern Japanese style. Certainly, if you travel in Asia you can immediately recognize the Japanese touch in hotels and office buildings by the lack of trees and, instead, the rows of low-clipped azalea bushes around them.

A curious aspect of the tree war is the primitive level of skill with which it is waged. Japan is the land of bonsai and is famous worldwide for its great gardening traditions. Many and varied are the techniques for pruning and shortening each twig and bough—gradual clipping over years or even decades to shape a branch as it grows, props to support old tree limbs as they droop, canvas wrappings to protect bark from cold and insects, and much more—sensitive techniques developed over centuries, of which until recently the West knew little. Yet tree pruning in Japan today is truly a hack job. No gradual, delicate work here—just limbs roughly chainsawed off at the base, with no treatment to protect against insects and rot. "What bothers me the most," says Mason Florence, "is the brutality of it. The trees look like animals mutilated or skinned alive in medical experiments."

A world of traditional skills in the arts of building homes and cities evaporated when postwar Japan despoiled its old neighborhoods. The destruction happened so quickly that these arts and crafts never had a chance to adapt to modern Japanese life, and today they seem to have lost relevance. The quiet, low-key comforts, the incredible finesse of detail found, for example, in Japan's old inns belong to an entirely different civilization from the shiny Bakelite interiors of Kyoto's new hotels. Similarly, in just a few decades Japanese public gardening technique went from tender pruning to brutal hack jobs.

A salient element in any comparison of Singapore's advanced city planning, which has given it the name Garden City, and Japan's is the treatment of trees. The drive from Changi Airport into downtown Singapore is one of the pleasures of the modern world. You whirl along a highway lined with a canopy of spreading trees—all newly planted in the past few decades—and under bridges from which flowering vines trail. Southeast Asian garden expert William Warren, in his book on Singapore, has included this highway and also the airport itself as examples of Asia's great gardens. He told me, "I was astonished at the devotion of the botanical staff in Singapore. These are well-educated professionals who love, really love, their work." In Japan, you will not find professionalism, and certainly nothing like love, among those who tend city streets. Work crews saw off branches according to a program drawn up by bureaucrats in downtown offices. Aside from a few showpieces, like Tokyo's Omotesando fashion street, you would be hard put to find trees arching over a road even in a small provincial town, and if you do, you had better enjoy it, photograph it, and treasure it, because it will probably not be there the next time you visit. Chainsawing is the law of the land.

Yet "Tokyo is a resort!" writes Sano Tadakatsu, director general of International Economic Affairs at MITI. It is because of the winter sun, he explains, so sadly lacking in northern European cities; the lack of sunlight drives Europeans to take those regrettable long vacations in their lovely holiday homes. In contrast, sun-drenched Tokyo is so marvelous that "even foreigners living in Japan do not want to have holiday homes," and in any case, "children born in this high growth era see nothing wrong with concrete buildings."

Sano is right. What happens to people living in cities like Tokyo? They get used to it. "Many people of my generation feel angry," says Igarashi Takayoshi, the author of a best-selling book on wasteful public works. "We have an idea of how nature should be, but the younger generation doesn't. Students are not shocked by images of environmental destruction the way I am—they got used to it growing up." Recently, Andrew Maerkle, the sixteen-year-old son of an American family in Osaka, and his parents and I had occasion to drive east from Kobe, through Osaka, and down the coast of the Inland Sea to the town of Izumi-Otsu, near the New Kansai Airport. For hours we drove along elevated expressways, giving us a view to the horizon of unrelieved industrial horror. In that bleak landscape live millions of people, in desolate rows of apartments barely distinguishable from the factories around them. Andrew gazed at the flashing billboards, the towering pylons for high-tension wires, the flaming smokestacks, the jumble of buildings stretching to the horizon without a tree or a park, and commented, "I read a lot of Japanese *manga* comics at school, and I was always impressed by their view of the future. Apocalyptic. Now I see where it comes from."

Just as people get used to bleak cityscapes, they come to feel at home with cheap industrial materials. Kyoto art expert David Kidd once said to me, "The Japanese have gotten so used to living with fake wood that they can't tell the difference between it and real wood. They think they're the same." A good place to see this confusion at work is the Arita Porcelain Museum, in northern Kyushu, dedicated to the traditional craft of hand-enameled Imari ceramics. The structure, designed in the rococo style, is built of concrete covered with plaster to look like stone; the dining-room tables are plastic, with printed wood patterns—this in a museum built at great expense to celebrate hand craftsmanship!

One does not expect this lack of understanding of materials in Japan, for "love of materials" is one of the most sublime principles of traditional Japanese art—with its unpainted wood, rough stone surfaces, and unglazed pottery. And yet modern Japan is notable for its persistent use of ill-processed plastic, chrome, highly glazed tile, aluminum, and concrete. These cheap industrial materials are everywhere. At a recent show at the Idemitsu Museum, famed as Tokyo's greatest museum of Asian ceramics, there was a bonsai at the entrance—in an orange plastic pot.

How could a nation that once seemed to have an inherent understanding of natural material fall into the unquestioning use of industrial junk? As with its destruction of the countryside, the explanation cannot be simplistic arguments about "Westernization" or about uniquely "Asian" values. It may be that the very tradition of using plain materials, without treatment or processing, underlies Japan's guileless use of plastic and aluminum today; Japanese builders are simply taking what they find in their environment and using it, as is. Another factor may be the traditional "love of reflective surfaces," once evidenced by gold screens, smooth lacquer, and the glint of polished swords. But the simpler, probably truer explanation is that Japan has embraced an old-fashioned idea of modernism, in which these bright shiny surfaces show that one is wealthy and technologically advanced, and quiet, low-key environments suggest backwardness. In any case, the key word is "shiny." Japan is caught in a time warp, its vision of the future derived from sci-fi movies of the 1960s.

The poor people, strong state policy has been in effect more or less since 1868, with only a few decades of relief (notably a brief cultural renaissance in the 1920s and another in the 1960s). For most of the past century and a half, Japan's leaders have single-mindedly aimed at foreign expansion, and this has distorted the nation's modern development. For hundreds of years during the Edo period (in fact, for most of its recorded history), Japan did not aim at conquering its neighbors, either militarily or economically; instead, it applied its energies to itself, and the results were not economic poverty or cultural stagnation, as one might suppose. Instead, Japan flourished, so much so that by the early nineteenth century it was, per capita, by far the wealthiest Asian nation and boasted some of the world's most beautiful cities, literally millions of superbly crafted traditional homes, and an incredibly rich cultural tradition that has since exerted a powerful influence on the rest of the world.

Commodore Perry's arrival in 1854 set off shock waves whose reverberations can still be felt today. Japan set out on a desperate effort first to resist and later to challenge the West, and while it achieved spectacular success, it did serious damage to its own cultural legacy. Today, the beautiful cities are gone, as are the superbly crafted homes, and the leisure that Edo people once had to create a great world culture. Nothing could be more ironic: pursuit of foreign gain at all costs ended up impoverishing the nation.

The paradigm established in the late nineteenth century under the influence of European nationalism was one of military conquest, and it has never really changed: Japan's bureaucratic leaders still think of economic expansion in terms of war. Military metaphors abound in business, government, and the press. Karel van Wolferen describes Japan's system as "a wartime economy operating in peacetime," and a crucial part of this economy is the principle of poor people, strong state. The military has always hated luxury, for it makes people lazy and soft, and from this point of view poor people, strong state is a classic military approach to governance, as we know from the history of the ancient kingdom of Sparta.

Plutarch reports that Lycurgus, when drafting the laws of Sparta, began with house design. Lycurgus decreed that ceilings should be wrought by the ax, gates and doors smoothed only by the saw. "Luxury and a house of this kind could not well be companions," Plutarch comments. "Doubtless he had good reason to think that they would proportion their beds to their houses, and their coverlets to their beds, and the rest of their goods and furniture to these."

In Japan, likewise, the poor people, strong state policy rests on cramped and poorly built housing. Matthias Ley, a German photographer based in Tokyo, told me that once, when he was taking a German publisher from Osaka Airport into Kyoto, the publisher looked out at a neighborhood on the outskirts of the city, a typical jumble of concrete boxes and electric wires, and asked innocently, "So this is where the poor people live?" The answer to that question was, unfortunately, No, this is where everyone lives.

A frequent misunderstanding about Japan is the claim that there is not enough land to support its large population, that Japan is "crowded," hence land costs are high. In fact, Japan's population density is comparable to that of many prosperous (and still-beautiful) European countries. Another myth is that, given how mountainous much of Japan is, the habitable land area is bound to be small. This begs the question of what is "habitable land." Hills did not stop Tuscany from developing

beautifully, or San Francisco, or Hong Kong. The problem lies
in land use.

In Japan, there are many laws restricting both the supply of
land available for housing and what can be built on it. With
homes prohibitively expensive—in the early 1990s banks were
arranging mortgages that would bind families unto the third
generation—the people are forced to save; banks then channel
these savings at low interest to industry. After the Bubble deflated in 1990, the government panicked, and since then national policy has been to prop up land prices at all costs.

One way that the government restricts land use is by rigor-
ously enforcing low floor-to-area ratios, unchanged from the
days when Japanese cities consisted mostly of one- and two-
story wooden buildings. The Sunlight Law and low FAR in big
cities like Tokyo and Osaka results in street after street of low
buildings even in expensive commercial areas. Another way in
which the government restricts land use is through outdated
regulations that subsidize owners who use their land as rice
paddies; large areas of Tokyo are still zoned for agriculture. A
third major obstacle to effective land use in Japan is that people
cannot easily convert most mountain land for residential or
commercial use. The virtual taboo against it dates to antiquity,
when mountains were thought to be the domain of the gods,
not of people. Given that most of Japan's landmass is mountainous, this effectively limits development to the crowded plainlands and valleys.

After Lycurgus had finished laying down the laws for Sparta,
he gathered the king and the people together and told them
that all was complete, except for one final question that he
needed to ask of the Oracle at Delphi. He made all the citizens
take a solemn oath that they would not alter a single letter of
his laws until he returned. Lycurgus went to Delphi and starved
himself to death there, so as never to return, and the people,

bound by their oath, maintained his laws unchanged for the next nine hundred years.

Japan is like this. Lycurgus left in about 1965, and since then nobody has changed anything. Land-use planners, for example, have never seriously examined the old taboo on mountain land, which has been a blessing in part, given the primitive state of Japanese city planning and the lack of environmental-impact controls. Although they have been replanted with cedar and honeycombed with concrete roads and embankments, at least the mountains have been spared the fate of the plainlands. On the other hand, this has driven up the cost of residential land elsewhere, which is why Japanese houses are 20 to 30 percent smaller than European homes and about three times more expensive, though they are built of shoddy, flimsy materials—plywood, tin, aluminum, molded vinyl sheets—and, as the Kobe earthquake proved, are not designed to be earthquake-resistant (the lead in this technology is now coming from the United States). Most houses are almost completely uninsulated; people usually heat their rooms with separate units (commonly kerosene heaters) and have no special ventilation for exhaust fumes. Discomfort—bone-chilling cold in winter and sweaty heat in summer—is a defining feature of Japanese life.

One important trend in domestic architecture is quietly transforming neighborhoods across the country: prefabricated housing. "Prefab" in Japan means *totally* prefabricated, with the entire structure mass-manufactured by giant housing companies and delivered to homeowners as one package. Prefab homes now account for a majority of new Japanese houses—and in this there is some progress, and also a final blow to the urban landscape. On the plus side, the new homes are cleaner and more convenient than the old houses they replace. On the minus side, they represent the victory of sterility. Inside and outside surfaces consist of shiny processed materials so unnatural as to be unrecognizable. One cannot say whether they are concrete, metal, or something else, although for the most part they are plastic, extruded in various forms, and colored and texturized to look like concrete or metal. Industrial materials have had the last word: people now live within walls and on floors made of material that might as well be in a spaceship. This might have some futuristic appeal except that the houses are designed with exactly the same clutter and lack of ventilation and insulation as before.

Saddest of all is the utter uniformity of the prefab houses. Neighborhood after neighborhood has seen whatever character it once had disappear before rows of mass-produced homes in the shape of Model A, B, or C, all clad in exactly the same gray shade of hybrid construction material. It's another cycle in Japan's descending cultural spiral, something that no mere upturn or downturn in the economy is going to affect.

In any event, very few people, including the rich, have homes to which they can invite strangers with pride. A dinner party in Japan means dining out. A wedding reception in the back yard? Unthinkable. Most Japanese, regardless of wealth, education, taste, or personal interests, pass most of their social lives in public spaces—restaurants, wedding halls, and hotel banquet rooms. Modern Japanese homes are not places where one can commune intimately with one's friends.

Lycurgus would have approved. One of his most effective laws was one that forced all Spartan men to eat at the same communal table, never at home. "For the rich," Plutarch wrote, "being obliged to go to the same table with the poor, could not make use of or enjoy their abundance, nor so much as please their vanity by looking at or displaying it. So that the common proverb, that Plutus, the god of riches, is blind, was nowhere in all the world literally verified but in Sparta. There, indeed, he was not only blind, but like a picture, without either life or motion."

The restricting of the population to cramped, expensive, and now characterless prefabricated housing made of low-grade industrial materials suited Japan's policy of benefiting old-line manufacturing industries at all costs. However, new industries like interior design can prosper only when people are comfortable and educated enough to develop a higher level of taste.

The results are evident in hotels and resorts. While Kyoto is famed for its lovely old inns, the city has no modern hotel of international quality. In Paris, Rome, Peking, or Bangkok, one can find modern hotels that incorporate local materials and design in such a way as to provide a sense of place, but Kyoto boasts not a single such instution. The big hotels (such as the Kyoto, Miyako, Brighton, and Prince), with their aluminum, granite, and glass lobbies, deny Kyoto's wood-and-paper culture in every way. Compare the wooden lattices and tree-lined entrance to the Sukhotai Hotel in Bangkok with the wall of dirty concrete and the narrow cement steps leading up to the Miyako Hotel, Kyoto's most prestigious. Stroll through the gardens filled with ponds and pavilions at the Inter-Continental or the Hilton in Bangkok, and then look at Kyoto Hotel's public plaza, a tiny barren area of granite paving surrounded by a yellow *plastic* bamboo fence. Drink a leisurely cup of coffee amid the greenery under the soaring teak-timbered vaults of the Hyatt in Bangkok, and then visit Kyoto's Prince, the hotel where most conventioneers stay, with its low ceilings and almost every surface of plastic and aluminum. For a nightcap, you could view the Bangkok skyline from the fiftieth floor of the Westin Hotel—surrounded by polished teak and rosewood paneling; or you could enjoy the floodlit rock and waterfall in the garden of the Royal Hotel in Kyoto—the rock being made of molded green fiberglass. One finds the same lack of quality in Tokyo, a city with only two attractive hotels, the Park Hyatt and the Four Seasons. In the case of the Park Hyatt, the low-key lighting, the elegant use of wood in hallways and elevators—all this was accomplished by shutting out Japanese designers. "We couldn't allow Japanese designers to be involved," the management told me. "They wanted to fill it with aluminum and fluorescent lights." And in the Four Seasons, where I noticed recently that the gold screens on the walls were antiques of high quality, I knew instantly that no Japanese designer would have chosen them. At the front desk, I asked who did the decor, and was told "designers from the Regent Chain in Hong Kong."

So far we have been speaking of big city hotels with hundreds of rooms; when it comes to small garden hotels or boutique hotels, the contrast with other advanced nations is even more striking. There was a brief period in the late 1980s, at the height of the Bubble, when price was no object, when a few brave developers created hotels of striking originality, such as Kuzawa Mitushiro's colorful Il Palazzo in Fukuoka, done in collaboration with Aldo Rossi. But with the collapse of the Bubble, developers settled back into the convenient old pattern of "business hotels," with their cramped rooms, flat decor, and limited facilities. It would be fair to say that the very concept of a boutique hotel has yet to exist in Japan. There is no such thing as New York's witty Paragon or W hotels, nothing with the minimalist chic of Ian Schrager's creations—just the standard shiny marble lobbies one sees everywhere, with rooms designed with basic industrial efficiency. "But hotels are not just places to sleep," says Schrager. "You're supposed to have fun there."

Today's younger Japanese designers, who have grown up in landscapes such as the one the Maerkle family saw when they drove from Kobe to Izumi-Otsu, or the equally horrifying vista welcoming visitors at Narita Airport when they take the Narita express train into Tokyo, work accordingly. As Lycurgus predicted, people proportion "their beds to their houses, and their coverlets to their beds, and the rest of their goods and furniture to these." Standardized shiny surfaces are what people really like and feel comfortable in. The victory of the industrial mode in Japanese life can be sensed in health spas, which, far from being relaxing natural retreats, look rather like clinics, with bright white corridors and attendants in surgical smocks. Boutique hotels, even were they to be introduced into Japan, would be bound to fail.

Tokyo and Osaka may boast a handful of attractive international hotels designed by foreigners, but the Japanese countryside remains solidly in the hands of domestic designers. Japanese resorts are so ill designed, so destructive of their surroundings, that in May 1997 the Environment Agency reported that 30 percent of all those surveyed did not live up to the agency's assessment criteria. By American, European, or Indonesian standards, that number would rise to more than 90 percent.

A good example of the sort of thing that happens can be seen in Iya Valley. Iya has Japan's last vine bridge, built by Heike refugees in the twelfth century and rehung with fresh vines regularly ever since. The Vine Bridge is Iya's most famous monument, visited by more than 500,000 people every year. What happened to it? The River Bureau flattened the riverbanks below with concrete; the Forestry Agency constructed a metal bridge right next to it; and resort builders then covered the surrounding valley slopes with concrete boxes and billboards. Travelers who have come from distant prefectures to get a view of the romance of the Heike line up on the metal bridge and take photographs, carefully framing the Vine Bridge to screen out the concrete and the billboards. The choice of accommodation is between *minshuku* (bed-and-breakfast in old homes) or a few big tourist hotels. *Minshuku* in old thatch-roofed houses sound attractive—and indeed would be, except that the interiors have been redone with synthetic veneer and fluorescent lights, and yet they still lack modern conveniences such as clean flush toilets and heated bathrooms. So a visit to the Vine Bridge in Iya is only, and just, that: one has seen the Vine Bridge, but there is little in the experience to relax the body or please the heart. In this, Iya's Vine Bridge symbolizes the anomalous fate of old cities like Kyoto and of rural scenery throughout Japan. Iya's mountains and gorges are nothing less than spectacular, the Vine Bridge itself a romance. Rich possibilities for cultural experience and travel are simply there for the taking—and yet a failure of "tourism technology" causes them to be ignored or damaged.

Ill-applied modernity can also be seen at the *onsen* (hot springs), which were one of Japan's most wonderful traditions. There are thousands of *onsen* in romantic environments beside rivers, atop mountains, and along pine-tree-clad seacoasts; they once boasted lovely buildings of wood and bamboo, exquisite service, healing hot waters, and the chance to relax amid beautiful natural scenery. You could lie in the hot water by an open window and watch the mist rise from the river or the trees around you.

Well, the *onsen* are still there, the hot water still flows, and the service is still good. But the ambience that made *onsen* uniquely relaxing is vanishing with the mists. Old *onsen* have been restored with lots of chrome and Astroturf, all the slapdash additions that damaged Kyoto; meanwhile, new *onsen* tend to look like cheap business hotels plopped down in the countryside or, at best, like bland white-and-gray bank lobbies.

It sometimes happens that enlightened owners manage to preserve the mood of an old *onsen* or design an attractive new one, but nothing can replace the lost rivers, mountains, and sea-coasts in which the *onsen* stand. Hardly a hot spring the length and breadth of Japan has not been in some way degraded by ugly, ill-designed resorts or civil-engineering projects. Robert Neff, the head of the Foreign Correspondents Club of Japan, writing about his search for "hidden *onsen*" far from the beaten track, summed up the situation sadly:

> As Japan's countryside gives way before concrete, plastic, automatic vending machines, and pachinko parlors, hidden *onsen* make us forget the passage of time. It is a joy when I can report that such places still exist. Alas, they are on the verge of extinction. When I visited them some years back, these places were wonderfully untouched. But when I go to visit hidden *onsen* nowadays all vestige of former scenery has been removed, and replaced with modern monstrosities totally out of keeping with the surroundings. Or new highways, dams, hideous bridges, ski lifts, ropeways, and electrical generating stations are built where they can be seen right out the front door. [Translated from the Japanese]

Onsen were a true cultural treasure, which would have appealed to travelers from around the world; if they had been developed with truly modern design and management, there is no doubt that Japan could have based a thriving international tourist industry on them. Not so now. A few lovely *onsen* do exist, but loveliness in Japan has become a luxury that few can afford. Most of the affordable *onsen* have become places "neither here nor there"—a mix of nice scenery and eyesores—places you might visit if you happened to be in Japan and had some free time, but not destinations you would cross an ocean or spend a lot of money to see.

The historian Gibbon, an expert on the rise and fall of empire, wrote, "All that is human must retrograde if it does not advance." Thirty or forty years ago, Japan had all the earmarks of modernism: technical finesse in manufacturing, clean cities, trains that ran on time. For bureaucrats, architects, university professors, and city planners, Japan seemed to have the perfect formula, and it needed only to develop on a grander scale along established lines. It was so deceptively reassuring that few observers noticed that time had stopped. Confident in their belief that their country had "got it right," Japan's leaders firmly resisted new ideas, whether domestic or foreign. Lacking the critical ingredient, change, culture in Japan took on modernism's outward forms but lost its heart. Without new attitudes and fresh knowledge, the quality of life in cities and countryside, as Gibbon could have predicted, did indeed retrograde. This is the paradox of modern Japanese life: that although it is known as a nation of aesthetes, there is hardly a single feature of modern Japan touched by the hand of man that one could call beautiful.

In 1694, the haiku poet Basho set out on his final journey, one that he expected to be his greatest—he was traveling from the town of Ueno near Nara to Osaka, where he planned to meet with his disciples, put an end to their bickering, and set the haiku world to rights. But it didn't turn out that way. Basho fell sick along the way and died, having accomplished nothing. As his disciples gathered around his bedside, he granted them one final haiku:

Stricken on a journey
My dreams go wandering round
Withered fields.

After the 1960s, fueled by one of the greatest economic booms in world history, Japan embarked on a journey to a brave new world. During the next few decades, the old world was swept away with the expectation that a glorious new world would replace it. But somewhere along the way Japan was stricken on its journey. It is now clear that there will be no glorious new, no sparkling extravaganza of the future like Hong Kong, no tree-lined garden city like Singapore, not even a Kuala Lumpur or a Jakarta. Only withered fields—an apocalyptic expanse of aluminum, Hitachi signs, roof boxes, billboards, telephone wires, vending machines, granite pavement, flashing lights, plastic, and pachinko.

9 Demons

The Philosophy of Monuments

"My name is Ozymandias, king of kings:
Look on my works, ye Mighty, and despair!"
—PERCY BYSSHE SHELLEY, "Ozymandias" (1817)

In ancient times, in faraway Izumo on the coast of the Sea of Japan, there lived a fearful eight-headed serpent, the Orochi. He ravaged the mountains and valleys far and wide, devouring the daughters of local villagers, and only when the god Susano-o vanquished him did peace come. Inside the Orochi, Susano-o found the sacred sword that still ranks as one of the three imperial treasures; nearby was founded Izumo Shrine, Japan's oldest. Since that time, the land of Izumo has been holy, so much so that the traditional name for the month of October is *Kannazuki* (the month without gods), because it is believed that in that month all the gods of Japan leave their native places and gather at Izumo.

Alas, all the gods of Japan cannot save the town of Yokota, in Izumo, from an enemy even worse than the Orochi: depopulation. In rural areas all across Japan, young people are fleeing to the cities, transforming the countryside into one giant old folks' home. The exodus of young people for the cities is a worldwide phenomenon, but in Japan it has been exacerbated by several factors. One is the centralization of power in Tokyo, which inhibits the growth of strong local industries. No Japanese Microsoft would for a moment consider having its headquarters in the equivalent of Redmond, Washington.

Other means of recycling the resources of the once agricultural countryside—retrofitted small-town businesses, resorts, vacation homes, tourism, parks—have not been explored, since, as we have seen, Japan's bureaucratic structures are aimed at manufacturing and construction, and little else. Civil-engineering projects and cedar plantations have not addressed core issues concerning rural areas in a postindustrial state. Worse, the new and useless roads, dams, and embankments make the countryside less attractive while failing to give it the advantages of city life. This scarred countryside does not offer appealing locations for companies to locate their headquarters or subsidiaries, for artists to set up ateliers, for retirees to build homes, or for quality resort developers to attract tourists.

What to do? With subsidies from the Construction Ministry, Yokota took its most picturesque valley and filled it up with a double-looped elevated highway complete with tunnels, bridges, concrete supports, and embankments. At one end, a brightly painted red bridge, lit by spotlights, spans the valley. The tunnels are decorated with dragon eyes, and eight viewing spots (the Orochi's eight heads) feature towering concrete pillars. Yokota proudly proclaims the "Orochi Loop" as Japan's longest highway circle. "An invitation to the world of the gods," sings the tourist pamphlet, and indeed it is a celebration of the gods of construction who rule Japan today.

When the Orochi Loop opened in 1994, Yokota hoped that the highway would become a tourist lodestone to vie with the fabled Izumo Shrine itself. But it turned out that city dwellers are not so impressed by what is basically just another road. There are far too many concrete pillars in Tokyo and Osaka already; why come all the way to Izumo to see more?

So it was time for Yokota to take the next step in *mura okoshi*, "raising up the village." *Mura okoshi* (there is also *machi okoshi*, "raising up the town," and *furusato zukuri*, "building up the old hometown"), civic-improvement schemes, are sweeping the nation. The process goes like this: Yokota built the Orochi Loop, thinking it would bring tourists in and keep the locals around. It didn't. So officials called in a consulting firm, which advised, "Leave things alone. Accentuate the natural beauty of the area. This is what tourists come to see." This advice was unwelcome, as it did not factor in the largesse of government subsidy money, so the town called in another group, with Allan West, an artist knowledgeable about *nihonga* (traditional Japanese painting), as a foreign adviser.

Yokota had a beautiful 1920s railroad station facing a nice town square, but in the 1970s the city fathers had rebuilt the shops with their backs turned to the station and the square. West suggested that they resurrect the town square and station, which would give back some life to the center of Yokota, and the citizens supported this, saying they were sick of having to hold their annual festival in the town-hall parking lot. But the officials wouldn't hear of this, as it didn't use enough money. They also dismissed the suggestion to bury telephone wires, because it went against the Construction Ministry's agenda for rural areas. Someone proposed refurbishing an ancient local temple, where the priest, a mah-jongg addict, had gambled everything away to local gangsters, who stripped the temple bare, right down to the ornamental tiles on the roof, and left it to rot. But the local officials showed no interest in fixing it up or restoring it.

Thus in the first round of *machi okoshi* in Yokota, an unnecessary elevated highway, specially designed to be twice the required length and have double the destructive effect, wiped out a scenic valley. In the second round, advice to restore the town square and temple went unheeded, and phone lines remained above ground. The third round was the construction of another monument: Yokota built a large museum to the art of sword-making, crowned by another Orochi, this one a helix of eight entwined stainless-steel tubes topped with dragon heads. This, too, failed to make Yokota an attractive place to live in or visit, and its depopulation continues. Soon it will be time for round four, and what form the next Orochi monument will take is anyone's guess.

"Dogs are difficult; demons are easy." Dogs are the simple, unobtrusive factors in our surroundings that are so difficult to get right; demons are grandiose surface statements. Anyone can draw a demon. Dogs are zoning, sign control, the planting and tending of trees, burial of electric wires, protection of historic neighborhoods, comfortable and attractive residential design, environmentally friendly resorts. Demons are Orochi bridges and multipurpose halls—any kind of monument, the bigger, more expensive, and more outrageous the better: "cultural" halls shaped in ovals or in diamonds, as ships or as flames; museums in huge tubes with rock gardens plastered on their curving walls, museums made to look like galactic starships, museums with no artworks at all. Rural villages have meeting halls and sports stadiums big enough for the Olympics. Cities fill in their harbors for futuristic metropolises as if they expected their size to double or triple.

When the Construction State meets disappointed civic pride, the results are such as the world has never seen before. Consider once again an example from Kyoto. When Japan Railways sponsored a design competition in the early 1990s for

the New Kyoto Station (completed in 1998), it attracted attention worldwide. Here was an opportunity to make up for the
damage done by the Kyoto Tower in 1965 and to re-establish
Kyoto as Japan's cultural capital. The proposed designs split into
two main categories: there were those who tried to incorporate
traditional Kyoto forms, for example, making the station look
like a large-scale *Sanjusangendo*, or Hall of the Thousand Bud-
dhas, one long narrow building with a tiled roof. As trains
arrived in such a station, passengers would feel they were
entering into Kyoto's past. The second category was of resolute
modernism. The architect Ando Tadao designed a square arch
(rather like the arch at La Défense in Paris), using a modern
form but drawing inspiration from Kyoto's history. When Japan
Railways built the old station, which runs east–west for blocks,
it cut Karasuma Road, Kyoto's north–south axis, in two, effectively severing the northern and southern halves of the city.
With the proposed arch, Karasuma Road would become whole
again, reunifying the split city, and the arch would be a reminder that Rashomon Gate, the fabled south gate of the
ancient capital, had once stood on this site.

Japan Railways and the city authorities turned all these proposals down, however, and chose one designed by Professor
Hara Hiroshi of Tokyo University. It divides the city as before,
and does away with every reference to Kyoto's history and culture. The New Kyoto Station is a dull gray block towering over
the neighborhood, so massive that Kyoto residents have taken
to calling it "the battleship." The pride of the station is a tall
glass-fronted entrance lobby that resembles an airport building.

Professor Hara has a reputation as an expert on ethnic architecture, yet at a glance nothing here would appear to be particularly "ethnic." But there are signs of the monumental
architecture peculiar to modern Japan, now as ethnic as kimono. We've seen it all before in the Orochi Loop, the aggres-

sive denial of—even attack on—the surroundings, the bombastic style, the architectural equivalent of sound coming from loudspeakers turned up to maximum volume. As Kyoto slides deeper into mediocrity, the station tries to impress by its sheer size. And, last, there are the cheap, functionless decorations. A plain gray box might not have been so bad, but Hara couldn't stop himself from adding things: miniature arches are built into the structure (apparently as a sop to Ando); the back of the station features external yellow stairways, red piping, and rows of porthole-like windows pasted onto the facade; and inside the giant entry lobby, escalators leading nowhere soar toward the sky. These are all features in which we see the influence of *manga*, Japanese comic books. The *manga* effect is reinforced in front of the station, where the first thing an arriving passenger sees is the Kyoto Mascot, a totem pole topped by big-eyed baby-faced children, molded in plastic. It's the equivalent of arriving in Florence and being greeted by Donald Duck.

The station's crowning glory is its so-called Cultural Zone, featuring a multipurpose entertainment center. As real culture disappears, these expressions of artificial culture, in the shape of cultural zones and halls, are a major source of revenue for the construction industry and hence a national imperative. Every year billions of dollars flow to such public halls; by 1995, Japan had 2,121 theaters and halls (up from 848 in 1979), and by 1997 it had 3,449 museums, the result of a museum-building rush unequaled by any other nation in the world.

Unquestioning foreign observers new to Japan often accept these halls and museums at face value. But most of these institutions satisfy no need aside from the construction industry's intention to keep building at public expense. The Kabuki actor Bando Tamasaburo says, "A multipurpose hall is a no-purpose hall." At the theaters, events are staged that are planned and paid for by government agencies, attended mostly by people to whom they distribute free tickets. The museums are echo chambers, empty of visitors, with a few broken pots found in archaeological digs or obscure contemporary artworks chosen by the architect.

For Japanese architects, cultural halls are a leading source of income, and designing them is a dream. The buildings need not harmonize with their surroundings, nor need they provide a community service or indeed fulfill any recognizable function, and this gives architects a free hand, to put it mildly. The result is a plethora of buildings that are fanciful to the point of being bizarre. In Fujiidera City, on the outskirts of Osaka, one can find an office building in the shape of a huge concrete boat. In Toyodama, a town with a population of 5,000, the Home of Culture is a ¥1.8 billion extravaganza in the shape of a multi-storied white mosque. The Desert on the Moon Hall (¥400 million), on the Miyado coast, is shaped like an Arabian palace, complete with bronze statues of camel riders in an artificial dunescape.

One can find many of the architectural wonders of the world in a monument somewhere in Japan. Tokyo boasts a French château at Ebisu Garden Place, a Gaudí-style walkway with curving mounds inset with broken tiles at Tama New Town, and a German village in Takanawa, Minato-ku Ward. "However," as the weekly magazine *Shukan Shincho* says, "just look around you at the sea of signs in kanji characters and kana alphabets, and in a moment your good mood crashes to earth in real-life Japan. Alas, however hard we strive to bring in foreign culture, in the end it is nothing but 'foreign-style.' On the other hand, maybe the inability to do anything for real could be called 'Japanese-style.' "

Hanker for Italy? You can find a Venetian palazzo in Kotaru, or an entire Michelangelo inlaid courtyard re-created at the Tsukuba Civic Center Building in Ibaragi. In Akita you can visit the Snow Museum, which keeps samples of snow in chilled display chambers. In Yamanashi, a Fruit Museum is housed in fruit-shaped glass-and-steel spheres described by the architect as "either planted firmly in the ground or attempting to reject the earth, as if they had just landed from the air and were trying to fly away." And in Naruto, Tokushima, the Otsuka Museum of Art houses a thousand renowned works of Western art—from the Sistine Chapel to Andy Warhol—duplicated on ceramic panels. In Tokyo, fanciful monuments are legion. Typical of the genre is the Edo-Tokyo Museum, a snouted metal body raised high on megalithic legs. The city built it to celebrate the culture of the Edo period. As one commentator has said, "What this look-alike of a *Star Wars* battle station has to do with Tokyo's past is a mystery. At any moment you expect it to zap the graceful national sumo stadium next door and reduce it to galactic dust."

Monuments come in two basic varieties: *manga* and massive. The *manga* approach is typified by functionless decoration—the stainless-steel tubes topped with dragon heads at the sword museum in Yokota, for example, or Asahi's Super Dry Hall in Tokyo, reported as "what can only be described as an *objet*, a kind of golden beet resting on a black obsidian-like pedestal. . . . This is the *Flamme d'Or* (Flame of Gold) representing, we are told, the 'burning heart of Asahi beer.' Or maybe the head on a glass of that same product. Or something from *Ghostbusters*. The flame is hollow, so serves no practical purpose at all. Call it architecture as sculpture." Known locally as the "turd building," Asahi's Super Dry Hall was designed by a French architect, replacing what the Tokyo historian Edward Seidensticker believes to have been the city's last remaining wooden beer hall, dating from Taisho if not late Meiji.

Into the massive category fall the supercities being planned for landfill in the harbors of Tokyo, Osaka, and Kobe, as well as fortresses like the Tokyo Municipal Office Complex in Shinjuku. The most lavishly funded monuments, like the New Kyoto Station, manage to combine *manga* and massive in one structure.

What both categories of monument have in common is excess. Braggadocio. In Shelley's famous sonnet "Ozymandias," the poet describes a traveler coming across the ruins of a gigantic statue in the desert. On the base of the statue, an inscription reads:

> *"My name is Ozymandias, king of kings:*
> *Look on my works, ye Mighty, and despair!"*
> *Nothing beside remains. Round the decay*
> *Of that colossal wreck, boundless and bare,*
> *The lone and level sands stretch far away.*

Japan has a bad case of the Ozymandias syndrome. "Boundless and bare, the lone and level sands" of miserable houses, ugly apartments, shadeless streets, bleak office buildings, and the clutter of signs and electric wires stretch far away. But Japan's planners seem to believe that the world will stand in amazement before these monuments, the larger and more strident the better.

Hence the pride that the town of Yokota takes in the fact that the Orochi Loop is Japan's longest highway cloverleaf. Other towns have built the longest stone stairway (3,333 steps), the biggest waterwheel, the world's biggest Ferris wheel (Yokohama waterfront), the biggest stewpot (six meters wide, able to feed 30,000 people), the biggest drum, the biggest sand clock, and the world's longest beach bench. In Tokyo, monuments on the drawing boards include Taisei Corporation's 4,000-meter cone-shaped building known as X-SEED4000. Its base would be six kilometers wide and it would sit above the ocean, housing 500,000 people. The reason for the name X-SEED is that, though shaped like Mount Fuji, the monument's height would exceed that of Mount Fuji by several hundred meters, so residents could enjoy looking down on the mountain.

Shimizu Corporation is proposing a far more modest 800-meter skyscraper (almost twice the height of the Sears Tower in Chicago), on pillars above a city. Kajima Corporation is pursuing a stacked structure, a so-called Dynamic Intelligent Building, which consists of several fifty-story structures piled on top of one another. Ohbayashi Corporation, for its part, has announced plans for the 2,100-meter Aeropolis 2001, whose shadow will darken the environs of Tokyo.

While these companies have put their plans on hold due to the bursting of the Bubble, their concepts are dear to the Construction Ministry's heart, and as we have seen in the case of Nagara Dam, once a concept, always a concept. Aoki Hitoshi, a senior specialist with the Construction Advisory Section of the Construction Ministry, says, "The construction companies put a great deal of work into developing them, and it seemed a shame not to utilize them. Aside from the military, development of such buildings is an ideal frontier in which scientific research can be extended. We hope that in the future this can be developed into a national project." How these structures will get around the Sunlight Law is a mystery, but in the case of monuments, ministries waive restrictions. Whatever it costs, something like these will surely get built.

Mile-high buildings are just the beginning. The grandiose visions of Japan's builders and architects go further—nothing less than reshaping the land itself. The new Comprehensive National Development Plan, or Zenso, is considering a network of expressways across the country, as well as mammoth tunnels and bridges linking all of Japan's islands, despite the fact that road, rail, and air systems already link them. The jewel in the crown would be a brand-new capital built on land far away from Tokyo; this will provide opportunities for monuments on a scale beyond anything yet imagined. Estimated by the government to cost ¥14 trillion, it will house 600,000 people in a 9,000-hectare site surrounding the National Diet, to be called Diet City. The construction work will essentially involve flattening an entire prefecture—and eight prefectures have passed resolutions urging that this new capital be built in their territory.

The architect Kurokawa Kisho proposes to expand Tokyo by creating a 30,000-hectare island in the bay, laced with canals and freeways. This island would be home to 5 million people, with an additional million housed in another new city built at the Chiba end of the bay and connected by a bridge. The cost of this scheme comes to around ¥300 trillion (twenty times the Apollo program), and it would require men and machines to level an entire range of mountains yielding 8.4 billion cubic meters of landfill (125 times what builders excavated to cut the Suez Canal), this on top of the 900 million cubic meters already shaved off the mountains of Chiba Prefecture to build the Tokyo–Chiba trans-bay bridge.

The world knows Japan as the land of the miniature, of restraint, of quiet good taste, of devotion to the low-key but telling detail. Nakano Kiyotsugu wrote a best-selling book published in 1993 in which he argued that the very core ideal of traditional Japanese culture was *Seihin no Shiso*, the "philosophy of pure poverty." By pure poverty, Nakano meant the simplicity of life of the eighteenth-century Buddhist monk Ryokan, famed for living happily in a thatched hut. Ryokan's chief pleasure in life was playing with the local children. "Pure poverty" inspired many of Japan's greatest works of literature, such as Kamo no Chomei's *Record of the Ten-Foot-Square Hut*, written in the early thirteenth century, which describes a life of meditation in a modest natural setting, and which set a pattern that the philosopher Yoshida Kenko and the poets Saigyo and Basho followed in later years; it reached its apex in the tea ceremony. Tea masters designed tearooms to be small, unobtrusive structures, made of humble woods and bamboo.

The philosophy of pure poverty penetrates every facet of traditional Japan. Visitors to Ryoanji Temple in Kyoto, home of the famous rock garden, will have seen a stone water basin in the garden at the back, whose motto is known to schoolchildren across the land: four characters are carved in it, surrounding a square hole in the center of the stone, which is a visual pun, since all four have the radical for "mouth," a square, in them. The message—the essence of Zen, one could even say of Buddhism in general—is *Ware Tada Taru Shiru*, which means "I know only what is enough." Another translation is "I know the limits, and that is enough." Nakano writes plaintively:

> When I speak of Japanese culture to foreigners, the problem always circles back to the way we live today, which is only natural. The reason I began talking about this side of Japanese culture is I wanted to say, "The Japanese products you see and the people making them are not all there is to the Japanese! *This* is what our traditional culture was!" While I know full well that it is being lost in today's Japan, it was my desire to introduce the best, the supreme point of Japanese culture.

If "pure poverty" and "knowing what is enough" were the supreme points of Japanese culture, where in the world did Japan's modern gigantism, the insistence on the biggest and the longest, the taste for the bombastic, come from? Within traditional culture itself, coexisting with pure poverty has been another tendency, a competitive streak. When the imperial court built cities like Kyoto and Nara, it did so with an eye over its shoulder at China and Korea. In Nara, the very first order of business was to devote all the energies of the state to building the Hall of the Great Buddha, intended to compete with the largest temples of the Tang-dynasty capital in Chang-An. Today's Todaiji, though a much smaller reconstruction, is still the largest wooden structure in the world.

Later rulers celebrated their reigns with undertakings such as the Great Buddha in Kamakura, Hideyoshi's Himeji Castle, and the Shogun's Palace in Edo, which are among the larger structures of the premodern world. In short, Japan also has a strong tradition of celebrating its rulers' power through impressive monuments. What is going on today may be a similar affirmation of wealth and power.

Thoreau wrote: "Many are concerned about the monuments of the West and the East, to know who built them. For my part, I should like to know who in those days did not build them— who were above such trifling." The answer is, of course, that none were above it. Every state, as it acquires wealth, goes through a phase in which it enjoys building bigger and taller structures. Versailles, the Houses of Parliament, the Empire State Building, the Sears Tower—these are all Western monuments. Newly industrializing Asian countries are headed one after another in the same direction, with mega-projects scheduled for China, Malaysia, and Singapore. From the Pyramids of Egypt to Malaysia's new Linear City (a twelve-kilometer mall and office building planned to straddle the Klang River in Kuala Lumpur), monument building would seem to be a universal need, perhaps even a basic human desire.

There is, however, one critical difference between ancient societies and those of today, and it is that raising huge monuments in pre-industrial times was *difficult*, involving massive mobilization of people and resources. Notre-Dame, the Forbidden City, the Potala Palace, Angkor Wat, the Vatican took centuries to complete. In contrast, the gigantic office towers and fanciful museums of today are apparently projects that even small and poorly developed nations can easily do. As the twenty-first century dawns, the construction of huge monuments is no longer a proof of advanced civilization. In other advanced industrial nations, the advent of a new skyscraper these days rarely brings more than a yawn—if not outright opposition. But Japan seems stuck in a pre-industrial mode in which such monuments still invariably astound and amaze. It's Japan's old competitive streak in action, but not updated to a newer model of development. Therefore Japan must keep building more and bigger and higher and grander in order to impress its citizens that it has "arrived," or, in the words of Nakaoki Yutaka, the governor of Toyama Prefecture, "so that people can feel they have become rich." Monuments prove to people that they live in a successful modern state. But of course the real test of a successful modern state is the degree to which it rises above such trifling.

Why is it that monument building has triumphed to such an extreme in modern times, while Japan's strong tradition of "pure poverty" has been swept away like a straw in a gale? It's a case of breakdown and imbalance—and this inability to keep a balance lies at the core of Japan's modern cultural trauma.

A clue to the problem may be found in what I call the theory of Opposite Virtues. Nations, like people in this respect, may pride themselves most highly on the quality they most lack. Hence "fair play" is a golden virtue in Great Britain, the country that attacked and subjugated half the globe. "Equality" was the banner of Soviet Russia, where commissars owned lavish dachas on the Black Sea and the proletariat lived no better than serfs. The United States prides itself on its high "moral standard," while perpetuating racial and moral double standards. And then there is *l'amour* in France, a nation of cold-blooded rationalists. Or Canadians priding themselves most on being so distinctively "Canadian."

In Japan we must look at the time-honored ideal of *Wa,* "peace." *Wa* means security, stability, everything in its proper place, "knowing what is enough." Yet a persistent irony of Japanese history since 1868 is that for all the emphasis on peace and harmony, they are exactly the virtues that Japan did not pursue. At the end of the nineteenth century, rather than settling back to enjoy its new prosperity, Japan embarked on a campaign to conquer and colonize its neighbors. By the 1930s, it had already acquired a tremendous empire in East Asia; this inability to stop led to its suicidal attack on the U.S. base at Pearl Harbor, as a result of which it lost everything. Something similar is happening again. Perhaps Japan values *Wa* so highly for the very reason that it has such a strong tendency toward imbalance and uncontrollable extremes.

Prewar history and Japan's present rush toward environmental and fiscal disaster indicate a fatal flaw in Japan's social structure. The emphasis on shared responsibility and obedience leads to a situation in which nobody is in charge, with the result that once it is set on a certain course, Japan will not stop. There is no pilot, nobody who can throw the engines into reverse once the ship of state is under way; and so it moves faster and faster until it crashes onto the rocks.

The rhythm is predictable. In studying traditional arts in Japan, one encounters the classic pattern of *jo, ha, kyu, zanshin,* which appears everywhere, from the wiping of the scoop in the tea ceremony to the dramatic finale of a Kabuki dance. *Jo* means "introduction," the initial start of a movement. *Ha* means "break"—when the movement breaks into medium speed. *Kyu* means "rush," the sprint at the end. These all lead to a full stop, known as *zanshin*, "leaving behind the heart," after which another cycle begins. A simple English translation of this sequence would be "slow, faster, fastest, stop." In the context of twentieth-century history, one might translate it as "slow, faster, fastest, crash." Japan never rests at *ha* but always continues to *kyu*, and nothing can stop it thereafter but catastrophe. *Zanshin.*

After recovering from its defeat in World War II, Japan set out to lead the world as a great industrial power. Pure poverty did not fit into this scenario; gigantic construction did. With industry and construction as the sole national goals, Japan turned on her own land, attacking the mountains and valleys with bulldozers, sweeping away old cities, filling in the harbors—essentially turning the nation into one large industrial battleship. Nobody can slow her as she steams full speed ahead toward a colossal shipwreck.

Another factor that prevents Japan from coming to its senses is the effect of the damage already done. Gavan McCormack has written, "The real and growing need is for imaginative projects designed to undo some of the damage to the environment: begin *de*-concreting the rivers and coast, demolishing some of the dams, restoring some of the rivers to their natural course." Such a process has in fact begun in the United States, but in Japan it is nearly inconceivable. Consciousness of environmental issues is so low and heedless development has already so damaged Japan's urban and rural settings that what it would take to repair them beggars the imagination. It's a self-fulfilling cycle: as the texture of city life and the natural environment deteriorates, there are fewer and fewer places in which people can enjoy the quiet, meditative lifestyle of "pure poverty," and fewer and fewer people who can appreciate what it ever meant.

A child brought up in Japan today may have a chance to travel to Shikoku's Tokushima Prefecture, but the closest he will come to enjoying its native culture is to see robots dancing in ASTY Tokushima's Yu-ing Hall. When he goes on family or school outings, bus tours will carry him not to famous waterfalls or lovely beaches but to see cement being poured at Atsui Dam. As Japan flattens its rivers and shoreline, and sheathes every surface with polished stone and steel, it is turning the nation into one huge artificial environment—a Starship *Enterprise*, though not nearly so benign. A Death Star. Aboard the Death Star, every megalomaniac sci-fi fantasy is a possibility.

At the deepest level we find ourselves face-to-face with what McCormack calls the "Promethean energy" of the Japanese people. With a thousand years of military culture behind them, a mighty energy propels the Japanese forward—to go forth, to do battle, to vanquish all obstacles. This is Japan's vaunted Bushido, the way of the warrior. During the centuries of seclusion before Japan opened up in 1868, this energy lay coiled within like a powerful spring. Once opened, Japan leaped forth upon the world with a voracious hunger to conquer and subdue—as Korea, China, and Southeast Asia learned in the 1930s and 1940s. And, despite the defeat of World War II, Japan has still not come to terms with its demon.

Economic analysts have seen the Bushido mentality in positive terms, as the motive force behind the long hours workers spend in overtime at their offices, taking few vacations, and devoting their lives to their companies. But Japan's unlimited energy to go forth and conquer is like a giant blowtorch—one has to be careful which direction the flame is pointing. In the past half century, Japan has turned the force of the flame upon its own mountains, valleys, and cities. McCormack writes:

> One of the more philosophically minded of Japan's postwar corporate leaders, Matsushita Konosuke of National/Panasonic, once advocated a 200-year national project for the

construction of a new island that would involve leveling 20 percent, or 75,000 square kilometers, of Japan's mountains and dumping them in the sea to create a fifth island about the size of Shikoku. He argued that only the containment and focusing of Japan's energies in some such gigantic project at home could create the sort of national unity and sense of purpose that formerly had come from war.

This is why Yokota had to build the Orochi Loop, Kyoto had to build the New Station, and Tokyo and Osaka have to fill in their bays. A demon escaped from the bottle in 1868, and it has yet to be tamed.

10 *Manga* and Massive

The Business of Monuments

Society is like sex in that no one knows what perversions it can develop once aesthetic considerations are allowed to dictate its choices.

—MARCEL PROUST

The building of monuments is now so important for Japan that it deserves to be studied as an independent sector of the economy. What follows is, I believe, the first step-by-step outline of the business and planning of monuments in either Japanese or English.

Government subsidies underpin it all. With construction so lucrative to bureaucrats and politicians in charge, building mania has overrun every part of Japan. Most of the "pork" goes to the countryside, since the Liberal Democratic Party, heavily dependent on the rural agricultural vote, has governed Japan with only slight interruptions for a half century, and it supports a policy of special rural subsidies, most of which are earmarked for construction. That is why the more remote the countryside, the greater the damage. A tiny mountain village like Iya Valley in Shikoku depends on construction for more than 90 percent of its income; government handouts for building dams, roads, and *kominkan* (community halls) are its very lifeblood.

In the case of halls and monuments, the Ministry of Home Affairs' Bonds for Overall Servicing of Regional Projects (*chisosai* bonds) channel much of the subsidies to local entities. Using *chisosai* bonds, towns can borrow up to 75 percent of the cost of their monuments from the government, which shoulders 30 to 50 percent of the interest. Subsidies also cover 15 percent of "ground preparation," including landfill and foundation work, which is often the most expensive part of construction.

In addition, Japan has a Monument Law. In the 1980s, Prime Minister Takeshita Noboru began with a onetime grant of ¥100 million to rural areas to use any way they wished. Had the money gone to "dogs"—planting trees, beautifying riverbanks—it might have led to real benefits, but it was intended for "demons," for striking monuments and attention-gathering events that are much more expensive. So with only ¥100 million, small towns could do nothing much. (Perhaps the biggest success story concerned the town of Tsuna, in Hyogo Prefecture, which used its money to buy a sixty-three-kilo gold nugget, and drew more than a million tourists to see it.) Takeshita followed up with a full-fledged law that provides subsidies to "specially targeted projects for building up old hometowns (*furusato zukuri*)," waiving interest on loans for "ground preparation" and facilitating *chisosai* bond issues. Even with subsidies, villages like Toyodama can hardly afford the expense of their mosques and museums, but with debt so easy and with bonds matched by government grants, provincial towns have not resisted; during the 1990s, small towns borrowed about a trillion yen for their monuments.

So the money is there (albeit on loan). The next step is to plan what sort of hall your town is to have, and planning a monument isn't easy. The architect Yamazaki Yasutaka, an expert in civic-hall construction, says, "They are not building these halls in order to vitalize culture. The aim is, through building halls, to vitalize the economy. To put it strongly, in the name of these halls, local governments are simply building whatever they want to build."

The journalist Nakazaki Takashi illustrates how a hall gets planned. When the village of Nagi in Okayama decided that it needed a monument, its first idea was a museum of calligraphy, but regional authorities pointed out that a monument is not a monument unless a famous architect designs it. So Nagi approached Isozaki Arata, and Isozaki told village officials that if they would allow him a free hand in designing a museum according to his own ideals, he would agree to do it. Flattered by the famous architect's attention and at a loss how to build a monument otherwise, Nagi agreed to Isozaki's terms. What the village got was a modern museum housing only three artworks, two by Isozaki's cronies and one by his wife, with a small token calligraphy gallery tacked on at the back. The three artworks (valued at ¥300 million) were included as part of the construction budget, but Isozaki never told the village the details of the fees the artists received; the total cost came to ¥1.6 billion, about three times the village's annual tax income. Takatori Satoshi, the director of the museum, said, "There was nobody in the village who could talk back. It could be that those who had some idea of what was going on were scared and didn't dare raise their hands."

The town of Shuto in Yamaguchi Prefecture (population 15,000) set out to build a community meeting place. The town fathers consulted with the construction-department head at the prefectural office, and in a scenario reminiscent of Nagi's, the department head called in his college buddy, the architect

Takeyama Sei, who proposed a concert hall. While this was far from the original purpose of a meeting place, and though Shuto villagers had little need for a concert hall, who were they to argue? The Shuto Cultural Hall (Pastora Hall) opened in 1994, a huge concrete block in the middle of rice paddies, with a rooftop performance space large enough to seat 1,500 people.

The next step after "planning" is "design." Commercial architecture accounts for most of the new buildings in Japan, which is of course true around the world, and in Japan these are designed largely by in-house designers working for giant construction firms and architectural agencies. These buildings share a common grayness, uniformity, and cheap commercialism. As for independent architects, their work generally falls into the two familiar styles: *manga* (comic-book fantasy) or massive (overwhelming office block).

The leader of the massive camp is Tange Kenzo, whose solid, single-piece constructions aim to impress with weight and majesty. This style dominated in the 1960s, when he designed the Olympic Stadium in Tokyo, and at first it featured traditional Japanese forms duplicated in concrete, such as pillar and post, or jutting roof beams. A turning point came in the 1970s, when Isozaki Arata insisted that it didn't matter if a building looked Japanese or Western. Japanese culture, he argued, had no core, so the architect was free to quote wittily from any tradition. This was the beginning of the *manga* style, with its emphasis on curious shapes and fantastic decorations. Architecture came to be seen as "contemporary art," as a form of sculpture.

The architects Ito Toyo, Shinohara Kazuo, and others took the next step when they invented the term *fuyu-sei*, "floating," to describe a type of building made of punched metal, colored plastic, and glass with a quality of temporariness and impermanence. This self-consciously trashy, cheap, shiny look caught on like wildfire, and it dominates mainstream architecture in Japan today, even inducing a "massive" builder like Hara to add *fuyu* touches to his New Kyoto Station.

During the high-growth decades of the 1960s and 1970s, two developments influenced architects in Japan. Kathryn Findlay, a British architect working in Tokyo, put it this way, "From the 1970s a number of Japanese architects felt that it was necessary to divorce architecture from society, economies, and city planning, and become a self-referential art." So in the first development Japanese architects considered that they should not be constrained by the buildings' environment. They felt no need to harmonize their buildings with cities, no requirement to site them vis-à-vis rivers or hills, and no need to take a backward glance at history. In a sense, Isozaki was perhaps right when he declared that Japanese culture had no core.

Of course, when architects sit down in front of their desks and start drawing, who knows what extraordinary visions may flow from their pens? Dreaming up castles in the air is part of what they are supposed to do. But in most modern contexts local history and the natural environment have tempered their dreams. In the 1930s, Le Corbusier drew up a plan for Paris that would have demolished the old urban center and replaced it with wide avenues fronted by rows of tall rectangular office blocks. He called this plan *Ville Radieuse*, "Radiant City." But Parisians dismissed Radiant City with horror, and today it is considered a byword for the misguided schemes of egotistical architects. The history of modern architecture in America is replete with the corpses of similar bizarre ideas.

A fierce argument rages between architects whose buildings are meant to stand alone as pure art, "object-oriented," and those whose structures meld into their surroundings "contextually." Mostly, city planners try to strike a balance between the two points of view.

In Japan, however, there is no "context," only "objects." Hasegawa Itsuko, the high priestess of the *fuyu* movement, has written: "At the opening [of an exhibition] we were shown a video of modern Japan. Scenes overflowing with people, cars, and consumer goods, scenes of chaotic cities and architecture, a confusion of media information, coexistence of traditional ceremonies and people's multi-faceted life of today—after seeing it once even I, who live amongst it, found myself completely exhausted." The logical direction out of this chaos is escape from the dreary and prosaic Japanese urban landscape. Any touch of variety, even something hideous, is a welcome release. Upon seeing the Hinomaru Driving School, a black building with a huge red globe emerging from it, Shuwa Tei, the president of a Tokyo architectural firm, said, "It's so ugly and unexpected it's endearing." Hasegawa sums it up: "Architecture that fits in with the city and leads people into various activities—through these alone we will not see liberated space. . . . We must aim at developing a liberated architectural scene worldwide, by conceptualizing architecture between time and space."

What this jargon means is that it is old-fashioned to design buildings that actually fulfill a useful purpose or improve people's lives, and it is more important to have buildings that are "liberated" from "time and space." An example of a liberated building would be Saishunkan Seiyaku Women's Dormitory in Kumamoto, designed by Sejima Kazuyo and commissioned by Isozaki Arata for a project known as Artpolis. This building from the early 1990s, intended to house young women employees of a pharmaceutical company, won the Japan Institute of Architecture's Newcomer's Prize. Judges praised it for its elegant modernism, which Sejima achieved by squeezing four women into each room of the living quarters and having a large common space; she based her concept on the Russian Supremacist view of housing. Design an uncomfortable, even miserable, apartment block of the sort you might find in Eastern Europe in the 1950s, and the Japan Institute of Architecture will award you a prize for elegant modernism.

Fuyu, "floating," could not be a better image for the rootless feeling of modern Japanese architecture. And designs abound for imaginary cities wholly unrelated to the real places where architects live. Recently, Isozaki curated an exhibition called "Mirage City—Another Utopia," featuring fantastical buildings to be located on the uninhabited island of Haishi, off Hong Kong. As Kathryn Findlay has said, "Mirage City sums up the attitude that architects here have: detachment and distance from the places where they build."

The second important development affecting architecture in Japan was the increase in money flowing to construction. On the crest of the monumentalist wave, Japanese architects had opportunities to design structures far more bizarre—and more numerous—than they could have imagined several decades earlier. Largesse from the construction industry funds glossy magazines and pamphlets advertising the work of Japanese architects to all the world.

Foreign designers find the wild and wacky fantasies of Japanese architects amusing, even enviable. What fun it must be to throw off the fetters and design as one might for a science-fiction set or a comic book! The international design community lionizes architects like Kurokawa and Isozaki. They have what architects everywhere desire but almost never have the luck to find: lots of money and total freedom.

The structures decorated with sheets or domes of perforated aluminum designed by Hasegawa Itsuko, Queen of Monuments, dot the landscape from the far north to the distant south. Her work, which epitomizes the *manga* school, also provides an opportunity to deploy the academic doublespeak used to glorify her aesthetic. The architect described her Nagoya World Design Expo Pavilion as follows:

> A distant view of this building emulates a misty landscape, with layers of perforated metal panels and see-through screens reflecting the atmospheric colors of the clouds and seas. The garden is reminiscent of the spiky rocks in Guilin, China or a group of chador-covered Muslim women. It is actually a rest area with custom-designed chairs made of perforated plywood and shaded by milky white fabric tents. Imaginary trees made with expanded metal sheets and FRP (Fiber Reinforced Plastic) change their appearance constantly by reflecting sunlight. A deformed geodesic dome "high mountain" is also clad with FRP and perforated metal sheets, and surrounded with a great sense of nature.

Let's think about this. Hasegawa's "great sense of nature" includes a "misty landscape" made of perforated metal sheeting, a "garden" of brightly painted plywood, and "trees" of aluminum and plastic cutouts borne on steel columns. Words cannot do justice to what this structure really looks like: a jumble of functionless, pseudo-tech decoration, with columns sprouting sheets of metal and plastic cut into squares and ovals. This is nature on the Death Star, not on earth. Pure *manga*.

And why not? What is the Nagoya World Design Expo Pavilion anyway but another monument with no inherent purpose? A clutter of sterile decoration is as good a design as any other, although what this has to do with nature is a mystery. Hasegawa's masterpiece is considered to be the Shonandai Cultural Center, built for the city of Fujisawa. It consists of a hodgepodge of huge spheres, littered with bits and pieces of glass and aluminum, with her trademark metal and plastic trees.

This she calls "architecture as a second nature." She goes on to say, "We thought that if we architecturally recreated a primal hill (which existed on the site before development) and established vestiges of nature hidden in the urbanity, then we could possibly find a new nature in the man-made environment." This, she believed, would help us move "from the 20th century history of exploitation to a more soft-edged symbiotic unity."

Let's return to our study of how to build a monument. Having achieved a "soft-edged symbiotic unity" in the design, the next step is to build, for construction is the whole point. The budgets sometimes make this comically clear: in an extreme case, the city of Ono in Kyushu had to fill its museum with replicas because no money had been set aside to buy art. The contractors, commonly chosen by closed bids, feed a percentage of the profits back to local politicians. Bureaucrats, architects, and laborers on the work crew all benefit.

Trouble arrives later, when the bills come due. Monuments are albatrosses for the cities and towns that commission them. Osaka has lost so much money on its waterfront projects that the prefecture has gone bankrupt and survives financially only by borrowing from the central government. The optimistic prognosis for the new Tokyo Bay projects is that expenditures will break even in 2034! Subsidies may cover construction, but they do not cover the management of monuments, as small towns have learned to their horror.

The operations headache goes back to the fact that most monuments do not satisfy any real need. In the case of Shuto's concert hall, the operating cost in the opening year was ¥30 million. This hall was one of Takeyama's greatest hits, combining architectural interest with high-tech acoustics, but since the village didn't need a concert hall it stands silent most of the year. The town of Chuzu (population 12,000) in Shiga is burdened with a combined cultural hall and health center (Sazanami Hall) dreamed up by the architect Kurokawa Kisho, which cost ¥2.2 billion to build and requires ¥44 million a year to manage. In order to maintain Sazanami Hall, the town had to cut its general expenditures from ¥20 million to ¥13 million—and this was only to cover operations, before it had to begin repaying its share of the construction budget (¥1.6 billion).

Tokyo has added the biggest behemoth to its extensive stable of white elephants. The Tokyo International Forum, beloved of world architectural critics for its curving glass walls following the train tracks near Tokyo Station and for its tall atrium, was completed for ¥165 billion in January 1997. It opened with a high occupancy rate, having rented out its meeting rooms to municipal agencies celebrating its completion. But within a few months occupancy had sunk to below 30 percent, with no hope for a revival in sight. Lovely though the atrium is, there was no need for it in the first place. Although it is labeled an "international forum," it is neither much of a forum nor international, though its upkeep is world-class: this elephant gobbles fodder to the tune of ¥4.6 billion a year. And the new Yokohama Stadium, constructed at a cost of ¥60 billion, has only one purpose—to host a few competitions in the Soccer World Cup planned for 2002. There is no long-term use in sight, and Yokohama expects maintenance fees to run into hundreds of millions of yen every year.

To make matters worse, all these halls and stadiums face fierce competition from one another. The commuting town of Sakae (population 25,000), an hour outside Tokyo, opened a multipurpose civic center in July 1995, with a hall that seats 1,500 people, welfare facilities, and a "community base" called

"*Fureai* [Get-in-touch] Plaza Sakae." Unfortunately for Sakae, the neighboring, even smaller towns of Inzai and Shiroi opened similar halls at the same time. Meanwhile, not far away, the cities of Matsudo, Sakura, and Narita all have big halls of their own. Sakae can't compete.

Small towns burdened with heavy operations fees turn again to mother's breast, the Construction Ministry, from which they can suckle more subsidies if they agree to build new monuments. The town of Igata is caught in such a cycle of dependency. Igata agreed to build three nuclear-power generating facilities in its environs in exchange for hefty grants (¥6.2 billion for the third plant alone). But the town used up all the money on multipurpose town halls and other facilities, so it approved expansion of the third plant in exchange for more subsidies. These did not suffice to return the village to financial health, for the cost of maintaining its empty monuments was so high that Igata exhausted the funds by 1995. Igata now has no choice but to accept another power station.

Managing monuments successfully is largely beyond the capacity of the bureaucrats who are in charge of them. In some cases, there is no choice but to give up the original purpose of the hall and recycle it. The town of Nakanita, in Miyagi Prefecture in Kyushu, led the way in the 1980s with its Bach Concert Hall, at the time the most high-tech concert hall in Japan, which today is used for karaoke contests and piano lessons.

The painter Allan West, who lives in Nezu, Bunkyo-ku Ward, in Tokyo, described his experience with a new center that opened in his neighborhood. The organizers intended to have an "international room" for crafts use by locals, so he stopped by to ask what their plans for the room were. They had no idea. He suggested that they install a printmaking press for public use, and gave them a catalog of presses. They weren't interested.

Yet they had taken the trouble to draw up regulations for the international room:

1. The room can be used only by groups of at least ten or eleven people.

2. At least seven of these people must live within a six-block area of Nezu.

3. They must pay ¥3,000 per person, per day.

4. They are not allowed to leave any materials at the hall.

5. A majority of a group's members must be present in order for them to use the room.

Allan then offered to buy and donate equipment for the room, but they turned him down. "It seemed like the building administration wanted to make their lives easier by making the facility impossible to use," Allan says.

Concerned about the low level of management know-how, the National Land Agency opened a course of study for people in charge of cultural halls in February 1995. According to Kogure Nobuo, the cultural-affairs director of the Local Autonomy Unified Center, participants come for one reason: "Their desperate problem is that they can't make ends meet."

One thing is clear: an entirely new service industry is in the making. Every year billions of dollars will flow nationwide to support tens of thousands of directors, curators, planners, office workers, and sales and custodial staffs. What is remarkable about this situation is that it runs counter to the official Japanese view that a service economy is not as viable, productive, or profitable as a manufacturing and construction economy. What, then, are we to make of the business of managing monuments, which employs so many people to provide for so little social need, creates no wealth, and relies almost entirely on public handouts for funding?

Grandiose slogans cover up this tawdry reality of Japanese cities and their monuments. Slogans have deep cultural roots—words, in ancient Shinto, are magic—and the ideals stated in words sometimes have a greater psychological truth than material reality. One can see this principle in action daily in the business or political world, where people will typically state the *tatemae* (official position) rather than the *honne* (real intent); nor is this seen as duplicitous. The *tatemae* may not reflect objective truth, but it describes the way things are supposed to be, and that is more important.

Also, in a military culture, slogans are the equivalent of shouts going into battle. Officials preface public activities in Japan with battle cries. In March 1997, the city of Kyoto published the results of its Fifth Kyoto 21 Forum, its title trumpeting, "An Avant-Garde City at the Turning Point of Civilization." That's the blood-stirring *tatemae*. The actuality is a blah industrial city that has temples on its outskirts lined with loudspeakers.

Every monument and new city plan has exciting slogans to go along with it. Take Okinawa, one of Japan's poorest regions. We hear that the Ministry of Posts and Telecommunications is going to develop an Okinawa Multimedia Zone aimed at creating an "info-communications hub for the entire Asia-Pacific region." Meanwhile, the Ministry of International Trade and Industry is planning something called Digital Island, and Okinawa officials are proposing the Cosmopolitan City Formation Concept.

Yokohama describes itself as "cultivating its image as a 24-hour international cultural city, a 21st-century information city, and an environmentally friendly, humanistic city rich in water, greenery and historical places." Alas, Yokohama, where trains and buses shut down after midnight, is not "24-hour"; nor is the city international (its old foreign community has largely disappeared); certainly it is not environmentally friendly or particularly cultural; and it is not especially rich in greenery or historic sites. The port does have a lot of water.

Imaginary towns like "Mirage City—Another Utopia" boast even more glamorous slogans than real cities. Mirage City, Isozaki tells us, is "an experimental model for the conceptualization and realization of a Utopian city for the 21st century—the age of informatics." It will feature "inter-activity, inter-communality, inter-textuality, inter-subjectivity, and inter-communicativity." In the slogan lexicon, "twenty-first century," "communication," "hub," "center," "cultural," "art," "environment," "cosmopolitan," "international," *joho hasshin* (broadcasting of information), *fureai* (get in touch), "community," "multipurpose," "Asia-Pacific," "intelligent," and words beginning with *inter-*, *info-*, or *techno-* and ending with *-utopia* (or variants: *-opia* and *-pia*) or *-polis* are favorites.

Slogans require a certain amount of care in handling, since their true intent is often far from their surface meaning. Take, for example, the term "symbiotic unity," *kyosei*, used by Hasegawa Itsuko to describe her metal-and-plastic trees. *Kyosei* literally means "living together," and it is a rallying cry for modern Japanese architecture, made famous by Kurokawa Kisho, who used it to justify proposals like the one for filling in Tokyo Bay by razing a mountain range. *Kyosei*, in other words, is exactly the opposite of "symbiotic unity with the environment."

There is a lesson here that has profound implications for the way foreign media report on Japan. It is all too easy to accept the slogans at face value and not question what is really going on. For example, the city of Nagoya made plans to wipe out

Fujimae, Japan's most important tidal wetland (after the loss of Isahaya), and use it as a dump site. Faced with local opposition, the Fujimae project is now on hold—although the future of the wetlands is far from secure. Yet Nagoya plans to host Expo 2005 based on the theme "Beyond Development: Rediscovering Nature's Wisdom." How many foreigners will attend Expo 2005, visit charmingly designed pavilions, listen to pious speeches about Japan's love of nature and about "rediscovering nature's wisdom," and never guess the devastation Nagoya plans for the wetlands right outside Expo 2005's gates?

In the case of modern Japanese architecture, foreign critics come as pilgrims to the holy sanctuary, abandoning critical faculties that they use quite sharply at home. Consider the following effusion by Herbert Muschamp, the architectural critic for *The New York Times*, on the Nagi Museum:

> Try to visit the Nagi Museum of Contemporary Art in the rain, when the drops form rippling circles within the square enclosure of a shallow pool and the steel wires that rise from the pool in gentle loops make it seem as if the drops have bounced off the surface back into the air, freezing into glistening silver arcs. Or go when it's sunny, go when it snows. Just go, or try to imagine yourself there. Though Nagi is barely a dot on the map, the museum is more startlingly original than any built by a major city in recent years.

The reader will recall that the Nagi Museum is the one that cost three times the village's annual budget, with only three artworks housed in three sections (in Muschamp's succinct description, "a cylinder and a crescent, both sheathed with corrugated metal, and a connecting rectangular solid of cast concrete"). Inside the cylinder, the artwork consists of a replica of the sand garden at Ryoanji Temple pasted onto the curving walls. "The museum, completed last year," Muschamp informs us, "is one element of a municipal program designed to strengthen the town's cultural life, partly in the hope of encouraging young people to remain in the town instead of migrating to the big city." If Muschamp really believes that three works of esoteric contemporary art housed in a tube, a crescent, and a block would keep young people from leaving this remote village, then he might also believe all the other slogans: that Kyoto is an avant-garde city at the turning point of civilization, that Okinawa is an info-communications hub for the entire Asia-Pacific region, and that the city of Nagoya is moving beyond development to rediscover nature's wisdom.

Observers sometimes find that what is most touching about the Orochi Loop is the naive faith of the people of Yokota in the wonders of "technology," and it brings a smile to city dwellers' lips when we think of how pleased the villagers have been with the Loop's big red-painted bridge, kept lit all night. But the same is true of the international art experts who write about modern Japanese design. What could be more quaint than architectural critics' unquestioning acceptance of weird monuments because they stand for that wonderful thing, "art"?

A friend of mine, William Gilkey, taught piano at Yenching University in Beijing at the time of the Communist takeover in 1949. He told me that when the propaganda and purges started, the professors and intellectuals were among the first to start mouthing slogans about "liberation of the proletariat" and about "sweeping away dissident elements." On the other hand, the common people of Beijing had better sense: greengrocers in the market simply ignored the political jargon for as long as they could without being arrested.

Likewise, the majority of the Japanese people aren't taken in by the slogans of monumentalism. They don't travel to visit either the Orochi Loop or the Nagi Museum. As we have seen, domestic travel is dwindling and international tourism is skyrocketing for the Japanese. They are not nearly so gullible as bureaucrats and art critics make them out to be. They know what a real museum is, and they know where to find it. According to gate receipts, the museum most frequently visited by the Japanese is not in Japan; it's the Louvre.

Unaware of the mechanisms of the Construction State that drive Japan to build monuments, and ignorant of the real history behind the founding of the Nagi Museum, Muschamp tells us, "It is peculiar, a century after artists rallied around the cause of art for art's sake, to find oneself in a museum created for art's sake. Strange because for what other sake should art museums exist?" If Muschamp only knew!

"A work of art?" wrote Mark Twain in his celebrated essay about James Fenimore Cooper's *The Deerslayer*.

> It has no invention; it has no order, system, sequence, or result; it has no life-likeness, no thrill, no stir, no seeming of reality; its characters are confusedly drawn, and by their acts and words they prove that they are not the sort of people the author claims that they are; its humor is pathetic; its pathos is funny; its conversations are—oh! indescribable; its love scenes odious; its English a crime against the language. Counting these out, what is left is Art. I think we must all admit that.

One could say much the same of the Nagi Museum, the Shonandai Cultural Center, the Toyodama Mosque, the New Kyoto Station, and of course the Orochi Loop. They have no order, system, sequence, or result; no reason for being except government subsidies to the construction industry. A highway loop smashing through a valley, a giant corrugated metal tube plopped in the middle of a scenic village, "new nature" in the form of a bulldozed hill lined with aluminum trees. What are these things, really? A sand garden pasted on walls—the humor is pathetic. Aluminum trees touted as "new nature"—the pathos is funny. Across the length and breadth of Japan, an encrustation of unneeded and unused public monuments tricked up as 1960s sci-fi fantasy—the waste of money is indescribable, the slogans are odious, and the academic jargon used to explain and justify it all a crime against the language.

Counting these out, what is left is Art. I think we must all admit that.

11 National Wealth
Debt, Public and Private

These days people borrow without the slightest thought, and from the very start they have no notion of ever settling their debts. Since in their own extravagance they borrowed the money just to squander it in the licensed quarters, there is no way for the money to generate enough new money to settle the loan. Consequently they bring hardship to their creditors and invent every manner of falsehood. . . . No matter what excuse some malevolent scheme of yours prompts you to invent, nothing can save you from the obligation of returning an item you have borrowed.
—IHARA SAIKAKU, *Some Final Words of Advice* (1689)

Gavan McCormack points out, "Japan is the world's greatest savings country, but it is also the world's most profligate dissipater of its people's savings." Despite five decades of continuous growth, making Japan the second-largest economy in the world, the nation is living beyond its means. After seeing the civil-engineering and monument frenzy sweeping Japan, we have a pretty good idea where the money is going. What remains to be seen is the results as they manifest themselves on the bottom line.

In 1990, a cartoon in a Japanese newspaper featured two couples, American and Japanese. The American man and wife, dressed in designer swimwear, were guzzling champagne as they sat in the whirlpool bath of their large, luxurious apartment. In the companion cartoon, a Japanese wife was hanging laundry out on a tiny veranda while her shirtsleeved husband read the newspaper in a cramped kitchen. Under the American couple the caption read "World's Largest Debtor Nation," and under the Japanese "World's Largest Creditor Nation."

Since then, the Americans have gone on living well, and the Japanese have gone on sacrificing, but by 1996 their country had become the world's largest debtor nation. Adding in so-called hidden debts buried in Ministry of Finance special accounts, Japan, with a national debt approaching 150 percent of GNP, has no relief in sight, as budgets, set by government ministries on automatic pilot, continue to climb. The Ministry of Finance's support for banks and industry through the manipulation of financial markets has had high costs. Interest rates of 1 percent or lower have dried up the pools of capital that make up the wealth of ordinary citizens: insurance companies, pension funds, the national health system, savings accounts, universities, and endowed foundations. The prognosis is for skyrocketing taxes and declining social services.

Besides the central government, local units across the nation, from heavily populated prefectures to tiny villages, are drowning in red ink. By 1998, thirty-one of Japan's forty-six prefectures were running deficits averaging 15 percent of their total budgets; six prefectures had reached the crisis level of 20 percent, at which point the central government had to step in and rescue them. Of these, Osaka Prefecture, reeling from a string of failed waterfront projects, is basically bankrupt, surviving on emergency cash infusions from the central government; its cumulative debt already topping ¥3.3 trillion, Osaka has been running annual losses of ¥200 billion per year since 1997. However, Osaka could still lose in the race to become the biggest prefectural bankruptcy, for the municipality of Tokyo also met disaster at the waterfront, and its shortfall for fiscal 2000 is three times larger than Osaka's, and growing.

Quantifying Japan's debt crisis is not easy, because its debts are so well disguised that nobody knows the exact figure. In a special pamphlet on the national debt, the *Yomiuri Shimbun* reported: "In addition to the general budget, there are 38 special accounts and the Zaito program, known as the 'second budget,' as well as debts of local governments. All of these are intertwined with one another, and have become a bloated monster." Here is one estimate: In 1999, revenue shortfalls for the official "first budget" came to ¥31 trillion, an astonishing 37.9 percent of expenditures. Measured as a percentage of national product, Japan's deficit came to 10 percent of GDP, jumping right off the scale when compared with the OECD average of 1.2 percent; the nearest competitor for big-deficit spending among advanced industrial nations was France, at 2.4 percent of GDP. Adding long-term bonds, by 1999 Japan's cumulative debt had risen to ¥395 trillion, amounting to 72 percent of GDP (the United States' gross federal debt, in contrast, comes to 64 percent of GDP). But this is not all. We need to take into account the shortfalls of municipal and prefectural governments, which come to ¥160 trillion. Add this to the national debt and the total jumps to ¥555 trillion, approximately 97 percent of GDP.

There is more. "Hidden debt" from the JNR Resolution Trust and Ministry of Finance budget manipulations; Zaito loans to bankrupt agencies such as the Forestry Agency, the Highway Public Corporation, and the Housing Public Agency; and additional trillions of yen in off-budget short-term "financing bills" brought the grand total to 118 percent of GDP, sur-passing even the notoriously spendthrift Italy, and making Japan the most heavily indebted of the twenty OECD nations. And that was 1999. By 2002, cumulative debt will have reached pos-sibly 150 percent of GDP. David L. Asher, of Oxford Univer-sity, claims that Japan's real debt could be as high as $11 trillion, or 250 percent of GDP, after Zaito loans and unfunded pension liabilities are added.

Bad as they are, these figures do not take into account dubi-ous reporting, such as the numbers game the Housing Public Agency plays with apartment sales, showing unsold units as sold in its official statistics. Turn over a stone among government agencies and strange things come crawling out. The Housing Public Agency's subsidiary, Japan Unified Housing Life (JUH), developed a large office tower in Shinjuku that opened in 1995. Given that this was a stagnant real-estate market, every-one was surprised to learn that the building was 95 percent leased—the tenants turned to be JUH itself and related compa-nies, which occupied the building at nearly four times market rents. Nobody knows the degree to which the cooked books of *tokushu hojin* and *koeki hojin* could drive up Japan's true in-debtedness.

Japan may have a high deficit but not to worry, economists ad-vise us, because the Japanese are such high savers that they have stored away in the banks more than enough money to pay their debt. Japan's high savings rate is the glory of its economy. For decades, American households consistently saved at only about one-third of the Japanese rate, leading the economist Daniel Burstein to label the two nations "grasshoppers and bees."

What the experts overlooked in the "Large GNP, Large Sav-ings" formula was that capital in Japan earns consistently low returns. For the past decade, Japanese government bonds have yielded between 0.2 and 3 percent, far below the United States' 5 to 8 percent. No feature of the Ministry of Finance's magic system charmed financial experts as much as this, for the sacrifice by the public for the good of the national economy seemed unbeatable. After the Bubble deflated, the Ministry of Finance, in an effort to prop up the stock market and the banks, lowered interest rates as far as they could go—the lowest levels in world banking since the early seventeenth century—which is to say, close to zero: in the latter half of the 1990s, interest rates on ordinary deposits earned their owners less than a quarter of 1 percent.

To get some idea of how such rates affect the lives of ordinary Japanese, consider the case of an average salaried employee. He retires with a lump-sum pension equal to about ¥20 million, half of which he will use to pay off his mortgage, leaving ¥10 million in the bank. At 0.25 percent, his deposit brings him about ¥25,000 in interest income; that's $200 a year. "It's not worth the effort of taking your money to a bank," says Senba Osamu of Daiwa Securities. "In a year, you'll have earned just enough interest to buy yourself lunch."

Large segments of the public have agreed with Senba, and banks report unprecedented use of safety-deposit boxes to store cash, while piggy-bank sales have risen at department stores. By 1996, the Seibu Ikebukuro Department Store stocked sixty-eight kinds of money boxes—for example, Paka Paka Kan, a container that clacks its lid when you pass, demanding to be fed ¥500,000 in 500-yen coins. A Seibu spokeswoman said, "There has been an increasing number of people who would rather use a piggy bank at home than a bank after interest rates declined with the end of the Bubble economy boom."

They knew much better uses for their money during the mercantile heyday of the seventeenth century, when Saikaku wrote his novels of city life in Kyoto and Osaka, lovingly counting out each *kamme* and *momme* (weights of gold and silver) that his protagonists made from lending at interest. A clever young man

> was able to loan out his one *kamme* at twelve percent annual interest, and by redepositing his earnings for thirty years, he found himself in possession of a tidy fortune of twenty-nine *kamme* nine hundred and fifty-nine *momme* eight *fun* four *rin* and one *mo*. He then withdrew the money from the bank, put it into a chest, and eventually managed to loan it out himself. Before long he had one thousand *kamme*. From then on he made money more and more rapidly until by the time he died he had accumulated the grand sum of seven thousand *kamme*, and his name was even entered into the social registry of the thirty-six richest men in the Capital. The way this man took one shingle and two one-*mon* coins from his father and turned them into a millionaire's fortune should serve as an example, just like a mirror, of what a merchant can do in this world.

That was a charming fairy tale of the past. Today, nobody can dream of retiring and living on interest in Japan. "I look at my bank account," says Ishigaki Hisashi, a retired auto engineer interviewed in *The New York Times*, "and you know, we get interest about twice a year—and I say, 'What on earth is this?' You can't say it's just interest, that it's just a small bit of money. We need it to live on. It's a matter of life and death."

Until recently, many economists saw the sacrifice made by Ishigaki as admirable because low returns for savers meant "free money for industry." The assumption was that an impoverished lifestyle for the people was somehow morally superior, and payouts to the public a waste of national resources. As we have seen, the idea derives from the poor people, strong state policy, a relic of military-style thinking that dates to the days of the samurai.

Oscar Wilde said that the mind of an antiquarian is similar to a junk shop in that "it is filled with dust and bric-a-brac, with everything priced above its proper value." Japan is just such a shop. When everything is priced above its proper value, it takes more money to accomplish less; in other words, capital has lower productivity. Low capital productivity has surprising results, and one of them is that the Japanese, saving for fifty years at far higher rates than the Americans, now find themselves with proportionately lower savings.

Simple mathematics shows that it takes a very short time for interest gains to equalize the totals achieved by a high savings rate. Assuming an interest differential of 10 percent, Americans saving a third of what the Japanese save end up, after about two decades, with exactly the same amount in the bank! Another ten years, and the Americans now have double the amount of the Japanese. While this calculation is very simplistic—the interest gap is narrower for savings accounts and wider for pension funds—one can see how it was possible for Americans to go on guzzling champagne in the Jacuzzi and still come out ahead. There is nothing strange about this. It's merely the principle of compounded interest, an iron law of capital, but one the Ministry of Finance overlooked.

While bureaucrats borrow against the future to build more monuments, something more serious is taking place behind the scenes, which threatens the system more than all the combined waste and losses to date. The national debt, Zaito, and *tokushu hojin* are mere lizards compared with the real Godzillas: massive underfunded insurance, health, pension, and welfare bills.

The problem arises from simple demographics: Japan is rapidly becoming the world's oldest country. With a birthrate that has fallen to 1.4 (the lowest in the world and possibly headed to 1.1 by 2007), the number of young people is shrinking, while the number of old people is burgeoning. In 1997, Japan surpassed Sweden in having the largest percentage of people aged over sixty-five among advanced economies—more than 17 percent. By 2020, this percentage will have soared to 25 percent. (By comparison, the numbers for the United States, China, and Korea will be 15 percent, 9 percent, and 10 percent, respectively.)

An aging population translates into trouble for Japan's pension funds and health-insurance plans, which must rely on a shrinking pond of productive workers to support an expanding lake of old and sick retirees. The figures point to an ever-increasing burden for the working population: in 1960, there were eleven younger workers supporting each retired person; in 1996, there were four; in 2025, there will be only two.

Nowhere is the problem so severe as the national health-insurance plan, where, on top of the demographic undertow, a tide of rising medical costs is dragging funds underwater. By 1999, 85 percent of Japan's 1,800 health-insurance societies had fallen into arrears, forcing them to take the radical step of halting payments for elderly policyholders because they simply could not afford to pay them.

In 1996, when the national health program reached the point where collapse was imminent, the Ministry of Health and Welfare began raising contributions and lowering benefits. Holders of employee health-insurance plans now pay 20 percent of their medical costs (versus 10 percent before), and health premiums have risen from 8.2 to 8.6 percent. In addition, the ministry is levying a ¥15 surcharge on each daily dosage of medicine, which translates into approximately a 30 percent tax on medicine.

Even this isn't enough to save the system. In raising premiums by a few tenths of a percentile, the Ministry of Health and Welfare has taken its first baby step. As one popular daily newspaper has observed, these measures amount to no more than "throwing water on a red-hot stone." During the coming decades, the share of the health bill that a salaried worker will have to bear is projected to rise to 2.5 times the present level. Even so, to fund the health costs forecast for the next decades, premiums will have to increase three times, to about 24 percent of salary by the year 2025.

An aging population is nobody's fault. If anything, it is the result of one of Japan's great modern successes—the lowering of the birthrate. In less extreme forms, an aging population is a fate that lies in store for all industrialized nations. Japan's real problem is its failure to plan for this inevitable fate. With a high GNP and a household savings rate of 13 to 14 percent (two and a half times the American rate), Japan has the wherewithal to amass pools of capital with which to support its aging population. Or so everyone believed.

Nothing comes for free—everything has its price, as the collapse of the Japanese insurance industry illustrates. Japanese households have turned to life insurance as a way of avoiding steep inheritance taxes, among the highest in the world. Indeed, the tax system essentially forces people to buy life insurance, which accounts for about 20 percent of household savings. And, as we have seen, MOF requires insurance companies to buy low-interest government bonds and invest in the stock market whenever the exchange begins to drop. After years of investing in stocks and bonds that produce no yield, insurance companies are showing zero, or even negative, returns.

Even this would not be so serious—just a case of running in place—but, in addition, life insurers are exposed to trillions of yen of bad loans extended during the Bubble. In the latter part of the 1990s, the eight biggest insurers wrote off trillions of yen in bad loans, but this is only a fraction of the real exposure, since *tobashi* techniques obscure most of the bad debt. The Ministry of Finance did its best to hide the damage (no insurance company had gone bankrupt since the war), but in April 1997, MOF could no longer cover for Nissan Mutual Life Insurance, which went belly-up with losses of ¥252 billion. Others followed. By October 2000, Chiyoda Mutual Life Insurance and Kyoei Life Insurance, Japan's eleventh and twelfth largest life insurers, had both collapsed, with combined liabilities of a whopping ¥7.4 trillion, in Japan's biggest corporate bankruptcies ever, with further bankruptcies and consolidations in sight. Reliable information about pension funds and insurance is sparse—so far, only a vague silhouette of the Godzillas looming over Japan in the coming twenty-five years is visible in the mist. At Nissan Mutual Life, for example, MOF knew that Nissan was bankrupt in 1995 but allowed the company to continue in business without publishing any report of its losses for two more years.

Extremely low interest rates have also heavily affected the nation's pension funds. In 1991, pension funds in the United States made a whopping 28 percent return on their investments; Japanese pension funds gained only 1 percent. By 1998, Japanese pension funds had made the lowest returns of pension funds worldwide, declining at a rate of *minus* 3.2 percent, while U.S. funds garnered 14.6 percent. The year before, the rate for the United States was a hefty 18 percent. Rates of return like these, compounded annually on immense pools of money, make a difference of literally trillions of dollars to public savings.

When Japan founded its national pension-fund system in 1952, planners set 6 percent as the minimum annual rate of return for employee savings plans. Pensions have not met this goal since 1991. One survey, in September 1996, showed that only 4 percent of corporate pension funds had sufficient reserves to make payments to pensioners, and since then the situation has deteriorated further. Dozens of pension funds are outright bankrupt, with assets worth less than the cumulative money paid in by participating workers. The number of pension funds in arrears has become such an embarrassment that the Labor Ministry lowered the minimum rate of return to 3 percent in 1995, and then to only 1 percent in 1997. Meanwhile, since 1998 a record number of companies have resigned from the national pension system—more than 800,000 companies simply don't pay premiums for their employees, even though they are legally required to do so.

As in the case of health insurance, the pension system cannot survive without lowering benefits and raising taxes. Pension premiums are rising rapidly, growing from 14.5 percent of salary in 1994 to 17.4 percent in 1997, and reports say they may even reach 30 percent by 2020. In addition, in 1994 the government raised the minimum age for beneficiaries from sixty to sixty-five. As many Japanese firms and government agencies mandate retirement at age fifty-five, this leaves workers with a ten-year gap after retirement before they can receive their pensions.

Private industry faces an exposure to unfunded pensions that could develop into one huge flat tire for Japan's manufacturing businesses; for some companies, the cost of funding pension shortfalls is approaching half of their net profits. According to a survey carried out at the end of 1999, 70 percent of Japanese companies did not have enough money set aside to cover their pension obligations. In fiscal 2000, MOF changed its accounting rules to better reflect pension liabilities (previously completely unreported), but the new rules left plenty of "cosmetic accounting" techniques in place to veil the true extent of the danger. Only a handful of large companies have divulged their pension shortfalls, but the numbers for the few that have are sobering: in spring 2000, Mitsubishi Electric announced that it owed ¥540 billion; Honda Motors and Toyota Motors were short ¥510 billion and ¥600 billion, respectively; Sony needed to make up ¥225 billion. While nobody knows the true number, the aggregate shortfall for companies on a national basis is estimated to reach tens or even hundreds of trillions of yen. Given corporate unwillingness to admit embarrassing facts and the worsening economic situation in the late 1990s, the true situation is probably much worse. To get a sense of scale, the World Monetary Fund estimated Japan's pension liabilities in 1997 at roughly 100 percent of GNP. As Jane Austen said, "An annuity is a very serious business." Life will not be easy for Japan's future pensioners.

A favorite mantra of economics experts is to say that Japan's debt is of less concern than that of other countries because it owes this debt mostly to its own people. While this is true, the fact remains that the Japanese people must repay the debt through taxes, and the burden will be crushing. By 2005, according to Gavan McCormack, government debt will run about "¥1,400 trillion, ¥11 million per head (say, two years' salary for an average worker). To repay such a sum with interest would call for a tax of ¥1.7 million per year every year for sixty years from every working citizen."

As McCormack points out, Japan can dispose of its debt in three possible ways: increase GNP (rapidly), tax, or inflate. An explosive growth in GNP is unlikely. So the next alternative is taxes, and over the next twenty-five years taxes could skyrocket to the point where they surpass notorious situations such as Sweden's. Withholdings that in 1997 took a bite of about 36 percent out of the average taxpayer's income are estimated to soar to more than 63 percent by the year 2020—and these tax increases do not take into account the burgeoning national debt.

The consumption (sales) tax rose from 3 to 5 percent in 1997—and there is strong pressure to raise it to 10 percent or more once the economy recovers. Indirect taxes, such as road tolls, surcharges such as the Ministry of Health and Welfare's tax on medicine, and a myriad of fees levied by other distressed agencies will also double and triple. Meanwhile, the level of services will decline, pension payouts will drop, and patients will be called upon to bear a larger share of medical costs. Add the rising consumption tax, and by 2025 the average Japanese citizen could end up paying up to 80 percent of his income to the government.

Obviously, this isn't going to happen—such high taxes would strain taxpayers to the breaking point. Hence it would seem that "printing money" (having the government buy bonds or deposit money in banks), thereby causing inflation, would be the obvious next step. But this, too, Taggart Murphy points out, may not work, since it would undermine the value of government bonds; at the same time, banks, grown cautious after the Bubble, might not turn around and lend the money to the public. We're back to the Mole Game: Cut down on government spending, and millions of people (including politicians) will be out of work. Raise taxes too high, and even the long-suffering Japanese public will rise up in anger. Print money, and government bonds lose their value. So what to do? Nobody knows.

All this comes of supporting an artificial regime so long that everyone's livelihood depends on it. So elaborate is this structure that to change any part of it threatens the whole; hence it is nearly impossible to make serious reforms. Facing a similar situation, Abraham Lincoln recounted the following story:

Two boys out in Illinois took a short cut across an orchard. When they were in the middle of the field they saw a vicious dog bounding toward them. One of the boys was sly enough to climb a tree, but the other ran around the tree, with the dog following. He kept running until, by making smaller circles than it was possible for his pursuer to make, he gained upon the dog sufficiently to grasp his tail. He held on to the tail with a desperate grip until nearly exhausted, when he called to the boy up the tree to come down and help.

"What for?" said the boy.

"I want you to help me let this dog go."

Some believe that the Japanese save according to "Confucian ethics." Others point to the fact that high land prices *force* people to save, since they have no alternative if they wish to own a home. In any case, Japan's stock of savings is not nearly as secure as it looks, for mice have gotten into the storehouse. Behind the scenes, personal and corporate debt is gnawing away at Japan's savings.

Surprisingly, and this runs contrary to the common wisdom about Japan, the Japanese people have an avid aptitude for debt. Credit-card use quadrupled from the mid-1980s to the mid-1990s. Of course, expanded use of credit cards is not what it seems on the surface, for the anti-consumer nature of credit in Japan means that most cards are highly restricted and do not provide much credit as we usually understand it: most people must pay their cards monthly in full. Even so, the public has developed its own form of *tobashi*, whereby borrowers withdraw money on one card to pay for another. "Buy now, pay later," with installment purchases and long-term lease arrangements, have led to the growth of giant leasing and consumer-credit companies. Installment buying is so popular in Japan that by the mid-1990s the Japanese were carrying more consumer debt per capita than Americans.

While the public pays for its debt with usurious interest

rates, industry has access to free money. Stocks and bonds pay negligible returns, and banks would never foreclose on businesses in their *keiretsu* grouping. In a world where banks hand out money for free, it would be easy to predict that companies might begin to pile up debt. That they did. Today (and for most of the postwar era), corporate debt in Japan has exceeded equity by an average of 4 to 1 (compared with 1.5 times to 1 in the United States). Allowing companies to leverage themselves far beyond what was considered safe in the West was one of Japan's most successful stratagems. It worked well in the high-growth era, but when exports reached a plateau and growth slowed in the 1990s, these companies found themselves saddled with huge surplus capacity. Suddenly they began to feel the heavy weight of debt on their shoulders.

Judging by history, one could even argue that the Japanese show a cultural bent toward wild, heedless borrowing. Perhaps it was a result of the traditional intense love of the moment. It is remarkable how many Kabuki and puppet-theater plays revolve around debt, or around the misuse of money entrusted to the hero or heroine. (In contrast, Chinese theater is obsessed with injustice and law courts—the misuse of power rather than the misuse of money.) One of the most famous moments in Japanese puppet theater is the scene known as *Fuingiri*, "Breaking Open the Seal," in the play *Meido no Hikyaku*. An Osaka shop clerk, Chubei, driven by his love for the courtesan Umekawa, breaks open the seal on a packet of gold coins consigned to him by his master. He knows the punishment will be death, but he can't stop himself. Debt owed by daimyo lords to moneylenders in Osaka brought down the Tokugawa Shogunate in 1868. Debt was the very key to Japan's pre-Bubble financial system, with its cycle of assets-debt-assets. And spiraling debt and misuse of funds intended for other purposes is the hallmark of the bureaucrats who run agencies such as the *tokushu hojin.* In the corporate sector, a giant millstone of debt hangs around the neck of Japanese industry. In short, the Japanese are anything but natural savers. On the other hand, who is? It is human nature to borrow—and here is where the bureaucrats guiding Japan's financial system made a mistake that has had serious consequences for society. They punished noncorporate borrowers with usurious interest rates.

In Japan, lenders can legally charge interest of 40 percent, the sort of rate for which Dante confined usurers to the third ring of the Seventh Circle of Hell. While corporations enjoy access to capital at near-zero interest rates, private individuals have no alternative but to turn to *sarakin,* "consumer loan companies," a nice name for loan sharks, who lend at official rates ranging from 30 to 40 percent, with actual rates sometimes reaching 100 percent. Failure to repay earns a visit from a crew of gangsters. The Ministry of Finance smiles on this system, because it believes such high rates dampen consumer borrowing. But despite MOF's best intentions, nothing will stop needy people from borrowing money. What consigning the consumer-loan business to gangsters did achieve was to drown millions of people in usurious debt. Saikaku remarks, "Of all the frightening things you can imagine, surely there is nothing as horrifying as having one's fortune ruined and being hounded by creditors. Nothing else even comes close."

Sarakin are the hopeless debtor's last resort, yet it is estimated that in the late 1990s borrowers from loan sharks amounted to 12 million people (one in eight adults). In fact, the only part of the Japanese banking system to grow appreciably during the 1990s was this one, with assets leaping 25 percent in some years. Of Japan's 12 million "deep debtors," 1.5 to 2 million are "heavy debtors" with no chance of repaying loans. Bankruptcy is not an alternative for most of them because it carries heavy social disapproval. Also, says Utsunomiya Kenji, Japan's leading bankruptcy attorney, "They haven't declared bankruptcy only because they don't know how." For most of them, however, the real reason for not declaring bankruptcy is the fear of gangsters. Just as the Yakuza (organized crime) plays a role in Japan's financial system at the high end, by fixing shareholder meetings so that nobody asks questions, it plays an even larger role at the lower end, as loan harvesters. No legal bankruptcy proceeding will prevent a group of burly crew-cut men from threatening your in-laws, pounding on your door at night, and calling you at your place of work twenty-five times a day. As a result, tens of thousands of people disappear each year in a process known as *yonige*, "Midnight Run." They discard their homes, change their identities, and move to another city, all to hide from the enforcers of Japan's consumer loans.

Traditionally, people must clear all debts by the end of the year, so New Year's Eve is the premier time for *yonige*. The 80,000 people who fled in the night in 1996 had nearly doubled by 1999, to 130,000, while estimated *sarakin* debts quadrupled, from about $45 billion to $200 billion. So popular is the Midnight Run that it has spawned a new business, *benriyasan* ("Mr. Convenient"), facilitators who help families flee their homes and who take care of their possessions while they are on the run. In 1999, Japanese television featured a new drama, *The Midnight Run Shop*, whose hero devises schemes for people to evade gangster loan enforcers. It's a *Mission: Impossible* for debtors, with each episode featuring a new clever escape: a disc jockey goes on the lam during a live show; a florist evaporates during a wedding.

Sarakin loans are not the only means by which Japan's financial system beggars the public. The nation has no lender-liability laws, leaving the public at the mercy of scam artists who prey on credulous old people and heavy debtors. Most notorious of the scams is so-called variable life insurance. In the late 1980s and early 1990s, banks and insurance companies colluded in selling these policies to homeowners, claiming that they would guard against high inheritance taxes. A homeowner would mortgage his house and invest the proceeds in an insurance policy but was not told the meaning of the word "variable"; namely, that payouts were not guaranteed. When investments made on their policies went south with the collapse of the Bubble, owners of variable insurance found that they owed more on their houses than their policies were worth.

Tazaki Aiko, age sixty-two, was a typical victim. The law prohibits banks from selling insurance, but they got around it as follows: In 1989, a salesman from Mitsubishi Bank began paying Tazaki visits, warning her about the high inheritance tax her family would face. Soon she received a call from someone at Meiji Life Insurance (one of the Mitsubishi *keiretsu* group of companies), offering her a variable insurance policy. Tazaki bought, and seven years later she faced eviction from her home.

Altogether, insurers issued 1.2 million such policies, leading to the public's loss of trillions of yen. In many cases, bankers and insurance-company salesmen were present together at the time the contract was signed. Victims have filed hundreds of lawsuits, and some of the plaintiffs have committed suicide. "Suicide is a tempting idea, because the longer you live the larger your debts grow. That is the nature of the insurance," says Oishi Satoru, the secretary for a plaintiffs' group. Yet to date, despite the damage done to the public, neither MOF nor the courts have punished a single bank or insurance official.

A system that favors gangster-ridden loan sharks as the established means of consumer credit, allows banks and insurance companies to practice financial scams with impunity, rewards savers with near-zero interest rates, and punishes debtors with interest rates of 40 percent and higher—it doesn't take an expert economist to predict what this will do to public savings over time.

Nor is the damage limited to individuals. When economists measure "public savings," they tend to concentrate on how much individual savers put in the banks, and overlook endowed trusts and charitable foundations. Japan's Ministry of Finance, intent on ensuring that labor and money go straight to manufacturing corporations, has discouraged charitable giving and volunteerism. Almost no tax deductions are allowed on charitable gifts, and severe hurdles have made establishing nonprofit foundations extremely difficult.

Yet trusts and foundations represent national wealth in a very real sense. In the United States, by 1998 there were more than 1.5 million nonprofit foundations with annual revenues of $621 billion, accounting for more than 6 percent of the GDP. Nonprofit organizations are so important that they make up their own sector of the economy, known as the "independent sector," which employs 10.2 million workers. Assets from these foundations are the fuel used to fire start-up companies and boost the capitalization of the stock market. The proceeds fund schools, hospitals, libraries, and myriad other institutions. The IRS grants about $12 billion in tax exemptions to foundations annually, and an additional $18 billion to individuals as charitable contributions—a total of $30 billion. That $30 billion makes up part of America's overall savings, even if it does not belong to individuals or companies.

In Japan, charitable giving is negligible. It stems from the lack of a philanthropic tradition, an undeveloped legal structure to regulate the work of nonprofit organizations, and tax disincentives. Only in 1998 did the government pass a law making civic groups eligible for nonprofit status, but the law provided no tax benefits either to the organizations themselves or to the people giving to them. For the foreseeable future, the lion's share of nonprofit endowment will continue to lie in *tokushu hojin* and *koeki hojin* established as *amakudari* nests for retired bureaucrats and feeding off government money. They are parasites on the national wealth, not contributors to it.

Canny fund managers in the United States have multiplied their funds' assets at fantastic rates. Yale University's assets rose from $3.9 billion in 1996 to $7.2 billion in 1998, while Harvard's rose from $9.1 to $13.3 billion during the same period, the two universities enjoying three-year returns on investments of 84.6 percent and 94.9 percent, respectively. Although these years were a bumper season for the stock market, and endowments do far less well in slow periods, foundation endowments grew tremendously during the 1990s. Meanwhile, Japan's foundations, their money invested in bank accounts earning no interest and in stocks making no yields, withered on the vine. By 1997, the assets of the twenty largest U.S. foundations came to twenty-two times the assets of Japan's twenty largest.

The difference between the United States and Japan is further underscored by the existence of something like the American Cancer Society, which in 1998 had more than two million volunteers, dispensed more than $100 million for research, and had assets of $1.1 billion. There is no private organization in Japan that functions on a scale remotely like this. By the beginning of the twenty-first century, total assets of American nonprofit groups could be estimated as approaching $2 trillion—a hoard of savings that Japan couldn't begin to match. And the difference lies not only in dollars in the bank but in a legal infrastructure and the expertise of millions of people in managing such funds.

It's difficult to compare university-endowment growths, since Japanese university endowments are one of the nation's great secrets—a textbook case of how hard it is to find accurate information in Japan. In the summer of 2000, an extensive

search of Web and newspaper databases and more than a dozen
e-mails to Web masters and college offices at Tokyo, Keio,
Waseda, and Doshisha universities drew a complete blank.
However, even without hard figures to go by, any visitor to a
Japanese college can see visible evidence—in substandard libraries and run-down facilities—of the beggaring of the universities as a result of low capital returns. In 1995, in the wake
of the subway poisonings by the fanatical religious group Aum
Shinrikyo, commentators marveled that Aum was able to re-
cruit elite scientists from leading universities, and its facilities
were much better. Trying to explain a piece of Aum machinery
before a television audience, a professor would say, "Well, the
one at my university is ten years old, and not nearly as sophisticated as Aum's, but you can get the idea."

One of the myths of the financial world is that the United
States is a model of laissez-faire capitalism and Japan is highly,
even overly regulated. Nothing could be further from the
truth. In the United States, regulations elaborated and enforced
by legions of busy lawyers hem in transactions on every side,
with rules punishing insider trading and mandating disclosure,
liability laws protecting investors, and myriad other devices
functioning to make the market more transparent and efficient
(and at the same time, of course, enriching the lawyers). It is
Japan that is unregulated. Where the Federal Reserve has between 7,000 and 8,000 banking inspectors, the Ministry of Finance had only 400 to 600, and, according to Richard Koo, a
senior economist at the Nomura Research Institute, "Of that,
only 200 are considered any good." Lack of financial supervision became such a scandal that the Diet removed this function
from the Ministry of Finance in the late 1990s, creating a new
Financial Supervisory Agency (to become the Financial Services Agency in January 2001). The new agency, however, has

only 310 inspectors, most of whom hail from its inept predecessors. The U.S. Securities and Exchange Commission employs 3,000 inspectors, versus about 200 in Tokyo and Osaka, whose work is mostly perfunctory. In Japan's financial world, gangster payoffs, insider trading, juggled books, defrauding of old people by insurance companies and banks, under-the-table payments to bureaucrats, usurious interest, special accounts for officials and politicians at securities houses—anything goes. It's wild and woolly out there.

In place of regulation, the Ministry of Finance has drawn rigid boundaries around Japan's financial world in an attempt to limit its range. Rather than clean the sharks out of the lagoon, the ministry chose a smaller lagoon. Circling round and round inside their little universe, MOF officials neglected to learn the new techniques of wealth creation that are redefining finance elsewhere in the world.

MOF is dragging its feet in legalizing derivatives, and the red tape for granting stock options to employees of start-up firms is so lengthy that so far only a handful of companies have applied for permits to do so. In any case, it takes an average of thirty years to list on the Tokyo Stock Exchange, so stock options are not much of an incentive. Pension-fund management, at the leading edge of financial sophistication outside Japan, is only in its most primitive stages, and MOF is still in a position to order managers to buy nonproductive stocks and low-yield government bonds. With rules of disclosure nearly nonexistent, investors lack confidence in listed firms and, as a result, the over-the-counter market languished.

To put it simply, Japan failed to develop mature financial markets—and the expertise that goes along with them. This means that money does not make money. Another way of putting it is that Japan has very low productivity of capital. It is one of the oddest paradoxes of modern Japan that in a nation seen worldwide as a paradigm of "capitalism," the bureaucrats in charge basically distrust money. This may result from the fact that in the early postwar years Japan's bureaucrats found *keiretsu* banks effective (and controllable), and in time the Ministry of Finance became addicted to a system. One might say that MOF's love of the system is far greater than its interest in financial health.

Japan's low capital productivity begs another comparison with ancient Sparta. Plutarch writes that Lycurgus, the founder of Sparta, ordained that Spartans must use iron money. Given that iron was of so little value and yet so heavy, the best people could do was lay up stocks of it in their closets. After a while, they ceased to have much interest in acquiring wealth and instead devoted themselves to military glory. Plutarch points out that "being iron, it was scarcely portable, neither, if they should take the means to export it, would it pass amongst the other Greeks, who ridiculed it. . . . For the rich had no advantage here over the poor, as their wealth and abundance had no road to come abroad by but were shut up at home doing nothing."

Japan has stored up a huge pile of savings, but the money is iron, shut up at home doing nothing, and the nation is paying the price, with the Tokyo Stock Exchange stagnant for a full decade, a crumbling welfare system, and securities firms that lack the expertise to compete abroad. In this there is a valuable lesson in what really constitutes culture and tradition. Entrenched Asian elites are very fond of appealing to hallowed "Asian values" as a means of clinging to power. MOF's distrust of the free use and flow of money would seem to have all the sanction of Japan's tradition of control by elite officials. On the other hand, it's important to realize that for all its bureaucratic background, Japan also has a freewheeling mercantile history. Distrust of the free flow of money is actually something new, an aspect of Japanese tradition that was relatively minor until after World War II.

When the U.S. Occupation confiscated the *zaibatsu* assets from their owner families, the bureaucracy as we now know it took control of the government. Salaried officials feared the robber-baron capitalists of prewar times and used every means in their power to rob them of the power of their money. That was how the present system got going. Today, the reason MOF fears the free flow of money boils down to a simple question of control. Money is power, and the ability to decide how money is used and invested is what keeps Japan's bureaucrats firmly in control. That said, the oddest part of the equation is the amazing disdain the bureaucracy shows for money. The figures for debt, bad loans, failed stock markets, and so forth are staggering enough to keep the leaders of most other countries lying awake at night in terror. Yet Japan's government agencies seem curiously unconcerned. Like spoiled society girls who grew up on ample trust funds, Japan's officials have never really had to learn what money is. When they needed it, there was always more from Daddy.

Edo townspeople knew better than to distrust and disdain money. The novelist Saikaku warned:

> Year after year the loss and senseless waste pile ever higher one atop the other: the blossoms of a merchant's flowering talents fall, his brocade robes are replaced by ones of paper, and finally, in the same way the seasons turn one to another, he is reduced to a faceless beggar. Consider all this and it should become apparent that for the merchant, in all his varied activities, there is simply no room for lack of heed.

Michael Phillips, an adviser to start-up companies in California, wrote a classic little volume in 1977 entitled *The Seven Laws of Money*. The Second Law was "Money has its own rules," which meant that no amount of goodwill or cleverness

˷ you beyond the simple laws of supply and demand, income and outgo, profit and loss, compound interest, and so forth. He writes: "The rules of money are probably Ben Franklin–type rules, such as never squander, don't be a spendthrift, be very careful, you have to account for what you're doing, you must keep track of it, and you can never ignore what happens to money." Yet for a while it became fashionable to believe in a mysterious new Japanese system that somehow transcended the Second Law. As Alan Blinder put it, "The amazing Japanese economy poses another challenge—one that has been barely noticed. I refer to Japan's challenge to received economic doctrine. Stated briefly and far too boldly, the Japanese have succeeded by doing everything wrong (according to standard economic theory). That should make economic theorists squirm."

The question of whether there really are "laws of money" is one of the most hotly debated topics among economists today. Karel van Wolferen warns against taking this view too far. He says:

That [there are laws of money] is what neoclassical economists, in other words, the vast majority of contemporary mainstream economists, are telling themselves and want everyone to believe. Keynes never thought so. And it fits in with American ideology, which is rarely recognized as an ideology. What Alan Blinder is referring to is perfectly accurate: Japan is definitely a challenge to received economic doctrine. Blinder once pointed out to me that the reason why this doctrine has become one, and why it is now rarely challenged, is because it had been made to fit the Anglo-American experience amazingly well. The reason why money does not have its own rules, like physics, is because there is an important political dimension to it. This notion is anathema to mainstream economists, which is why you get so much certainty where none is warranted.

There is no doubt that countries can structure the means of production and the use of capital in many different ways depending on their political structures, with "Russian communism," "Japanese capitalism," and "Anglo-American capitalism" being only three of numerous varieties. In that sense, van Wolferen is correct in reminding us that economics does not have ironclad laws of cause and effect, like physics. By Western standards, Japan's banks are almost all bankrupt—yet they continue to function. Many other aspects of Japan's unique form of credit-ordering also baffle outside economists—and, most remarkably, despite the Bubble and all the pain it has engendered, the whole system is basically still intact, ready for the next period of economic expansion.

However, the meltdown in Russia and a decade of doldrums in Japan suggest that while cultural factors can make some difference, certain underlying rules of money do exist and will in time assert themselves. The interesting lesson to be learned from Japan is that the effects of an economy's defying "laws of economics" will not necessarily show themselves as classical theorists would predict. Instead, they go underground, re-emerging in surprising forms elsewhere. At a bank in Tokyo, you can make 10 plus 10 equal 30 if you like—but somewhere far away, at a pension fund in Osaka, for example, it may be that 10 plus 10 will now equal only 15. Or even farther away, implications of this equation may require that a stretch of seashore in Hokkaido must be cemented over.

The Ministry of Finance did not get away with ignoring all the classical rules, for the bankruptcy of pension funds, insurance companies, and banks, the stagnant stock market, six years of zero-to-negative growth, and millions of people in debt to loan sharks are cold, hard facts that cannot be ignored. The argument over whether there are laws of money has to do partly with what sacrifices you are willing to take to maintain an "unscientific" system. Japan is willing to drive its national debt to stratospheric levels, flatten its mountains and rivers, and bleed its savers dry in order to support its system. So the system endures.

Back in the seventeenth century, when Saikaku penned his racy stories of townspeople in the cities of Osaka and Kyoto, shopkeepers knew differently. In Saikaku's world, people had to repay debts, money earned interest, quick-thinking businessmen prospered, while their competitors went bankrupt. Even staid Confucianists understood these things. In 1813, the Confucian scholar Kaiho Seiryo wrote: "Everything under heaven and earth is a commodity. And it is a law of nature that commodities produce new commodities. From paddies is produced rice, and from gold is produced interest, and there is no difference between them. For the forests to produce timber, the sea to produce salt and fish, and for gold and rice to produce interest is a law of the universe." Saikaku's sharp-witted shopkeepers and Confucian academicians alike would find today's so-called Japanese Model—where debts don't matter, money earns no interest, and no established company ever fails—absolutely incomprehensible.

This brings us to one of the most profound implications of the Bubble and Japan's financial troubles as the nation enters the twenty-first century: the source of these troubles does *not* lie in the economy or even in financial weakness per se. I'm definitely not predicting the collapse of Japan industrially—or even financially (although the strain is terrific). Neoclassical Western economists are very wrong if they believe that Japan is about to crumble. The entire system can continue for two reasons: strong resources, and what one could call "the sacrifice."

As for resources, Japan has piled up tremendous industrial capacity as well as savings in the bank—and these can support the status quo for years or possibly decades to come. "The sacrifice" refers to the fact that a nonclassical economic system can indeed be sustained, but, when the system strays very far from reality, at an ever-increasing sacrifice. The question is: What is a nation willing to sacrifice? In Japan's case, the answer is: everything.

The process of propping up the system that created Japan's Bubble wreaks untold havoc on society. These days the trend among the more penetrating writers, both Japanese and foreign, is to analyze Japan's financial problems in political terms. I, on the other hand, see them as part of a "cultural trauma." We are probably all talking about the same thing. Japan's financial system has fallen far, but it has a long way to go before real value asserts itself. In the meantime, the distortions of the financial markets will continue to manifest themselves as distortions in society and as depredations on the environment.

"There is a solid bottom everywhere," Thoreau writes. "We read that the traveler asked the boy if the swamp before him had a hard bottom. The boy replied that it had. But presently the traveler's horse sank in up to the girths, and he observed to the boy, 'I thought you said that this bog had a hard bottom.' 'So it has,' answered the latter, 'but you have not got half way to it yet.'"

12 Education
Following the Rules

In governing the people the sage empties their minds but fills
their bellies, weakens their wills but strengthens their bones.
He always keeps them innocent of knowledge and free from
desire, and ensures that the clever never dare to act.
—LAO-TZU, *Tao-te Ching*

The inability to slow down or turn back from disastrous policies has been Japan's core problem in the twentieth century, so
it is natural to wonder why. This brings us to education, which
shapes the way people ask questions of themselves and their environment. Neither Japan's system nor the lengths to which it
goes once it is set on autopilot are conceivable in a society in
which people ask many questions. Plutarch tells us, "King
Theopompus, when one said that Sparta held up so long because their kings could command so well, replied, 'Nay, rather
because the people know so well how to obey.'"

The fear of speaking one's mind in Japan dates to feudal days.
Closed to the outside world and ruled by a military class for
350 years, Japan developed far-reaching techniques of social
control. Sumptuary laws prescribed which woods the four

classes of society could use in their houses, the shapes of their gates and doorways, and the materials of the clothes they wore. Temples and shrines had to join sects registered with the shogunate, and nonorthodox faiths were outlawed. The feudal virtues of loyalty and self-sacrifice became popular and abiding themes in Kabuki and puppet theater: parents killed their own children to protect those of the lord; joint suicide was a favorite ending of love stories.

No country in the world could have been more fertile ground for totalitarianism. But control of the human mind is more difficult than it appears. The provinces boasted dialects and character of their own, to the extent that outlying fiefs were almost independent states. (The government did not succeed in bringing Shikoku's Iya Valley under control until 1920, when workers carved the first road through its canyons by hand.) In the cities, class divisions created the stuff of variety: pompous samurai, meditative monks, soft-mannered craftsmen, and unruly, sensuous townspeople. Nothing could be more colorful and chaotic than the "floating world" of old Edo.

With the opening of Japan in 1868, *Wakon Yosai* (Japanese spirit, Western technology) became the rallying cry of the Meiji Restoration, and in the case of education *Wakon Yosai* involved a marriage between the old feudal desire for total control (*Wakon*) and compulsory education, introduced from the West (*Yosai*). Standardized textbooks, uniforms, school rules, marching in lockstep around the school grounds, bowing in unison— these regimens were able to achieve what 350 years of isolation could not: a triumph over regionalism and individuality. It was probably Japan's single most serious modern maladaptation.

Yet the opening up of Japan initially sparked a great outpouring of creative energy, culminating in the so-called Taisho Renaissance. Taisho, strictly speaking, refers to Emperor Taisho's reign (1912–1926), but as a cultural term people use it to describe the years from about 1910 until 1930. This was the era when Okakura Kakuzo was writing *The Book of Tea*; when Kabuki, traditional dance, and martial arts were taking the shape we see now; and when rich industrialists built the art collections that today form the core of Japan's museums. Great writers such as Akutagawa Ryunosuke and Izumi Kyoka wrote some of the most fascinating and inventive literature in Japanese history. Kimono design, architecture, and music flourished, and a young democratic movement began to stir.

However, only a thin stratum of society breathed the liberating air of the Taisho Renaissance. The great mass of the people were studying in militarist fashion in the schools, with children lining up in rows in the schoolyard and shouting *"Banzai!"* By the 1930s, this generation came into power, sweeping away the fragile Taisho freedoms and instituting the *kenpeitai* (secret police), censorship, and the fanaticism that drove Japan to war.

With the loss of the war and removal of military control and censorship, it was commonly assumed that Japanese education had entered a glorious new era. And, indeed, much of the credit for Japan's remarkable rebirth after the war can be laid to its well-organized educational system. This system is second only to the nation's elite bureaucracy in its appeal to foreign experts, who have devoted many books and articles to the skills that Japanese children master—so many more, it seems, than Americans or Europeans. There is no doubt that Japan's educational system produces a dedicated workforce, and that these "corporate warriors" are the engine behind Japan's tremendous industrial strength. Obedience to authority, instilled in people from the time they are small children, makes Japanese society work very smoothly, with far less of the social turmoil and violent crime that have plagued other countries. All this is on the plus side of the balance. But there is a minus side, which, like so many other modern Japanese problems, has to do with once-good ideas carried too far.

Luckily for us, the psychiatrist Dr. Miyamoto Masao, formerly of the Ministry of Health and Welfare, has put Japan on the couch, and here he can function as our guide into modern Japanese education. According to Dr. Miyamoto, foreign experts have gone wrong when they accept the *tatemae* (officially stated position) fed to them by the authorities rather than the *honne* (real intent) of education as practiced in the schools. Facts memorized for exams are only a by-product, for the real purpose of education in Japan is not education but the habit of obedience to a group, or, as Dr. Miyamoto puts it more strongly, "castration":

> Driving through the English countryside, you see many sheep grazing on the hillside, which brings a feeling of peacefulness. This peacefulness is exactly what the bureaucrats want to obtain in Japanese society. But I want to emphasize that they want this peacefulness because their ideal image of the public is one where people are submissive and subservient. With such a group people are easy to control, and the system does not have to change. How do the bureaucrats manage to castrate the Japanese so effectively? The school system is the place where they conduct this process.

Lesson One is the importance of moving in unison. The British writer Peter Hadfield describes accompanying his daughter Joy on her first day to a Japanese kindergarten, which began, as many kindergartens do, with a roll call. After that came a class when all the students had to sit quietly while the teacher taught them how to fold pieces of paper. Only then did she allow the children to go outside:

They scattered outside in different directions, and Joy ran straight for the swings. But no sooner had the children started playing than a barrage of piano music came through a set of loudspeakers, and they all ran like soldiers on parade to the center of the playground. They then went through a series of aerobic exercises to the accompaniment of the music. In other words, they were getting all the exercise they had been getting on the swings and climbing frames, but together, and in response to a set of rules. Finally, the kids were allowed to run around—but not just anywhere. They ran around together, in a circle, in a counter-clockwise direction.

But not all of them. Consternation ensued when Joy started running in the clockwise direction:

> The teachers gently encouraged her to run the "right" way, and silently appealed to me for help. I was proud of my daughter for taking a stand, and proud of her for not just following the crowd. But in the end she has to be part of the system or she will suffer for it. "Turn around, Joy," I said in the end, coaxing her with my hand. "Go the same way as everyone else."

Lesson Two is to learn that it is a crime to be different. Dr. Miyamoto reports that when one of his friends put her child in kindergarten, the teacher advised her to bring steamed rice for her child's lunch. "Why?" the mother asked. The teacher answered, "If children bring fried rice or sandwiches, some other child may want to have that, and it is not a good idea for children to feel they want something different. If everyone brings steamed rice, then nobody is going to wish for something they cannot have."

The natural corollary of Lesson Two, unfortunately, is xenophobia. The idea that foreigners are aliens and should not be allowed to mix with the Japanese is an idea for which schools lay the groundwork very early. There are many examples of this, but I'll offer just one: In January 1996, the Iwakuni City Office banned children of U.S. military personnel from the city's nursery schools, because, it explained, the facilities were "getting full." Yet at that time only three American infants could be found in Iwakuni's sixteen schools.

After kindergarten, students enter Japan's compulsory-education system proper, where schooling takes on the military cast it will have until the end of high school. "Attention!" was the first word that my cousin Edan, age nine, learned in primary school in 1993 in Kameoka. At the beginning of each class, all students must stand up, hands at their sides, "at attention." Walking in unison, with announcements from loudspeakers, continues throughout the day, and as the children grow, new rules about dress and hair are added, and often uniforms are required.

Teachers assign children to a *kumi*, or "group," a unit the child will stay with until graduation. "Students of the same kumi usually play together during recess, study together during the long class time, and even eat together during lunchtime in their assigned seat, all within the four walls of the kumi for two years in a row," writes Benjamin Duke, the author of *The Japanese School: Lessons for Industrial America*. He continues:

> The kumi mentality obviously builds within its members a strong feeling of "we and them." Them, the outsiders, are just that, those outside the group. Japanese children often use a special phrase during play, *nakama hazure* [cut off from the group], to distinguish between those outside the group and those inside. *Nakama hazure* has the special feeling of not being part of the intimate group and, therefore, of being re-

jected by it. It is often used in a taunting manner. Few children want to be rejected by their peers. Most make maximum efforts to be accepted by the group and remain securely within it.

The *kumi* system is certainly a lesson for future workers in industrial Japan, perhaps the biggest lesson they ever learn. As the noted scholar Edwin Reischauer has written:

> Their emphasis is on the individuals' own groups—the "we" of the classroom, company, or nation as opposed to the "they" of all other groups. It is somewhat frightening to realize that in the uniformity of Japanese education all the children of a given age group are learning precisely the same lesson in much the same way on the same day throughout Japan, emerging with the same distinctive and often exclusive ideas about their own little groups or the large group of Japan. Broader world interests are given lip service, but in reality very little emphasis is given to the essential "we" group of humanity.

In grade school, subtle distrust of foreign people and things becomes a part of the curriculum. It's not intentional; the schools do not consciously set out to teach xenophobia. But so innocent are Japan's educationalists of the real issues of racism or ethnic bias that they end up teaching a condescending, if not fearful, attitude toward foreigners anyway. Textbooks depict foreign products as dangerous and Japan as the victim of international pressures. A typical lesson reads, "Chemicals prohibited in our country have been used on some of the food imported from foreign countries. It would be terrible if chemicals that harm humans would remain on the food." Many textbooks feature photos of angry American autoworkers bashing Japanese

cars, to impress upon children that the Japanese suffer fro
rational foreign hatreds.

Nevertheless, in view of their power in the international
economy, the Japanese learn that they must get along with
these difficult foreigners. "At first, because of differences in language and culture, work didn't go well," a character in a textbook states, referring to a Japanese factory abroad. "When we
tried to have morning assembly before work, or radio calis-
thenics [exercising in unison to recorded music], they said,
'Why do all of us have to do this?' When we tried to cut tardi-
ness and waste, they said, 'You're too strict.' " One little girl in a
textbook cartoon series concludes, "Working with foreign people is awfully difficult." The undercurrent: foreigners are lazy
and unable to understand our advanced Japanese ways—dealing
with them is a painful trial. Perhaps this is not the message that
was originally intended, but it is the message that comes across,
not only in this example but consistently in Japanese class-
rooms.

There is one more important lesson to be learned: schooling
in Japan involves a surprising amount of pain and suffering,
which teaches students to *gambare*, a word that means "to persevere" or "endure." On this subject Duke writes: "To survive,
the Japanese people have always had to *gambare*—persevere, endure—because life has never been, and is certainly not now,
easy nor comfortable for most Japanese." Definitely not. Even
when suffering is not naturally present, schools add it artificially. Elementary-school students must adapt their bodily
functions to the rules—or suffer. The city of Kyoto, for instance, did not provide toilet paper to elementary and junior-
high schools during most of the 1990s. Morihara Yoshihiro, a
member of the Kyoto Municipal Board of Education, said,
"Students should carry tissues with them, and if they use the
toilet in the morning at home, they won't have to do so at

school." Students may not change out of their winter uniforms
even if the weather is hot—everyone must sweat until the ap-
pointed day comes for the change into spring clothes.

Life in grade school is wild, heedless abandon compared
with what follows in junior high and high school. Hair codes
and uniforms become nearly universal, with everything prescribed, right down to the socks. Boys wear military-style uniforms with brass buttons, and girls wear a sort of sailor suit.
In 1996, Habikino City, near Osaka, introduced uniforms for
teachers as well.

The uniforms and dress codes are intended to enforce harmony. "In my mind," Dr. Miyamoto writes, "the concept of
harmony means an acceptance of differences, but when the
Japanese talk about harmony it means a denial of differences
and an embrace of sameness. Sameness in interpersonal relationships means a reflection of the other, the basic concept of
which derives from narcissism."

Punishment for dress- and hair-code infringements can be
severe. In one case, teachers stopped a student in Fukuoka Prefecture at the school gate and ordered him to go home after he
refused to get the regulation buzz haircut. Later, they allowed
him back, but he was separated from other students and made
to study by himself in an empty room—in solitary confinement. "Psychologically speaking hair symbolizes power," says
Dr. Miyamoto, "and at the same time it is an expression of one's
thoughts, emotions and conflicts. . . . As you may recognize,
through hair, the educational system demands that students
share the illusion that all Japanese are the same."

From hair and dress, the rules extend in the hundreds to
issues that go beyond the schoolyard. Many schools require
children to wear uniforms on weekends; others decree that students may not buy drinks from vending machines on their way
home from school. And often violence enforces these rules.

Corporal punishment is illegal, but this is often a case of *tatemae* rather than *honne*. For one thing, teacher violence carries no legal penalty. So widespread is teacher violence that at the trial of Miyamoto Akira, a teacher in Fukuoka who killed a girl by striking her on the head and shoulders, the line of defense was that the court should not single Miyamoto out because teachers everywhere commonly strike pupils. Pupils in the regular educational system fare better than those who are sent to special schools and seminars (boot camps, basically) whose purpose is to toughen them up. These schools are known for their shoutings, beatings, and physical privations; indeed, parents send their children to them expressly so that they will undergo such privations. The severe discipline at these schools often leads to injury, and sometimes to death.

While teachers sometimes resort to physical punishment, most of the violence in the schools is among the students themselves. The acceptance of violence against those who are weaker than you is a part of Japan's educational process, as it enforces group unity. Given the intense pressure to conform from kindergarten onward, Japanese students frequently turn to bullying, known as *ijime*. *Ijime* is a national problem, and it results in several much publicized suicides of schoolchildren every year. With a girl, it starts with being called *kusai* (smelly) or *baikin* (bacteria), and eventually takes the psychologically crushing form of not being talked to, or being shunned when she approaches. One girl interviewed by a reporter said that she thought what she had done wrong was to be outspoken—or perhaps she was too tall.

As the writer Sakamaki Sachiko has said, "An odd nuance of speech or appearance is enough to invite ostracism, and in a society where conformity is everything, no stigma weighs heavier than the curse of being different. Too fat or too short, too smart or too slow—all make inviting targets. Many Japanese children who have lived abroad deliberately perform poorly in, say, English classes so as not to stand out." With boys, *ijime* can result in severe hazing. In the case of Ito Hisashi, a thirteen-year-old in Joetsu, a city north of Tokyo, *ijime* began when his friends ignored him; later they stripped him naked in the school bathroom, doused him with water, and extorted money from him. His father found him swinging by the neck from a basketball hoop.

There is very little recourse against this kind of bullying, since in Japanese schools it is the one who is bullied who is considered to be at fault. While teachers take an official stand against *ijime*, they tend to encourage it indirectly, through their own emphasis on obedience to the group. In a nationwide conference of the Japan Teachers' Union in 1996, most teachers agreed: "It can't be helped that in severe cases of bullying the bullied student skips school for a while." But only 11 percent thought it was appropriate to suspend the bullies. Kodera Yasuko, the author of the best-selling book *How to Fight Against Bullying*, found that when she complained about her daughter's having been bullied, school authorities and the other parents dismissed the problem as hers, not theirs. Dr. Miyamoto says, "Bullying the weak is considered psychologically abnormal and a sign of immaturity in the West. But in Japan it's accepted."

Students who have studied abroad are obvious targets; so alien is their upbringing to that of their classmates that educationalists have created a new word for them: *kikokushijo*, "returnees." *Kikokushijo* attend special schools to reindoctrinate them into Japanese society. Foreigners are another matter. For decades, the Ministry of Education refused to accredit the special schools attended by many of the children of Japan's 680,000 resident Koreans; these schools teach the same subjects that are taught in other high schools, in the Japanese language, yet until 1999 the ministry pressured high schools and universities not to admit students who had graduated from them.

Far more effective than violence or overt Ministry of Education pressure in enforcing obedience and group identity are behavioral patterns of walking, talking, sitting, and standing in unity, which are instilled through drills and ceremonies, typically to the sound of broadcast music and announcements. These begin in kindergarten and continue in ever more elaborate form right through to graduation from high school. Many of the drills involve the repetition of stock phrases known as *aisatsu*, usually translated in English as "greetings," a ritualistic round of hellos, thank-yous, and apologies. These make up an important part of Japanese etiquette, and are one of Japan's attractive features in truth, smoothing the flow of social life and contrasting sharply with curt New York and rude Shanghai. At the same time, *aisatsu* are the ultimate tool in teaching conformity, for their reflexive use makes it unnecessary for students to think up original responses by themselves.

The effect of the violence administered by their peers and of the broadcast round of drills and rituals is to make Japanese students very good boys and girls indeed. Dr. Miyamoto compares Japanese schools with the château in the famous sadomasochistic novel *Story of O*. In the château, where O is locked up, she learns to become a good sex slave by following every little rule to avoid being whipped—and she learns to cherish the reward for good behavior, which is also a whipping. "O became a prisoner of the pleasure of masochism. . . . Now let's replace the château with Japan's conformist society, O, with a salaryman, and masochistic sex with work."

So far, I have dwelled on the ways in which schools teach children to behave and conform, not on the curriculum, and that is because obedience is largely what Japanese education is about. "In some sense it appears that Japanese schools are training students instead of teaching them," Ray and Cindelyn Eberts wrote. (Dr. Miyamoto goes so far as to call the Ministry of Education the "Ministry of Training.") Nevertheless, what of the curriculum that teaches so much mathematics and science—the envy of foreign educational experts?

It is true that Japanese children score consistently higher on mathematics tests than students in most other countries. However, they have only a middling rank in science, and even in math their scores drop as soon as tests diverge from application of cookie-cutter techniques and focus on questions that involve analysis or creative thought.

Literacy itself is a famed accomplishment of the Japanese educational system, and Japan's high percent of literacy is often compared with low numbers in Europe and the United States. But, according to recent studies, absolute illiteracy—the inability to read and write—accounts for 0.1 to 1.9 percent of the American population, and it is very nearly the same percentage in Japan. Experts have never properly defined "functional illiteracy," and researchers take it to mean all sorts of things, from the ability to read and write well enough to do a job to the ability to fill out an application form or understand a bus schedule. (If the test is how well a person understands forms and bus schedules, then I, for one, would definitely rank as a functional illiterate.) Based on such criteria, people have come up with figures for functional illiteracy in the United States that range from 23,000,000 to 60,000,000, or 40 percent of the population.

In Japan, on the other hand, functional illiteracy is not a concept. There is no way to know what the results would be if it were measured in ways similar to those used in the United States. One can only hazard a guess. For example, what is one to make of the fact that the favorite reading material of wage earners coming home on evening trains is not books or newspapers but *manga* comics? *Manga* now account for a huge share of Japanese publishing—as much as half of the magazine market. The point is not that Japanese schools fail to make their students literate—clearly, they do—but that they are not necessarily doing it better than schools in other countries.

To pass examinations in Japan, students must learn facts, facts that are not necessarily relevant to each other or useful in life. The emphasis is on rote memorization. The Ministry of Education reviews all textbooks and standardizes their contents so that pupils across the country, both in public and private schools, read the same books. Unfortunately, the "facts" are not necessarily the facts as the world sees them—especially the history of World War II. The 1970s and 1980s saw frequent protests from China and Korea, for example, when the ministry tried to insist that all textbooks describe Japan's "invasion of the continent" as an "advance into the continent." Officially approved texts teach that the facts of the Nanking Massacre are "under dispute"; recently, they finally mentioned "comfort women" (women who were forced to serve the Japanese army as prostitutes) but did not say what they did. There is no information about the infamous *kenpeitai* (secret police), who administered a reign of terror before the war, no description of Japan's colonial rule in Korea, and so forth. The authorities have effectively removed from students' education the period 1895–1945, a crucial half century in world history. Courts have ruled that the purpose of the ministry's textbook review is strictly to check facts, but it has become another unstoppable process that officials hold dear. In recent years, textbook review has gone beyond war issues to other matters: the ministry scratched a sixth-grade textbook because the onomatopoeic sounds that a poet used to describe a rushing river differed from the officially recognized sounds. Textbooks may not mention divorce, single-parent families, or late marriage. Or pizza.

The ministry commented, "Pizza is not a set menu for a family."

It is bad enough when bureaucrats in Tokyo start telling families what they may think about eating for dinner, but there is another, more serious problem: the facts taught in school are not the ones that university entrance exams test for! Students must therefore attend cram schools (*juku*) after school—two-thirds of all students aged twelve to fifteen attend *juku*, which accounts for between two and four hours each day. In addition, extracurricular activities like sports or music clubs function along the lines of paramilitary organizations, with a host of extra duties that exhaust both students and teachers.

This brings us to another vital and distinctive rule of Japanese education, which sets Japan apart from every other nation in the world (with the possible exception of North Korea). It is the principle of keeping a student busy every second. This successfully eliminates any time for independent interests and results in constant fatigue. "Children often tell me, 'I'm tired,' " says Kanno Jun of Waseda University. "They are busy with school, cram-school, and other activities—way beyond their natural limits." Sleep deprivation is a classic tool of military training, its use well documented in the prewar Japanese army. Being constantly exhausted and yet exerting oneself to *gambare* is one of the best lessons in masochism. One private poll of sixth-graders in Tokyo found that one in three students went to bed at midnight, at the earliest, because they were studying for *juku*.

One paradox of Japan's educational system is that *juku* is considered necessary: if the school system is as advanced and efficient as its proponents claim, this would not be the case. What are the real purposes of these institutions? One is obvious: to fill students' heads with more facts. A similar scenario in the

United States would have the majority of American high-school students studying for SAT tests and nothing besides this: they would go to cram school in the afternoon, memorize every word and fact ever asked on an SAT, and strictly avoid everything else. They would stay up until 1:00 a.m. every night memorizing these words and facts.

In the *juku*, students are learning another important lesson: the hard work, the sacrifice, the exhaustion, the resigning of one's interests and personality to the demands of impersonal rules—this is what *juku* really teach. The American Ray Eberts relates the following exchange with his friend Mr. Uchimura:

"If Japan's schools are so very good, why do you have to spend so much money for extra education?"

"The children do not learn what they need to know to pass the exams for university in public schools."

"Well, what are they doing in school, then?"

"They are learning to be Japanese."

The effect of rules, discomfort, violence both by teachers and by bullies, boring standardized textbooks, *juku*, paramilitary sports and music clubs, and sleep deprivation is just what one would expect: Japanese children hate school. They hate it so much that tens of thousands of students stay away from school for at least a month each year in a phenomenon known as *toko kyohi*, "refusal to attend school." A poll of fifth-graders showed that, out of six countries, children in Japan were the most dissatisfied with their homeroom teachers and the least likely to find school fun—and by a wide margin. Another poll found that only 21 percent of Japanese students said they were interested in their classes, versus 78.2 percent worldwide.

These numbers point to the fact that, under the surface, profound trouble is brewing in Japan's educational system. School in Japan is monochromatic: there's no room, or time, for a student to pour him- or herself into a personal hobby (as opposed to paramilitary club activities), or to read literature, do volunteer work, go to the zoo, get in touch with nature, or learn about other countries. The whole regimen makes sense only if one is determined to battle through "exam hell," go to college, and become an obedient blue-suited salaryman or even more obedient salaryman's wife. If not, there is no place for you. For the good boys and girls, all goes well. But what of the "bad" ones? In an era of relative wealth and leisure, when children do not feel threatened by poverty as their parents did, students who opt out of the salaryman route tend to opt out of education altogether. They reach a point where they simply snap under the pressure—the Japanese word is *kireru*—and from then on, the only thing that matters to them is the color of their hair or the speed of their motorbikes. The result is schoolrooms filled with rebellious, rude, even dangerous kids—the exact opposite of what the repressive educational program set out to create!

Karl Taro Greenfield, author of *Speed Tribes: Days and Nights with Japan's Next Generation*, describes his experience as an English teacher in a high school south of Tokyo, a low-level school whose students were not going to college or aiming at white-collar jobs. "These kids were friendly, jovial, and totally uninterested in learning English," Greenfield writes. "Most of them slept during class, others kept up a steady stream of jabber, and when I tried to quiet them, they simply walked out. This was the vaunted Japanese educational system? The condition I had stumbled upon, a sort of *kireru*—the nihilism that animates many left-behind Japanese kids—was broader than I realized."

If tattoos and pierced tongues meant a liberation of the spirit, then all this might bode well for Japan. But what we are seeing is not necessarily a flowering of individualism. The tattoos, the dyed hair, and the pierced tongues all follow more or less the same pattern; even the rebels remain very true to their group dynamics. These youth are unlikely to be the ones who rise above the Construction State and give thought to the environment, or decide to have an impact on local politics, become entrepreneurs and set up Internet companies, or break free of inhibitions and befriend foreigners. Rather, we are seeing an unpredictable nihilism, the birth of a new and truly dispossessed class. What effects this will have in the future on society can only be guessed.

One might think that the grueling training children undergo in their teens would continue at an even more strenuous level in college. But in fact the opposite happens. Once a student enters university, the pressure suddenly lets up. There is no need to study, because grading is lenient, and companies that hire college graduates pay little attention to grades. When a student starts his first job, no matter what he has learned at college he will have to begin training all over again in corporate orientation seminars. Since a university education matters so little for his future, the next four years spent on it are sheer play.

For those who go to college, that is, which is relatively few. The Japanese educational system does not entice students to aim for higher education, and less than a third do (versus almost two-thirds in the United States, a proportion that includes technical schools, however, while the Japanese figure does not). Gary DeCoker, a professor of education at Ohio Wesleyan, points out, "The big difference is that U.S. junior colleges lead to four-year colleges or to jobs, but in Japan they are mostly finishing schools for women."

And there is a wide disparity between education for men and women: the percentage of men going to college is 40.7 percent, versus 22.9 percent for women. This is a prime example of the ways in which the Japanese educational system perpetuates social backwardness. When the university in my town of Kameoka, Kyoto Gakuen Daigaku, tried to open a women's college in the 1980s, the Ministry of Education refused to allow it, since it considered that more women attending four-year colleges would create social disharmony because the women would seek jobs that major companies reserve for men. Through "administrative guidance," the ministry forced Kyoto Gakuen Daigaku to make the women's division a two-year vocational school.

The odd thing about Japanese higher education is that it seems so removed from the priorities of Japanese society. Graduate schools are poorly funded and organized and accomplish almost none of the important research and development work found in European and American universities. Only 6 percent of college graduates in Japan go on to graduate school (versus 15 percent in the United States) and, again, men outnumber women by two to one. Even the best colleges are run-down and dilapidated, with shabby, half-deserted laboratories, trash-littered grounds with uncut weeds, and poorly stocked and managed libraries. Mori Kenji, a professor at Tokyo Science University, observes, "Industries were in trouble [in the 1990s] and realized they needed basic science if they hoped to develop their own original technologies." So industry leaders paid a visit to Tokyo University, Japan's most elite institution. "They came to see what was going on and were shocked to discover that there had been few improvements since their student days."

Tokyo University (Todai), the very pinnacle of the elite, is an academic shambles by European or American standards. Todai graduates make few important contributions to world scholarship or technology; they go straight into government ministries, where they proceed to collect bribes, lend money to gangsters, falsify medical records, and cook up schemes to destroy rivers and seacoasts—with hardly a dissenting voice from their colleagues or professors. Few important schools in advanced countries can be said to have contributed so little of social value. As *Nihon Keizai Shimbun* puts it, the work of the elite schools is "to take the finished products of high schools and industry, pack labels on them and ship them out. They are like 'canning factories.' At the 'factories,' they are labeled 'XX Bank,' 'YY University,' but they only ship the same standardized product." Karel van Wolferen points out that Todai graduates have become the elite because of a selection process that rewards those with stamina in examinations, not necessarily those with superior talents. He writes: "There is no doubt that Todai graduates tend to be 'bright,' but many Japanese with capable minds of a different cast are discarded and doomed permanently to operate on the fringes. Much capacity for original thinking is wasted. The Japanese ruling class is far more thoroughly schooled than it is educated."

Edwin Reischauer comments, "The squandering of four years at the college level on poor teaching and very little study seems an incredible waste of time for a nation so passionately devoted to efficiency." What are we to make of this? The situation is doubly strange because the Japanese do not usually do things by half measures. The only possible answer is that Japanese society functions in such a way that the nation seems not to need universities. "By the time he reaches age 18, the Japanese child has become a perfect sheep," Dr. Miyamoto writes. "As sheep on the meadow are not concerned with freedom, to most university students in Japan, freedom as a concept is not important." In other words, by the time students arrive at college, the training process is already complete. Universities are superfluous.

Japanese universities are one giant *tatemae* erected to the idea of advanced education. In the bureaucratic state, where training as an adult begins in the company or ministry, there is no social need for them. The fact that serious learning takes place not in college but in industry goes far in explaining the lack of variety of new technologies developed in Japan. Without the wide-ranging and inventive research in universities that would lead to advanced knowledge of the environment and to new theoretical sciences, Japan's best minds devote themselves to one narrow band of human activity: skills in making, building, and marketing things.

Henry Adams once wrote, "Nothing in education is so astonishing as the amount of ignorance it accumulates in the form of inert facts." Their heads filled to overflowing with facts fed them by the Ministry of Education, Japanese students are surprisingly lacking in common knowledge. In February 1996, Azby Brown, an American teaching at a Japanese architectural college, noted these results of a study he had done: When he tested his architectural-design graduate students, he found they could not read hundred-page Japanese tracts, or summarize longer books. No one recognized the Guggenheim Museum, or knew in what century the Phoenix Pavilion, the famous Heian temple featured on ¥10 coins, was built. Only one student knew when World War II had taken place. They didn't know what Islam was and had never heard of Muhammad. One student thought Christianity started in A.D. 600.

Professor Duke is right in arguing that the Japanese educational system succeeds in producing a "loyal, literate, competent, and diligent worker," but he is wrong in believing that this success lies in how much Japanese students know. It is precisely the lack of independent knowledge that makes these workers so loyal, competent, and diligent. They have not been taught analytical thinking, the ability to ask unusual or creative questions, a sense of brotherhood with the rest of mankind, or curiosity about and love for the natural environment. The blame for modern Japan's environmental disaster falls squarely at the feet of the educational system, because it teaches people never to take personal responsibility for their surroundings. This leaves none but a few rebellious souls to notice or cry out when rivers and mountainsides are paved over.

Aware to some degree that the Japanese public suffers from this kind of ignorance, the Ministry of Education has dreamed up another "demon," the concept of *shogai gakushu,* or Lifelong Learning. The idea is that as the number of older retired people increases, the nation should give them the chance to study in their old age: English classes, tea ceremony, or other hobbies. Lifelong Learning suits the Construction State well, for it justifies the building of countless multipurpose Lifelong Learning Halls, but there is one little problem that lies in the word "lifelong." Take people who as children in school were discouraged from thinking for themselves. Deny them the time then and later, as working adults, to develop interests of their own: how can you expect them suddenly to acquire a taste for learning in their old age?

Nothing is more difficult to change than a policy that once worked and works no longer. Training people to be corporate drones succeeded in an era when manufacturing was the source of all wealth, and Japan could easily and cheaply import technology. But with a new age of services and information management dawning, and with software becoming a huge and costly industry, flexible and inventive minds are called for, yet flexible and inventive minds are exactly what the Japanese system tends to stamp out.

Mired in bureaucratic inertia, Japanese schools have been very slow to update the curriculum: in 1994, a Ministry of Education survey found that two-thirds of Japan's public-school teachers could not operate computers, and matters had improved only very slowly by the end of the decade. In late 1998, Japan ranked fifteenth in the world for Internet users per capita, falling far below the United States and some European nations, and lagging behind Hong Kong, Korea, and Singapore. It is one of the curious and unexpected twists of modern times that Japan, thought to be enamored of advanced science, has been so slow to embrace the new world of information technology—for most of the 1990s, it positively spurned it.

The reasons for this curious twist are many, including overpricing (Internet fees far higher than those in the United States or Hong Kong), overregulation, and fear on the part of conservative-minded leaders who foresee that the individualistic Internet threatens Japan's social cohesiveness. "It is true that multimedia will offer surprising advantages in some fields," an editorial in *Asahi Shimbun* said in October 1994. But it warned, "It is, however, still a wild card to our society as a whole. We should not be in a hurry."

And, indeed, Japan has not been in a hurry. The sluggish growth of its economy in the 1990s is ample proof of this. American entrepreneurs built huge businesses centered on information technology over recent decades: an Apple, a Microsoft, a Netscape, an Oracle, an Amazon.com—nothing like these developed in Japan. The two leading Japanese software developers, Ascii and Justsystem, are tiny in comparison with their American competitors, and both of them are bleeding red ink as Microsoft gobbles up the Japanese market. Justsystem's main product, a word-processing software called Ichitaro, maintained 80 percent of the domestic market until 1996, but by

1998 that percentage had fallen to 40 percent and was dropping rapidly.

Japan, however, must do what the rest of the world does, especially if it involves industry—and this means that sooner or later the Internet is coming to Japan. As the millennium turned, there were signs that Internet-based businesses had at last begun to prosper in Japan, with Yahoo! Japan stock rising to stratospheric heights and numerous government programs aiming to encourage entrepreneurs. But, for Japanese industry in general, change will not come easily, for workers fear to suggest new ideas lest the group ostracize them. The patterns of *ijime* extend deeply into corporate life. When Dr. Miyamoto angered his superiors at the Ministry of Health and Welfare, his boss ordered other employees not to speak to him, and even the tea girls not to deliver tea to his desk. Childish though these techniques may seem, for the average employee, taught from childhood never to offend the group, there is no psychological protection against them. How do you train people to become adventurous entrepreneurs when their education has taught them that this is precisely what they should not be?

This was brought home to me as I was editing this book in the spring of 2000, and found myself sitting in Tokyo's Keio Plaza Hotel coffee shop one day. Next to me was a young man interviewing another young man for a position in a start-up company, and I couldn't help eavesdropping. The earnest young interviewee, when asked to outline his strategy for a new start-up business, replied, "*Aisatsu*. It's vital for company morale that everyone say 'Good morning,' 'Good afternoon,' and so forth regularly and respectfully." It might seem charming that the young man thought this way, that there's a corner of the world where things like *aisatsu* still matter; on the other hand, while he's busy working on getting his *aisatsu* just right, the Internet whizzes of Hong Kong, Singapore, and Bangalore are going to leave him in the dust.

I saw the interviewer involuntarily move away, and I could see from his body language that this discussion was over. In spite of the pressures for conformity, there is a generation of adventurous young Japanese who are well aware of what will be needed to compete in the big wide world. The great question is whether there will be enough of them to make a difference.

As we have seen throughout this book, the Japanese people see the trouble their nation is in far better than foreign experts with emerald glasses firmly fixed on their noses. The public is disappointed with the educational system, and the press resounds with calls for reform. As Prime Minister Hashimoto said in his 1997 New Year's address, "The present education system just crams knowledge into children's heads. It values memorization too much. The system doesn't allow children to decide dreams, hopes and targets by themselves." In a report delivered to Prime Minister Obuchi in January 2000, a blue-chip commission headed by Hayao Kawai, the director general of the National Research Center for Japanese Studies, concluded that Japan's society is "ossified," and that adherence to rules and conformity have "leached Japan's vitality." The commission called for individuality and more support for risk-takers. Unfortunately for Japan, at the very moment when change is necessary, education—and society as a whole—appear to be headed toward more regimentation, not less.

13 After School

Flowers and Cinema

Tell me, gentle flowers, teardrops of the stars, standing in the garden, nodding your heads to the bees as they sing of the dews and the sunbeams, are you aware of the fearful doom that awaits you?

—OKAKURA KAKUZO, *The Book of Tea*

The question of how Japan's postwar educational system has affected its culture would make a book by itself. But certain trends are clear, as people's adult lives come to mimic the schoolyard, and can be summarized in a general way. Nakano Kiyotsugu has written:

Looking around modern Japan, I don't know why, but invisible rules have grown up everywhere. Lifestyle, human relations, clothing, deportment—each of these is enclosed in a framework. Just as the audience at a wedding stands up, sits down, and points their camera as directed by the MC, so people are bound up in rules. None of these rules is required by law, yet nobody dares disobey or they will be cast aside by the group. The younger they are the more people seem strongly attached to the rules, and they follow the others in their dress, possessions, hair styles, language, and topics of conversation. A foreigner would probably be surprised at the way they all seem to be dressed in uniform.

Magazines have observed that young wives with their children in Tokyo parks seem to form in cliques marked by similar clothes, hairstyles, and speech patterns—members of one, for example, will all have dyed hair. The groups even dress their toddlers in identical fashion. One woman, whom the others had initially shunned, later asked, "What did I do wrong?" It turned out to be the way she scolded her child—it wasn't the same way the other women scolded their children. The media call these groups Park Moms, as opposed to Park Gypsies, outcast mothers who are accepted by no group. A book published in 1996 entitled *Park Debut* counsels mothers on how to survive in the parks: "Newcomers should always take a low posture" and "Imitate the elder bosses."

Once admitted to a Park Mom circle, one can participate in its joint activities. The group keeps the women busy with parties, excursions, and *kairan-ban* (revolving registers), in which they take turns looking after and calling up the others. This is an exact repeat of the uniforms, rules, and nonstop busyness these women experienced as students. It also repeats the school hierarchy and the bullying. One Western observer notes, "Some of these women have imposed a rigid hierarchical system not so different from that of the Japanese political and business worlds. Senior mothers pull rank, signal who is acceptable and who is not, and decide what activities will be engaged in and when. Some even set a dress code."

And their husbands? They stay at the office until late at night, even if there is no work to do, and come home exhausted. Anyone who spends much time in Japan is struck by the obvious signs of sleep deprivation visible in the faces of the businessmen on trains and buses. The masochism these men learned so well at school has carried over into adult life.

When a woman complimented Whistler on his paintings of misty London bridges and remarked on how close they were to real life, Whistler replied, "Alas, madame, real life is catching up." Real life in Japan is catching up with its grade-school regimen. Trained since childhood to follow orders broadcast on loudspeakers, the Japanese today are addicted to public announcements. Japan suffers from a severe case of noise pollution. Hotel lobbies, department stores, and train stations reverberate with taped messages advising people not to forget things, to hand in their tickets, to be careful of this and beware of that, and to walk on the left.

Loudspeakers are fitted into every new escalator in public places, with tapes advising people on the most rudimentary behavior. The escalators at the Kyoto railroad station say, "When getting on the escalator please hold the belt and stay behind the yellow line. For those with children, please hold their hands and stand in the middle of the step. If you are wearing boots or thin shoes, they can get caught in the cracks, so please take extra care. It is dangerous to put your head or hands beyond the belt." There is an announcement at Narita Airport that reminds you to keep walking after getting off the escalator, and at the platform for trains to downtown Tokyo, a taped voice alerts passengers, "Your ticket is valid for the train and car shown on the ticket."

People have become so addicted to recorded *aisatsu* and commands that they feel lonely without them. Nowhere in modern Japan can one get away from a recorded voice thanking you for coming, giving you information, apologizing for an inconvenience, commanding or warning you—all this accompanied by a chorus of beeps, buzzes, chirps, and gongs.

The most common words you will hear are *kiken* (danger) and *abunai* (hazardous). Daily life in Japan is filled with peril— unless people follow the rules. A ride on any public conveyance—bus, train, or subway—is an endless round of *kiken*, followed by orders: Don't leave anything behind; stand back while the train pulls in; don't rush to get in; don't get your fingers caught in the door; stay in line. National parks, rock gardens in Kyoto, ski resorts, university campuses, temples, and shrines reverberate with recorded messages and sound effects. There is no escape. With the clamor at home on television, the ear-shattering fanfare of sounds at the pachinko parlor, and recorded voices, beeps, and gongs in all public spaces, the Japanese spend a major part of their waking lives in a sea of noise.

Useless announcements are not, of course, unique to Japan. In New York City, public-address systems in the subway urge commuters not to make trains late by holding the doors open; taxis broadcast recorded warnings, spoken by celebrities, to fasten your seat belt and not to forget your belongings when getting in or out—something that even Tokyo's cabs haven't got around to doing. Nevertheless, the noise pollution in the West and in Southeast Asian countries (so far) is mostly limited to public transit—one would rarely expect to hear loud announcements on every escalator, in gardens, parks, and churches. And repeated not once but endlessly. In Japan, it's a case of excess, of announcements carried far beyond a reasonable limit. And uncontrollable excess is the defining quality of Japan's modern cultural crisis.

In a famous haiku, Basho wrote, "Silence / Into the rocks seep the voices of cicada." Today, there would be no place for Basho to be alone with his thoughts, for seeping into the rocks would be an announcement from a chartered police-department Cessna overhead: "Let's remember to fasten our seat belts. When crossing the road, let's look left and right. This is Such-and-Such Police Department." The writer Fukuda Kiichiro points out that public agencies spend tax money to broadcast this sort of message because they have misunderstood the concept of "public service." Staffed with *amakudari* officials who have no idea how to benefit the public in any real way, agencies dream up these announcements so that "in the end it's a burlesque comedy put on by agencies such as the Transportation Safety Association as an alibi so they can say, 'Look! We're doing something!' " Another unstoppable tank of officialdom goes rumbling over the landscape. The same spirit of total dedication that has buried Japan's rivers takes over.

This, however, explains only the announcers, not the audience. The key question is why the Japanese public accepts and even craves all these commands and warnings. Fukuda writes:

> One could say that social control in Japan has come to invade the private realm to an extreme degree. Of course "control" does not take place if we have only people who want to control. It's a necessary condition to also have a majority of people who wish to be controlled. It's the same mechanism that sociologists call "voluntary subjugation." That is, people who wish to be controlled struggle to bring about control over themselves. It's related to the fact that children in high schools and students in universities never tire of having their teachers advise them what to do. Japanese college students are not adults who bear rights and responsibilities—they should all be called "children."

The operative word in the above paragraph is "children." Apart from the addiction to sound effects, the most remarkable aspect of Japan's public announcements is their sheer childishness. The level of nonsense in what Fukuda calls the Kindergarten State can strain credibility. Buses at Itami City urge riders to use soap. At Hayama, a beach south of Tokyo, a recorded voice tells bus passengers, "If you have come from a long way, please rest before entering the sea. If you are drowning, please shout for help."

The long and the short of it is that Japan's postwar educational system is turning the Japanese into children. That the air everywhere rings with warnings of "Danger!" "Hazardous!" cries out for psychological study—it certainly gives insight into people's timidity in stepping out of line. Commentators in Japan have discussed the problem of this infantilization at length; the social critic Fukuda Kazuya wrote a book entitled *Why Have the Japanese Become Such Infants?* The effects of infantilization on Japan's modern culture are far-reaching. As we have seen, *manga* comics now account for nearly half of Japan's publishing business. The old words that defined Japanese culture—such as *wabi* (rough natural materials) or *shibui* (subdued elegance)—have been replaced by a new concept: *kawaii* (cute). Japan is awash in a sea of cute comic froggies, kitties, doggies, and bunnies with big, round, babyish eyes.

The big eyes are a favorite with young girls—the determining audience for modern Japanese design. One magazine editor claims that "the limit on eye size comes when they get so big the shape of the face is distorted." You can hardly buy a household object—a bar of soap, a pencil, a blanket, a trash can, an electric fan, or a stereo set—without a big-eyed baby face printed somewhere on it. Gone are the days when the sleek Walkman defined Japanese industrial style. Today, while American and Taiwanese computer makers sweep the world with innovative and elegant designs, the main thrust in Japan is toasters in the shape of Hello Kitty.

The educational system has the effect, as Dr. Miyamoto has noted, of freezing children's emotional development at the level before they need to take adult responsibility for their lives; after decades of such a system, the end result is a massive national nostalgia for childhood. Comments Merry White, the author of *The Material Child: Coming of Age in Japan and America*, "We in the US are said to be a youth society, but what we really are is an adolescent society. That's what everyone wants to go back to. In Japan, it's childhood, mother, home that is yearned for, not the wildness of youth."

In this there is a sobering reminder for those who expect that the new Japanese youth are going to cast off the trammels and bring revolutionary change to their country. If wild hairdos and tattoos meant wild and liberated people, then perhaps there might be some hope. But wild is not what it's about; it's about becoming a baby again.

If one were to look for the chief influence of Japanese modern culture on the outside world, it would definitely be in toys, games, comics, and fashion for children. In the United States and Europe, Japanese products such as Hello Kitty and Pokémon have been huge hits, but they appeal abroad almost exclusively to boys younger than twelve and girls younger than fifteen. As they mature, adolescent boys turn from Pokémon to games created by Americans and British designers, such as Myst or Doom, girls set aside Hello Kitty and start reading *Seventeen* or *Elle*. The same is true of *anime* (animated films), very few of which appeal to adults as did Disney's *The Prince of Egypt*; most series, such as *Dragonball Z*, beloved of nine-year-old boys, and *Sailor Moon*, a favorite of ten-to-fourteen-year-old girls, appeal to preadolescents.

It's a very different story inside Japan. Cute creations like Pokémon are targeted largely at adults, and the manufacturers of cute are among the few Japanese companies whose domestic profits actually grew during the 1990s stagnation. Sanrio, the maker of the Hello Kitty line (now expanded to more than fifty cute characters), grosses more than $1 billion a

year through sales and licensing. Since the 1980s, animated
films have taken first and second position in domestic cinemas
almost every year, leaving films with real-life adult actors dead
at the box office. Today, about half of all domestic film revenues
come from *anime*.

The conquest of cute happened slowly, taking about thirty
years to sweep all before it. The first step was when cute toys of
the 1970s became cult objects for adult women in the 1980s;
the next step was when, as Japan sank into recession in the
1990s, young male wage earners developed a taste for big-eyed
cuddly creatures, and by the end of the century the conquest
was near-complete. In 1999, a stuffed doll called Tare Panda
with a round face, droopy eyes, and a soft body swept Japan,
selling $250 million worth that year alone; most of the buyers
were adult men. Takemono Katsunori, a thirty-four-year-old
company worker in Tokyo, enthused, "A mere glance at it
makes me melt."

Mary Roach powerfully evokes the extent to which cute has
conquered:

> To anyone who knows Japan . . . the pull of the cute is a
> powerful and omnipresent force. The Japanese are born into
> cute and raised with cute. They grow up to save money with
> cute (Miffy the bunny on Asahi Bank ATM cards), to pray
> with cute (Hello Kitty charm bags at Shinto shrines), to have
> sex with cute (prophylactics decorated with Monkichi the
> monkey, a condom stretched over his body, entreating,
> "Would you protect me?"). They see backhoes painted to
> look like giraffes and police kiosks fixed up like gingerbread
> houses. . . . Teenage boys tattoo themselves with Badtz-
> Maru, the Sanrio company's mischievous lumpy-headed
> penguin. Salarymen otherwise indistinguishable in their gray
> suits and cigarettes buy novelty cell phone straps adorned

with plastic charms of their favorite cute characters: Thunder Bunny, Cookie Monster, Doraemon the robot cat. Cute is everywhere. They're soaking in it.

Japan is indeed soaked in cute, to the extent that it is no longer merely an amusing sidelight—one could fairly call it the cultural mainstream, and its influence reaches everywhere, from cinema to traditional arts.

Ikebana flower arranging provides a good opportunity to see how Japan's new environment and educational system are influencing the traditional arts. At the March 1997 official ikebana showing of the Tokyo Branch of Ikenobo School, Japan's oldest and most prestigious, with a lineage that dates to the sixteenth century, it could be seen that about half of each arrangement consisted of plastic. Flower arrangers wrapped petals around glitter hearts; they stapled stems to wires and rods; they draped branches with fiberglass mist and hung them with cutouts made from sheets of blue and orange vinyl; they painted thorns with acrylics, and encrusted leaves with Christmas-tree icicles. A lifetime spent in an ugly city surrounded by a degraded countryside will have its effect. Nature, for Japan's new flower masters, is half vinyl, wire, rubber, and paint. The one thing one might say in defense of this is that it honestly reflects the environment.

Even more thought-provoking in this Ikenobo show was the technical level of the arrangements. Those stapled and cutout leaves, glitter hearts, and the rest were put together with the amateurish zest one might find in a fourth-grade classroom. Flowers glued with epoxy mingled with bits of metallic foil and tubes of pink jelly—these are the work of children, not of adults.

While we are on the subject of flowers, there is no better field than this to study Japan's new "manual approach" to the arts, an outgrowth of the educational mode of telling students exactly what to think and do about everything. Flower schools such as Ikenobo and Hara have taken to diagramming their arrangements. Branch A stands at an 87-degree angle to the ground; Branch B turns away at a 32-degree angle to the right; and Branch C leans at precisely 55 degrees to the left. The tips of the branches must end within a triangle, with sides of such-and-such length.

Foreigners, and even Japanese new to a study of traditional arts, may assume that this rigid diagrammatic approach is a part of the tradition. But the opposite is true. Ikebana was a meditative practice, heavily influenced by Zen, taxing to the utmost the artist's spontaneous skill and sensitive observation of nature. Trying to duplicate a geometric shape was definitely not the point. Ikenobo Senno, the founder of the Ikenobo School and the father of ikebana, in the famous preface to his seminal essay on flowers in 1542, went out of his way to stress that the aim of ikebana was not to enjoy a shape but to bring out the basic nature of a flowering branch or tree, thereby mystically pointing the way toward the secrets of the universe.

From this point of view, what we see in modern ikebana books is a denial of everything that ikebana once stood for. The same goes for the modern tea ceremony, which also has manuals demonstrating how to sit and stand at every instant of the ceremony, and where to lay the utensils—exactly so many centimeters from the edge of the tatami, no more, no less. All this has the look and feel of tradition, but it's definitely not tradition. The rules in these manuals are newly invented, written especially for adults who have graduated from Japan's postwar schoolrooms.

All of this is not to say that Japan's culture, modern or traditional, has become hopelessly childish. The great fashion designer Miyake Issey, the inspired flower arranger Kawase Toshiro, the architect Ando Tadao, and other fine contemporary artists have shown a profound understanding of Japanese tradition and combined this with a contemporary outlook. The world rightly admires these great artists, yet back home in Japan they do not represent the mainstream, and in private they despair at what they see going on around them. For every exquisite pleated Issey vest sold in Aoyama, youngsters in Harajuku are buying myriad *kawaii* garments with oversize socks, sailor suits fringed in lace, purses embellished with the smiling face of adorable three-year-old Chibi Maruko-chan, and shoes that squeak. In the time that Ando completes one pure abstract structure, Hasegawa Itsuko and her followers have raised dozens of *fuyu*-type monuments across the land, each a kindergarten-style concatenation of fiberglass, metal cutouts, and plywood. For every lady pleased by Kawase's simple arrangements of a few flower petals and branches, tens of thousands of Ikenobo followers labor on *manga*-esque creations of foil and vinyl. The future belongs to them.

Well, not completely. I had an interesting encounter at that ikebana show that illustrates in a nutshell the difference between how the Japanese and foreigners look at Japan's cultural crisis. As I was walking down the rows of flower arrangements, I came across a young American woman who was studying ikebana in Tokyo and her middle-aged Japanese lady friend whom she had brought along to see the show. "Isn't the Japanese love of nature wonderful?" the American woman commented to me. "I guess so," I replied. "But I see here some vinyl, here some fiberglass and leaves stapled to painted cardboard. Where's the nature?" The American ikebana practitioner grew angry. "Treating flowers this way is traditional!" she exclaimed.

The Japanese woman, who had not said a single word, joined in at this point. It turned out that she was not an ikebana practitioner herself; she had come along merely to see the art form that her foreign friend was so enthusiastic about. She had been walking around feeling vaguely uncomfortable, but in such a prestigious location and with her friend oohing and aahing, she had not felt confident in expressing her doubts. Hearing me, she relaxed and gave vent. "Yes!" she exclaimed. "These things are monstrous. This is environmental degradation, that's what it is!"

The American woman was typical of a phenomenon: the foreigner who converts to Japan, as one might convert to a religion. For her, announcing that flower arrangements of this type were "traditional" had all the weight of quoting the Bible. Tragically, she was unaware of how removed such arrangements really are from tradition; but she exemplified the many foreign writers, especially on culture, who continue to purvey modern Japanese arts to the world as unquestioning devotees. It's because of the existence of such converts that the real troubles in Japan's environment, design, architecture, and cinema have never been expressed in the foreign media. For foreign students of Japan, it has been a long and chronic case of the Emperor's New Clothes.

The Japanese woman, however, had a healthy and natural response; she didn't care about tradition: ugly was ugly. Or, at a deeper level, she instinctively understood what the tradition should have been, and could feel without knowing exactly why that these arrangements were all wrong. The Japanese are not so nostalgic about their own culture that they have become blind to its problems. And in this lies the hope for revitalization and change.

One of the most fascinating phenomena of the new Japan is the explosion of wacky youth fashion, which is hugely influencing young people all over East Asia, and drawing a lot of attention in the Western press. The "look" is by now familiar from many a magazine article: spiky dyed hair, face entirely smoothed in heavy makeup to a shiny copper or caramel complexion, shaved and painted eyebrows, and high clunky shoes—plus lots of cute Hello Kitty accessories. The impact on East Asia is, in a sense, a healthy one, in that Asians are finally discovering their own identities, and the new styles coming out of Japan are in many ways better suited to their local cultures. Terry McCarthy writes: "Despite the marketing muscle of American record companies and film studios, there is an inevitable cultural short-fall—Asians may watch the American shows, but the bronzed, buffed bodies of *Baywatch* are not something that most Asian teens could (or even would) aspire to." Nineteen-year-old fashion student Watanabe Eriko puts it succinctly: "It's stupid for the Japanese to compete with Western designers. . . . We should be selling our own Eastern styles to Asia, because Asians have the fashion sense and bodies to complement Japanese designs. Why must we go to Europe to dress tall blondes? Our aesthetic matches black hair and slimmer bodies better."

The question is whether the new fashion means a cultural renaissance is on its way, as many of its supporters believe, or whether it is just, well, fashion. Ever since World War II, one of the favorite themes of Western journalism about Japan is the New Youth, and regularly, about once every year or so, *Time* or *Newsweek* devotes special articles to this subject. The youth are going to change, they are going to overturn the old order, because they wear miniskirts, or because they sport nose rings and dye their hair. It's a natural inference to make, because in the West free sexual and fashion mores have traditionally been linked to free thinking, viz. Woodstock. However, in Japan the situation is different in that such freedoms have always been allowed so long as people toe the line with regard to their families, work, social hierarchies, and so on. In other words, sex and fashion are delinked from politics. This was true even in the seventeenth century, when Jesuit missionaries fresh from imperial Beijing, where most people dressed in drab blue or black, arrived in Japan to find a colorful "floating world" of brilliantly dyed silks, incredible towering hairstyles, and long flowing sleeves. Compared to that in China, life in Japan looked like wild abandon, and yet at the time Japan was one of the most tightly controlled societies on earth.

Ian Buruma quotes an essay by movie director Oshima Nagisa (known for the film *In the Realm of the Senses*) in which he describes a meeting with a conservative politician. The politician says mores have the power to change society, but the director thinks otherwise. "Here Oshima puts his finger on the sorest point of Japanese politics—'it is not, as the LDP Dietman said, that mores have more power to change society than politics; rather the forces unable to change society through politics shift to manners and mores.' " One could argue that the extreme fashions of the youth represent precisely that: a veiled protest against the established order. Whether it signifies real change in the society is still an open question.

In any case, the youth fashion does underscore the extreme groupism of the young in Japan. Seventeen-year-old girls set the trend. "It's not how much they spend," says Ogino Yoshiyuki, editor of a teen magazine, "it's that they all buy the same things. So if someone has a $10 product, they can sell lots of them." Tim Larimer writes: "If an item is hot, like pagers—they're called pocket bells in Japan—a manufacturer can get almost 100% market penetration and fast. 'If it is really powerful, it can take less than a week,' says Ogino. Once 5% of the teen girl population takes a liking to something, he says, 60% will join the bandwagon within a month. A few weeks later, everybody will be on board. The hard part is predicting what the famously fickle teenage girls will next anoint as *kawaii*."

There is no better mirror of a nation's life than its movies, and Japan's cinema perfectly reflects the nation's modern cultural malaise, for it is a tale of nearly unbroken decline over three decades. Once boasting masters such as Kurosawa Akira and Ozu Yasujiro, Japan has recently produced only a few films of moderate world success. The number of good films is so low that at the 1994 Kyoto International Film Festival the usual *Japan Film Today* program was replaced by a retrospective of older films—the most recent from 1964. "Japanese audiences see Japanese art films as introverted, gloomy, and sentimental, and Japanese entertainment films as trash," says Okuyama Kazuyoshi, a former vice president of Shochiku, Japan's largest film producer. "They've basically given up on them."

Japanese cinema's golden age, from the 1950s through the early 1970s, coincided with the period of highest economic growth. In 1960, 545 domestic films captured almost four-fifths of the market. Admissions reached a billion people at 7,457 theaters. Since then, however, the industry has shrunk astonishingly, losing as much in quantity as in quality. In 1993, a mere 238 domestic films caught less than a 40 percent share. In 1996, admissions were 120 million people at 1,828 theaters. In other words, the number of films dropped to half, theaters declined to one-fourth, and admissions collapsed to one-eighth of earlier totals. Of this drastically shriveled market, foreign films captured a 72.4 percent share in 1998. In the past forty years, Japanese film has so thoroughly lost its audience that it exists more as a symbolic industry than as a real one.

Today, Kurosawa's and Ozu's films from the 1950s and 1960s stand as enduring masterpieces, exerting an incalculable influence on American and European directors. But, unfortunately, cinema followed a pattern similar to what we have seen in other areas of Japanese life: in the early 1970s, trouble set in, and the wind mysteriously went out of the sails. Studios found a way to take it easy by producing remakes of such comedies as *Otoko wa tsurai yo*, known for its star, the lovable vagabond Tora-san—of which approximately two were produced every year since 1969. In 1996, *Otoko wa tsurai yo* was showing in its forty-eighth episode, but then Tora-san died and everyone thought the series would finally be laid to rest. By that time, profits from *Otoko wa tsurai yo* accounted, by some calculations, for more than half of Shochiku's annual movie income. Even though Tora-san's audiences had been dwindling every year, and the longtime star was dead, Shochiku couldn't stop. That year, it announced that a replacement had been found and the series would go on as before—albeit under a different name. Only with the collapse of Shochiku as a movie producer, which followed soon afterward, did the series finally come to an end.

In the late 1980s, there was a brief resurgence in Japanese cinema with the director Itami Juzo's off-beat comedies, notably the 1986 film *Tampopo*. Twelve years later, in 1997, Suo Masayuki's *Shall We Dance?* achieved some success in the United States, yet in between there were very few films that have been popular at home or abroad. Curiously, like the decline in the Japanese environment and the decay of its old cities, the collapse of Japanese cinema has gone nearly unnoticed abroad. In general, there is a persistent time lag in the world's perception of Japan. In the mid-1970s, American industry failed to perceive quality in Japanese cars, steel, and electronics, even though companies such as Honda and Sony had established themselves as powerful competitors since the early 1960s. Michael Crichton's 1992 novel *Rising Sun* (filmed in 1993) depicted an all-powerful Japan about to gobble up a defenseless America—by which time the Bubble was burst and Japan was headed into a decade of stagnation and retreat from world financial markets.

For manufacturers the gap was about ten years; for Crichton it was only three years; but for foreign filmgoers the gap stretches back decades. Nostalgia for a great aesthetic era has made time stop: After all, Kurosawa's and Ozu's great films, far from being "contemporary cinema," as they are usually portrayed, go back nearly half a century; they belong to the vintage of *The King and I* and *Lawrence of Arabia*. When it comes to more recent productions, what gets shown abroad is highly selective. Foreign art houses screen only the best of Japan's independent filmmakers, and this small but talented group saw a small renaissance in the 1990s. Beat Takeshi's *Hana-bi* and Imamura Shohei's *Unagi* received critical acclaim abroad, *Unagi* as co-winner of the Palme d'Or at Cannes in 1997 and *Hana-bi* as winner of the Golden Lion at the 1997 Venice Film Festival.

But independent art films do not a cinema industry make. While Japanophiles at international filmfests are enthusiastic about pictures the Japanese audiences have shunned—or never heard of—the domestic industry has continued its downward slide. A big percentage of movies produced in Japan today are porno flicks (as much as 50 percent in the early 1990s, somewhat lower today, since porno is moving to television, depriving filmmakers of even this market), and a high proportion of the rest are made for children. In the summer of 1998, the top domestic film was *Pokémon*, aimed at six-to-ten-year-old boys. It was the sixth-highest-grossing Japanese film ever, and in November 1999 a sequel grabbed the top of the charts in the United States, grossing $52 million in its first week—success like this among ten-year-olds blows adult art-house favorites like *Hana-bi*, *Unagi*, *Tampopo*, *Shall We Dance?*, and the rest right out of the water.

To give Japanese cinema its due, box-office success is a contentious issue among film lovers. Cinema critic Donald Richie comments, "World success is based on whether the pictures sell themselves or not. They are in the category of products— judged not by how good they are but by whether they sell. Since Japan's independent films are not intended for that, to judge them by this standard is a false equation. Every year there are a few good films that reflect Japanese realities, unlike the others that reflect no such thing, and a small but highly articulate audience goes to see those." This brings us to a core question: What constitutes "art" in film? An argument could be made that art lies in achieving creativity within the constraints of an art form: hence it's essential to a sonnet that it have fourteen lines, to a haiku that it have seventeen syllables. In the case of cinema, which was from its very inception a popular art, one of the necessary constraints would seem to be that it appeal to the public. From this point of view, winning the hearts and minds of viewers is not an ancillary issue; it's central. When a director creates a film that entertains and at the same time establishes his unique aesthetic viewpoint, he has created a work of cinematic art. Otherwise, his film is lacking a core ingredient.

Japanese film was not always unpopular. Kurosawa's *Seven Samurai* was one of the box-office successes of all time when it was released in 1956. This brings us back to "the image of a wilted peony in a bamboo vase, unable to draw water up her stem." Every year, according to Richie, out of about 250 films, there are 10 to 12 really good ones. But by and large the public avoids them. Obviously there should be room in cinematic culture for small experimental or independent films that appeal to a specialist audience. Nevertheless, a successful film industry requires that some films of quality make money. Japan is not unique in that it produces a number of good independent or experimental films every year—practically every country in the world does so, including America despite Hollywood, India despite Bollywood, and Hong Kong despite kung fu. One could say that Japan is lacking the interface between quality film and the marketplace. The quality is there, but the skills of presenting that quality to the public in an entertaining and appealing way are missing.

Commercial success is important for another reason, which is that for most film industries, even in the best of times, the more experimental films survive as a luxury: the existence of a large moviegoing audience means that there can be art houses that show offbeat films and small groups of dedicated fans who see them. A successful film industry can *afford* offbeat productions. Richie notes, "Nowadays an Ozu or a Kurosawa wouldn't be allowed to make films because the film studios couldn't get their money back." Thus a decline in the box office has eventually affected quality. Says Richie, "Thirty years ago, I was on a committee to choose the best Japanese films, and it was an embarrassment, there were so many of them. Now it's equally embarrassing because there are so few. With the failure of films to make money, producers tightened the moneybags. Only company hacks were allowed to produce films, because they followed the formulas."

How is it that the nation which gave the world Kurosawa is now producing *Pokémon* and not much more? It has partly to do with the "autopilot" syndrome we have met in other fields, a dependence on patterns set in the 1960s and never revised. Shochiku became so addicted to the *Otoko wa tsurai yo* series that it couldn't stop making these movies even when the star died—and its dependence on the income from the series was so severe that when the series finally ended, Shochiku itself died. Another reason—perhaps the most important one—was the abandonment of the adult market in favor of children. In the 1980s, "studios devoted themselves instead to churning out light entertainment for the mass teenage audience," the film critic Nagasaka Toshihisa says. As cinema expert Mark Schilling observes, "Mainstream Japanese cinema, which used to mean classics like Kurosawa's *Shichinin no Samurai* (*Seven Samurai*, 1954), and Ozu's *Tokyo Monogatari* (*Tokyo Story*, 1953), is now primarily entertainment for children on school holidays."

Godzilla is worth looking at because it epitomizes this history. The monster Godzilla debuted in 1954, and by the end of the

1990s, he had appeared in more than twenty films. In the West, *Godzilla* is something of a joke, synonymous with campy low-tech effects, but standards in Japan are now so low that critics polled at the prestigious bimonthly *Kinema Junpo* (*Cinema Journal*) voted it one of the twenty best Japanese films ever made. Each *Godzilla* film since 1989 has been among the top five money earners of the year for Toho, the company that produces them; *Godzilla vs. Destroyer* was the top-grossing movie of 1996.

It is not only in *Godzilla* and *Otoko wa tsurai yo* that old themes are repeated endlessly. *Ekimae* (*In Front of the Station*) had twenty-four installments from 1958 to 1969; *Shacho* (*Company President*) had forty remakes between 1956 and 1971. And there are numerous others, including the popular new comedy series *Tsuri Baka Nisshi* (*Idiot Fisherman Diary*), headed for its tenth installment. Repeats dominate the market: in 1996, thirteen of the top twenty films were installments in series. Hollywood is not averse to series, viz. *James Bond*, *Indiana Jones*, *Star Wars*, *Lethal Weapon*, and so forth, but generally speaking these are not cookie-cutter series but sequels based on a successful first movie, with very different stories, casts, directors, and actors. Formulaic series of the Japanese type flourished commonly before World War II: Westerns, Abbott and Costello, Laurel and Hardy, etc., and they exist today at the lower end of the movie market in the horror and high-school genres: *A Nightmare on Elm Street*, *Friday the 13th*, and so forth. But they are sideshows to the real business of Hollywood. Outside of Japan, producers learned long ago that cookie-cutter series, unless aimed at a niche market such as teenagers, soon lose their audiences.

In light of what we know about Japan's educational system, it should come as no surprise that cinema would devolve into this endless repetition of old formulas. In *Godzilla* we can also see the way in which insularity, another trait perpetuated by the school system, manifests itself in film. In 1962's *King Kong vs.*

Godzilla, Arikawa Sadamasu, the cinematographer, recounts, "director Ishiro Honda saw King Kong as a symbol of America, Godzilla as a symbol of Japan, and the fighting between the two monsters a representation of the conflict between the two countries." In one striking scene, Godzilla's burning breath sets fire to King Kong's chest hair. The theme continues in later films such as 1990's *Godzilla vs. King Ghidora*, in which Godzilla battles U.S. troops fighting the Japanese in 1944. Caucasians from the future then capture him and devastate modern Japan with a three-headed dragon—their aim being to force the country to buy foreign computers. Such is the level of "internationalization" in Japanese cinema: filmmakers cannot get beyond the idea that the Japanese are all alone, victims of foreign monsters.

There is one bright spot in this otherwise gloomy picture: *anime*. In contrast to the independent films, whose self-conscious artistic inventions do not attract a mass audience, *anime* have been top grossers for more than a decade. Innovative and visually striking, *anime* shared the lead box-office spots with foreign films for most of the 1990s. They tackle taboo subjects rarely seen in mainline film, such as war crimes and unethical business practices. *The Heisei Badger War* (1994) vividly depicted modern environmental destruction.

One could argue that independent films and the repetitive products of the Big Three filmmakers are both irrelevant to modern Japanese cinema. Porn and *anime* are overwhelmingly where the money and the audiences are. Japanese *anime* are the industry's most profitable export item. Those by the renowned producer Miyazaki Hayao (the director of 1997's hit *Princess Mononoke*, the highest-grossing Japanese film ever, and *The Heisei Badger War*) rise to a very sophisticated artistic level, yet unlike independent films, they are loved by the public—not only the Japanese public but young people worldwide.

Yet, as great as their success has been, even in *anime* we can
see the telltale marks of stagnation. For one thing, *anime* never
developed technically: while Japanese studios continued to
paint pictures on celluloid with skills little changed from the
1930s, Pixar and Disney were inventing brand-new digital
technology with dazzling visual effects that amazed the world
in *Toy Story*, *A Bug's Life*, and *Fantasia 2000*. Furthermore,
nothing can disguise the fact that in the end *anime* are essentially a children's medium. The really big hits, such as *Pokémon*
and *Sailor Moon* (a favorite of the early-teen girl set), have none
of the intellectual or aesthetic appeal of the famed works of
Miyazaki Hayao—they are simply cute screenplay for little kids,
and their very success underscores the vacuum at the adult end
of the spectrum. In his closing years, Kurosawa sighed in an interview, "There is no hope for Japanese film companies. They
have to be destroyed and rebuilt. . . . The people accept only
films they can understand, and what they can understand are
only films with cats and dogs in them, not the modern world."

Cinema provides a superb window into Japan's modern troubles, because all the patterns that afflict other aspects of national
life come together here. One is monopoly. Three large companies—Toho, Toei, and Shochiku—have controlled most of the
theaters and monopolized the business. They are shackled by
the same seniority system that rules the rest of corporate Japan,
with the result that producers prefer to work only in-house or
with established directors with whom they have long-standing
ties. In contrast to the frenzied telephone calling and "pitch-
ing" of new ideas that goes on in Hollywood, a deathly calm
rules in Japan's studio offices.

We can sense the dead hand of bureaucracy weighing upon
cinema: for decades, zoning rules made it hard to build theaters
in suburbs and newly grown "bed-towns." Cinemas did not

benefit any branch of officialdom—so they haven't been built. In contrast, pachinko is a huge source of income for the police, whose retired officers run pachinko associations. (The police also profit massively from prepaid pachinko cards through their ownership in the card finance companies.) Therefore every tiny village and hamlet must raise a pachinko parlor.

Monopoly bred boredom among the public, and this actually had some good results in that the Big Three ceased to rely on their own products and started to buy independent films and put their own logos on them. This has been one way that independents break through. The other way is to find motion picture houses that are unaffiliated, and quietly these are increasing. After 1996 the number of movie theaters began to grow, for the first time in half a century, as American-style multiplexes entered big-city suburbs. Most of these, however, have foreign backing, such as Warner Bros., so it remains to be seen what these new theaters will do for the domestic industry.

By the end of the century, the Big Three were quietly running out of money. The budgets of Japanese films ran to a few million dollars at most, a scale of magnitude smaller than Hollywood's. In 1997, Shochiku reached the point where annual receipts from its entire movie division totaled only ¥3.4 billion—approximately $30 million, which would hardly produce one modest Hollywood feature. By 2000, Shochiku had given up: it sold its famous studio complex at Ofuna, fired most of its production staff, and retired from filmmaking, keeping only its distribution licenses. The Big Three had become the Big Two. As funds dried up, technological advance in film simply ceased. There were few inventive minds to spur innovation and no money to pay for it.

In 1995, I helped prepare the English subtitles for a Shochiku film, and I visited the famous Nikkatsu studios where so many of Japan's postwar films have been produced. I felt

I'd stepped into a time tunnel: machinery decades old, camera-men standing on old orange crates to get height, piles of wires snaking over earthen floors, almost no computerization, no ad-vanced lighting techniques—all in an aluminum Quonset hut.

There are other problems besides lack of money and out-moded technology, notably the degraded environment. The cities and countryside are so changed that it is difficult to pro-duce a film with a beautiful backdrop, which Kurosawa com-plained about in his last days. When he directed the van Gogh episode in his *Dreams* (1990), he had to scour the entire coun-try to find a site with no modern buildings or electric pylons where he could reproduce a French cornfield. Most other directors don't have the time, the budgets, or the obsessive perfectionism of Kurosawa, so they make do with painted backdrops, close-ups of leaves and running water, well-manicured temple and shrine grounds—hence the stilted, arti-ficial quality of most recent Japanese films that take place in a natural setting.

While Japanese film was slowly sinking into quicksand, the rest of the world did not stand still. The contrast with the pop-ular success of Chinese filmmaking in recent years could not be more striking (although when we speak here of China, we are combining three very different societies: mainland China, Taiwan, and Hong Kong). Chinese films not only won awards from international juries but packed audiences into theaters worldwide. Ang Lee's 1993 *The Wedding Banquet* received an Oscar nomination and racked up global profits. Chen Kaige's *Farewell, My Concubine* took top prize at Cannes in 1994 and was named best foreign film in polls of Los Angeles and New York film critics.

In contrast to Japan's focus on the under-sixteen market, Chinese films appeal to adult audiences at three levels: high, middle, and low. There are the grand historical dramas by Chen

Kaige; the domestic comedies of Ang Lee; and action thrillers by Jackie Chan and John Woo. Chinese society, with all its injustices, offers rich ground for the cinematic imagination. Japan's controlled modern life seems to offer little room for either grand drama or action thrills. If there is any hope for Japanese film, it lies in comedy, as is evidenced by the fact that the two most internationally successful Japanese films of the past fifteen years, *Tampopo* and *Shall We Dance?*, were both comedies. When a director like Suo takes Japan's bland society for his springboard, as he did in *Shall We Dance?*, there are rich comic possibilities. Unfortunately, very few directors are able to make Suo's leap. As Nagasaka has written, "The same narrow, insular, and complacent attitude that explains Japan's response— or better, the absence of a response—to the gulf war can be seen in the repetitive and unadventurous products of this country's motion picture industry."

Finally, there is the problem of insularity. While Japanese directors went on making movies in the vein of self-pity and fear of foreign monsters, the Chinese walked right into the lair of the Hollywood beast and won him over. Ang Lee and Emma Thompson worked together on 1995's award-winning *Sense and Sensibility*. John Woo's *Broken Arrow*, starring John Travolta, and Jackie Chan's *Rumble in the Bronx* fought for the lead spot in U.S. box offices in March 1996, and since then Lee, Woo, and Chan have continued to produce hits. In 2000, John Woo swept America once more with *M:I-2*, the *Mission: Impossible* sequel. So many ambitious Chinese directors and actors have followed them that Hollywood now sports a mini–Hong Kong in its midst.

Chinese contemporary film is notable because it sought a new market abroad. Hong Kong directors moved to Hollywood because their own film industry declined. As for the mainland, most of the films by internationally renowned Chi-

nese directors have not been popular at home, and the ones
that had the potential to be were held back or repressed by
government censors. Chinese directors began, as Japanese independents did, with niche marketing, aiming their products at
foreign festivals. In the next stage, however, Chinese films
parted ways with Japanese. They moved out of the art houses
and became international hits.

By 2000, U.S. studios were producing movies by Tsui Hark
and Ang Lee in Hong Kong. "What makes Hong Kong cinema
successful is its energy and spirit, and I was mindful to harness
that," said Barbara Robinson, the manager of Columbia Pictures Film Production Asia. Meanwhile, Peter Chan, freshly returned to Hong Kong from directing *The Love Letter* for
Dreamworks SKG, announced in May 2000 that he was founding a company to produce Asian films for Asians—and that he
would begin by linking up with Thai and Korean directors.

As for Japan, there has never been a successful joint Western-
Japanese or Asian-Japanese film, or any highly regarded Japanese
film set in another country. There are no crossover directors or
producers; and since Toshiro Mifune in the 1960s and 1970s,
there has never been a major crossover actor from Japan, as
there have been from Hong Kong and China. In recent years,
Taiwan-born Kaneshiro Takeshi has made a name for himself in
the avant-garde films of Wong Kar-Wai, but he is no match for
the big international stars such as Chow Yun-Fat, Michelle
Yeoh, Jet Li, and Vivian Wu. Thomas McLain, a film-industry
lawyer in Los Angeles, sums it up: "The Japanese entertainment
industry is in the dark ages."

Education is a subject fraught with emotion, given that it is one
of the chief means whereby a nation maintains its cultural identity. Conservative politicians and the Ministry of Education
vigorously defend Japan's educational system for doing just that,

but the problem is: Which cultural identity is being preserved? As we have seen in the case of ikebana and the tea ceremony, much that masquerades as hallowed tradition today is in fact brand-new.

The uptight manual-bound tea masters of today bear very little resemblance to their playful forebears. Now a tea master has to consult a reference book to tell him which flower to place in the *tokonoma* alcove during the rainy season. But in early Edo, Kobori Enshu, when his guests entered the tearoom after an afternoon shower, simply took a bucket of water and splashed it in the *tokonoma*. Students of ikebana diligently calculating the exact angle of each flowering branch may think they are studying "tradition," but the angles and triangles come from another planet from the mystical world of Ikenobo Senno.

When Nakano Kiyotsugu confessed himself baffled at the new rules that seem to have sprung up in daily life, he was telling us that the rigidly conventional lifestyle of today is in fact something new. Nothing like the strict adherence to rules we see today ever existed in Japan before. For all the shoguns' attempts at control, the Edo period was a riot of variety and eccentricity. Saikaku and his freewheeling townsmen friends would find today's incessant announcement of *aisatsu* greetings, the rules telling everyone what to do at every moment, very much at odds with their experience.

Even at the height of mid-twentieth-century militaristic fanaticism, there was more room in Japan for characterful individuality than there is today, as one discovers when one meets older Japanese. People who were educated before the war (now in their seventies and eighties) seem to have kept more of their humanity than students of recent years. Among this older generation, one constantly meets cultured, questioning people, often with a sly sparkle in the eye and a wicked tongue. And, of course, in the confused years immediately after World War II, education was especially relaxed. This relative openness in education bore fruit in the 1960s and 1970s in a cultural rebirth similar to the Taisho Renaissance of the 1920s. In business, this was the era when upstart entrepreneurs at Honda and Sony created giant international corporations not linked to the large *keiretsu* groupings. In the cultural sphere, the cinema directors Kurosawa and Ozu, the fashion designer Miyake Issey, the writer Mishima Yukio, the architect Ando Tadao, the Kabuki actor Bando Tamasaburo—names that symbolize Japan's modern cultural achievement—all of whom were educated before the war or in the two decades after it, did their finest work.

The window of opportunity stayed open only for one generation, about twenty years. Behind the scenes, opposing forces were at work as the bureaucrats solidified their grip on power and the cement began to set on the teaching system. While artists flourished in the 1960s and 1970s, schools were training the next generation according to a detailed regimen more far-reaching than anything Japan, or the world, had ever seen. By 1980, these students had matured and the story of the Taisho Renaissance repeated itself. A gray curtain—or, rather, a colorful banner decorated with big-eyed baby faces—descended over Japan. Among the artists who dazzled the world so briefly, few have any successors who can hope to duplicate or transcend their achievements. From here on in, it's Hello Kitty, and ikebana flowers glued to tubes of pink jelly.

In the 1930s, the secret police stifled Japan's intellectual and artistic freedom with the help of truncheons and handcuffs. In the 1980s and 1990s, kindergarten teachers, armed only with loudspeaker systems, do the same work much more effectively.

14 Internationalization
Refugees and Expats

When the inside had become so solidly inside that all the
outside could be outside and the inside inside.
—GERTRUDE STEIN

On the day that Merit Janow and I had coffee on the terrace of
the Oriental Hotel back in 1996 and the idea for this book first
came to me, the thing that struck us most forcefully at the time
was the vibrant international life in Bangkok—the Germans,
Chinese, Japanese, Americans, and Thai intermingling in business and social life—and the lack of anything like this in Japan.
No country is as obsessed as Japan with the word *international*;
you will find it used as a name for everything from hotels to
taxis to soap, and you can hardly get through a single hour in
Japan without reading, hearing, or saying *international* at least
once. Yet few modern nations have erected such high barriers
against foreign people and ideas.

Japanese and foreign commentators take it as a commonplace
that with time Japan is becoming steadily more international.
But it could be said that Japan is headed in the opposite direction—back to a quiet form of isolation. The doors to real access

to Japan remain firmly closed to foreigners; meanwhile, young Japanese men and women with talent and an international mind-set are leaving their country. This emigration has been going on for a long time, but it picked up pace in the 1990s.

Indeed, escapees from Japan's rigid internal systems have been going abroad since the nineteenth century. Often, they are from disadvantaged backgrounds and have suffered disapproval from their families and from institutions in Japan. When they succeed abroad, they are lionized as heroes at home, after which they can return and engage in activities they could not have initiated within Japan. This is how it was with Fukuzawa Yukichi (1834–1901), the father of modern education, and with Ozawa Seiji in the 1960s, who moved to America after Japan's leading orchestra, sponsored by the national broadcasting company NHK, went on strike against him and refused to play. Ozawa Seiji is one of a number of prominent artists to base themselves abroad. Others include the musician Sakamoto Ryuichi, the composer of the score for the film *The Last Emperor*; Ishioka Eiko, who won an Academy Award for her costume design in Francis Ford Coppola's *Dracula*; and Senju Hiroshi, the painter whose *Waterfall* installation won a prize for the Japan Pavilion at the Venice Biennale in 1995. All of these artists live in New York.

The trend continues. Son Masayoshi, often called Japan's Bill Gates, was born the son of Korean immigrants, a minority group that suffers social ostracism, much of it officially sanctioned. "Being of Korean background, I thought as a child that things might be pretty hard," Son says. So while still in school he moved to the United States. By the time he went to the University of California at Berkeley, he was already a successful young entrepreneur; he made a million dollars in his early twenties when he sold a pocket-translator invention to the Sharp Corporation. "In the United States, people come from all over the world, all races, all backgrounds," Son says. "And they're all doing what they want, many scoring huge successes. When I saw that, I became more open. It freed my soul."

In the early 1980s, Son returned to Japan and founded Softbank, which in one decade grew into Japan's largest software distributor and publisher of computer-related magazines. Winning the right to use his Korean last name took longer (naturalized citizens cannot use their foreign names but must choose from a list of officially accepted Japanese names), but he achieved that feat in 1993, after an extended struggle with the immigration authorities. Today, Son is the golden boy of Japanese information technology and is frequently in the news as he buys up software and information businesses around the world.

While the phenomenon of escapees from Japan is an old one, there is a significant difference between the situation in the late Edo-Meiji period and conditions today. Japan at the turn of the century was a poor, backward nation struggling to throw off centuries of feudal stagnation. It was not free politically, and few Japanese spoke a foreign language or had much experience of the outside world. For educated people, the only way to acquire necessary skills was by going abroad, and it was only natural for farmers and manual laborers to try to escape poverty by immigrating to Hawaii or Brazil.

But Japan is now a free democracy, has few overt controls over the media, and is famed for its high technology. All Japanese study English as children in grade school, and tens of millions of them have traveled abroad. In addition, Japan is rich. It is a situation verging on the incredible that modern Japanese would lack access to up-to-date information or business opportunities within Japan. And yet the flow of refugees continues.

It begins with doctors. The National Institutes of Health (NIH) in Bethesda, Maryland, have more than 350 Japanese doctors in

residence at any one time. Each doctor represents the department of a certain hospital in Japan, and when his three-year
term is over, his department sends a replacement, a system that
has gone on for decades. The reason is that basic research in
Japan is understaffed, weakened by bureaucratic inertia, and
limited by a lack of freely shared and reliable data.

Not all of these doctors return to Japan. Many of the brightest and most innovative remain in the United States. Dr.
Kakere Ken, a specialist in cancer cell division, has been at NIH
since 1967. "The reason I stayed at NIH is because I could
freely pursue basic research [here]," Dr. Kakere says. "Creative
work is valued in American medical research. In Japan, I could
only have researched in one narrow category. Also, in [Japa-
nese] institutions, with their vertical hierarchies, there is little
exchange between people—this is another difference from
America."

Doctors have symbolic importance because they exemplify
the process by which Japan learns from the West. During the
Edo period, medicine alone was officially sanctioned as a field
of foreign study; scholars flocked to Nagasaki to learn skills
from the Chinese and the Dutch. One could say that medicine
is the only truly indispensable modern technology. Many of us
might enjoy taking a journey to the past for the experience of
living with candles and traveling by horseback, but who would
be willing to forgo modern medical treatment? From that point
of view, medicine is the queen of technology, and it was indeed
the only thing from the West that premodern Japan really
wanted. Therefore it is all the more surprising that today, nearly
one hundred and fifty years since Commodore Perry arrived,
medical advances still do not originate in Japan; they continue
to come from the West, and Japanese doctors continue to flee
to the West and stay there. As one Japanese newspaper put it,
"In the field of basic research, human exchange between Japan

and America is basically a one-way street—Japan absorbs knowledge from the United States." Dr. Kimura Shikiko, a woman doctor who has been with the NIH since 1987, says, "The appeal [of an American career] is that whether you are a woman or a foreigner, you will be able to pursue your research based on the merits of your work." In Japan's medical world, young people, women, the outspoken, and the inventive stand no chance of recognition.

The problems afflicting medicine apply to advanced technology in general. Consider Nakamura Shuji, the inventor of important breakthroughs in blue lasers, the Holy Grail of the consumer-electronics industry. Blue lasers allow for far greater data storage and for images much superior to those available today, but nobody had been able to produce a sustained beam of blue laser light until 1999, when Nakamura developed one that beams light for up to ten thousand hours. His employer, Nichia Chemical, now leases the technology to the electronics giant Pioneer; this may be one of the finest achievements of postwar Japanese technology.

So what happened to Nakamura? Not only was he not rewarded or promoted (he earned $100 each for his five hundred patents in the 1990s) but when he decided to leave Nichia, no Japanese company even made him an offer. He attributes this to the fact that he graduated from a minor university and worked at a small firm in the provinces. In February 2000, he therefore took a job as a researcher at the University of California at Santa Barbara. He says, "No bonus, no big position. This is a Japanese company. So I go to the U.S.A."

Another example of how hard it is for independent-minded inventors or entrepreneurs to get ahead in Japan is Okabe Nobuya, who runs a company that makes science-fiction effects for movies and television. He invented a program that allows games makers to vary the background scenery on the screen, but he could not interest Japanese manufacturers. "Japan is like the army with everyone in senior-junior relationships," he says. "But it's not manly to stick around complaining, so I'm finding my own solution." He took his program to a convention in San Diego and soon had multiple orders. Okabe has since moved most of his company to Hollywood.

Meanwhile, JETRO (Japan External Trade Organization) has set up a fund called Tiger's Gate 2000 to nurture young Internet entrepreneurs in Japan. However, the condition of JETRO's support is that the young tigers move to the United States and learn how to do business there. Okabe sells software in the United States because he cannot find buyers at home; JETRO actually requires that young Internet start-ups leave the country! Such are Japan's up-and-coming entrepreneurs: their success depends on the degree to which they avoid Japan. This is true even for Son Masayoshi, whose high-tech acquisitions were garnered largely in the United States, not Japan. The source of Son's leveraged money has been Japan, but the growth areas of his business are abroad.

It isn't only individuals who are fleeing Japan but businesses as well. The most celebrated example is Honda Motors, which in the 1980s quietly transferred its base of operations from Japan to the United States, which now accounts for more than half of Honda's production and sales. Honda expects exports from Japan to continue to fall in the coming years and is betting the company's survival on cutting loose from Japan.

Hundreds, even thousands of companies are slowly but surely moving their base of operations abroad. This is why Sony was willing to take massive losses in Hollywood (more than $2.5 billion) when it purchased Columbia Pictures: there would be no purpose in buying or developing Japanese movie studios, since the Japanese movie industry has almost completely collapsed. Sony's only way forward was to expand in the United States.

Today's refugees also include top athletes. Nomo Hideo, a pitcher for the Los Angeles Dodgers (and later several other teams), epitomizes this new type of Japanese refugee. Nomo was a very successful pitcher for the Kintetsu Buffaloes, but Japan's rigid baseball world limited his prospects. Among other things, he disliked the "endurance exercises" that are a feature of Japanese sports. Endurance exercises, such as *hashirikomi* (deep running) or *nagekomi* (deep throwing) basically involve running or throwing until you drop. It's an approach to sports training that has obviously developed from the military–style emphasis on *gambare* (endurance) taught in the schools, and it is common in most Japanese athletic programs, though it has little to do with developing muscle strength or athletic skill.

When in the spring of 1995 Nomo quit the Buffaloes and in the summer of that year joined the Dodgers, there was a cry of outrage from the Japanese press. The newspapers labeled him an "ingrate" and accused him of loving money, not sports. In short order, Nomo went on to become a sensation in the United States, winning the National League Rookie of the Year Award and being dubbed "the Tornado" by the media. When he was asked what he liked about baseball in America, Nomo explained that Americans really *enjoyed* baseball, whether they were players or spectators. The key to Nomo's departure lies in the word *enjoy*, in contrast to *endure*. Nomo's escape opened the floodgates. In 1997, another star, Irabu Hideki, left Japan to join the Yankees; and in December 1999 the popular player Sasaki "the Devil" Kazuhiro went off to join the Seattle Mariners. So many successful players have left that baseball clubs had to change the rules in order to allow easier departure to the United States. In October 2000, Japan's most popular baseball

star ever, Suzuki Ichiro, made his farewells, to a standing ova-
tion from 26,000 fans, as he, too, set out for the U.S. majors.
The situation in Japanese baseball was like ballet under the
U.S.S.R.—raise a star, and the first thing he wants to do is de-
fect.

Many refugees are people who are at the top of their professions. An inventor like Nakahara Shuji is nothing less than an
international technology superstar, and yet he had no choice
but to leave Japan. We are not dealing with the poor and disadvantaged here, or with the politically oppressed, such as those
who fled Nazi Germany or China after the massacre at Tianan-
men Square. It must surely be unique in world history that a
free and wealthy society in a time of peace has become unattractive to the brightest and most ambitious of its own people.
But this is what the stranglehold of bureaucracies and entrenched systems in Japan is achieving.

The flight of native talent abroad is an old story in Japan, almost
a cliché. What is less known is that a significant shift is taking
place in the makeup of Japan's resident foreign population. Expats who have lived there for decades are making a quiet exodus. In 1995, Otis Cary, then seventy-four, the dean of Kyoto's
foreign residents, announced that he was planning to return to
the United States. Cary, who was born in Japan and spent most
of his life there, received an award from the emperor for a distinguished career spanning more than forty years as a professor
at Doshisha University. Among the foreigners in Kyoto, his
name was synonymous with love of the city. Nevertheless, Cary
voiced no regrets. "It will be a relief to me," he said.

David Kidd, a legendary art dealer (forty years in the Kyoto
area), and Dan Furst, active in the theater world (ten years),
both moved to Honolulu more than a decade ago—and others
followed. John McGee, a distinguished Canadian who was head

of Urasenke Tea School's International Department, resigned in 1999 and left Kyoto after twenty-seven years. The most common conversation I have these days is with foreign friends from Japan who are moving to the United States, South America, Hong Kong, or Bangkok. The second most common conversation is with the gloomy people who for one reason or another see no way out.

The elite of fast-track investment bankers who were stationed in Japan transferred to Hong Kong and Singapore in the early 1990s, leaving second-string players in Tokyo. Long-established foreign communities in Kobe and Yokohama, dating to Meiji days, have shrunk to nearly the vanishing point, and international schools are closing. There is a clear shift among Westerners from long-term residents to short-term employees who come to Japan to make some money and then move on.

At the same time, the absolute number of foreigners in Japan nearly doubled in the 1990s. But one must look at the numbers carefully. The largest foreign group in Japan is the 640,000 Koreans, descendants of forced laborers brought over in the 1930s and 1940s. Many are third- or fourth-generation residents in Japan, speak no Korean, and are indistinguishable from the average Japanese.

Japan maintains a tight immigration policy, accepting fewer Vietnamese or other refugees than any other developed country, for example, and making foreign spouses wait decades before they are granted permanent residence. Yet there is a need for unskilled labor, and the way to meet this is to welcome South American descendants of Japanese emigrants. The great increase in foreign residents in Japan has been in this group of *nikkei*, foreigners of Japanese descent, from Brazil and Peru (from 2,700 in 1986 to 275,000 in 1997). While this group includes many intelligent and ambitious young people, very few of them manage to surmount Japan's high barriers to joining the mainstream and carve out successful careers. Sadly, most of them are doomed to live their days at the bottom of the social pecking order, doing work that modern Japanese shun. It will take generations for them to assimilate, and it will not be easy: in the summer of 1999, rightist gangs paraded through the Brazilian neighborhood in the town of Toyota, home of the automobile company and of a large concentration of *nikkei* workers, demanding, "Foreigners go home!" Even Japanese blood doesn't count for much, it seems.

If you remove Koreans and *nikkei* laborers from South America from the statistics, the remainder of the foreign population in Japan is minuscule, less than 0.4 percent of the total population. There was a time in the late 1980s when there was widespread debate about allowing foreign workers without Japanese blood into the country. But after the Bubble burst, the government tightened regulations. Japan turned back at the brink.

In the days of *sakoku*, "closed country" (1600–1869), when the shogunate restricted the Dutch and Chinese to the port of Nagasaki, Dutch traders lived on Dejima, a small artificial island in Nagasaki Harbor connected by a causeway to the mainland. Only with special permits could the Dutch pass over the causeway, and the authorities usually granted these only during the day. At night the Dutch had to return to Dejima, where their guardsmen locked the gate behind them. Modern-day rules that restrict foreigners to certain discrete corners of Japanese society and keep them out of the mainstream can be traced to Dejima. And the dream of a physical Dejima for foreigners has never faded. During the days when I worked for American real-estate developer Trammell Crow, I ran across many national and local development plans that called for getting all the foreigners to move into special apartment buildings designed just for them—often on landfill islands.

Recently a young friend of mine, the child of a Chinese father and a Japanese mother, joined a large coffee company as a new employee. The personnel department called him in and told him, "We see that you carry a Chinese passport. It is our policy not to give management positions to foreigners. Please change your nationality." As this story makes clear, foreigners in Japan cannot expect career advancement.

There is one niche, however, a "Dejima of employment," that is specially allotted to foreigners. It is the job of creating and selling propaganda. Japan issues such a massive volume of advertisement about itself, for both foreign and domestic consumption, that propaganda production deserves to be considered an industry in its own right. A surprisingly large percentage of the Europeans and Americans employed in Japan are working on selling Japan abroad, ranging from the Western students of architecture and gardens whose job is to preach Japanese culture to the world to thousands of spokesmen retained by religious foundations, banks, and trading houses. Yet of the expats I have known over the years who work for Japanese institutions, only a handful enjoy substantive responsibility. Most work in "international departments," where their assignment is to polish up speeches or edit newsletters and magazines whose content is largely glorification of their company, industry, town, or art form.

The involvement of foreigners in producing propaganda obviously has an important effect on how Japan is seen by the rest of the world, so important that hardly a book on Japan in recent years has not mentioned it. Patrick Smith (*Japan: A Reinterpretation*) and Richard Katz (*Japan: The System That Soured*) refer to these committed Japanophiles as the Chrysanthemum Club.

One of the most fascinating questions about Japan as a field of study is the deep commitment, amounting to religious conviction, that is often experienced by foreign experts. It's a strong testament to the enduring appeal of Japan's arts and society. Typically, a foreigner discovers in Japan something, whether it be modern architecture, cinema, or the school system, that he thinks is of value, and thenceforward makes it his mission to explain it to the world. When he writes about his field he will speak about its good points, since these are what attracted him. What would be the point of criticizing, since the goal is to open people's eyes to the wondrous thing he has found in Japan?

This is what happens: I have a foreign friend who is a cinema critic. He is well aware of the meltdown that has taken place in Japanese cinema and speaks about it quite bluntly in private. But when it comes time to pen an article, he sifts through the dross for a few good filmmakers who have produced something worth looking at in the past decade and writes about the special aesthetic qualities of their work. What his foreign readers see is more praise for the wonders of Japanese film; the deep problems of the field never make it into print.

It's a natural thing to do and, since the goal is to introduce abroad those things that are really praiseworthy in Japan, an admirable one. In that sense, I am proud to number myself a member of the Chrysanthemum Club. When it comes time for me to write my book about Kabuki, it's not going to be about the fact that Kabuki is degrading in quality, losing both its audience and its creative artistry; it will be about the great actors I have known and seen, and about their achievements, which rival the best in world opera or ballet. That's what a Kabuki book should be.

It's a matter of selectivity. Japan experts are not necessarily as blind or worshipful as their writings may lead us to believe. Rather, as well-meaning introducers of Japanese culture abroad, they naturally end up in the role of editors and censors, choosing the striking and beautiful film clips and leaving the rest on the cutting-room floor. In any case, one thing is true: commentators on Japanese culture by and large are not dispassionate reporters; for better or for worse, they are in the position of "selling Japan." I believe this goes a long way toward explaining why foreign writing on Japan tends to be so admiring and uncritical.

While the Chrysanthemum Club members' dedication to Japan is often genuinely felt, it is also true that many of them owe their livelihood to Japan. Overseas, propaganda can be extremely profitable, especially for Washington lobbyists and Ivy League academics. However, for those toiling in international departments within Japan, propaganda is rarely more than a low- to medium-wage job, a sad substitute for founding one's own business or rising to an executive position in a Japanese company. One needs to be a very committed Chrysanthemum Club member to stick around.

During the 1990s, there was an important shift in Japan's place in the world, and it had to do with the renaissance of China and Southeast Asia. For foreigners coming to Asia during the decades following the war, it was nearly impossible to live securely in China, and for decades Vietnam, Burma, Cambodia, and Laos were completely closed. Since the late 1980s, all this has changed. Southeast Asia, though it suffers from severe boom-and-bust cycles, is the scene of frenzied economic activity. There is a wealth of new business opportunities in banking, manufacturing, writing, and other fields, and, unlike Japan, where foreigners are mostly restricted to low-level international-department positions, there are genuine opportunities to advance. In Bangkok, I know dozens of foreigners who own and operate their own businesses; in Japan, only a handful. Perhaps Japan is to be commended for keeping its arts and industry strictly to itself, and not allowing "neo-colonialists" a foothold. Whatever the right or wrong of it, the bottom line is that Japan is not an attractive location for outsiders (or at least individuals, as opposed to big corporations) to set up shop.

For forty years after the war, Japan was not only "Number One" in Asia—it was the "Only One." Now, although its economy is still larger than all the other Asian nations combined (including China), the balance is rapidly shifting, and in the process Japan is becoming merely one of many. Foreigners interested in Asia—not only Westerners but Asians themselves—now have a much wider field in which to play out their ambitions.

That it is becoming "one of many" in a revitalized East Asia is a healthy development, and by no means a discredit to Japan. However, this does mean that there is competition for brains, for the people who make international culture spark: bright entrepreneurs, writers, designers, artists, and so forth. The nation will find it more and more difficult to draw the best and the brightest to its shores unless it makes being in Japan more attractive. At the moment, unfortunately, Japan is following the opposite tack. It's becoming harder, not easier, to find an independent position in a Japanese company; and nearly impossible, as before, to strike out on one's own.

Japan's shrinking international appeal is visible in many ways, not least in the sluggish growth of its foreign-exchange program. In 1983, the Nakasone administration announced a goal of increasing the number of foreign-exchange students to Japan to 100,000 by the end of the century. By 1999 there were only 56,000 (a number achieved after several years of decline in the 1990s), despite a steady increase in Japanese government scholarships. And many of the students are in Japan only as their second choice. A conversation with a Taiwanese student in Kobe gave me some insight into the lack of interest on the part of

Asians in coming to Japan. When he decided to pursue higher education in Japan, his family was bitterly opposed. "Japan is where poor and ignorant people go," his parents said. This reminded me of my two groups of friends in Thailand. One consists of farmers in a poor village built on stilts in the rice paddies of northern Thailand, where I often travel on vacation. A surprising number have a sister in Japan or dream of going to work in Japan. My other group of friends are cosmopolitan Bangkok dwellers, affluent, and destined to lead Thailand's big businesses and banks. They travel to the United States, Hong Kong, Singapore, China, or Australia. Japan is almost completely off their horizon.

Why is this? One reason is that Japan, while maintaining a competent standard in many industries, and intellectual or artistic pursuits, does not lead the way in any single field. Nobody would come to Japan to study the leading edge. This is especially true for university education, which, as we have seen, has not been a serious priority for Japan. All the effort went into grade school and high school. As a result, universities do not offer programs that can compete at an international level. When *Asiaweek* did a cover story in May 2000 on MBA schools, only five Japanese universities made it into the top fifty in Asia, and none into the top ten; they were outclassed by MBA schools in Australia and in Thailand, Singapore, Hong Kong, and Korea. And this was in East Asia, where MBA schools are relatively new and still at a disadvantage to the West. On a world scale, Japan's graduate schools simply fall off the list.

Nor does Japan's supposedly advanced lifestyle appeal much to middle- or upper-class Asians. "To many Southeast Asians living here, Japan is the poorest country in the world—in terms of lifestyle," says Yau-hua Lim, an Indonesian of Chinese ancestry living in Tokyo. "The Japanese have such pathetic lives. They may think Indonesia is a poor country, but we have larger houses, we can afford a car and a maid. It's easy to go to the beach on weekends. After living in Tokyo, my concept of rich and poor has really changed."

Who comes to Japan from Asia? Menial laborers, less qualified or poorer students dependent on Ministry of Education handouts, and low- to mid-level employees of Japanese multinationals sent there to study for a short time. The most promising students usually do not come to Japan, or if they do they soon leave; over time, this will surely have an effect on Japan's international role.

Meanwhile, in the place of real internationalization, Japan abounds with Dogs and Demons–type events and programs designed to give the appearance that admiring foreigners are flocking there. Towns and organizations spend huge amounts to host conventions in Japan, and the speeches at these conferences are given prominent space in the media. Japanese magazines regularly feature earnest advice from overseas experts. Living here, one sees token Japanese-speaking foreigners on almost every variety show. Most famous of such programs is the wildly popular TV show *Strange Things About the Japanese,* hosted by comedian Beat Takeshi, in which a panel of foreigners, fluent in Japanese, debates a Japanese audience and one another with a great deal of sound and fury. The program has a positive side in that it introduces citizens from many countries conversant in Japanese—something new to most viewers. On the other hand, the program is essentially comedy, tending to underscore the position of foreigners as freaks within the society: there is no moderation, and the debate consists mostly of vociferous sound bites shouted by people with plaques around their necks reading "South Korea," "France," "Benin," etc. Reporter Howard French points out, "Although it may open windows on other worlds for its viewers, for some the zoolike aspect of the program, with its raucous, inconclusive debates, might almost seem to advertise Japan's conservative virtues. For all the giddy freedom of foreigners, the disorder subtly recommends the tranquillity of a uniform society governed firmly by rules understood by all." The speeches, advice, and television debates look and feel exotic, but they have little to do with real involvement by foreigners in Japanese business or culture. It's the voice of Hal again, reassuring everyone that Japan is indeed international.

Considering Japan's stalled internationalization, we come back to the principle of *Wakon Yosai*, "Japanese spirit, Western technology," the rallying cry of the Meiji Restoration from which Japan has never deviated. Fukuzawa Yukichi, a pioneer early traveler to Europe in the 1850s, wrote a widely read book about his experiences, in which he described his puzzlement upon discovering that foreigners were free to buy land in the Netherlands. "If a foreigner buys land, doesn't that mean that he could build a castle or a military fort on it?" he asked. That thought hadn't occurred to his Dutch friends, but something like it has never faded from the minds of the Japanese public. There is a fear that allowing foreigners entry into the nation's life would give them terrifying power. And so they have been kept at arm's length.

As we have seen in Japanese education, an attitude of wariness, if not fear, toward foreigners is imparted in the schools. Hence the refusal of many people to rent homes or apartments to foreigners, or the appearance of signs on bathhouses warning them to stay out. The Japanese are so cut off from meaningful contact with people from other countries that they are unaware of ethnic or national sensitivities, as may be seen in the stream of racial slurs made by leading politicians. In May 2000, Ishihara Shintaro, the mayor of Tokyo, publicly attacked Koreans, Taiwanese, and Chinese living in Japan, saying, "Atrocious crimes have been committed again and again by *sangokujin* [a derogatory term for foreigners] who have illegally entered Japan. We can expect them to riot in an earthquake." He was referring to the notorious aftermath of the Great Kanto Earthquake of 1923, when in fact the opposite happened: angry Japanese mobs rounded up and murdered thousands of Koreans. The important thing to note about this slur was that Ishihara refused to retract it, and that *Yomiuri Shimbun*, one of Japan's major daily newspapers, criticized not the governor but the outcry in the media. Ishihara remained more popular than ever, with more than 70 percent of the callers to the city office supporting him.

The lack of foreigners in Japan is not accidental; it results from laws and social frameworks especially designed to keep them out, or, if they are allowed in, to hold them on a very short leash. Bureaucrats restrict the import of goods from overseas, the media (newspapers, cinema, and television) portray Japan as the victim of dangerous foreigners, and business cartels raise high barriers to prevent outsiders from gaining a foothold. Internationalization in Japan is a concept at war with itself, for no matter how much lip service is paid to internationalization, the country's basic policies have been to keep Japan closed.

Plutarch, commenting on Lycurgus, said, "He was as careful to save his city from the infection of foreign bad habits, as men usually are to prevent the introduction of a pestilence." Such is Japan. In the upper echelons of government and business, though one might find one or two men who did a stint at graduate school at Stanford or perhaps taught at Harvard in an exchange program, there is no one in a position of influence whose mind was shaped abroad at a young age.

The Ministry of Education, having by the end of the century fired all the foreign teachers at national universities who had longtime careers in Japan, and bankrupted the American colleges established in Japan during the 1990s, can breathe easy. It has successfully protected Japan against the "pestilence of foreign bad habits." Closing the door to foreign influence on education is one of the biggest drags on real change, for with business and bureaucratic leaders all educated to have exactly the same mind-set, new ideas can rarely gain the ears of those who are in power. A truly different point of view cannot reach the top.

Traditional cultures everywhere face the problem of how to resist the overwhelming assault of Western, primarily American, civilization. The problem is not limited to Asia or Africa; Europe, too, has agonies over this issue. Some countries choose to erect legal, religious, or customary barriers to the outside world. For those who are studying how to use this model, Japan provides a good test case. Erecting barriers can have unintended effects, for, strangely enough, foreigners can help to preserve the local culture; what was quintessentially Japanese in its material culture might have survived better had there been more foreigners and Japanese with a broad worldview to appreciate it.

One could blame the decline of Japan's countryside and historic towns partly on the lack of foreigners—tourists, of course, but also others who might have an impact on design and preservation, such as resort and hotel operators, scholars, artists, or independent entrepreneurs. In Europe, preservation of natural and historic beauty did not come about as a means of pleasing tourists; it sprang from a long civic tradition among the people themselves, and tourism was a by-product. In Asia, however, modernization came so quickly that such civic traditions had little time to grow up; instead, rampant development is sweeping all before it. One of the few forces standing in the way of the development wave has been tourism. Foreigners living and traveling in countries like Vietnam, where the ex-

plosion of tourism is bringing in higher standards of design
and service, have directly contributed to the restoration of old
neighborhoods and the revival of traditional arts. But by keeping foreigners at arm's length, Japan never really felt the impact
of international levels of taste—and thus the conquest of aluminum, fluorescent light, and plastic was complete. It's an anti-
intuitive twist, one of the great ironies of modern East Asian
history: allowing the foreigners in revives local culture; keeping
them out helps to destroy it.

When the Japanese describe their country, they will often use
the word *semai*, "narrow," "cramped," "crowded." The idea is
that Japan's landmass is too small to support its population
properly. Of course, there are many nations with less habitable
land and higher population densities, including some of the
most prosperous countries of Europe and East Asia. Taiwan,
South Korea, the Netherlands, and Belgium have higher population densities than does Japan; Britain and Germany have
slightly lower but roughly comparable densities. *Semai* is not a
physical property; *semai* is in the mind. It's the emotional consequence of Japan's rigid systems, which bind individuals and
keep out the fresh air of new ideas from abroad.

The result is explosive. Japan is a nation of people bursting to
get out. This has happened before. In the 1930s Fascists in both
Germany and Japan defended their expansionist plans by claiming that they needed Lebensraum. After Japan's defeat in World
War II, its hunger for its neighbors' land subsided but did not
disappear entirely. In the 1980s, the Ministry of International
Trade and Industry had a pet project that consisted of sending
tens of thousands of Japan's old people to Australia, where they
could live in vast retirement cities, the presumption being that
Japan does not have the land or the resources to provide a good

life for its aging population. But today the emphasis is not on land but on opportunity. From one point of view, the pressure on talented people and top-notch companies to move out is a strength. It fuels Japan's international expansion. Japanese presence in Southeast Asia is massive, with Japanese factories accounting for as much as 10 percent of Malaysia's GNP. Picking up the *Guide to Japanese Businesses in Thailand* is a sobering experience: the volume is as thick as the Yellow Pages of a small American city, listing thousands of companies. Shifting their focus overseas may be beneficial to Japanese businesses over the long term. But in the short term it bodes even greater stagnation, because it further reduces business and employment opportunities at home.

One can glean a sense of the hunger to get out of Japan from *Newsweek's* Japanese edition, August 14, 1996, which offered its readers a special ten-page feature on the top-ten locations for living abroad. The headline read "Escaping Japan. Living Abroad Is Just a Matter of Making Up Your Mind!" "Living abroad is a dream? No, certainly not," the article begins. "There are people right now living pleasant lives in lands across the sea. . . . A place where just taking a walk in the morning makes your heart beat faster with excitement. Where the bustle of activity in town is not tiring but energizing—surely cities like this exist somewhere in this wide world." There follow photos and rankings of Edinburgh, Santa Fe, Bologna, Penang, Auckland, and so on, as places for the Japanese to move and start a new life, concentrating on an unspoiled natural environment, large comfortable houses, and a vibrant traditional culture. Sato Sachiko, the wife of a Japanese businessman living in Strasbourg, says, "When I think of returning to Japan, I get depressed."

Why should she get depressed? The word *semai* gives us a

strong hint, and Nomo's use of the word *enjoy* instead of *endure*
brings us close to the answer. The school system, the bureaucracy, and the oppressive rules and hierarchies to which they
give rise are dampening the Japanese people's spirit. In short,
Japan is becoming no fun. Sasaki Ryu, a fifteen-year-old student who was interviewed in *Asiaweek* in May 1999, sums up
the mood in Japan today:

> I dream of going to a college in the U.S. School is so boring
> here. All the kids in my class think alike and everybody wants
> to be in a group. I'm quite sick of it. I like baseball, and
> when I see how some Japanese baseball players have made it
> in the States, I really admire them. Japanese players are good
> too but somehow the individuality of the American players
> draws me. I know it will be tough, but I'm ready to try.
> Young Japanese people have no dreams. I don't want to be
> like that.

This brings us full circle—from the Japanese people's relationship with the outside world to their feelings about their
own country. Stalled "internationalization" has very little to do
with anything international; rather, the problems spring from
troubles within. As Ian Buruma comments, "The main victims
of the bigoted, exclusive, rigid, rascist, authoritarian ways of
Japanese officialdom are not the foreigners, even though they
are at times its most convenient targets, but the rank and file of
the Japanese themselves."

When "young people have no dreams," when a great inventor gets "no position, no bonus," when school, work, and sports
are a matter of "endure" rather than "enjoy," when cities and
countryside are losing their beauty and romance—that's a case
of becoming no fun. And what an incredible reversal of Japan's
own tradition this is! This nation had a countryside that was

pure romance, as we can see from the haiku of Basho and the ecstatic tales of foreign travelers until very recent times. Even during the strictest days of the old Edo Shogunate, there was ample time and freedom to enjoy life; indeed, Saikaku's merchants and scholars in the "floating world" refined their pleasures to the point that almost every occupation and amusement they touched became high art.

Nor did the fun die out in the nineteenth century. Forty years ago, it was still possible for young entrepreneurs, like the men who founded Sony and Pioneer, to dream of creating new businesses and of succeeding on a global scale. And there was even a time, for several decades after World War II, when Japan was a more hospitable place for foreigners; in fact, the nation's international reputation coasts on the nostalgia of foreign experts for this era of relative openness that lasted right into the 1980s. Everyone can remember how much fun it used to be—one could hardly think of anything less Japanese than being no fun. And yet this is what Japan is doing to itself.

Whatever the foreigners may do or think, it is far sadder to see so many Japanese leaving—or dreaming of leaving—when their country offers so much by way of natural and cultural treasures, as well as one of the world's most affluent economies. It's another case of "a wilted peony in a bamboo vase, unable to draw water up her stem." The treasures are still in Japan, but people cannot enjoy them. Saikaku says, "Whether you happen to be a businessman or an artisan, never move from a place that you are accustomed to. . . . There is nothing quite as painful to observe as people packing up their belongings while the pots on the stove are still warm."

15 To Change or Not to Change

Boiled Frog

If I don't drive around the park,
I'm pretty sure to make my mark.
If I'm in bed each night by ten,
I may get back my looks again.
If I abstain from fun and such,
I'll probably amount to much;
But I shall stay the way I am,
Because I do not give a damn.
—DOROTHY PARKER, "Observation"

The question at the beginning of the twenty-first century is: Can Japan change? The picture is not without hope. Japan has made abrupt about-faces, to the point of completely reinventing itself twice during the past 150 years, and could possibly do so again. But what if Japan cannot change? In seeking an answer, let's take another look at the bureaucracy.

Bureaucracy is the core institution of government, for its

mission is to intelligently allocate the resources of the state. If it provides that service efficiently, it does its job. Japan's bureaucracy, riven with corruption and guilty of massive misallocation of funds in almost every area, fails this simple but crucial test. An indurated bureaucracy is Japan's single most severe and intractable problem, responsible for bringing the nation to the brink of disaster in the 1990s. The Ministry of Finance, for all its mistakes, is just one of many government agencies, and the damage it has done cannot compare with the Construction Ministry's burying the nation under concrete, the Forestry Bureau's decimating the native forest cover, the Ministry of International Trade and Industry's needlessly damming the Nagara River, or the Ministry of Health and Welfare's knowingly allowing 1,400 people to become infected with AIDS. So angry is the public that the last decade has seen bookstores overflow with books attacking officialdom, from Asai Takashi's 1996 best-seller, *Go to Hell, Bureaucrats!*, to Sumita Shoji's 1998 *The Wasteful Spending of Officialdom*. The public is ready for change.

During the past few years, it has become fashionable to speak of Japan's "three revolutions." The first occurred after 1854, when Commodore Perry arrived with his "black ships"and forced the opening of Japan. Within twenty years, Japan discarded a system of feudal rule that went back almost eight centuries, replacing it with a modern state ruled by the army, wealthy businessmen, and government officials.

After the nation's defeat in World War II, a second revolution took place, under the guidance of General Douglas MacArthur and the U.S. Occupation. MacArthur dismantled the army and broke the power of the prewar capitalists—and in their place the bureaucracy took over, creating the Japan we see today.

It's now time, many believe, for a third revolution, which will differ from the previous two in one important way: pressure from foreign powers sparked both of the earlier revolutions; they did not spring from among the Japanese themselves. This time around, however, there is no foreign pressure. Nobody outside Japan is concerned about the fate of its mountains and rivers; nobody will arrive in a warship and demand that Japan produce better movies, rescue bankrupt pension funds, educate its children to be creative, or house its families in livable homes. The revolution will have to come from within.

It could. Dissatisfaction is rife, as may be gleaned from the many angry and frustrated people who are quoted in this book. Some readers might wonder how I can say such harsh things about Japan. But it is not I who say these things. Fukuda Kiichiro calls Japan a Kindergarten State, and Fukuda Kazuya asks, "Why have the Japanese become such infants?" Kurosawa proclaimed that Japanese film companies are so hopeless they should be destroyed. Asai Takashi titled his book *Go to Hell, Bureaucrats!* Nakano Kiyotsugu complains, "I don't know why, but invisible rules have grown up everywhere," and Professor Kawai carries this much further in his report to the prime minister, declaring that Japan's society is "ossified," and that conformity has "leached Japan's vitality." Dr. Miyamoto Masao describes Japanese education as "castration"; Inose Naoki compares Japan's environmental ills and bad-debt crisis with the unstoppable march to war in the 1930s. The people of Kyoto rose up and fought the construction of the Pont des Arts. In short, there is a strong and vocal body of opinion within Japan that recognizes its troubles and is increasingly prepared to fight for change. In this lies great hope. The question is whether the mood of dissatisfaction will ever gain enough momentum to seriously affect Japan's forward course. One can make good arguments for revolution, and—sadly—even better ones for another decade or two of stagnation.

In the realm of politics, the early 1990s saw unprecedented

anger within an electorate that was among the world's most docile. In 1993, the ruling Liberal Democratic Party (LDP) lost its majority for the first time in forty years, and an opposition coalition, led by Prime Minister Hosokawa, took over briefly. The opposition, however, was no match for the bureaucrats. When Hosokawa sought financial information from the Ministry of Finance, the bureaucrats stalled, and there was nothing that the prime minister's office could do. Within six months, Hosokawa was out, and former members of the LDP, now scattered into a number of splinter parties, took over again. The electorate settled back into apathy, and at present the old LDP stalwarts are firmly back in power, beholden as before to bureaucrats and large businesses. In the political sphere, the score is Status Quo 1, Revolution 0.

One of the sharpest observations made by Karel van Wolferen is that the Japanese bureaucratic system has never relied on public approval for its legitimacy and power; it works in a separate dimension, far above and removed from the democratic process. As we have seen, even when voters do oppose ruinous construction projects and sign petitions requesting referendums, local assemblies are free to ignore them, and usually do. Outside observers see criticism in the media and hear complaints from average Japanese, and jump to the conclusion that these feelings will be translated into political action. The dissatisfied Japanese people are going to rise up and take matters into their own hands! But so far this has never happened.

Nevertheless, there is movement below the surface. Despite what Marxist theory tells us, the masses rarely start revolutions. The instigators tend to be the educated middle class and disgruntled low-level officials, what one might call "the soft underbelly of the elite"—and the soft underbelly is hurting. Since the publication of *Lost Japan* in Japanese, I am sometimes asked to speak on panels or write for specialist publications, even to act as a consultant to government agencies. What I have found is that the mid-levels of many organizations—mostly people in their forties—are disillusioned and frustrated by their inability to make changes. Mid-level disillusionment is a highly subjective area. There are no statistics on this subject, and elite-track officials and company employees don't write books and articles, which leaves me with very little in the way of published quotable material. I have only my own experiences to go by.

In 1994, I wrote an article lambasting the dreary displays and shoddy interiors of the Ueno National Museum. Soon afterward, at an opening, I met one of the top officials in the agency that runs the museum. He approached me, and I steeled myself for an angry denunciation of my article—only to hear him say that he personally thinks the mismanagement of Japanese museums is a disgrace. But despite his lofty position in the hierarchy there is little he can do. At the moment, the "soft underbelly" is hurting, but even elite managers are powerless against the inertia of their agencies.

The same official did manage to bring in a team of experts from the Smithsonian to give advice on modern museum management. To put most of that advice into practice he will have to wait—as enlightened middle-level bureaucrats and executives across Japan are waiting—for stodgy seniors to retire, or for their department to fall into such disarray that they can finally seize the initiative. This group of would-be reformers are like Madame Defarge in Dickens's *A Tale of Two Cities*, a secret revolutionary who sat for years in her tavern quietly knitting the names of hated aristocrats into her shawl. When the revolution finally came, she took her place at the foot of the guillotine, counting as the heads rolled. A lot of people in Japan are waiting to count heads.

You can hear the drumbeat of coming revolution in the rising level of anger in public opinion, fueled to a great extent by the sheer embarrassment of falling behind. There is considerable chagrin as the gaps between Japan and the United States, Europe, and newly wealthy Asian states widen. The thrust of the educational system is to make people highly competitive, and the hierarchical social structure gets people into the habit of ranking ethnic groups and nations as "higher" and "lower." Naturally, they would like to stand at the top of the pyramid, and this leads to obsessive comparisons between Japan and other countries. This is where the frustration comes in.

When millions of Japanese travel abroad and return from Singapore's beautiful and efficient Changi Airport to the grim environment of Narita, the disparity is too strong to ignore. The decline of the Tokyo stock market, against a backdrop of explosive growth in New York and London, has been an agonizing spectacle for Japan's financial community. By the end of the century, Chinese-directed films featuring major Hollywood stars regularly took top spots in American box offices, and Chinese stars had become household names; in contrast, Japan's greatest success was *Pokémon*, a movie for ten-year-olds. The Japanese sense the contrast between the bright lights and excitement outside, and the mediocrity inside. They are embarrassed.

Yet while the groundwork exists, there is no assurance that the revolution will come. Against the dissatisfaction felt by the public is arrayed a complex system of bureaucratic control, infinitely more subtle than anything ever achieved in Russia or China in their Communist heydays. In order to visualize what is involved, let's do a "thought experiment" and ask ourselves what it would take to dismantle just a few bricks of the bureaucratic edifice—the system of licenses for aerobics instructors, for instance. The mind's screen goes blank, because the scenario whereby the Japan Gymnastics Association, the Central Association for Prevention of Labor Disabilities, and the

Japan Health and Sports Federation will voluntarily disband and give up their lucrative permit businesses is simply unimaginable. What, then, can be done about the tens of thousands of other agencies and special government corporations—all working in secrecy and against whose fiat there is no recourse?

The public may be able to combat the bureaucracy over certain high-profile projects such as the Pont des Arts, or well-publicized scandals such as dioxin contamination. But power lies in the details, in the thousands of tiny Pont des Arts–type monuments rising quietly in every city and hamlet, in the myriad unreported dump sites not covered by the media, and deep in the impenetrable thicket of regulations in the form of unwritten "guidance" hemming in the life of the nation.

For those who hope that Japan is headed in the direction of greater freedom, it is sobering to see how brand-new industries create cartels in the old pattern. The Internet? Providers established the Japan Network Information Center (JPNIC) as the entity that approves new domain addresses. The JPNIC set to work right away, putting up the same barriers to outsiders and upstart businesses that we find in older cartels. For example, the JPNIC does not approve addresses unless they use Japanese Internet providers—despite global guidelines worldwide that say local authorities shall show "no preferential treatment for customers of a particular data network." It's the old game of using a cartel to keep the foreigners out. Meanwhile, the JPNIC raised registration fees to the point where it costs four times more to list a new domain than it does in the United States. The result of battening down the windows to the Internet— the very room that everyone thought was going to bring fresh air into Japanese industry—is that by 1998 Japan had only 0.3 percent the number of domains in the United States, and ranked twenty-first in the world for domain names per capita.

Multiply this cozy cartel by a million, and you'll get a sense of the complexity and power of the system. Seeking to reform the gigantic structure of the bureaucracy is a project overwhelming in its scale, involving nothing less than a radical change in social mores; the entire country would be turned upside down and inside out. That is exactly what Japan's leaders dread: they fear that if they make too many changes the whole jerry-built edifice of bureaucratic management will collapse and the nation will sink into anarchy. This anxiety acts as a powerful brake against change. For the moment, Madame Defarge faces a very long wait.

There has been much talk in recent years of *Kaikaku*, "reform," and while the bureaucracy has made a few timid steps toward reform, especially in finance and trade, *Kaikaku* is hampered by one major flaw: it aims, by and large, to shore up the status quo. Bureaucrats find ways, in classic Dogs and Demons fashion, to make small, nonessential changes, rather than tackle serious structural problems both in the industries they control and in their own systems of management. The phrase *Kisei Kanwa*, used for "deregulation," is highly symbolic, for it means "relaxation of the rules." It does not imply a discarding of the rules.

Here's how it works. Gas prices in Japan average 2.7 times world levels due to a law forbidding direct import. After 1996, deregulation allowed JAL, the national airline, to buy fuel abroad—but JAL cannot use this gas on domestic routes, and sulfur- and lead-content standards are designed to exclude South Korean gas. Contractors, pressured by the cartels they belong to, will not unload shipments bought through newly opened channels. Even after deregulation, foreign gas still cannot enter Japan directly.

In 1997, Japan finally legalized transplants from brain-dead patients. The "legalization" involved so many compromises and restraints that two years later only one liver transplant and one heart transplant had taken place. Although the law has changed, dozens of desperately ill patients continue to raise money to travel abroad for organ transplants, as they have been doing for decades. For all intents and purposes, such transplants remain illegal in Japan.

In response to strong public discontent, the government set *gyosei kaikaku*, "administrative reform," as a priority for most of the 1990s, but the real work in dismantling the top-heavy edifice of Japanese officialdom lags. Instead, in a titanic demonstration of *tatemae* conquering *honne*, much of the effort has gone into *renaming* the ministries. As of January 2001, several ministries have changed their names (and some have disappeared, subsumed into larger entities). For example, the Construction and Transport ministries are being combined with the National Land and Hokkaido Development agencies into a Land, Infrastructure, and Transport Ministry. At tremendous expense, these new ministries will shuffle personnel and departments between them, setting up new signs and offices to indicate their new functions—and then will go on to do business more or less as before. Halfhearted reforms such as this are endemic, and highly deceptive, if taken at face value. As for the investigations and scandals in government ministries, once public anger dies away, it's back to business as usual. "Reform" of this nature would be called "stagnation" in any other country.

William Sheldon, famed for his studies in anthropometry, drew a distinction between two fundamental types of human psychology, inspired by the mythical Greek brothers Epimetheus and Prometheus. Epimetheus always faced the past, while Prometheus, who brought fire to mankind, looked to the future. An Epimethean values precedent; a Promethean will steal fire from the gods if necessary in order to advance humanity's progress. In thinking about Japan's future, it's a good idea to briefly step aside from the mechanisms of bureaucracy and pc itics and look at psychology.

So far, the psychology of reform has been almost exclusively Epimethean: forced by public opinion, bureaucrats make minimal, often purely symbolic changes, while exerting most of their energies to protect the status quo. Reforms look backward, toward shoring up established systems, not forward to a new world. In general, Japan has settled comfortably into an Epimethean mind-set, and this is central not only to reform but to the overall question of how Japan failed to become a modern country. Modernity, if nothing else, surely means a love of the new. However, as we have seen repeatedly in this book, if new technology was not aimed at export manufacture—like cameras or cars—it never took root. Society frowns on people who steal fire from the gods. Too much fire too fast would undermine the role of officials in the Cold Hearth Agency, who tell people what to do with their flameless hearths, and it would bankrupt the powerful Hot Stone Cartel, whose existence depends on a lack of fire.

At the moment, the trend is toward an increasingly Epimethean bent. Change will get harder, not easier, as the population ages. At the very moment when Japan needs adventurous people to drastically revise its way of doing things, the population has already become the world's oldest, with school registrations on a strong downward curve. Older people, by nature, tend to be more conservative than young ones, and as they tip the balance of the population, it will be harder to make changes.

Meanwhile, youths, whom one would ordinarily expect to be full of energy and initiative, have been taught in school to be obedient and never to question the way things are. Young people are thinking about shirts printed with bunnies and kitties—with platform shoes to match, and some really amazing makeup ther than about heavy issues like the environ-

ostalgia for the past is a natural reaction in
of the systems that now slow the nation down
.... source of its success only a decade ago. One cannot
underestimate the shock that true globalization would bring to
a social system and economy like Japan's, which depends so
much on being cut off from the world. Mikuni Akio writes:

> Under great economic and political pressure, foreigners have
> been allowed into certain designated sectors of the economy
> [such as Nissan Automobiles and Long Term Credit Bank].
> The government is finding it an expensive proposition to
> compensate those hit by this first taste of genuine market
> forces, and understandably quails at the prospect of pacifying
> the millions who would suffer in a full-scale opening of the
> economy. Opposition in Japan to further liberalization, de-
> regulation or globalization is thus steadily gathering momen-
> tum.

So strong is the longing for the past that there is a good
chance that Japan will turn reactionary. The success of the
rightist politician Ishihara Shintaro, the author of the popular
Japan That Can Say No series and the mayor of Tokyo, augurs
for a political step backward, not forward. Ishihara and his
group blame Japan's troubles on evil foreigners, especially the
United States. In academia, a quiet sea change is taking place.
In the decades after World War II, leftists and rightists argued
heatedly over national policy, with leftists often wielding the
upper hand in the control of universities. However, by the end
of the 1990s the leftists were in full retreat, and nationalist
thinking took over the academic vanguard. The new national-

ism may prevent Japan from looking inside at what the nation has done to itself.

A popular argument among Japan watchers is that as Japan becomes more international, people's perceptions will gradually come to harmonize with the outside world. There is some truth to this, for while internationalization at the official level has largely been a conspicuous failure, millions of Japanese have traveled and lived abroad. Every organization has at least one, and maybe even dozens of people, with international experience working within its ranks.

On the other hand, it was perhaps naive to imagine that foreign travel would broaden Japanese horizons. One of the most remarkable phenomena of the 1980s and 1990s is the creation of special worlds abroad made just for the Japanese. Most Japanese tourists travel in groups, and their itinerary consists of a "package"—including attractions, hotels, and restaurants that cater only to them. In Thailand, for example, the Japanese have their own entertainment street lined with "Members Only" signs, and even their own crocodile farm, which insulates them from having to deal with Thais and tourists from other countries who visit the ordinary crocodile farms.

Recently, an interviewer questioned veteran Japanologist Donald Richie about a statement in his book *Inland Sea* (1971) in which he predicted that as the Japanese traveled abroad in greater numbers, they would become more like everybody else. Richie replied, "I meant that when people got out and saw how other people lived and felt, they would not be able to come back with any complacency. I was exactly wrong. I hadn't envisaged Jalpak. The Japanese go abroad in a package; they have their own crocodiles, and their own flags and their own must-see stops. This is the way the vast majority travel, and they are not touched."

As for refugees and longtime expats leaving Japan, few will mourn their exodus. Their departure from Japanese shores serves only to remove destabilizing influences, and well-heeled "international departments" will quickly replenish the missing foreigners with new ones, better behaved and more manageable than the old. "What is in store for Japan?" asks Kamei Tatsuo, the former editor of the influential opinion journal *Shincho 45*, with an ironic smile. "We will go back to *sakoku* of the Edo period. We Japanese like it that way."

How on earth did Japan get itself into such trouble? Iida Hideo, a finance lawyer, describes what he calls the Boiled Frog syndrome: "If you drop a frog into a pot of boiling water, he will jump out immediately and be saved. If you put him in warm water, he feels comfortable and does not notice when you slowly raise the temperature." Before the frog knows what is happening, it's cooked.

The Boiled Frog syndrome is what comes of failing to change as the world changes. Techniques such as *tobashi* keep the water lukewarm, hiding disastrous mistakes. The policy of shoring up insolvent firms and wasteful government agencies at public expense creates no incentive for those in charge to rethink their mistakes. Meanwhile, the government croons the public to sleep with reassuring lullabies about Japan's unique form of government by bureaucracy, and its superiority over the degenerate West, exemplified by Sakakibara Eisuke's book *Japanese-Style Capitalism as a Civilization*.

Death at a slow boil is also behind the sad condition of Japan's rivers, mountains, and seashores, as well as the landscapes of towns and cities. Ill-planned development, monuments, and bizarre public works have ravaged all these parts of the national heritage—but the heat doesn't scald, because the propaganda of "ancient culture" and "love of nature" continues to lull the public into blissful unawareness.

Radical change will come only when conditions have grown completely intolerable, and in Japan's case that day may never come. To put Japan's financial troubles into context, we must remember that it remains one of the wealthiest countries in the world; the bankrupt banks and deflated stock market are not going to deprive most people of their television sets, refrigerators, and cars. From this point of view, Japan remains a reasonably comfortable place to live.

In using the word "comfortable," I would never suggest that Europeans, Americans, or most middle-class Southeast Asians envy such a lifestyle. For the Japanese, cramped low-quality housing, lack of time for private life, and a degraded environment in cities and countryside are so all-pervasive that most citizens can hardly imagine an alternative. Goals set in the 1950s and 1960s—to own television sets, toasters, and cars—froze to where even now they define the limits of Japanese modernism. As long as people get to keep their toasters, very few will complain if it becomes a little harder to buy a house, or their companies make more severe demands on their time, or their surroundings get a little uglier. Such things seem such a normal, even predestined and unavoidable part of life that it is hardly worth thinking about. Japan has trained its population to believe in the old military virtues of hard work and endurance. Hence people will bear hardships without necessarily asking how they might avoid or decrease them, especially if the hardships are quiet in the coming.

The best word to describe Japan's modern plight is *Chuto Hanpa*, which means "neither this nor that"—in other words, mediocrity. Stunning natural scenery exists, but rarely does it truly uplift the heart, for somewhere in the field of vision the

Construction Ministry has built something hideous and unnecessary. Kyoto preserves hundreds of temples and rock gardens,
but a stream of recorded announcements disturbs their meditative calm, and outside their mossy gates stretches one of the
world's drearier modern cities. The educational system teaches
children facts very efficiently, but not how to think by themselves or to innovate. The nation has piled up more savings than
any other people on earth, and at the same time sunk into a
deep quagmire of personal, corporate, and national debt.
Everywhere we look is the same mixed picture—that is, *Chuto
Hanpa.*

Japan's ability to rescue itself will depend partly on the rate
of technological advance in business, but here, too, *Chuto Hanpa*
rules. Despite an industrial structure aimed single-mindedly at
international expansion, there is no question that, technologically, Japan fell behind in the 1990s. Again and again, Japanese
firms and agencies were slow to see that their industries were
entering new paradigm shifts—for example, the shift in television from analog to digital. In the early part of the decade,
MITI encouraged electronic firms to pour billions into developing high-definition television based on analog technology. It
seemed that another Japanese monopoly was about to be established—and then a small Silicon Valley start-up figured out how
to do it digitally, and all the money went down the drain
overnight.

That Japan bet wrong was merely unfortunate; the most
telling aspect of these fiascoes is the attempt by government to
force people to continue in the use of clearly outmoded technology. A similar pattern afflicts medicine, where, in an effort to
protect domestic pharmaceuticals, the Ministry of Health and
Welfare refuses to approve foreign drugs. As a result, the Japanese are denied medicines that are in common use around the
world for the treatment of arthritis, cancer, and numerous other

ailments from headache to malaria. Rather than use a foreign drug with proven value, the MHW encourages local firms to produce copycat medicines with little or no efficacy and sometimes with terrible side effects. These are known as *zoro-yaku*, "one after another medicines," because firms put them out one after another. In order to protect the *zoro-yaku* business, the MHW collaborates with drug companies in hiding deaths from side effects. In one notorious case in the 1980s, the MHW allowed drug firms to continue distributing a *zoro-yaku* polio vaccine even after it had killed dozens of children, the aim being to protect the makers from the financial loss of recalling unused supply.

After decades of producing *zoro-yaku*, and failing to test or monitor medicines properly (the United States' FDA has a hundred drug inspectors, while Japan's MHW has two; the FDA has elaborate drug-testing protocols, while the MHW has none), Japan's pharmaceuticals are hopelessly behind in technology and today have only a tiny international presence. Where the big European and American drug makers are inventing revolutionary treatments for arthritis, Alzheimer's disease, and cancer, not to mention drugs like Viagra and Rogaine, Taisho Chemical, one of Japan's major pharmaceuticals, is pinning its hopes for foreign expansion in Asia on Lipovitan D, a sweet tonic drink that has no medicinal benefit. The very existence of a word like *zoro-yaku* should set off alarm bells for those who believe that Japan is dedicated to technological advancement. Medicine and biotechnology rank among the biggest growth industries in the world—and Japan is missing the boat.

Computer software is another major business that Japan has neglected to develop. Japan imports leading-edge software from Microsoft, Apple, and Oracle; it exports computer games for children. Most surprisingly, Japan also failed to make the leap in chip manufacture, once an area of great strength. Manufacturers did not advance from DRAM production to microprocessors, and thus abandoned the high end of the industry to Intel. Korea and Taiwan, meanwhile, have moved in from below and are eating the Japanese alive at the lower end of the chip business. By 1999, all of Japan's major chip makers were reporting huge losses, while American and other Asian manufacturers had a bumper year. In the area of satellites and rockets, Japan's NASDA space agency, after spending billions of dollars to develop a "Japan-only" rocket, has suffered a humiliating series of failures, most notably in November 1999, when the launch of an H-2 rocket went so badly that ground control had to order it to self-destruct.

All this said, the Japanese have one of the world's most sophisticated industrial infrastructures, which annually runs a huge balance-of-trade surplus with the rest of the world. Sony's visionary leaders created a truly international corporate culture that continues to make world-class innovations. The Japanese have commanding leads in LCD screen technologies, as well as in numerous niche fields in precision machinery. So secure are Japanese monopolies in certain specialist components that hardly a computer or advanced industrial device can be built without them. Steel firms and shipbuilders boast some of the world's most efficient factories. Car manufacturers, though greatly weakened, are still a towering presence in world markets.

It's a story of strengths inherited from the industries of the 1970s balanced against severe weaknesses in the industries of the new millennium. Technology in Japan is good, but not nearly as good as was once thought; it's "neither here nor there"—that is, *Chuto Hanpa*. Because of this mix of qualities, Japan will not crash. There is more than enough industrial power to support the population at roughly present standards.

On the other hand, given its deep systemic weakness in finance and technology, Japan is not going to boom. The long-term prognosis is for more *Chuto Hanpa*, with GNP growth slow, unemployment edging upward, and the debt burden mounting year by year.

Part of the undertow against change is Japan's dream of becoming the leader of Southeast Asia. The old desire for empire, previously called "the Greater East Asian Co-Prosperity Sphere," never completely faded, and in recent years it is enjoying new life. Japan is pouring huge amounts of industrial capital, ODA funds, monetary loans, and cultural grants into Southeast Asian nations in the hope of integrating Thailand, Malaysia, Indonesia, and other nations into a new Asian bloc, with Japan at the helm.

The dream is that Southeast Asia will join hands with Japan and act as a new engine for industrial growth; Japan will then take center stage once again, and all the old policies will be vindicated. Typical of the group of theorists beating the drum for a new co-prosperity sphere is Professor Shiraishi Takashi of Kyoto University's Centre for Southeast Asian Studies, who argues that Southeast Asia at the dawn of the new century must now "choose" between the United States and Japan for its model and controlling partner. The choice, of course, should be Japan.

Shiraishi represents a strong body of academic and official opinion that is angry at foreign criticism of Japan, especially what Shiraishi calls "stereotypical Anglo-American triumphalist statements that both the Japanese model and developmental authoritarianism are now bankrupt." He longs for the old days when Japan produced an economic miracle without having to update or rationalize its internal systems. "Free-market ideas of legal contracts, impartial regulations, and transparency are all fine, and perhaps these are all portfolio investors need," he says with some bitterness. "But can we rely safely on markets for long-term investment for industrialization, technological development, and, above all, human-resources development?"

Shiraishi's question—what to rely on?—touches on many of the questions raised in this book. The value of free markets is only one issue; there are numerous others, such as the role of bureaucracy and the importance of clear and correct information to the efficient running of a modern state.

Getting Southeast Asia to "choose now" between the United States and Japan is Japan's last big bet at the beginning of the twenty-first century. Perhaps Japan will indeed win the bet and succeed in reviving its old hegemony over Southeast Asia. Backed by new industrial might based on control over Southeast Asia, and with a whole new continent of rivers and valleys to profitably cement over, Japan's academics and bureaucrats will not then feel that they need to give a backward glance at home to ravaged cities, sterile countryside, and a culture of big-eyed baby faces. All complaints can be easily dismissed as "Anglo-American triumphalism," and Japan can revert happily to business as usual.

Perhaps, but then again, perhaps not. For one thing, Southeast Asian nations may not feel that their only choice is between the United States and Japan, or that they have to make a choice at all. The world is a far more complex place than Shiraishi dreams—including a newly unified Europe, a powerful China, and wealthy tigers and dragons in Asia itself, such as Hong Kong, Singapore, South Korea, and Taiwan. Meanwhile, Japan's internal problems affect its position in Southeast Asia, as the elites of these countries discover that Japan is not the cultural or economic paradise they expected. "Korean business is following America rather than Japan," says Kang Dong Jin, director of Paxnet, a South Korean financial-information Web site. "Korea has seen America enjoy a decade of prosperity and Japan the opposite, so in some ways the choice is easy."

Foreign observers, Western and Asian alike, are asking whether ideal "human-resources development" means millions of construction workers flattening valleys at government expense—and lackluster tourist and software industries. When Thailand's telecommunications agency suffers huge losses from being forced to install the failed PHS cellular system; when educated Indonesians like Yau-hua Lim start saying, "The Japanese have such pathetic lives," hopes that the leaders of Thailand and Indonesia will "choose" Japan as their preferred and exclusive model dim.

The Asian Bet, like many other modern Japanese policies, is likely to turn out neither heads nor tails but something in between—that is, *Chuto Hanpa*. Japanese industry already has a huge presence in Southeast Asian nations, and Japan's voice in policy is likely to grow. On the other hand, it's doubtful that these nations will sign on the dotted line to unquestioned Japanese leadership.

For the next few decades, Japan has enough savings to coast on. This is Japan's tragedy, for only bankruptcy could shock people out of *Chuto Hanpa*. After the Asian crisis of 1997–1998, Korea, which did not have the luxury of relying on its savings, was forced to make major structural changes. By 1999, the results were making themselves seen in a jump in growth and a revivified political life.

However, Japan has not yet suffered such a shock, and despite the loud calls for change, one cannot underestimate the public's complacency. Schools have taught people to ask few questions and to follow a routine, to "endure." The propaganda machine continues at full tilt, with the voice of Hal reassuring everyone that the rivers and lakes are beautiful, the banking mess has been cleared up, recovery is around the corner, Japan's "unique model" is superior and will lead Asia, have a nice day. Children who have grown up in the *Chuto Hanpa* environment of Japan's cities and countryside reach adulthood knowing of no other way to live.

The feeling that it is "too late" exerts a psychological undertow in all Japan's cultural and environmental movements. People naturally wonder what is the merit of enacting new zoning and environmental legislation when the cities and countryside have already been damaged almost beyond repair. What it would take to restore Japan's rivers, mountains, and seaside to ecological health boggles the imagination. What do you do? Strip cement away from river bottoms, grow vines over concrete embankments, cut down the *sugi* cedar plantations? How will you keep the vast number of people who depend on construction employed? These are difficult questions, and only a determined few have the bravery to face them.

Meanwhile, the bureaucracy continues on autopilot for one simple reason: the funds are still flowing. There is no lack of money to continue to build highway loops in the shape of eight-headed dragons and fill in a few more meters of Osaka Bay. Foreign economics experts insist that Japan "must" rein in its overspending on construction, but why must it? The country is eating into its savings—of this there is no doubt. But for the time being there are still trillions of dollars of assets in savings, much of it deposited in the postal-savings system, one giant piggy bank for the bureaucrats to play with.

At the turn of the century, hopes for the future remain balanced between revolution and stagnation. Stagnation is most likely in the absence of a major shock to the system, such as a wholesale economic crash. But revolution could happen. The world is full of surprises—who would have imagined in 1985 that by 1990 the whole of Eastern Europe would have shaken off Communism? It is exactly such a surprise that millions of Madame Defarges are quietly waiting for.

Sadly for Japan, a crash is highly unlikely. The chances are that for the next decade or two there will never come a moment when the nation stares disaster right in the face. The water will remain lukewarm, and the public will sleep comfortably in a soup of *Chuto Hanpa* while their country slowly degenerates. When it comes time to carve the epitaph for "Japanese-style capitalism as a civilization," the legend on the tombstone will read "Boiled Frog."

Conclusion

E pur si muove.

But it does move.

—GALILEO GALILEI, said under his breath after he was
forced to recant his belief that the earth moved
around the sun (1632)

In contrast to most books by Europeans and Americans on
Japan, this one has avoided the words "Japan must" and "Japan
should," for I do not believe that foreigners should make demands on Japan. Nothing is more damaging to U.S.-Japan relations than Washington's noisy insistence that Japan rationalize
its financial markets, boost domestic demand, and so forth. It
enrages—rightly—politicians like Ishihara Shintaro, who resent
American insolence, and it frightens the average citizen, who is
aware of how misguided such advice often is. For example,
American pressure to "pump-prime" the economy does real
damage, for pouring money into public works only exacerbates
Japan's worst problem, which is its addiction to government-
subsidized construction.

Writing this book has not been easy, for many of the issues raised here are close to unknown overseas. It has been challenging to describe in a believable way Japan's cultural trauma, so beyond most people's experience in Western countries that it strains credibility. Yet the situation that I have been describing is all too real, and the hope for the future, I believe, lies in seeing the condition of modern Japan for what it is—only from recognition and understanding will come change. I have written to describe and not prescribe.

That said, it would be ingenuous to claim that I have no personal hopes for Japan. For one who loves Japan's culture and its rivers and mountains, the disaster overtaking cities and countryside has been heartrending to witness. I've written this book for my Japanese friends and millions of others who have so far had very little voice in the foreign media, who feel as sad and angry as I do. Although I'm skeptical of Japan's ability to change (the very roots of the tragedy lie in systems that repress change), in my heart I dream of change.

Modern Japan is an emotional minefield. Old-line Japanologists, in my view, are so convinced that their duty lies in preaching Japan's glory that these subjects deeply frighten them. People are afraid to open the closet, afraid that the sight of the skeletons inside might undermine what they love about Japan, and fearful, too, lest the high-powered international forums they belong to do not invite them back to future meetings. While this situation has changed in recent years with regard to finance, it is still largely true when it comes to culture. The popularizers of Japanese culture, the people who write about Zen, flowers, the tea ceremony, architecture, design, and so forth, are still writing as if they hadn't noticed that there is trouble in Eden.

But there is trouble, and it has happened once before in the past century when a similar process led the nation into disaster.

One may easily draw parallels between the collapse of the
Taisho Renaissance of the 1910s and 1920s and the Heisei Depression of the 1990s. In both cases, systems of inflexible government and education stifled a generation of freedom and
creativity. The same mechanisms that caused Japan to veer off
course before World War II—a ruling elite guiding a system
aimed single-mindedly at expansion—are at work today.

Over the years, foreign observers have looked with envy at
the "Japanese paradigm," in which the goal of the economy is
to expand at all costs, and not necessarily to benefit the citi-
zenry. The virtue of this paradigm lies in the sacrifices the people make in exchange for national economic power. But it is
time to review this paradigm and take a long look at Japan's
concrete-shrouded rivers, shabby cities, stagnant financial markets, Hello Kitty–fied cultural life, and mismanaged resorts,
parks, and hospitals, and to see them for what they are. Perhaps
Japan's twentieth-century history is not that of a nation that has
successfully adapted to modernity but one that has twice maladapted, with calamitous results.

In asking ourselves at the deepest level what happened to Japan,
it helps, oddly enough, to look again at ikebana flower arrangement. One day in the fall of 1999, I broached a question to the
flower master Kawase Toshiro. It was something that had long
been troubling me: What is the real difference between old-
style ikebana and the monstrosities that pass under that name
these days? One can regret the use of wire and vinyl cutouts,
the way flowers and leaves are stapled and folded together, the
way manuals diagram arrangements in terms of exact angles at
such-and-such degree—but all of these things, however distorted, do have roots in the tradition. What is the crucial difference? Kawase's answer was that modern flowers lack *jitsu*—that
is, "reality." Traditional flowers had a purpose, whether it was

religious or ritual; people in those days had a mystical respect for the wonders of nature and used their arrangements as a way of seeking and responding to the creative breath of the cosmos. Nowadays, all this is lost. There is no purpose except decoration for its own sake, no inquiring after the nature of plants and flowers themselves. Instead, the flowers are just "material," not much different from any other material such as vinyl and wire, used any which way to serve the whimsical needs of the arrangers. In short, there is no *jitsu*, no spiritual purpose, nothing that connects with the inherent forces of nature—just empty design.

Kawase's comment was a profound one, for lack of *jitsu* carries over into every field in Japan today, and can be said to be at the very root of the country's present cultural malaise. The construction frenzy (building without purpose), architecture (design without context), education (facts without independent thought), new cities (destroying the old), the stock market (paying no dividends), real estate (making no returns), universities (irrelevant to education), internationalization (keeping out the world), bureaucracy (spending without regard to real needs), finance ("virtual yen"), cinema (aimed mostly at children, not at adults), company balance sheets ("cosmetic accounting"), the Environment Agency (unconcerned with the environment), medicine (copycat drugs improperly tested), information (fuzzy facts, secrets, and lies), airports (bad for people, good for radishes)—the whole edifice is lacking in *jitsu*.

The gap between Japan's way of doing things and the realities of modern life, both international and domestic, is extreme—there is no other way to put it. It is this that leads me to call Japan a case of failed modernization. Japan's elaborate Dogs and Demons monuments are a sort of defensive bulwark, a desperate attempt to shore up its embattled systems against the crushing weight of real value. The strain can only worsen,

explain

yet in the end reality will prevail—the earth *does* move around
the sun.

Japan has departed so far from *jitsu*, I believe, because during
the past century the nation did not in fact respond well to new
ideas coming from the West, as classical "modernization theory"
preaches; instead, Japan has had one long, agonizing struggle
with these ideas, and the struggle is by no means over. As in the
1930s, the nation is repeating a pattern whereby huge initial
success eventually leads to disaster. In the early stages, Japan
finds its own innovative way to do what the West does—and
with spectacular results. We should remember that it is only a
decade or so ago that the whole world was studying Japanese
management, manufacturing, finance, and merchandising techniques. In the second stage, however, these very innovations
that amazed the world are carried too far; the whole system
goes onto automatic pilot, and the ship runs up on the rocks.

The cultural troubles are long-term and chronic. There is a
way out, of course, and it's the way of *jitsu*—getting back in
touch with reality. The reality that Japan needs to get back to,
however, is not necessarily reality as it is seen in the West but
Japan's own moral and cultural roots. As we have seen repeatedly in this book, much that parades as quintessentially Japanese
today—for example, money that earns no interest and companies that cannot fail—would be unrecognizable to Saikaku and
the hearty tradesmen of old Edo. The manualized flower
arrangements are a denial of everything that flower masters
taught for centuries; the bombastic architecture a slap in the
face to a long tradition of restraint and aesthetic sensitivity; the
smiling baby faces an absurd end to the sophisticated adult culture that gave us Noh drama, Basho's haiku, sand gardens, and
so much more. Most tragic of all, the construction frenzy that is
a core part of today's distorted system is destroying the very

land itself, the land that the Japanese have always considered to
be sacred.

The result of Japan's war with *jitsu* has been to tear apart and
ravage most of what Japan holds most dear in its own culture,
and this lies at the root of the nation's modern cultural malaise:
people are sick at heart because Japan has strayed so far from its
true self. The challenge for the Japanese in the past two centuries was how to come out of isolation and assert themselves
in the world, and in this they succeeded brilliantly, to the extent
that Japan is now one of the world's most powerful nations.
Success came, however, at tremendous internal cost. The challenge of this century will be how to find a way home.

Notes

Endnote Reference Key

[J] = Japanese language
[J/E] = Japanese and English language

ABBREVIATION	PUBLICATION
AB	*Asian Business*
AEN	*Asahi Evening News*
AERA	*Asian Shimbun Weekly AERA* [J]
ASJ Almanac 1999	*Asahi Shimbun Japan Almanac 1999*
AW	*AsiaWeek*
AWSJ	*Asian Wall Street Journal*
FEER	*Far Eastern Economic Review*
JT	*Japan Times* (Osaka)
MDN	*Mainichi Daily News* (Osaka)
MS	*Mainichi Shimbun* [J]
NKS	*Nihon Keizai Shimbun* [J]
NKW	*Nikkei Weekly* (Tokyo)
NWA	*Newsweek* (Asia edition)
NWJ	*Newsweek* (Japanese edition) [J]
NYT	*The New York Times*
NYT International	*The New York Times*, International Edition
Saikaku	Ihara Saikaku, *Some Final Words of Advice*, trans. Peter Nosco (Tokyo: Charles E. Tuttle Company, 1980)
SD	*SD (Space Design) Magazine* [J/E]
SS	*Sankei Shimbun* [J]

"STN," YS Yomipack	*Yomiuri Shimbun "Yomipack,"* "Shakkin Taikoku
	Nippon"[J]
TMA	*Time* (Asia edition)
YDN	*Yomiuri Daily News* (Tokyo)
YS	*Yomiuri Shimbun* [J]

I The Land: The Construction State

15 "dismayed by the unrelieved banality": Jane Faulders, "Perfect Citizens in a Land Without a Script," quoting Robert MacNeil, *JT*, 17 October 1996.

15 The River Bureau has dammed: See Andrew Pollack, "Japan's Road to Bankruptcy Is Paved with Public Works," *NYT*, 10 March 1997.

15 the United States . . . not to build any more dams: "State, Groups Wrangle Over Dam Construction," *JT*, 28 September 1994.

15 dozens more are scheduled to be dismantled: Andrew Murr, "A River Runs Through It," *NWA*, 9 August 1999, 19.

15 plans to add 500 new dams to the . . . 2,800: Brian Mertens, "Sinking in Cement," *AB*, March 1999.

17 ¥630 trillion: "Japan to Drop 1994 Public Works Pledge," *JT*, 19 April 1997.

18 giant concrete tetrapods: See Pollack, "Japan's Road."

18 "The seashore has hardened": "Shinrin Hakai," *Shukan Post*, 16 December 1994.

18 South Carolina mandated: "Surfers ride the environmentalist wave," *JT*, 13 November 1998.

19 construction market in Japan is the largest: *ASJ Almanac 1999* (Tokyo: Asahi Shimbun, 1998), 167. The 1997 figures vary between ¥83 and ¥75 trillion.

19 versus 2 percent in the United States: "Desirable Form of Road Investment in the 20th Century," *MERI's Monthly Circular*, March 1998; and Pollack, "Japan's Road."

20 the share of GDP . . . had risen: "Stimulus set to smooth recovery," *NKW*, 15 November 1999.

20 40 percent of expenditures to public works: See Brian Woodall, *Japan Under Construction* (Berkeley: University of California Press, 1996), 15; and Gavan McCormack, *The Emptiness of Japanese Affluence* (New York: M. E. Sharpe, 1996), 33.

20 A good percentage . . . goes to the politicians: See Ken Belson, "Japan's Government Should Rethink Public Works Policy," *MDN*, 5 November 1996; Woodall, *Japan Under Construction*, 4, 12.

21 they own 90 percent of the company's stock: Inose Naoki, *Nihongoku no Kenkyu* (Tokyo: Bungei Shunju, 1997), 73.

21 bureaucrats who once worked: " 'Family' firms hogging road contracts," *YDN*, 5 November 1997.

21 one in five jobs in Japan depends on construction: *ASJ Almanac 1999*, 167; Woodall, *Japan Under Construction*, 29; Jon Herskovitz, "Tough Times for Contractors," *The Journal*, November 1998, 11.

22 *Miyamoto*: "You mean": Miyamoto Masao, *Straitjacket Society*, trans. Juliet Winters Carpenter (Tokyo: Kodansha International, 1995), 82.

23 the general budget for 1999: *NKW*, "Budget Breakdown," 28 December 1998, 3; *"STN,"* *YS Yomipack*, 1 December 1996, 6.

23 "Bureaucrats are very skilled": Sato Kenichiro, quoted in Mertens, "Sinking in Cement," 22.

24 the last flood, in 1957: "Mayor defends development of Japan's largest wetlands," *NKW*, 7 July 1997.

25 "The result might have been": Cited in Naito Yosuke, "Environment watchdog said asleep," *JT*, 7 June 1997.

25 "The current ecosystem": Ibid.

26 "We have also studied": "Mayor defends," *NKW*, 7 July 1997.

26 "dam-building frenzy": Frederick Pearce, cited in "U.K. Expert Pulls Plug on Japan's Dam Policy," *YDN*, 1996.

26 ¥200 billion per year: Benjamin Fulford, "Water Shortages Flow from Many Currents," *NKW*, 9 September 1996.

26 blocked by large dams: Pollack, "Japan's Road."

26 additional demand projected: "Nihon Kinkyu Shujutsu wo Yosu, *SS*, 23 February 1997.

27 cost of this facility: Gavan McCormack, "Afterbubble: Fizz and Concrete in Japan's Political Economy," *Asia Pacific Magazine*, May 1997.

27 "You can't just tell us now": Inose, *Nihongoku no Kenkyu*, 61.

28 Shimane Prefecture's plan: Hirao Sachiko, "Shimane Plan to Fill in Lake to Make Farms Stirs Distrust," *JT*, 24 March 1996; "Senior LDP official visits Nakaumi," *JT*, 12 August 2000; Murakami Asako, "Lake reclamations scheme canceled," *JT*, 31 August 2000.

29 Nakaoki Yutaka: Quoted in Suzuki Yumiko, "Bullet-Train Debate Quickens as Vote Nears," *NKW*, 23 September 1996.

31 "the forests are a nuisance": "Shrine Woods Called Development Model," *JT*, 10 September 1995.

33 pollarded stumps: G. Taaffe, "Good Luck and Health Come in Trees," *JT*, 26 February 1997.

34 "They say, 'Please kill' ": Quoted in "Noise Pollution Draws Most Complaints in Kyoto," *YDN*, 22 May 1996.

34 "how Japanese women": Cited by Anastasia Stanmayer and Murakami Mutsuko, "In a Cold Sweat," *AW*, 24 January 1997.

37 "What's the difference": Donald Richie, interview with author, Tokyo, 1 April 1997.

37 "earthquake hazard": "Kamakura Residents Angry Over Landslide Barrier Project," *MDN*, 19 November 1995.

38 "Earthquakes, volcanoes, floods": Cited in Hirooka Koji, "Crisis on the Horizon," *Rivers and Japan* 7 (August 1995): 7.

39 "It was only when": Patrick Smith, *Japan: A Reinterpretation* (New York: Pantheon Books, 1997), 318.

42 "This country is": "The Landslide Disaster," *MDN*, 9 December 1996.

43 "It was in 1953": Mitsuoka Akashi, "Nihon no Kawa wo Kataru, no. 38, Shirakawa (Kumamoto)," *Shukan Shincho*, 9 September 1999.

44 "One particularly outspoken chap": Lee Kwan Yew interview, *TMA*, March 1996, 20.

46 "If someone's got a dam": Quoted in Murr, "River Runs Through It," 19.

46 legislatures have refused to conduct referendums: *Japan Wetlands Action Network: National Report, May 1999*, sec. 2.12, *http://www.yin.or.jp/user/rdavis/jawanreport.txt*

47 concrete production in Japan: *Inaka: The Japanese Countryside, Kyoto Journal* 37 (June 1998): 81.

47 spending on public works: "Contract Value up for Public Works," *NKS*, 24 May 1999.

47 Igarashi Takayoshi: Quoted in Mertens, "Sinking in Cement."

49 Margaret Loke: Quoted in *Inaka: The Japanese Countryside*, 80.

49 "In the case of Miyagase Dam": Quoted in "How About an Excursion to Miyagase Dam?," *Rivers and Japan* 7 (August 1995): 22.

49 "It won't be easy": Matsumoto Shinji, quoted in J. Ryall, "Next Big Tourist Destination—the Moon," *JT*, 22 June 1996.

50 Utopia Song: Quoted in Woodall, *Japan Under Construction*, 65.

2 Environment: Cedar Plantations and Orange Ooze

52 Japan had replanted: "Forests in Trouble," *NKS*, 28 April 1997.

53 recommends wearing protective gear: Yoshida Reiji, "Pollen Count Up This Spring," *JT*, 5 March 1997.

54 "If we had this kind of money": Quoted in M. Hoffman, "Flushed Down the Toilet," *MDN*, 8 December 1996.

54 Forestry Agency debt: "Forestry agency may face privatisation," *NKW*, 30 September 1996.

54 Lumber prices: James Sterngold, "Japan's Cedar Forests Are Man-Made Disaster," *NYT*, 17 January 1995.

54 Forestry Agency workforce: "Forestry agency," *NKW*, 30 September 1996.

54 A recent survey: "Broad-leaf Forests," *MDN*, 31 August 1996.

55 "more important than production": Cited in George Wehrfritz, "Green Heat," *NWA*, 7 October 1996.

55 in place of human labor: "Agency Seeks to Streamline Forestry," *JT*, 22 November 1995.

55 "We've passed into another dimension": Inose, *Nihongoku no Kenkyu*, 41.

55 "The reforestation policy": Shitei Tsunahide, quoted in Sterngold, "Japan's Cedar Forests."

56 Doctors investigating: See Karel van Wolferen, *The Enigma of Japanese Power* (New York: Alfred A. Knopf, 1989), 55.

56 Ministry of Education told a textbook publisher: Peter J. Herzog, *Japan's Pseudo-Democracy* (Kent: Japan Library, 1993), 203.

57 Only in 1995: "Minamata Plaintiffs Lose Suit," *JT*, 12 July 1994; "Minamata Victims Accept Plan," *JT*, 1 November 1995.

57 In two separate cases: "Air-Pollution Hearings Are Resumed," *JT*, 2 October 1994.

58 in the United States . . . stringent rules: "SARA Title III Fact Sheet: The Emergency Planning and Community Right to Know Act," Environmental Protection Agency Web site, January 1993, 28 March 1996, EPA 550-F-93-002, January 1993 Factsheet.

58 companies . . . would merely be required: "Industrial Chemical Flow to Be Monitored," *MDN*, 23 July 1994.

58 no environmental-impact assessment law: Takagi Yukio, "Environmental Assessment Law Is Natural Step Forward," *NKW*, 25 November 1996.

58 "It's difficult to deal": Quoted in "U.S. Base Miffed by Incinerator's Fallout," *JT*, 2 November 1995.

58 Despite serious incidents: "Arsenic Remains in Farm Water," *JT*, 14 February 1996.

59 Operators of small incinerators: "Gov't to set dioxin emission limits," *MDN*, 26 August 1997.

59 an incinerator in Nosecho: "Dioxin threat stirs communities to action," *NKW*, 19 January 1998; "The burning issue," *The Economist*, 25 July 1998.

59 "To single out dioxin": Quoted in "Dioxin threat," *NKW*, 19 January 1998.

59 California ruled: "NCUA OMD RULE 3-4-100: Airborne Toxic Control Measures for Emissions of Dioxins from Medical Waste Incinerators, Regulation 3, Section 4," 12 May 1991. 28 March 1997, *http//:www.epa.gov/opptintr/tri/trirules.htm*

60 interview with a section chief: Asahi TV News (Channel 6), 6:30 p.m., 29 March 1997 (transcription and translation by Bodhi Fishman).

61 the city of Tokorozawa: "City admits it knew of dioxin levels," *MDN*, 7 September 1997.

61 Yatozawa Waste Water Cooperative: "Reveal water data, waste co-op is told," *JT*, 22 February 1996.

61 a well in Tsubame: "Carcinogens Found in Well Water in 41 Prefectures," *MDN*, 3 December 1995.

62 no regulations: "Panel Takes Aim at Polluters," *JT*, 21 February 1996; "Agency Urges Measures to Fight Water Poll," *JT*, 29 November 1995.

62 "We were in a great hurry": "Hasty Quake Cleanup Causing Pollution," *JT*, 2 March 1996.

63 "Even if underground water": Kawamura Kazuhiko, quoted in "Pollution becomes Kobe's new foe," *NKW*, 16 September 1996.

63 a little tour: See Michael Hoffman, "Poisoned Powerhouse," *MDN*, 22 May 1995, reporting on the essay published in *Friday*, 27 May 1995.

64 Yoshizawa's fine: "Soil firm accused of damaging gov't land," *MDN*, 1 November 1995.

64 "If this continues": Ohashi Mitsuo, quoted in Suzuki Yumiko, "Japan Running Out of Space for Waste," *NKW*, 9 December 1996.

65 "Almost all waste": Suzuki Yukichi, quoted in Hoffman, "Poisoned Powerhouse."

65 "Why do we have to shoulder": Ohta Hajime, quoted in Suzuki, "Japan Running Out."

65 "Japan's economy is supported": Quoted in Hoffman, "Poisoned Powerhouse."

65 A private research firm: See Frank Gibney, Jr., "Taking on the Trash," *TMA*, 16 June 1997.

66 A study of twenty sites: See "Tougher rules eyed for waste," *JT*, 22 September 1994.

67 "an experimental basis": Matsui Tadashi, "Microbe technology used to combat oil spill," *YDN*, 26 February 1997.

67 Kevin Costner: Seno A. A., "Costner's High-Tech Act Opens in Japan," *AW*, 7 February 1997.

67 "This time": Yamada Tatsuya, "Nakhodka spill shows nothing learned from past," *AEN*, 15 March 1997.

67 "a large number of blankets": "MSDF ships dispatched to clear oil," *JT*, 9 April 1997.

68 ¥3.6 billion: See Mark Shreiber, "The dreaded outdoor boom," *MDN*, 17 July 1994.

69 recycling coupons: "Kaden shori hiyo maebarai," *NKS*, 7 April 2000.

69 "If we dig up landfills": "Residents battle to expose the truth about a toxic landfill site," *AEN*, 11 September 1998.

70 "Japan's nature conservation": "Japan environment groups try to avert extinction," *NKW*, 24 November 1997.

71 River Bureau of the Construction Ministry: "River Bureau construction fund smells fishy," *MDN*, 2 October 1996.

71 full-color advertisement: "Shizen to Jinkobi no Chowa" (Denpatsu advertisement), *Shukan Shincho* (December 1995).

72 "We expect that it will play": "Hiyoshi Damu he Yo koso!," *Ninomachi*, 2 September 1998.

73 "I have come to realize": Kimoto Yoko, letter to the author, 1999.

74 "Whenever I find": Harada Taiji, quoted in "Nihon no Genfukei wo Motomete," *NKS*, 19 November 1998.

3 The Bubble: Looking Back

77 $3 trillion likely yet to go: Brian Bremner, "Japan's Real Crisis," *Business Week*, 18 May 1998, 42.

79 ¥2.8 trillion: "Gama no tsuge de tagaku no kabutorihiki," *Tokyo Shimbun*, 15 August 1991; "Onoe Nui ki ni naru 'kakushi zaisan,' " *Shukan Bunshun*, 31 August 1995.

79 one-fifth of Bubble-era values: "Japanese Property: Get Real," *The Economist*, 22 March 1997.

80 golf-club developers: "Yotakukin 'jucchoen' shokan de toraburu zoku-shutsu, koredake no 'abunai gorufujo,' " *Shukan Shincho*, 24 April 1997; Nakamoto M., "Golf clubs get bunker mentality," *JT*, 6 June 1996.

80 with her bank-manager patrons: "Onoe Nui ichiban tayori ni suru," *Shukan Bunshun*, 14 January 1993.

80 bad loans . . . surpass ¥77 trillion: "Analyst Sees Further Drop in Property Prices," *MDN*, 10 October 1996; "Details, Details," *The Economist*, 17 January 1998.

80 cost of rescuing Japan's banks: David E. Sanger, "Japan's Bad Debt Is Now Estimated Near $1 Trillion," *NYT*, July 30, 1998; Sheryl WuDunn, "Wounded Giants," *NYT*, 24 November 1995.

81 rates ranging from 5 percent: Robert Zielinski and Nigel Holloway, *Unequal Equities* (Tokyo: Kodansha, 1991), 15, 154.

82 average P/E ratios in *depressed* Japan: "Stock Indexes," *AW*, 2 July 1999; Mano Teruhiko, "Stock market is sitting on a stack of dry firewood," *JT*, 22 January 1996; "Bank losses pull down total profits of listed firms," *NKW*, 8 April 1996.

83 average *review period*: See J. Friedland, "Japanese entrepreneurs can't get financing," *FEER*, 30 June 1994; Yoshito Denawa, quoted in Peter Landers, "American Accents," *FEER*, 31 July 1997.

83 Son Masayoshi, Japan's Internet wizard: "New Stock Market Plan Holds Promise for Companies, Investors," *NKW*, 21 June 1999.

84 crash came even harder for real estate: "Land prices drop for 4th year in a row," *MDN*, 20 August 1996; "Analyst sees further drop in property prices," *MDN*, 10 October 1996; Henny Sender, "The Big Chill," *FEER*, 31 August 1995.

85 only nine U.S. banks: McCormack, "Afterbubble: Fizz and Concrete."

85 the average rating of major banks: "Japanese Banks: Too Early for Optimism," Executive Summary. Moody's Investor's Service Web site, 30 June 1999, *http://www.moodys.com/cgi-bin/pr.exe*

85 two Japanese banks in world's top ten: "Financial Indicators," *The Economist*, 10 July 1999.

85 "In order to preserve": Moriaki Osamu, quoted in "Furyo Saiken 'Zoshoku' de Kinyu Kiki ha Owatte nai," *Shukan Shincho*, 9 September 1999.

86 compares the bank to the *Yamato*: Ohmae Ken'ichi, quoted in "Built for comfort, not for speed," *The Economist*, 6 November 1999.

87 "The competitive advantages": Zielinski and Holloway, *Unequal Equities*, 16.

88 "Harmony [*Wa*] is to be valued": "The Seventeen Article Constitution of Prince Shotoku," Tsunoda Ryusaku, William Theodore de Bary, and Donald Keene, eds., *Sources of Japanese Tradition* (New York: Columbia University Press, 1958), 48.

88 "the spring breezes stilled": Saikaku, 118.

90 foreign brokerage houses were handling: "Headlong Retreat," *FEER*, 5 November 1998; "Kukyo no nikkei shoken, Joi 10sha hairezu," *NKS*, 5 January 1998; Sam Jameson, "Brave New World," *AB*, January 1998.

90 Yamaichi Securities: Yokota Kazunari, "Securities Giant Stands Above Rivals in Profits," *NKW*, 28 April 1997; "Ex-Yamaichi official reportedly says securities regulator knew of losses," *NKW*, 2 February 1998; " 'Kaigai nara mienai,' Bogai shori, Matsuno-shi aun no 'Shido,' Yamaichi-gawa 'Osumitsuki eta,' " *NKS*, 30 January 1998.

90 "Just as the U.S. brokers": Saito Atsushi, quoted in "Beaten abroad, battered at home, Nomura looks for success in Asia," *MDN*, 27 June 1995.

90 "We are just asset eaters": Sanada Yukimitsu, quoted in Henny Sender, "The Game Changes," *FEER*, 3 October 1996.

91 money lent to Thailand: "Tai yushi, hogin ga kahan," *NKS*, 5 January 1997.

91 Japan's banks . . . are writing off: M. Ishizawa, "Banks boost Asian alliances," *NKW*, 16 February 1998.

92 "What's left if this fails?": Alicia Ogawa, quoted in "Beaten abroad," *MDN*, 27 June 1995.

92 monthly turnover at NASDAQ: "World Stocks," *AW*, 11 August 2000 and 11 June 1999; Sato Makoto, "Nasdaq to give initial issues online fast track," *NKW*, 21 June 1999.

93 "a quick outline": Jathon Sapsford, " 'Mr. Yen' Will Get New Job, Expanding His Market Power," *AWSJ*, 3 July 1997.

93 began to water down the standards: "Japan's 'Big Bang' financial reforms considered big bust," *The Nation* (Bangkok), 17 June 1997; Jathon Sapsford and David P. Hamilton, "Tokyo May Dilute Key Big Bang Reform," *AWSJ*, 24 December 1997.

94 By 1998 this figure: E-mail attachment from Tokyo Stock Exchange Web master, "TSE Equity Financing Factsheet," 19 March 2000, *www.adm@tse.or.jp*

94 number of companies listed: Sato Makoto, "Tired TSE turns 50 with rivals at its heels," *NKW*, 19 April 1999.

94 the Tokyo and Osaka stock exchanges: Japanese figures from e-mail attachment from Tokyo Stock Exchange Web master, "TSE Equity Financing Factsheet," 19 March 2000, *www.adm@tse.or.jp*, and e-mail from Ikeda Yuji, assistant manager of International Affairs, Osaka Securities Exchange, 17 March 2000, *y.ikeda@ose.or.jp*; U.S.A. figures from NASDAQ Web site, "Monthly Market Data," 10 April 2000, *http://www.marketdata.nasdaq.com/asp/*

98 "Japan and the United States have realized": R. Taggart Murphy, e-mail to the author, 24 February 2000.

99 Tokyo Stock Exchange's foreign section: "No Easy Turn of Foreign Tide from TSE," *NKW*, 8 January 1996; and "Foreign Section," *JT*, 1–5 June 1999.

100 London listed 522 foreign firms: London Stock Exchange Web site. "The London Stock Exchange: Key Statistics and Comparisons," 10 April 2000, *http://www.londonstockexchange.com/stats/keystatistics/comparisons.html*; just under 10 percent of all trading: Len A. Costa, "They List in the US but Trade at Home," *Fortune*, 5 July 1999; trading on NASDAQ's foreign section alone: NASDAQ's "Monthly Market Data," 10 April 2000, *http://www.market data.nasdaq.com/asp*, and Tokyo Stock Exchange Web site, 1999 Annual Report, 11 April 2000, *http://www.tse.or.jp/english/about/annual99.pdf*

100 TSE and Asian firms: Mertens, "Tokyo Stock Exchange Bids to Go Asian"; and "Schlumberger to Delist from TSE," *NKW*, 10 February 1997.

4 Information: A Different View of Reality

103 "Men take their misfortunes": Ihara Saikaku, "What the Seasons Brought to the Almanac-Maker," in Donald Keene, ed., *Anthology of Japanese Literature* (New York: Grove Press, 1995), 350.

105 "When people say": Hayashi Chimio, "Amerika bunka no mayakusei," *SS*, 31 October 1998.

106 A headline announces: "Nippon Trust sells choice Kyoto site," *JT*, 2 March 1994; and "Hokkaido Bank sells assets to write off loans," *MDN*, 23 March 1996.

107 Jusen nonperforming loans: "Jusen Collateral Worth One-Quarter of Outstanding Debt," *JT*, 8 February 1996; and "Juso Used Three Sets of Figures to Deceive Lenders on Bad Loans," *MDN*, 22 January 1996.

107 the bank showed investigators: "Juso Used Three Sets," *MDN*, 22 January 1996.

107 "not approaching a state of danger": "MOF Misjudged Loan Problems in 1992," *MDN*, 26 January 1996.

108 "in a week or two": Jathon Sapsford, "Firm Hands Make Japan's Banks Toe Line," *AWSJ*, 9 February 1999.

108 "Even if we told the truth": Fulford, "New bad-loan disclosures still not the full story," *NKW*, 27 November 1995.

109 "Contracts are assigned": Inose, *Nihongoku no Kenkyu*, 73.

109 auditors at government agencies: "Most public requests for audits fail," *JT*, 12 February 1996.

110 "not for the public": "Nagano bid files up in smoke," *AEN*, 16 January 1999; and Donald MacIntyre, "Sushi, spas, geisha: How Nagano got the games," *TMA*, 1 February 1999.

110 New Tokyo International Airport: "Lack of financial disclosure derided," *JT*, 13 December 1995.

110 law proposed by the Ministry of Justice: "Panel proposal limits public's right to get government information," *MDN*, 11 March 1996.

110 "it was impossible": "JHL inflated land value to grant loan to Collins," *MDN*, 16 June 1996; and "MOF Misjudged Loan Problems in 1992," *MDN*, 26 January 1996.

110 "the culture of deceit": Quoted in Frank Gibney, Jr., "Ending the Culture of Deceit," *TMA*, 26 January 1998.

111 "We just want to avoid": "Machida school board cracks under pressure," *MDN*, 20 January 1996.

111 "[We did it] believing": "Tourism poster fetes beaches sans nuclear plants," *JT*, 15 May 1996.

112 "Guidelines for Measures to Cope": "Kanagawa cops kept 'manual' to hide scandals," *YDN*, 25 November 1999.

112 "Many journalists have become": Quoted in Sakamaki Sachiko, "Paper Chasers," *FEER*, 20 March 1997.

113 "With such a close relationship": Quoted in "Interview: Digging up Dirt in High Places," *Newsweek*, 23 August 1999.

114 *Loving Couples, Divorcing Couples*: "Fuji Yarase Tsuma, AV Jo datta," *Tokyo Supotsu*, 16 November 1999.

114 "[In 1992] an NHK documentary": Sebastian Moffett, "Slipping Standards," *FEER*, 25 April 1996.

114 "The camera is focused": R. Sumner, "Reader's Forum," *MDN*, 12 August 1995.

115 Monju nuclear reactor leak: "Report on nuclear safety postponed after Monju leak," *MDN*, 14 December 1995.

116 "Donen was more concerned": "Monju operator takes flak for leak-video coverup," *JT*, 22 December 1995.

116 "We know that the plutonium": Eric Johnston, "What's the purpose of Monju?," *MDN*, 7 February 1996.

117 nobody ever informed them: "PNC didn't warn visitors about fire," *JT*, 17 March 1997; "Radiation leak is 20 times 1st report," *AEN*, 16 March 1997; and " 'Monju' Doyo, matamoya Shittai," *YS*, 13 March 1997.

117 radioactive tritium leaks: Suzuki Yumiko, "Coverup exposure scorches nuclear agency," *NKW*, 21 April 1997.

117 Tokai's nuclear plant safety lapses: See "Iho Tejun Kaisha ga Shonin," *SS*, 3 October 1999; and "N-plant failed to repair safety equipment for 17 years," *YDN*, 25 November 1999.

117 Measures to deal with the accident: "Japanese Accident Is a Tale of Small Steps Not Taken," *ASWJ*, 9 October 1999; *TMA*, 18 October 1999.

118 "Improving management techniques": "Clinton orders safety review of nuclear installations," *JT*, 3 October 1999; and "Nuclear safety management stressed," *China Daily*, 11 October 1999.

118 "Oh no, a serious accident": "The Lessons of Tokaimura," and "A Dangerous Wind," *NWA*, 11 October 1999; and "Too Hot to Handle," *TMA*, 11 October 1999.

119 "The water level has not dropped": Takagi Shogo, "Donen reneged on deal to waterproof nuclear-waste pit," *MDN*, 3 September 1997; and "Hoshasei busshitsu ga choki roshutsu," *SS*, 27 August 1997.

119 "It's true that the storage": Takagi Shogo, "Donen misused renovation budget," *MDN*, 29 August 1997.

119 "A small character named Pu": Johnston, "What's the purpose of Monju?"

120 so unconcerned were Donen officials: "Workers at Tokai nuke plant played golf on day of explosion," *MDN*, 19 March 1997.

120 "By the end of March": Jonathan Sprague, "Plugging the Dike," *AW*, 26 February 1999.

121 nuclear plant in Hamaoka: "N-plant fire blamed on paper towels," *MDN*, 26 January 1996.

121 Kato Hisatake: Howard W. French, "Japan Debates Culture of Covering Up," *NYT*, 2 May 2000.

122 Mitsubishi Motors cover-up: "Daimler Is Seeking Change at Mitsubishi," *International Herald Tribune*, 5 September 2000; Miki Tanikawa, "Mitsubishi Shares Tumble After Police Raid on Headquarters," *NYT*, 29 August 2000.

122 milk producer Snow Brand: "Bad Milk Raises Old Fears: Where Are the Watchdogs?," *TMA*, 31 July 2000.

123 "DA chief richest among Cabinet ministers": *MDN*, 17 February 1996.

123 "It's my corporate secret": "In Other Words," *FEER*, 18 February 1999.

124 "Systematic misinformation": Karel van Wolferen, e-mail to author, 8 February 2000.

124 "The report is not ideal": Abe Takeshi and Arima Hiroki, "Japan's global-warming report under fire," *AEN*, November 1995.

124 Official estimates of the bad debt crisis: "Details, Details," *The Economist*, 17 January 1998.

125 Fujimura Shinichi, Japan's leading archaeologist: "Kyusekki Hakken Netsuzo," *YS*, 6 November 2000; and "Archaeological Find Exposed As Fake," Associated Press, 6 November 2000.

129 "I have yet to see the man": Saikaku, 180-81.

5 Bureaucracy: Power and Privilege

133 ¥320 million in six years: Ohmae Ken'ichi, *Heisei Kanryo Ron* (Tokyo: Shogakukan, 1994), 295, 300.

133 "It's because we are assured": "Tokushu Hojin Kaikaku," *NKS*, 8 March 1997.

134 *amakudari* who run semi-government agencies: Ibid.

134 more than 2 million people: Ibid.

135 "When you seek to abolish": Robert Orr, *NKW*, 19 August 1996.

135 Government bureaucrats spend billions of yen: See "Officials Partied on Taxpayer Funds," *JT*, 19 December 1996; and "Gunma officials pilfered ¥367 million," *MDN*, 12 November 1996.

136 Social critic Inose Naoki: Inose, *Nihongoku no Kenkyu*, 234–35.

138 Yamaichi Securities: "Ex-Yamaichi official reportedly says securities regulator knew of losses," *AWSJ*, 5 February 1998; and "Kaigai nara mienai," *NKS*, 30 January 1998.

138 Hamanaka Yasuo: Andrew Pollack, "Japan Weighs Benefits of Loosening Rules," *International Herald Tribune*, 19 November 1996.

138 If a supermarket sells aspirin: Ibid.; Emily Thornton, "Deregulation Dawdle," *FEER*, 29 September 1994; "Regional Briefing," *FEER*, 29 August 1996.

139 construction industry payments to politicians and bureaucrats: Woodall, *Japan Under Construction*, 40; and Tom Weverka, "Anatomy of a Megaproject," *Tokyo Time Out*, February 1995.

139 bid-rigging inflating cost of construction: Woodall, *Japan Under Construction*, 40.

140 "compare very favorably": Ezra Vogel, "The Strides That Japan Still Needs to Take," *JT*, 22 March 1997.

140 "Japanese civil servants": Fingleton, *Blindside*, 130–31, 167–69.

141 MITI's vice minister, Makino Tsutomu: "Not an Open and Shut Case on Wining and Dining," *AEN*, 30 March 1997; "Six MITI Officials Punished in Izui Case," *MDN*, 6 December 1996; "More Politicians Tied to Izui Cash," *JT*, 13 November 1996.

141 Izui Jun'ichi and Hattori Tsuneharu: "Izui Allegedly Gave Hattori ¥4.9 Million," *JT*, 25 January 1997; "Izui Okura kanbocho no futomei bubun," *Daily Gendai*, 27 January 1996; "Kambo kokuzei ni 'atsuryoku,' " *MS*, 23 February 1997.

142 "For a bureacrat from": Peter Landers, "Limited Exposure," *FEER*, 12 February 1998; Yamai Norio, "No-rio," *AERA*, 26 January 1998.

142 Koyama Hiroshi and MHW: "WaiWai," *MDN*, 1 December 1996; "Kono Kancho," *Daily Gendai*, 5 December 1996.

143 payment to Nakajima Yoshio: Edward W. Desmond, "How the Mighty Have Fallen," *TMA*, February 19, 1996.

143 loans to Koike Ryuichi: "Dai-Ichi Kangyo Loaned ¥3 billion to Sokaiya-linked Company," *MDN*, 6 April 1997; and Richard Hanson, "Nomura Achieves Impossible—Again," *Asia Times*, 10 March 1997.

6 Monuments: Airports for Radishes

146 The costs are astronomical: "Maitoshi Akaji 2000 Oku En," *SS*, 21 February 1997.

147 Teleport Town's projected shortfall: B. Fulford, "Skyscraper Market Hits Bottom," *NKW*, 19 February 1996; and Aita Kaoruko, "A 'Futuristic City' Drowns in Red Ink," *JT*, 12 September 1995.

147 "I don't have a good feeling": "A Fountain of Ill Feeling in Chiba," *MDN*, 7 April 1996.

147 "Milan of Japan": Kawai Koshiro, "Gifu Aims to Restyle Itself as Milan-type Fashion Center," *NKW*, 18 December 1995.

148 "Although no one openly says so": " 'Shortcut' Cost ¥130 Billion but Will Have Little Use," *AEN*, 10 March 1997.

148 Hakata Bay project: Yoshida Reiji, "Boondoggle, Bird Threat Seen in Hakata Port Projects," *JT*, May 1996.

148 MAFF construction budget: Hoffman, "Flushed Down the Toilet."

149 Disaster Treatment Center: Eric Johnston, "Japan Red Cross in Hot Water," *JT*, 6 March 1997.

149 "This money was collected": Ibid.

150 "Japan is still a developing country": Quoted in Pollack, "Japan's Road to Bankruptcy."

150 "Good projects are a luxury": Brad Glosserman, "Top economist sees the good in Japan," *JT*, 29 June 1998.

151 postal-savings accounts deposits: Chris Gay, "A Life of Its Own," *FEER*, 27 March 1997.

152 the official "first budget": "Cabinet OKs ¥52.89 trillion 'zaito,' " *JT*, 26 December 1998; "Budget Breakdown," *NKW*, 28 December 1998; and "Trust Fund surplus faces 50% cut at Finance Ministry," *NKW*, 11 January 1999.

153 Japan's real national debt: Gay, "A Life of Its Own"; and "JNR Debt Set at ¥70 Trillion," *JT*, 26 April 1997.

153 *koeki hojin* figures: "Saabei: Fueru Koeki Hojin," *NKS*, 13 January 1997.

153 MITI and Ministry of Education *hojin*: Inose, *Nihongoku no Kenkyu*, 220.

154 Highway PC debt: Ibid., 93–95.

154 Highway Facilities Association revenues and fees: Ibid., 99, 106.

154 agencies operating service areas: Ibid., 102–4.

155 New Development Materials Company: Ibid., 190.

155 people send letters to Hong Kong: Ohmae Ken'ichi, "Vox Populi," *FEER*, 20 March 1997.

156 boat and auto and bicycle racing: Inose, *Nihongoku no Kenkyu*, 218, 219, 226.

156 "[Racing money] is not checked": Ibid., 227; and "Kinkyu Shujutsu," *SS*, 21 February 1997.

157 "There is enough cash flow": Quoted in Fulford, "Deft Accounting Hides Finance Sector's Ills," *NKW*, 14 October 1996.

157 "in a week or two": Quoted in "Corruption is a Problem for the Whole Nation," *MDN*, 13 February 1997; and Sapsford, "Firm Hands."

158 "Even if underground water": Quoted in "Pollution becomes Kobe's new foe," *NKW*, 16 September 1996.

158 "The current ecosystem": "Environment watchdog said asleep," *JT*, 7 June 1997.

159 public works planned: Inose, *Nihongoku no Kenkyu*, 30, 119.

159 "Why not go and connect": Ibid., 70.

159 plans to fill in Osaka Bay: McCormack, *Japanese Affluence*, 31.

160 "At the moment, our citizens are waiting": Inose, *Nihongoku no Kenkyu*, 82.

7 Old Cities: Kyoto and Tourism

163 "To that end, most": Philip Langdon, "Renovating a Classic Campus," *Yale Alumni Magazine*, November 1998.

163 "We literally tore": Ibid.

164 "Today, the celebrated dining room": Marlise Simons, "Proud Castles Stripped and France Is Scandalized," *NYT*, 15 February 1996.

164 "How must Kyoto appear": Tayama Reishi, in Nakajima Yoshimichi et al., eds., *Shizukasa to wa Nanika* (Tokyo: Daisan Shobo, 1996), 145.

168 forty thousand old wooden homes: "An Irreplaceable Loss to the World," International Society to Save Kyoto (ISSK) pamphlet, 1997.

169 "In its scale": Tayama, in *Shizukasa to wa Nanika*, 146.

170 "In a historic city": Peter Landers, "Edifice Complex," *FEER*, 11 September 1997.

170 "Visitors can enjoy": Ibid.

170 "There must be many foreigners": Kato Shidzue, "100 years, 100 views," *JT*, 9 November 1996.

173 "the formless, brutal": Quoted in Faulders, "Perfect Citizens."

173 disappearing historical monuments: Yoshida Reiji, "Wrecking ball threatens historic buildings," *JT*, 23 March 1997.

174 "Work has started": Shoji Kaori, "Once-frivolous Fukugawa turns tough," *JT*, 13 June 1996.

174 "I look at Fukagawa": Ibid.

176 "I visited an old couple": Marc Keane, e-mail to author, 23 June 1997.

178 Sarah Cummings: Linda Inoki, "Fresh ideas keep old traditions alive," *JT*, 29 June 2000.

179 "There will be no electricity": "Depopulated mountain village turns back the clock," *JT*, 18 September 1994.

180 "war on service-ization": See Fingleton, *Blindside*, 54.

181 international tourism's export earnings: "Tourism Highlights 2000," World Tourism Organization (WTO) Web page, 29 March 2000, *http://www.world-tourism.org/esta/monograf/highligh/hl.pdf*

181 spending $532 billion: "1998 Statistics Summary," World Tourism Organization (WTO) Web page, 30 June 1998, *http://www.world-tourism.org/commhead.htm*

182 domestic travel figures: "The value of tours," *NKW*, 12 February 1996.

182 Ise-Shima's tourist arrivals: Sano Noboru, "Ise-Shima senses a tourist boom over the horizon," *AEN*, 6 November 1999.

182 Japanese traveling abroad: "Overseas travelers decline . . . ," *NKW*, 14 June 1999; Kanabayashi Masayoshi, "More Japanese Opt to Travel in Asia in July and August," *AWSJ*, 10 August 2000.

183 number of foreign visitors to Japan: "Getting Around More These Days," *AW*, 11 February 2000.

183 South Korean figure: Wada Keiji, "Promoting Tourism in Japan" (paid supplement), *NKW*, 23 September 1996.

183 Japan's tourism deficit: "Tourism Highlights 2000," World Tourism Organization (WTO) Web page, 29 March 2000, *http://www.world-tourism.org/esta/monograf/highligh/hl.pdf*

185 "For Hong Kong's Wong Chun Chuen": Tanikawa Miki, "Fun in the Sun," *FEER*, April 1997.

185 "China has the potential": Sasaki Sei, "Can China save Japan's tourism industry?," *NKW*, 28 June 1999.

186 "*building a broad range*": "Meeting Foreign Tourists' Needs" (paid supplement), *NKW*, 23 September 1996.

186 "passionate romantic Tokushima": "A Treasure Trove of Tourist Temptations" (paid article by Tokushima Prefecture), *AEN*, 21 October 1998.

186 "At Atsui Dam": "21 Seiki no Kokudo Tsukuri," *Mizusumashi*, 1 July 1998.

188 "Pontocho is part": Saino Hiroshi, "Pontocho ni awanai Pari no geijtusubashi, Kokusai koryu he no gokai," *MS*, 20 September 1997.

8 New Cities: Electric Wires and Roof Boxes

197 In the countryside, a "priority policy": Allan West, interview with author, Tokyo, 25 March 1997.

200 "It's absolutely not necessary": Kathryn Findlay, letter to author, 30 April 1997 (quoting from conversation between architect Tajima Noriyuki and K. Findlay, June 1996).

200 "The scale was distinctly": Christine Hawley, "Disclosure and Surprise," *SD*, no. 9511 (November 1995).

201 "New Japan does not like trees": Donald Richie, *The Inland Sea* (Tokyo: John Weatherhill, 1971), 16.

202 "What bothers me the most": Mason Florence, conversation with author, Bangkok, March 1997.

203 "I was astonished": William Warren, conversation with author, Bangkok, 15 December 1997.

203 "Tokyo is a resort!": Sano Tadakatsu, "A Favorable Southern Aspect," *Look Japan*, August 1996.

204 "Many people of my generation": Quoted in Mertens, "Sinking in Cement."

204 "I read a lot of Japanese": Andrew Maerkle, conversation with author, March 1997.

209 Japanese houses are smaller: *ASJ Almanac 1999*, 212.

212 "But hotels are not just places": Daniel Eisenberg, "Where It's Chic to Sleep," *Time*, 4 October 1999.

213 Environment Agency reported: "Shizen Hakai nara Jigyo Chushi," *YS*, 23 May 1997.

215 "As Japan's countryside": Robert Neff, "Hiyu wo hakai suru kanko bijinesu: Kiita Nihon, Mita Nihon," *Shukan Shincho*, no. 14 (1996). (Translation by author from Japanese translation of English original.)

9 Demons: The Philosophy of Monuments

220 West suggested that they resurrect: Allan West, interview with author, Tokyo, 25 March 1997.

223 3,449 museums: *ASJ Almanac 1999*, 166.

224 Desert on the Moon Hall: Okura Kango, "Toyodama bunka no sato, Omocha ni sareru zeikin," *Shukan Bunshun*, 24 November 1996.

224 "However, just look around you": " 'Gaikoku Fuu' Shin-Tokyo Hakkei," *Shukan Shincho*, 23 November 1996.

225 "either planted firmly": Hasegawa Itsuko, "Museum of Fruit, Yamanashi," *SD*, November 1995.

225 "What this look-alike": Todd Crowell, "After the Bang," *AW*, 21 March 1997.

225 "what can only be described": Ibid.

226 plans for tall buildings: McCormack, *Japanese Affluence*, 62.

227 "The construction companies put": "Construction Ministry casting eyes to the sky," *MDN*, 4 October 1994.

228 a brand-new capital: "Final report advises construction of new capital start by year 2000," *MDN*, 14 December 1995.

228 30,000-hectare island: McCormack, *Japanese Affluence*, 61–62.

229 "When I speak of Japanese culture": Nakano Kiyotsugu, *Seihin no Shiso* (Tokyo: Soshisha, 1992), 209.

233 "The real and growing need": McCormack, *Japanese Affluence*, 66.

234 "Promethean energy": Ibid., 65.

234 "One of the more philosophically minded": Ibid., 66.

10 *Manga* and Massive: The Business of Monuments

237 *chisosai* bonds and subsidies: Nakazaki Takashi, "Ha-do Tsukutte, Sofuto ni Kurushimu," *AERA*, 15 August 1994.

237 Tsuna's gold nugget: McCormack, *Japanese Affluence*, 66.

237 small towns borrowed: See Nakazaki, "Ha-do Tsukutte."

238 "They are not building": Quoted in Nakazaki, "Ha-do Tsukutte."

238 "There was nobody in the village": Okura, "Omocha ni sareru zeikin," *Shukan Bunshun*, 24 November 1996; and Nakazaki, "Ha-do Tsukutte."

239 Shuto Cultural Hall: Nakazaki, "Ha-do Tsukutte."

240 "From the 1970s a number": Kathryn Findlay, letter to author, 30 April 1997.

241 "At the opening [of an exhibition]": Hasegawa Itsuko, "In Search of Global Architecture" (author's translation), *SD*, November 1995, 10.

241 "It's so ugly": "In Other Words," *FEER*, 13 March 1997.

241 "Architecture that fits in": Hasegawa, "In Search," 11.

241 Supremacist view of housing: Kathryn Findlay, letter to author, 10 April 1997.

242 "Mirage City sums up": Findlay, letter to author, 30 April 1997.

243 "A distant view of this building": Hasegawa, "Nagoya World Design Expo Pavilion," *SD*, November 1995, 76.

244 "architecture as a second nature": Ibid., 89.

244 The optimistic prognosis: "Tokyo Bay project won't break even until 2034," *MDN*, 10 February 1996.

245 Sazanami Hall maintenance: Nakazaki, "Ha-do Tsukutte."

245 Tokyo International Forum costs: Nokura Megumi, "Trendy Tokyo Int'l Forum in the red," *MDN*, 27 July 1997.

245 Yokohama Stadium maintenance fees: "Zeikin Mudazukai no Genba," *Shukan Gendai*, 18 March 1997.

245 Sakae civic center: Nakazaki, "Ha-do Tsukutte."

246 Igata's cycle of dependency: "Zeikin Mudazukai," *Shukan Gendai*, 18 March 1997.

247 "It seemed like the building": West, interview with author.

247 "Their desperate problem": Quoted in Nakazaki, "Ha-do Tsukutte."

248 Okinawa proposals: Brad Glosserman, "Intelligent Island, Take 2," *JT*, 18 December 1996.

248 "cultivating its image": "Minato Mirai 21 district features fantastic facilities," *JT*, 22 March 1997.

249 "an experimental model": Isozaki Arata. "Mirage City—Another Utopia," preface, online exhibition catalog, 11 July 1997, *http://www.nttcc.or.jp/special/utopia*

249 city of Nagoya made plans: Stephen Hesse, "Garbage trucks ready to roll as Nagoya trashes wetlands," *JT*, 15 September 1998.

250 "Try to visit the Nagi Museum": Herbert Muschamp, "In Japan, Art and a Museum Breathe as One," *NYT*, 6 October 1996.

252 "It is peculiar": Ibid.

11 National Wealth: Debt, Public and Private

254 "These days people borrow": Saikaku, 119–20.

254 "Japan is the world's greatest": McCormack, "Afterbubble: Fizz and Concrete."

255 local units drowning in red ink: "Slump puts cities in bankruptcy peril," *NKW*, January 1998.

256 Osaka's annual losses: "Maitoshi akaji 2000 oku en . . . ," *SS*, 21 February 1997.

256 "In addition to the general budget": *"STN,"* YS *Yomipack*, 4.

256 Japan's deficit compared with OECD average: "Budget Breakdown," *NKW*, 28 December 1998; Morishita Kaoru, "Government debt soars to

new heights," *NKW*, 24 May 1999; and Morishita Kaoru, " '99 budget not a hit in markets," *NKW*, 28 December 1998.

256 Japan's cumulative debt: "Government Debt hits ¥394 trillion," *NKW*, 29 June 1998; and Bruce Bartlett, "It Doesn't Pay to Pay Down the Debt," *The Wall Street Journal Europe*, 12 July 1999.

256 shortfalls of municipal: "Slump puts cities in bankruptcy peril," *NKW*, January 1998.

256 "hidden debt" and real debt: "Government Debt hits ¥394 trillion," *NKW*, 29 June 1998; and Brian Bremner, "Japan's Real Crisis," *Business Week*, 18 May 1998.

257 showing unsold units as sold: Inose, *Nihongoku no Kenkyu*, 136–41.

257 Shinjuku office tower: Ibid., 150.

257 "grasshoppers and bees": Daniel Burstein, *Yen!: Japan's New Financial Empire and Its Threat to America* (New York: Simon & Schuster, 1988), 114.

257 Japanese government bonds: "Financial Indicators," *The Economist*, 3 July 1999.

258 "It's not worth the effort": Sheryl WuDunn, "The Heavy Burden of Low Rates," *NYT*, 11 October 1996; and "Consumers Continue Saving In Spite of Low Interest Rates," *MDN*, 31 October 1995.

258 "There has been an increasing number": "What Better Place for Your Money Than a Bank Safe?," *MDN*, 5 December 1995; and Tim Cribb, "Savings Find New Expressions in Low-Interest Japan," *MDN*, 8 February 1996.

259 "was able to loan out his one *kamme*": Saikaku, 84.

259 "I look at my bank account": Quoted in WuDunn, "Heavy Burden."

261 percentages of people over sixty-five: Sakamaki Sachiko, "No, Thanks," *FEER*, 3 April 1997; and "65 sai ijo ga sojinko ni shimeru wariai" (graph), *NKS*, 13 January 1997.

261 younger workers supporting retired persons: Todd Crowell and Murakami Mutsuko, "Living Beyond Its Means?," *AW*, 30 August 1996.

261 health-insurance societies in arrears: "Kenporen ga Ichiji Toketsu," *NKS*, 24 April 1999.

261 raising contributions and lowering benefits: "Health Ins. Plan for Small Firms in Dire Straits," *NKW*, 20 January 1997; and "LDP, Allies Discuss Increasing Public's Share of Medical Costs," *JT*, 20 December 1996.

262 premiums will have to increase: "Health Ins. Plan for Small Firms in Dire Straits," *NKW*, 20 January 1997; and *"STN," YS Yomipack*, 31.

262 Or so everyone believed: Jacob M. Schlesinger, "The More the Japanese Save for a Rainy Day, the Gloomier It Gets," *AWSJ*, 21 July 1998.

262 life insurance and household savings: "A Yen to Save," *NKW*, 7 October 1996.

263 Nissan Mutual Life: "Nissan Mutual Ordered to Shut Down Operations," *JT*, 26 April 1997.

263 Chiyodo Mutual Life Insurance and Kyoei Life Insurance: Naito Minoru, "Life insurance industry losing stable image as failures mount," *NKW*, 23 October 2000; and "Prudential to Rescue Kyoei," *AEN*, 24 October 2000.

263 Japanese and U.S. pension funds: Henny Sender, "Coming of Age," *FEER*, 31 August 1995; and Bruce Kelly, "Pension Funds Show Strong Returns," *Pensions and Investments,* 25 January 1999, 20.

263 reserves of corporate pension funds: "Many Firms Lack Funds to Pay Pensions," *MDN*, 10 September 1996; and Suzuki Yumiko, "Pension Liabilities Pinch Companies Harder," *NKW*, 18 March 1996.

264 minimum rate of return: "Labor Ministry to Lower Savings-Plan Min. Rate," *NKW*, 13 January 1997; and "Welfare Annuity Funds Facing Crisis," *MDN*, 15 December 1995

264 800,000 companies: See "Kosei Nenkin ga moraenai," *AS*, 16 April 2000.

264 minimum age for beneficiaries: "Nenkin Iryo," *Daily Gendai*, 20 February 1997; Crowell and Murakami, "Living Beyond Its Means?"

264 Private industry faces: "Yen to Save," *NKW*, 7 October 1996; "70% of firms face pension shortfall," *AEN*, 8 November 1999; and Mark Cutis, "Privatizing the World's Pensions, Japan 'Crisis at Hand,' " Nomura International PLC, Washington, D.C., 17 October 1997.

264 Only a handful of large companies: Chester Dawson, "Defining Moment," *FEER*, 27 April 2000.

265 "¥1,400 trillion": McCormack, "Afterbubble: Fizz and Concrete."

265 63 percent by the year 2020: Sumiya Fumio, "Economic Council Sees 'Catastrophic Scenario,' " *NKW*, 4 November 1996. Author's note: 63 percent = 35.8 percent + a pension fund increase of 12.2 percent (from 17.4 percent to 29.6 percent) + a health service increase of 15 percent (from 9 percent to 24 percent).

266 "printing money" may not work: See Taggart Murphy, "Inflation scare won't loosen purse strings," *JT*, 16 March 2000.

266 "Two boys out in Illinois": Anthony Gross, *Lincoln's Own Stories* (New York: Garden City Publishing, 1912), 221.

267 Credit-card use and installment buying: Sonni Efron, "Japanese charge into debt at furious rate," from *Los Angeles Times*, quoted in *Japan Times Weekly*, 28 September 1996.

268 corporate debt in Japan: Bremner, "Japan's Real Crisis."

269 loan sharks' rates: Velisarios Kattoulas, "Midnight Run," *NWA*, 11 January 1999.

269 "Of all the frightening things": Saikaku, 120.

269 assets leaping 25 percent: *NKW*, 10 February 1997; and Efron, "Japanese charge."

270 "Midnight Run": "Recession snarls bankruptcy system," *NKW*, 21 December 1998; "13 People Arrested in Fraud," *JT*, 25 January 1997; Utsunomiya Kenji, quoted in Efron, "Japanese charge."

270 *The Midnight Run Shop*: Kattoulas, "Midnight Run."

271 Tazaki Aiko: Murakami Asako, "Variable Ins. Risks Went Untold," *JT*, 13 April 1996.

271 "Suicide is a tempting idea": Oishi Satoru, quoted in Saito Rieko, "Variable Insurance Policyholders Place Hope In Lawsuits," *MDN*, 6 February 1996.

272 U.S. nonprofit foundations: Paul Ventura, "I. Some Statistics About the Not for Profit Sector in the United States," March 1997, *http://www .sover.net/~paulven/statcite.html*

273 Yale and Harvard assets: Yale Web page, "Fact Sheet—Statistical Summary of Yale University," 10 March 2000, *http://www.yale.edu/oir/factsheet.html# InstitutionalFinances*; and Harvard Web page, "Fact Book," 10 March 2000, *http://www.holyoke.harvard.edu/factbook/*

273 assets of U.S. and Japanese foundations: See "Japan Foundation Center," 20 April 2000, *www.jfc.com*

273 American Cancer Society: American Cancer Society Web page, "1999 Fact Sheet," 10 March 2000, *http://www2.cancer.org/about_acs/*; and "Budget Report," 10 March 2000, *http://www.cancer.org/annReport/tex_04.htm/*

273 total assets of American nonprofit groups: Independent Sector home
    page, "Key Findings," 13 April 2000, *http://www.independentsector.org/
    GandV/s_keyf.htm*; and National Center for Charitable Statistics Web page,
    "Non-profit Fact Sheets," 13 April 2000, *http://nccs.urban.org/factsht.htm*

274 "Of that, only 200": Sanger, "Japan's Bad Debt"; Desmond, "How
    the Mighty"; Robert Koo, quoted in Jathon Sapsford, "Japan's Healthier
    Banks May Hold Key," *AWSJ*, 27 August 1998; editorial, *NKW*, 30 June
    2000.

275 200 inspectors in Tokyo and Osaka: Shimizu Yasumasa, "New charges
    push back Nomura plans," *NKW*, 23 June 1997.

275 red tape and stock options: "Ban on Stock Options Lifted, but Rules Limit
    Eligible Firms," *NKW*, 12 February 1996.

275 over-the-counter: "Weak Investor Confidence," *NKW*, 14 April 1997.

277 "Year after year the loss": Saikaku, 33.

278 "The rules of money": Michael Phillips, *The Seven Laws of Money* (Boston:
    Shambala, 1993), 20.

278 "The amazing Japanese economy": Alan Blinder, quoted in James Fallows,
    Looking at the Sun (New York: Pantheon, 1994), 207.

278 "That [there are laws]": Karel van Wolferen, e-mail to author, 16 February
    2000.

280 "Everything under heaven and earth": Kaiho Seiryo, "*Keikodan*," trans. Alex
    Kerr, in Tsukadani Akihiro and Kuranami Shoji, eds., *Nihon Shiso Taikei 44:
    Honda Toshiaki, Kaiho Seiryo* (Tokyo: Iwanami Shoten, 1970), 222.

281 "There is a solid bottom": Henry David Thoreau, *Walden*, "Conclusion."

12 Education: Following the Rules

285 "Driving through the English countryside": Miyamoto Masao, " 'Castra-
    tion' the Major Goal for Japanese Education, and Its Relation to Deregula-
    tion" (paper presented at University of Oxford and University of
    Cambridge, 20 October 1995), 6.

286 "They scattered outside": Peter Hadfield, "With Respect," *MDN*, 3 March
    1996.

286 "If children bring fried rice": quoted in Miyamoto, " 'Castration' the Ma-
    jor Goal."

287 Iwakuni City Office banned: "Nurseries ban kids from U.S. base," *JT*, 18 January 1996.

287 "Students of the same kumi . . . The kumi mentality": Benjamin Duke, *The Japanese School: Lessons for Industrial America* (New York: Praeger, 1986), 24.

288 "Their emphasis is on": Edwin Reischauer, quoted in Duke, *The Japanese School*, 24.

288 "Chemicals prohibited": Gary DeCoker, " 'Internationalization' in Japan's Elementary School Social Studies Textbooks: First Lessons in Government Ideology," in Thomas Rohlen and Christopher Bjork, eds., *Education and Training in Japan*, vol. 2 (London and New York: Routledge, 1998), 191–214.

289 "At first, because of ": Ibid., 11.

289 "To survive": Duke, *The Japanese School*, 24.

289 "Students should carry": "Paperless society goes to the toilet," *MDN*, 13 July 1994.

290 Habikino City: "Assembly OKs uniforms despite teacher outcry," *JT*, 29 March 1996.

290 "In my mind": Miyamoto, " 'Castration' the Major Goal."

290 solitary confinement: "Pupil put in solitary for refusing haircut," *JT*, 20 June 1994.

290 "Psychologically speaking": Miyamoto, " 'Castration' the Major Goal."

291 So widespread is teacher violence: "Corporal punishment on trial," *JT*, 1 December 1995.

291 One girl interviewed: Janet Ashby, "School bullying rooted deep in Japanese society," *JT*, 1 March 1996.

292 Ito Hisashi: Sakamaki Sachiko, "Fates Worse than Death," *FEER*, 29 February 1996.

292 "It can't be helped": "Bullied kids should take leave: poll," *JT*, 30 January 1996.

292 Kodera Yasuko complained: Kodera Yasuko, quoted in Edward W. Desmond, "Battling Bullies," *TMA*, 12 September 1994.

292 "Bullying the weak": Miyamoto Masao, quoted in Sakamaki, "Fates Worse than Death."

293 "O became a prisoner": Miyamoto Masao, "Conformity, Masochism and Freedom" (paper presented at the American Chamber of Commerce, Tokyo, 15 June 1995), 4.

293 "In some sense": Eberts, *The Myths of Japanese Quality* (Upper Saddle River, N.J.: Prentice Hall PTR, 1995), 226.

294 "Ministry of Training": Miyamoto, "Conformity, Masochism."

294 in math their scores drop: Sumiya Fumio, "Colleges rapped for not teaching skills," *NKW*, 25 November 1996.

294 absolute illiteracy in the United States and Japan: Eberts, *Myths of Japanese Quality*, 230.

294 functional illiteracy in the United States and Japan: Duke, *The Japanese School*, 60; and Jonathan Kozol, *Illiterate America* (Garden City, N.Y.: Anchor Press, 1985), 4–5, quoted in Eberts, *Myths of Japanese Quality*, 231.

295 *Manga* now account: Benjamin Fulford, "Comics in Japan not just funny business," *NKW*, 17 February 1997.

295 "advance into the continent": For a detailed discussion of how the Ministry of Education handles prewar history in textbooks, see Ian Buruma, *Wages of Guilt* (London: Vintage Press, 1994).

295 the ministry scratched: Gary DeCoker, Department of Education, Ohio Wesleyan, e-mail to author, 26 November 1997.

296 "Pizza is not a set menu": Peter Hadfield, "Japan puts the pizza in purdah," *The Nation* (Bangkok), 9 July 1997.

296 "Children often tell me": Kanno Jun, quoted in Sakamaki, "Fates Worse than Death."

296 poll of sixth-graders: Inagaki Emiko, "Exam hell explodes bright children," *AEN*, 1 December 1996.

297 "If Japan's schools": Quoted in Eberts, *Myths of Japanese Quality*, 216.

297 Japanese children hate school: Arai N., "Truancy figures bare societal flaw," *JT*, 31 January 1996; "Days of shame in the halls of learning," *JT*, 10 November 1996; and Eberts, *Myths of Japanese Quality*, 225.

298 "These kids were friendly": Karl Taro Greenfield, "The Hardest Lesson," *TMA*, 3 May 1999.

299 Japanese students in higher education: *Japan Almanac 1997* (Tokyo: Asahi Shimbun, 1998), 240; and Eberts, *Myths of Japanese Quality*, 225.

299 "The big difference is": Gary DeCoker, e-mail to author, 26 November 1997.

300 percentage of men going to college: *Japan Almanac 1997*, 240.

300 men outnumber women in graduate school: Ibid.; and Irene M. Kunii, "The Seeds of Science," *TMA*, 28 April 1997.

300 "Industries were in trouble": Mori Kenji, quoted in Kunii, "Seeds of Science."

301 "to take the finished products": " 'Nan no Tame' Kotaenaku Iroaseru Erito," *NKS*, 5 May 1997.

301 "There is no doubt": Karel van Wolferen, "The Right to Rule," in *The Enigma of Japanese Power* (New York: Knopf, 1989), 308–9.

301 "The squandering of four years": Edwin Reischauer, quoted in Duke, *The Japanese School*, 24.

301 "By the time he reaches": Miyamoto, " 'Castration' the Major Goal," 6.

302 "Nothing in education": Henry Adams, cited in Eberts, *Myths of Japanese Quality*, 225.

302 Azby Brown's study: Azby Brown, "School Daze," *Tokyo Journal*, February 1996.

302 "loyal, literate, competent": Duke, *The Japanese School*, 24.

304 Ministry of Education survey: "Computers not teachers' forte," *JT*, 5 November 1994.

304 Japan ranked fifteenth: "Asia Lagging Behind at Logging On," *AW*, 4 December 1998.

304 "It is true that multimedia": David Lazarus, "Multimedia foe speaks with forked tongue," *JT*, 23 October 1994.

304 Justsystem's main product: "The battle with Ichitaro is already over," *NKW*, 23 March 1998.

306 "The present education system": Sato M., "Reform fervor faces cold reality," *NKW*, 13 January 1997.

306 "leached Japan's vitality": "Panel recommends dramatic changes in Japanese society," *The Japan Times Weekly*, 29 January 2000.

13 After School: Flowers and Cinema

307 "Looking around modern Japan": Nakano Kiyotsugu, *Seihin no Shiso* (Tokyo: Soshisha, 1992), 212.

308 "Newcomers should always": Mary Jordan, "Ties that bind Japan enmesh park moms," *JT*, 24 November 1996.

308 "Some of these women": Ono Satomi, "Koen Habatsu ni Mama ha Funsen," *AERA*, 19 May 1997, 61–63; and Jordan, "Ties that bind."

311 "One could say that": Nakajima Yoshimichi et al., *Shizukasa toha nanika* (Tokyo: Daisan Shobo, 1996), 24, 46.

312 "If you have come": Ibid., 47, 87.

312 *Why Have the Japanese. . . ?*: Fukuda Kazuya, *Naze Nihonjin ha kakumo yochi in natto no ka* (Tokyo: Kadokawa Haruki, 1996).

312 *manga* comics now account: Ibid.

312 "the limit on eye size": Quoted in Fulford, "Comics in Japan."

313 "We in the US": Merry White, quoted in Mary Roach, "Cute Inc.," *Wired*, December 1999, 337.

313 Sanrio's grosses: Ibid., 336.

314 domestic film revenues from *anime*: Andrew Pollack, "Japan: A Superpower Among Superheroes," *NYT*, 17 September 1995.

314 "A mere glance": Quoted in Tanikawa Miki, "Japan's Cuddly Cure," *TMA*, 9 August 1999, 20.

314 "To anyone who knows Japan": Roach, "Cute Inc.," 333–34.

319 "Despite the marketing muscle": Terry McCarthy, "Export Machine," *TMA*, 3–10 May 1999.

319 "It's stupid for the Japanese": Ibid.

320 "Here Oshima puts his finger": Ian Buruma, *The Missionary and the Libertine* (New York: Random House, 2000), 21.

320 "It's not how much they spend": Tim Larimer, "She's a Material Girl," *TMA*, 3–10 May 1999.

320 "If an item is hot": Ibid.

321 "Japanese audiences": "Tokyo fest of films goes to Kyoto," *JT*, 2 August 1994; Okuyama Kazuyoshi, quoted in Mark Schilling, "New Signs of Life in Japanese Cinema," *Japan Quarterly* (October–December 1994), 450.

321 the industry has shrunk: "The not-so-big screen," *NKW*, 24 February 1997; Schilling, "New Signs of Life," 450; and " 'Titanic,' other hits lift film distributors," *NKW*, 7 September 1998.

323 porno flicks: "Reviving Japanese cinema," *MDN*, 11 August 1994.

323 sixth-highest-grossing Japanese film: Mark Schilling, "Indiana Jones' Japanimation cousin," *JT*, 15 September 1998.

323 $52 million in its first week: "Pokemon Zenbei Ichi-i," *NKS*, 15 November 1999.

323 "World success is based": Donald Richie, conversation with the author, 28 June 2000.

325 "Nowadays an Ozu or a Kurosawa": Ibid.

325 "Thirty years ago": Ibid.

325 "studios devoted themselves": Nagasaka Toshihisa, "The Failure of Japanese Film," *Japan Echo* 18, no. 3 (autumn 1991), 3.

325 "Mainstream Japanese cinema": Schilling, "New Signs of Life," 451.

326 *Godzilla vs. Destroyer*: James Bailey, "I'm truly torched, my dear," *MDN*, 15 December 1995; and James Bailey, "Summer ghost story seems hauntingly familiar," *MDN*, 25 July 1997.

326 in 1996, thirteen: Bailey, "Summer ghost story."

327 "director Ishiro Honda saw King Kong": Bailey, "I'm truly torched, my dear."

327 *Godzilla vs. King Ghidora*: Bailey, "I'm truly torched, my dear."

328 "There is no hope": Kurosawa Akira, quoted in P. McGill, "In the emperor's field of dreams," *AEN*, 12 September 1998.

329 Shochiku reached the point: "Corporate dissatisfaction builds up to dramatic coup," *NKW*, 26 January 1998.

330 the van Gogh episode: McGill, "Emperor's field."

331 "The same narrow": Toshihisa, "Japanese Film," 88.

332 "What makes Hong Kong": Karen Mazurkewich, "Setting Sail in the Same Boat," *FEER*, 20 April 2000.

332 Peter Chan announced: See Karen Mazurkewich, "Hollywood Jumps In," *FEER*, 4 May 2000.

332 "The Japanese entertainment industry": Thomas McLain, quoted in Nigel Holloway, "Star Struck," *FEER*, 11 January 1996.

14 Internationalization: Refugees and Expats

336 "Being of Korean background": Son Masayoshi, quoted in "Japan's Bill Gates strikes it rich in cyberspace," *MDN*, 20 June 1996.

338 "The reason I stayed": "Beikoku ni iku nihonjin ishitachi," *SS*, 28 June 1996.

338 "In the field of basic research": "Beikoku ni iku," *SS*, 28 June 1996.

339 "The appeal [of an American career]": Ibid.

339 "No bonus, no big position": Nakamura Shuji, quoted in Chester Dawson, "Inventor with the Blues," *FEER*, 9 March 2000.

339 Okabe Nobuya: Sebastian Moffett, "The New Mavericks," *FEER*, 20 June 1996.

342 "It will be a relief": Otis Cary, quoted in C. Hay, "Doshisha's Otis Cary, 74, bids sayonara," *JT*, 29 October 1995.

344 "Foreigners go home!": Tim Larmer and Tashiro Hiroko, "Battling the Bloodlines," *TMA*, 9 August 1999, 19.

348 there were only 56,000: *ASJ Almanac 1999*, 251; "Preparing to welcome foreign students," *JT*, 12 August 2000.

349 MBA schools in Thailand: "Best Full-Time Programs," *AW*, 5 May 2000.

349 "To many Southeast Asians": Yau-hua Lim, quoted in Carol Hui, "In the eyes of the beholder," *JT*, 16 September 1996.

350 "Although it may open windows": Howard W. French, "TV Invents What Japan Sorely Lacks: Impoliteness," *NYT International*, 27 April 2000.

351 "Atrocious crimes": Tim Larimer, "Rabble Rouser," *TMA*, 24 April 2000, 22–25.

355 "When I think of": Quoted in "Kaigai ni Sumu," *NWJ*, 14 August 1996.

356 "I dream of going": "Changing Times, Altered Expectations," *AW*, 7 May 1999.

356 "The main victims": Buruma, *The Missionary and the Libertine*, 252.

357 "Whether you happen to be": Saikaku, 148.

15 To Change or Not to Change: Boiled Frog

358 "If I don't drive": Dorothy Parker, "Observation," in *The Portable Dorothy Parker* (New York: Penguin Books, The Viking Portable Library, 1928), 112.

364 Japan had only 0.3 percent: Michael Zielenziger, "Entrepreneurs finding obstacles to Japan's Web," *Austin American-Statesman*, 1 August 1998.

368 "Under great economic": Mikuni Akio, "How Japan's Financial System Is Administered and Protected by the Government: What Is to Be Done?" (paper presented at conference What Is to Be Done, Amsterdam, February 3–5, 2000).

370 "What is in store": Kamei Tatsuo, conversation with author, Tokyo, 8 November 1994.

370 "If you drop a frog": Quoted in Fulford, "Deft Accounting."

370 *Japanese-Style Capitalism as a Civilization*: *Bunmei to shite no Nihongata Shihonshugi* (Tokyo: Toyo Keizai, 1993).

373 In one notorious case: Fallows, *Looking at the Sun*, 239.

373 the United States' FDA: "Clinical trial system condemned," *MDN*, 22 July 1994.

374 launch of an H-2 rocket: "Trust in NASDA crashes after 2nd launch failure," *YDN*, 17 November 1999; and "H2 Uchiage Shippai," *NKS*, 16 November 1999.

375 "stereotypical Anglo–American": "SE Asia must toss between Japan and the U.S.," *The Nation* (Bangkok), 31 July 1999.

376 "Korean business is following America": Mark Magnier, "South Korea speeding away on info-superhighway," *JT*, 21 August 2000.

Index

421

Exodus への すすめ